*"Your fyre shall burn no more"*

*José António Brandão*

# "Your fyre shall burn no more"

*Iroquois Policy toward New France
and Its Native Allies to 1701*

University of Nebraska Press, Lincoln and London

Library of Congress
Cataloging-in-
Publication Data
Brandão, José António, 1957–
Your fyre shall burn no more :
Iroquois policy toward New
France and its native allies
to 1701 / José António Brandão.
p.   cm.
Includes bibliographical
references and index.
ISBN 0-8032-1274-7 (cloth : alk. paper)
1. Iroquois Indians — History —
17th century.   2. Iroquois Indians —
Politics and government.   3. Canada —
History — To 1763 (New France)
I. Title.
E99.17B83   1998
971.01 — dc21
97-9846 CIP

1001641081

*a Dorvalino e Salomé*

# Contents

# Tables and Graphs

# *Preface*

The Five Nations Iroquois were, and to some extent still are, the great "bogey-men" of seventeenth-century Canadian history. Schoolchildren in both French and English Canada were introduced to the stories of Canada's heroic first settlers struggling to overcome adversity and settle a new land. Adversity had two faces: one was the harsh environment, one of the great themes of Canadian literature. The other face was Iroquois and inevitably was painted for war. If contemporary sensibilities have led to kinder treatment of natives and the environment in textbooks, they had not when I began my education. Then the "cruel" wars the Iroquois waged against New France were the fires that forged the metal of Canada's "new" peoples.

Often, that was all the exposure to the history of the Iroquois most Canadians received. Even if one carried on to university, one could hope to learn little more than that—certainly not in the general textbooks that were assigned reading. If one was fortunate enough to land at a university that taught the history of New France (it is surprising how many places in Canada do not consider essential the history of the nation before 1763), one might learn more about early Indian-European contact, but with rare exceptions the Iroquois were still used as a means to make points about European valor. Through no foresight of my own I ended up at the University of Toronto, where W. J. Eccles, one of those rare exceptions, taught.

Nonetheless, if the focus on the Iroquois was to study them in their own right, the warfare they waged and their hostility toward New France were still central concerns of most readings. This suited me just fine since political and military history interested me. Yet fascinating as research into aspects of Iroquois-French relations was, I also found it perplexing. The documentary record did not really seem to support aspects of the views espoused in the secondary literature and raised questions to which I could find no answers. I was encouraged to pursue the questions my research raised and, thinking that I was undertaking nothing more than an interesting research puzzle, I did just that. The search for answers to those questions led to graduate school and, eventually, to this book.

What follows is not a social history of the Iroquois. No attempt is made to offer a comprehensive explanation of all aspects of Iroquois life and culture. Only aspects of culture and society relevant to explaining Iroquois relations with the French and their allies are treated. Nor is this a history of Iroquois relations with all the groups in the Northeast. The focus of this study is the nature of Iroquois-French relations seen from the perspective of the Iroquois. But, for several reasons, Iroquois relations with a variety of native and European groups cannot be avoided. Iroquois relations with the Hurons, for example, were part of the overall policy considerations of the Iroquois. What happened between these two groups could, or more likely did, influence Iroquois policy toward the French. Equally important, the Hurons and many other groups were allies of the French. Thus French relations with the Hurons or other natives were also likely to have an impact on Iroquois policy toward New France.

Neither is this a study of the "Beaver Wars"—it is doubtful they ever existed as such. Yet the specific interpretation of Iroquois relations with natives and Europeans that is embodied in this phrase cannot be overlooked. In various shapes and guises, especially since 1940, this interpretation has influenced the way that scholars of the Iroquois and of New France have viewed Iroquois-French relations. It is at the very heart of the historiography of this subject and is so deeply entrenched and widely accepted that it has become heresy in some circles to even question it. Inevitably, I found myself caught up in this debate. It seemed important to establish why the Beaver Wars interpretation should be reconsidered, if not rejected, before I could present my own explanation for Iroquois actions toward New France. For these reasons, it possibly receives more attention than it merits. However, the purpose of this work remains to elucidate what the Iroquois hoped to accomplish in their dealings with the French in New France before 1701. This year was chosen as a cutoff date because I felt that the one hundred or so years before 1701 were a "manageable" amount of history to cover. Conveniently, one of the periodic cessations of warfare that marked Iroquois-French relations began that year.

The book begins with a discussion of the historiography of the Beaver Wars and shows how that literature has come to dominate the interpretations historians of New France have presented of Franco-Iroquois relations. Subsequent chapters deal with the way the Iroquois governed themselves, the role warfare played in their culture, and how their culture and warfare were affected by contact with European society. These chapters can be viewed in two distinct although not contradictory ways. Since all of these elements are central to the various versions of the Beaver Wars interpretations, and since my reconstruction of these aspects of Iroquois culture is often at variance with the accepted view, these chapters can serve as detailed refutations of most of the unfounded assumptions at the heart of the Beaver Wars interpretations. They are, however, intended to establish a context within which to interpret Iroquois actions. Much of our understanding of Iroquois policy is derived from records of their actions, not from documents that reveal what they said or thought. For this reason it is extremely important that those actions and behaviors be viewed as the Iroquois understood them—in ways that made sense to *their* culture. Finally, the last five chapters outline Iroquois policy toward the colony of New France and its native allies.

Throughout the work numerical data are presented. This information is distilled from tables that can be found in various appendixes at the end of the book. The reasons for including each of these tables, the sources from which they were compiled, the methods used, and caveats are discussed in detail preceding each table. However, a word about why a quantitative approach was used in part may not be out of order here.

I used a quantitative approach to this subject to try to arrive at precise numbers for elements of interpretations that have often been based on imprecise "impressions" of what the documents revealed. It was not an endeavor to supplant documentary sources; rather, it was an attempt to extract more information from those traditional sources. The historical record on the Iroquois, like all historical records, is imperfect. But if evidence is fragmentary, all the fragments should be considered, not just a random or select few. Moreover, to recognize that the available sources are limited is no reason not to mine them to their fullest extent. I use the statistical data culled from the documents in full recognition of their limitations. But I remain convinced of the need to take those data seriously into account.

It may seem that I am obsessed with documentation. This is partly true. Native history, more so than in other fields of historical inquiry, requires a great deal of imagination and hypothesis building because Indians had no written language, although among some native societies pictographs and oral histories served as records for specific events. Thus although there is a record of Indian actions as noted by Europeans, the historian of Indian groups is usually left to speculate about the concerns or the goals that motivated those actions. This is equally true of portions of this work. However, since it is my contention that much of Iroquois history written in the past century is based on unsupported speculation and assumptions, I feel a need to establish as clearly as possible the basis of my interpretation. This means providing in as much detail as possible the evidence I have relied on, as well as showing how and why I have used those data. Given the paucity of sources for some facets of Iroquois history and our inability to answer key questions about aspects of Iroquois development, some of our understanding of that history must remain speculative. But conjecture cannot remain a basis for history—especially not when evidence for portions of that history exists.

When I defined my topic and began my research, I had no idea where my questions might lead me. When I completed it, I had no notion of the audacity of some of the answers I had arrived at. The latter has, however, been made more than abundantly clear in responses to my doctoral dissertation (on which this book is based), to presentations made at conferences, and to papers submitted for publication. Naive as I may have been when I began, and as unprepared as I was for some of the responses to the results of my research, I recognize that my conclusions are, in key places, at odds with what others have written about the Iroquois. This, however, did not stem from any desire to rehabilitate the image of the Iroquois in Canadian history, nor to question a historiographical tradition of Iroquois-Indian and Iroquois-European relations that was over a hundred years old. What I wanted to do was resolve what appeared to be inconsistencies between the views of the Iroquois presented in the books I read and the documents on which those books were based. As I pursued my education in matters Iroquois, it became evident that the discrepancies between the secondary literature and the historical record were, in places, so vast that an inaccurate picture of the Iroquois had developed. My research led me to conclude that resolving the questions that had intrigued me and presenting a more accurate picture of the Iroquois required challenging aspects of existing interpretations.

The end result is, of course, for others to judge. I claim no hold on the truth about the past. I hesitate even to speak of truths about certain events. I view my efforts in less ambitious terms. When I began studying the Iroquois, all I wanted to do was answer some questions and satisfy my curiosity about them and their history. I have not found all the answers I sought, nor do I want to stop searching; certainly my curiosity about the Iroquois remains unabated. However, the rules of the historical discipline require finite limits to such a process. This, then, is the status report on my understanding of Iroquois relations with the French and some of their Indian neighbors in the seventeenth century. If it differs from that of others, that is as it should be. If it leads to debate about the Iroquois, all the better.

TECHNICAL NOTE

All spelling and punctuation in quotations follow the original source. The exceptions are the abbreviations for *the*, *they*, and the ampersand, which have been spelled out fully. Spelling of French and Indian proper names and of place-names are as found in the *Dictionary of Canadian Biography* and the *Historical Atlas of Canada*, respectively. Spelling of Indian tribal names follows the practice of *Handbook of North American Indians*, volume 15, *The Northeast*. The dates given, with one exception, are as they appear on the document cited. Dates in the French and Dutch sources were in the New Style, while those in English sources were in the Old Style. Throughout the seventeenth century, Old Style dates were ten days behind those in New Style. Thus 25 April 1680 N.S. in New France was 15 April 1680 O.S. in New York. Similarly, the new year began on 1 January N.S. and on 25 March O.S. In English documents, dates between January and March were often written with both years (for example, 12 February 1674/75). In these instances only the date in the new year is used here (12 February 1675).

Where I quote from French-language documents that have appeared in published translation, I have relied on the existing translations. All other translations from the French are mine.

# Acknowledgments

Over the course of my studies I have had the support of many people and institutions without whose help completion of this work would not have been possible. John Sheppard and Allan Hux helped develop my interest in history. Professor W. J. Eccles encouraged me to pursue my curiousity about the Iroquois and suggested the topic that led to a doctoral dissertation and this book. Professor Eccles's insistence on solid documentary proof for my assertions and the example of his scholarship have shaped my approach to the study and practice of history. The Ontario Graduate Scholarship Program, the Social Sciences and Humanities Research Council of Canada, and Laven Associates provided financial support for my initial research efforts (the latter as part of an annual construction worker and truck driver "internship"). The good fathers at the Maison des Jésuites in St. Jérôme extended me every kindness during my stay with them, and Father Lucien Campeau generously allowed me to consult the material he had compiled from various Jesuit archives in Rome and Paris for his *Monumenta Nova Franciae*. Monsieur Pierre Gasnault, Conservateur en Chef of the Bibliothèque Mazarine in Paris, kindly arranged to have a microfilm copy of "Nation Iroquoise" made for me.

This book has benefited immeasurably from the input of many people who have read earlier versions of all or part of the manuscript. Joseph Ernst and Daniel Perrault forced me to come to terms with "economic" interpretations of Iroquois warfare and pushed me toward defining what others meant by that term and what I understood by it. Ramsay Cook and Jim Axtell struggled courageously to improve my prose, and W. J. Eccles and Conrad Heidenreich corrected far more errors of fact than I would like to admit. Thanks to their efforts there are fewer errors and unfortunate turns of phrase than when this book began its life.

To Conrad Heidenreich, however, I owe a special thanks. As a result of our discussions over the years, ideas were fleshed out, concepts sharpened, overlooked details discovered, and obscure place references and native groups identified. His unstinting willingness to share his vast knowledge of this period and of the native peoples of the Northeast saved me countless hours of research and even more errors. The errors that remain are of my own making—sometimes at the cost of ignoring good advice.

Lastly I wish to thank my friends and family: my friends for their support and belief that I would finish my dissertation and that it would become a book before they retired; my wife, Mary, and my son, Robert, for putting up with the privations that inevitably come with a husband and father who is an underemployed graduate student/researcher; my kid sister, Maria, because she typed and improved everything I have ever submitted while managing to complete her own university education and raising a family; my parents, Dorvalino and Salomé, for constant support, moral and fiscal, over the years. They uprooted their lives to come to "the New World" to give their children a better future and made every sacrifice required to make it so. *Esto livro e dedicado os meus pais. É pouco recompense para todos os seus sacrifícios, mas por entretanto tem de chagar.*

*"Your fyre shall burn no more"*

# Introduction

In the seventeenth century the Five Nations Iroquois Confederacy was composed of the Seneca, Cayuga, Onondaga, Oneida, and Mohawk nations. When first encountered by Europeans they may have numbered over twenty-five thousand people (see appendix C). Their villages were located south of Lake Ontario in an area bounded by the Genesee River on the west and the Mohawk River on the east. Aside from their tribal homelands, the Five Nations also claimed land north and west of Lake Ontario, and some tribes contended that the lands around present-day Montreal were once occupied by them. Despite these traditions, and nineteenth- and early-twentieth-century beliefs of Iroquois origins in Canada, current archaeological work suggests that the groups that came to be known as the Five Nations developed in the area south of Lake Ontario or migrated from further south.[1]

Along with geography, the Five Nations shared a culture and system of government. The Iroquois were an Iroquoian linguistic group, traced descent through the female bloodline, and divided work and many social activities along gender lines. While men cleared the forest for fields, women planted and harvested the crops. Men did the hunting, but women usually carried and cleaned the game. Women raised the children and mourned the dead, but curing the sick fell to men. If the activities each sex was expected to perform did not always reflect a balanced division of time and labor, they nonetheless illustrate the symbiotic relationship between men and women in Iroquois society.

The Iroquois lived in longhouses—so named because of their long, narrow construction—which stood in contrast to smaller, rectilinear European houses. Each longhouse was occupied by one or more extended families, about thirty people in all. The families usually included a mother, her children, and her daughter's children. Husbands did not live with their wives; instead, they lived in the same household as their mothers, brothers, and sisters.

Iroquois villages varied in population, from several hundred to two thousand, and were usually palisaded. Every few decades, old villages were abandoned in favor of new ones with fewer pests, more abundant supplies of wood, and fresh fields to cultivate the staple crops of beans, squash, and corn. The fields, located outside the palisades, belonged to the village rather than individuals, but it is likely that individuals tended their particular parts of the communal field. Each village and each tribe was self-sufficient and sustained itself by hunting, fishing, and farming. The Iroquois traded among themselves for mostly ceremonial and social reasons, and they appear to have engaged in little trade with other groups.

Before contact with Europeans, the Iroquois had no metal tools. Fishhooks were made from animal bones. The tips of spears and arrows used for hunting (and warfare) were made of stone (flint), as were axes and all sorts of scraping tools. Cooking vessels were made of clay. The Iroquois were also a "clothing-optional" society. Indeed, most adult Iroquois wore little more than a loin covering during the summer—some wore nothing at all—and children went about naked. During the winter, fur robes were worn, leggings covered the legs, and moccasins protected feet from the worst of winter.

The Iroquois, of course, had a spiritual life. They attempted to communicate with spirit beings who could influence almost all aspects of their daily lives, from hunting and warfare to crop yields. They also believed in an afterlife. Each person was responsible for dealing with the spirits or gods that inhabited his world, each undertaking the appropriate act of supplication or thanksgiving. Some individuals, usually referred to as shamans or medicine men, had the ability to deal more directly with the spirit world. These individuals were consulted for advice and for curing illnesses. The Iroquois also had communal ceremonies of thanksgiving, such as at harvest time.

Central to Iroquois culture and government was their clan system, the social structure by which descent was traced and familial relationships were established. The clan system, however, did more than define relationships among people in villages. It facilitated joint actions among villages and tribes because of the social linkages it provided. The mechanisms by which clans made decisions also served as the basis for decision-making in villages, between villages, between tribes, and among the members of the League of the Iroquois as a whole. This unification of the five tribes into a confederacy took place during some unknown period before contact with Europeans. The Iroquois worked out differences that had led to war among themselves and made a League of Peace.

Despite their traditions of peace, warfare was an important part of Iroquois life. Fortified villages were hard to construct with the tools they had at hand, and the Iroquois would not have built them had they not been necessary. Despite the importance of war, the Iroquois did not have a standing army. All males old enough to fight could, and most likely did, participate in warfare. Some men, proven warriors, commanded a following. Such leaders organized large groups for (defensive and offensive) military actions. At other times they may have led small groups to attack others to avenge previous losses. Individuals not normally considered war leaders also undertook raids for this purpose.

Indeed, it was their warfare against natives and Europeans that made them so important in the history of northeastern North America. In particular, the warfare of the Iroquois played a large role in shaping the course of the religious, political, social, and economic history of New France. It is not surprising, then, that their warfare first attracted, and continues to hold, the attention of historians of the Iroquois, New France, and other native groups in the Northeast. The hypothesis that has come to dominate historians' explanations of Iroquois hostilities in the seventeenth century, the period of heaviest fighting, is known as the Beaver Wars interpretation. It is a view of events quite old and it has been modified over the years, but aspects of it continue to shape the understanding of Iroquois-Indian and Iroquois-European history (see chapter 1).

Yet, the Beaver Wars interpretation rests on little or no evidence and on assumptions of a type of culture and behavior that is at odds with what the documentary record reveals about the way Iroquois culture functioned. Take for example the view that the Iroquois attacked Huron fur brigades in order to rob them of the furs they were carrying to the French. In most works that have adopted the Beaver Wars interpretation, this is stated to be a prime motive of war. Following the historical practice, a few raids are cited as examples of this general pattern. The impression left is that this was a widespread practice. But none of the works indicate how many Iroquois attacks were launched against fur brigades, nor what percentage of all Iroquois attacks those against fur brigades represented. These are important considerations in assessing the relative merit of this "new" motive for warring since most European contemporaries indicated that the Iroquois did not war to steal. My study of Iroquois raids against natives and Europeans reveals that attacks against fur brigades represented a very small percentage of all Iroquois warfare (see table D. 1 ).

Thus despite their much-studied past and the historical consensus about the nature and motivation of Iroquois society in the seventeenth century, I believe there is a strong need to reconsider aspects of Iroquois culture, politics, and warfare in the years before 1701. This book looks at one aspect of the Iroquois past, that of their history with and policy toward New France and her native allies in the seventeenth century.

# CHAPTER ONE

# Iroquois-French History and Historians

Until the 1940s the religious, secular, and nationalist ideologies that produced differing perspectives on New France's history and evolution also shaped the interpretations of French-Iroquois relations written by the colony's historians.[1] But as history divided itself into subfields and specialized areas of study, and as monographs on the Iroquois and other native groups became available, historians of New France began to incorporate those findings into their own works. The result was that no longer did the Iroquois become enemies of New France because Champlain had attacked them in 1609. No more were Iroquois incursions against New France and her native allies seen as one more challenge thrown by God at the little Catholic colony to test its mettle. No more were the battles against the Iroquois the anvil on which a brave new French society was hammered out on the St. Lawrence River.[2] After 1940 the Iroquois attacks against New France were viewed as part of a general pattern of economic warfare waged to gain control of the fur trade from the Hurons and their French allies. This view of events has come to be known as the Beaver Wars interpretation.

The roots of the Beaver Wars explanation for Iroquois wars can be traced back to Francis Parkman, the American historian of New France. This interpretive model was given its fullest treatment by George Hunt in 1940 and has come to dominate the way historians of the Iroquois have accounted for Iroquois relations with a wide range of European and native groups. It is not really clear when the term "Beaver Wars" was coined. Neither Parkman nor Hunt uses it to explain Iroquois aggression. It appears to have worked its way into the literature as a generalization for the elaborate theory that, reduced to its simplest form, argues that the Iroquois waged war to obtain furs. Historians of New France writing after 1940 concurred with the findings of these authorities, and their interpretations of French-Iroquois relations reflected the growing predominance of the Beaver Wars theory. Yet Hunt did not work in a vacuum. By the time his book was published, most of the ideas he espoused had been current for decades.[3] It was in part the longevity of those ideas, and the popularity of "economic" explanations of history, in both Canada and the United States, that gave Hunt's work such currency when it appeared over fifty-five years ago. Unfortunately, ethnocentrism, specious logic, and little or no evidence are at the heart of the Beaver Wars interpretation that has served historians of New France so long as a basis for their explanations of the nature of Iroquois-French relations.

If Francis Parkman can be credited for being among the first, if not the first, to contribute to the development of the Beaver Wars theory, that is certainly not the interpretation he is known for, and his contribution has remained obscured by his more sensational pronouncements. Parkman was among the first and most widely read of New France's historians. His history of New France was written as a tragic tale of a colony doomed to fail. In the struggle between Protestant liberalism and Catholic absolutism and feudalism, liberalism was destined to triumph.[4] Parkman's writings on Indians reflected a similar duality of purpose. In most of his works the Indians, especially the Iroquois, figured prominently. Parkman's treatment of Indians reflected his interest in them and allowed him to make a larger point about their inevitable destruction as a consequence of their inability to adapt to civilized ways and because they stood in the way of progress.[5] More important to Parkman, focusing on the Iroquois served as a means to tell a great story. In an early journal entry, made while hiking in the Berkshire Mountains, Parkman revealed most of the sentiments that would shape his writings on the Iroquois. While the "fierce savages" who "roamed like beasts" in the Northeast had passed away, Parkman found that the "scenes of fear and blood" that marked that passing were "not without a horrid romance."[6] The Iroquois, then, added color and drama to a bold but tragic tale of adventure and furnished a moral lesson about the eventual progress of Protestant liberalism and civilization.[7]

Despite the importance of Indians to Parkman's narrative, he did not think much of them. They were, along with blacks, "outcasts of humanity."[8] In his works he missed few opportunities to cast natives in a negative light. Parkman might call a headman a chief or a sachem, but "greasy potentate" was also possible. Children were almost invariably found "screeching."[9] The derogatory term *savage* was used to qualify nearly all aspects of Indian action and behavior: Indians were a "race of savages"; Indian negotiators were "savage politicians"; surprised Indians were "awe-struck savages"; Indian minds were "thoroughly savage"; and groups of Indians were "savage hordes."[10]

However, it was not enough for Parkman's purpose to portray Indians in denigrating terms. To add drama to his story, to portray the Iroquois as liberty's instrument to help to destroy New France, as well as to show how inevitable was the fall of Indians before progress, they had to be worthy opponents, and he thus stressed their "fierceness." Parkman often used animal imagery to depict Iroquois actions and describe their behavior. Iroquois warriors, he wrote, "followed like hounds," "prowled like lynxes," and when shot, went down "foaming like slaughtered tigers."[11] In one egregiously purple passage, the Iroquois were made out to be both animals and mad: "The threatened blow had fallen, and the wolfish hordes of the five cantons had fleshed their rabid fangs in a new victim."[12] Indeed, Parkman's antipathy toward Indians extended to deliberately falsifying evidence to make them appear irrational and to diminish their actual roles in historical events.[13] The negative, even hostile images of the Indians in Parkman's work reflected a deep-rooted belief that Indians were an inferior race. As far as Parkman was concerned, Indians, Iroquois included, were incapable of reaching the social and intellectual levels required to be "civilized."[14] To support these conclusions he drew on the then controversial and now discredited theories of craniologist S. G. Morton. Morton related intelligence to cranial capacity. Since Indians had, on average, smaller heads than Europeans, Morton and his followers concluded that they were less intelligent. Even the obvious inconsistencies in this theory did not force Parkman to rethink his acceptance of it. Parkman, for example, found it "remarkable that the internal capacity of the skulls of the barbarous American tribes . . . [was] greater than that of either the Mexicans or Peruvians." But since the areas of the skull that were largest were the regions "of the animal propensities," it was easy enough to explain the "ferocious, brutal, and uncivilizable character of the wild tribes."[15] By today's measure, Parkman would be labeled a racist. The worst that can be said, however, is that by the standard of his day he was as ethnocentric as most and less enlightened than some.[16]

Given Parkman's biases and purposes, it is not hard to understand his explanations of Iroquois wars against the French and other natives. The fullest explication of the nature and causes of Iroquois hostilities is found in Parkman's history of the Jesuit missions in New France, published in 1867. Iroquois wars, in general, were products of an "insensate fury" and "mad ambition." Indeed, the very "organization" and "intelligence" of the Iroquois were "merely the instruments of a blind frenzy." The wars against the Hurons and Algonquins in the midseventeenth century were clearly efforts at "annihilation" during a period when the Iroquois were in the "transports of pride, self-confidence, and rage for ascendency."[17] This same "audacious pride and insatiable rage for conquest," coupled with a "homicidal frenzy," accounted for Iroquois attacks against the Neutrals, Eries, and Susquehannocks.[18] Warfare waged against the French was, in part, due to a desire for revenge for Champlain's attacks against the Iroquois in 1609 and 1615, fueled, no doubt, by that "insensate fury." Access to guns, provided by the Dutch, furnished the Iroquois with the means to carry out their plans.[19] It should be stressed that the desire for conquest and annihilation seem to have had no broader purpose. It was the product of these various "savage" and "irrational" passions of the Iroquois.[20]

This is the interpretation for which Parkman has come to be known. It has been dismissed, and rightly so, for its ethnocentric assessment of the character of the Iroquois and for the superficial delineation of their motives.[21] However, this is a modern reaction to Parkman's work. Many of Parkman's contemporaries thought his book and his views of the Iroquois quite sound.[22] Yet few of those who read Parkman for his views on the Iroquois relied on this version of events when writing of the Iroquois themselves. Some years later he offered another motive for Iroquois wars, and it was this interpretation that his contemporaries came to use to explain Iroquois relations with Europeans and natives.

Writing in 1869 Parkman sought to explain Iroquois wars against the Miamis and Illinois in the 1680s. Certainly Iroquois "ferocity" had a role to play in these wars,

> yet it was not alone their homicidal fury that now impelled them to another war. Strange as it may seem, this war was in no small measure one of commercial advantage. They had long traded with the Dutch and English of New York, who gave them, in exchange for their furs, the guns, ammunition, knives, hatchets, kettles, beads, and brandy which had become indispensable to them. Game was scarce in their country. They must seek their beaver and other skins in the vacant territories of the tribes they had destroyed; but this did not content them. The French of Canada were seeking to secure a monopoly of the furs of the north and west; and, of late, the enterprises of La Salle on the tributaries of the Mississippi had

especially roused the jealousy of the Iroquois, fomented, moreover, by Dutch and English traders. These crafty savages would fain reduce all these regions to subjection, and draw thence an exhaustless supply of furs, to be bartered for English goods with the traders of Albany.[23]

In his biography of Frontenac, published in 1877, Parkman offered a more precise analysis of Iroquois motives:

> This movement of the western Iroquois had a double incentive,—their love of fighting and their love of gain. It was a war of conquest and of trade. All five tribes of the league had become dependent on the English and Dutch of Albany for guns, powder, lead, brandy, and many other things that they had learned to regard as necessities. Beaverskins alone could buy them; but to the Iroquois the supply of beaver was limited. The regions of the west and northwest, the upper Mississippi with its tributaries, and above all, the forests of the upper lakes, were occupied by tribes in the interest of the French . . . whose traders controlled their immense trade. . . . It was the purpose of the Iroquois to master all this traffic, conquer the tribes who had possession of it, and divert the entire supply of furs to themselves, and through themselves to the English Dutch.[24]

In these passages are most of the essential elements of what has come to be the Beaver Wars interpretation—the dependence on European goods, the implicit destruction of Iroquois culture, the extinction of beaver in Iroquois lands, and the attempt to divert the furs of others to trade for needed goods. Parkman made no attempt to support the central assumptions of this hypothesis with documentary evidence. As far as Parkman was concerned, there was no reason. It was obvious to him that native culture was inferior to that of Europeans and that the Iroquois would naturally see the advantage of European goods over those they produced themselves. This view flowed naturally from his negative conceptions of Indians. In short, the basis of the Beaver Wars theory rests on an ethnocentric belief in the superiority of European society; at heart it is as inherently biased as Parkman's view of Iroquois character.

Nonetheless, it remains significant that, while not denying Iroquois "ferocity" as a motive, Parkman stressed an "economic" motive—the desire to control the fur trade for material gain—as the cause of the wars of the 1680s. He did not try to use this motive to explain Iroquois wars against any other groups in this or earlier periods. He did state that the Iroquois hunted on the lands of the Hurons and others, but this seems to be an effect of the wars produced by "homicidal fury" rather than a cause of those wars. The implications of this view for Iroquois relations with the French were left unstated, but they seem clear nevertheless: to revenge and "insensate fury" one must now add the motive of competing to control the fur trade as causes of the Iroquois wars against New France.[25]

The next phase in the evolution of the Beaver Wars interpretation was the development of the view that Indians were, in some ways, like Europeans. Unlike Parkman, the next generation of historians did not try to establish what the Iroquois were like; they assumed they were like Europeans, or at least had similar attitudes in analogous situations. In its crudest form, this view ignored the cultural context of the Iroquois altogether. The more refined versions contended, even if they did not demonstrate, that cultural change had led the Iroquois to become acculturated to European ways. Among values shared by Iroquois and European was the desire for accumulation of material wealth. While this attitudinal change in historians was an important step away from the virulent ethnocentrism of Parkman, it led to an image of the Iroquois as distorted and as far off the mark as Parkman's.

The transformation of the Iroquois from ruthless warriors to what one scholar has called "capitalist entrepreneurs in moccasins"[26] began in earnest in 1915 with the publication of Peter Wraxall's manuscript of "An Abridgement of the Records of Indian Affairs contained in Four Folio Volumes, transacted in the Colony of New York from the year 1678 to the Year 1751."[27] In the introductory essay editor Charles McIlwain first suggested that the Iroquois were acting as "middlemen" in the trade between natives and English.[28] Given the centrality of his views to later historiography, they are worth quoting at length. According to McIlwain,

> The great role of the Iroquois was that of middlemen between the "Far Indians" and the English, a role which enabled them not only to obtain material benefits, but to retain that position of superiority over the Indians of the eastern half of the United States which they had probably first secured through their knowledge of the white man's firearms, but could now no longer hope to hold by mere force alone. . . . They hoped to retain by peaceable means what they could not expect any longer to keep by force. This could be done by alliance and by trade alone, and by English trade alone. . . .
>
> The Iroquois were fully alive to the great advantages their situation

gave them. It became, therefore, a consistent part of their policy to do their utmost to induce the nations of the interior to desert the French and accept English goods. . . .

The very existence of the Five Nations depended on this. There were no beaver left in their own country. As early as 1671, we have a French memoir to the effect that hardly a single beaver could be found south of Lake Ontario. The Iroquois had to get their beaver from the Indians farther west or get none, and beaver they must have or lose the rum, the clothing, guns and ammunition which had become necessary to their happiness and even to their existence. . . . Particularly important to them at one period were the Hurons and the Tobacco Nation, who were in such a position geographically that they could intercept all furs coming from the west to Canada. To intercept trade there was to turn it southward, where it must pass through the Iroquois country to Albany. It is easy to see the bearing of conditions such as these on the story of the Indians at this time,—the Fox Wars, the desperate struggle with the Hurons, the war between the Iroquois and the Illinois, the alliance between Iroquois and Miamis, the general influence of the Iroquois over the tribes as far as the Mississippi. It is little wonder the Iroquois valued a connection with the English which lay at the bottom of such influence and power.[29]

In part, this interpretation was little more than a repetition of what Parkman had claimed some forty-six years earlier. McIlwain again mentioned the dependence on European goods, the lack of furs among the Iroquois, and how the Iroquois tried to divert the fur trade in order to trade for those goods upon which they had become dependent. But he went farther than Parkman did and claimed that these items were vital to Iroquois survival. Which trade goods were more important was not specified. New as well was the claim that these were causes of the wars against the Hurons and Petuns, even though he indicated, based on one source, that the Iroquois ran out of furs only in 1671, some twenty years after both those tribes were dispersed by Iroquois invasions. But the most significant departure from past interpretations was the claim that the Iroquois were acting as middlemen in the trade between the western tribes and the English. By acting as middlemen, the Iroquois would reap some material advantage and maintain political superiority over other native groups. Whether that "material advantage" was profit, the general purpose of being a middleman, is not made clear. Iroquois political goals were achieved, one assumes, by controlling access to cheap English trade goods.

What is lacking from McIlwain's interpretation is any documentary evidence to substantiate it. Like Parkman, he claimed that the Iroquois were dependent on European goods, but offered no evidence to support that contention. His interpretation also suggested that the Iroquois were trading for profit, as middlemen did, and that they were using that position for political purposes. But in Iroquois society, accumulation of personal wealth and working purely for the sake of making a profit, or material gain, were alien motives.[30] He ignored this aspect of Iroquois society and did nothing to show how it had been altered so that these foreign concepts became part of Iroquois culture. It was not unreasonable to claim that the Iroquois were trying to use the fur trade for political ends, but again, McIlwain provides no examples of this behavior.[31]

McIlwain also failed to furnish evidence to prove that the Iroquois acted as middlemen. Parkman's analysis of Iroquois motives, especially the 1877 version, might appear to hint at middlemen behavior, but McIlwain did not cite Parkman in support of this claim. Moreover, a careful reading makes it clear that Parkman was contending that the furs were getting to the English because the Iroquois were forcibly taking them from the other tribes and trading them to the English for goods for themselves, not because they were taking English trade wares to those tribes in return for furs.[32] In support of his assertion that the Iroquois and English valued their relationship because it gave power to the Iroquois and furs to the English, McIlwain cited a passage from the work of eighteenth-century French historian Charlevoix.[33] In it McIlwain may have thought he saw support for his description of the Iroquois as middlemen, but that is not the case. Charlevoix wrote, "It is not that the Iroquois are great hunters; but rather that they often carry off from our allies and Voyagers the furs which these are bringing to Montreal, [and] they engage many nations, and often even our Coureurs de Bois, to trade with the English of New York, and the profit, which they draw from this trade, centered necessarily in their country, keeps them in the English interest."[34] It seems clear that Charlevoix means that the English got the furs because the Iroquois took them from others, or encouraged others to trade directly with the English, and not because they were middlemen. Whether the "profit" the Iroquois derived from their actions was economic or political, Charlevoix did not state. In short, neither the older aspects of the growing Beaver Wars thesis nor its additions were substantiated by McIlwain's work.

Lack of evidence did not hinder the acceptance of McIlwain's interpretation. In 1925 it formed the basis of Louise Kellogg's analysis of the role played by the Iroquois in the development of Wisconsin and the Northwest. In 1930 Harold Innis used it to explain the role of natives in the fur trade in his seminal work,

*The Fur Trade in Canada.* And in 1933 John Brebner, in his work on the exploration of America, argued that as early as 1615 the Iroquois and Huron were competing middlemen in the fur trade and that this was the cause of their wars at the time Champlain began his explorations.[35] The single most important use of the Beaver Wars thesis came in 1940 with the publication of George Hunt's *Wars of the Iroquois.* It was the first modern work of history devoted to explaining the wars of the Iroquois from the perspective of the Indians. Hunt put all the features of the Beaver Wars thesis to use in his effort to explain the causes of Iroquois wars against a wide range of native groups.

Hunt's work began with the generally accurate assumption that in northeastern North America trade was a significant basis of early Indian-European contact and relations. Unfortunately, he then proceeded to develop a highly speculative picture of changes in native society as a result of trade-based contact. He believed that the advent of permanent European settlements permitted the "constant participation of every native" in the trade and that natives "were usually frantically eager" to do so. The result was a change, "almost overnight," in the "fundamental conditions of the aboriginal economy." The fur trade became the determining factor in Indian-Indian relations and, as old skills were lost, Indians became dependent on European goods for survival and fought each other for the furs that would purchase those goods.[36] Providing absolutely no evidence to support this appraisal of the consequences of early Indian-European contact on the various cultures in the Northeast, he applied these conclusions to the Iroquois.[37] Taking his scenario as proven, Hunt then explained all major aggressions in the years before 1690 as products of Iroquois economic necessity. To survive in their geographic location, the Iroquois had to gain a middleman status in the fur trade. Because of dependency on European goods, their socioeconomic survival required attaining such a position. The Hurons, however, controlled this function. When the Iroquois ran out of their own furs and could not get any by peaceful means, they made a decision to dislodge the Hurons, even if it meant destroying them. For Hunt it was this singular and persistent motive that accounted for the Iroquois wars against the Hurons and other native groups.[38]

One of Hunt's underlying assumptions was that the Iroquois were pretty much like Europeans, at least in that they waged war for economic reasons.[39] By showing that the Iroquois acted as middlemen (that is, they were motivated by materialism and economic self-interest) and that wars were produced by desires to attain that position, he would support that broader thesis.[40] Unfortunately, in order to support the hypothesis that the Iroquois were middlemen,

Hunt assumed that his views about culture change and economic self-interest were self-evident. This allowed him to interpret Iroquois actions, especially their warfare, in light of those views. Hunt's interpretation of those actions then served as proof for his views of cultural change and warfare being brought on by economic concerns. This is circular sophistry. Moreover, as Allen Trelease has pointed out, Hunt based his middleman interpretation on few references, distorted his sources, and found "clear-cut evidence where actually it was obscure or non-existent."[41] Also, as Hunt's reviewers pointed out when his book was published and as Trelease stressed again twenty-two years later, Hunt ignored all the other factors that motivated the Iroquois to war.[42] Revenge, pride, and the need for captives for adoption and torture all continued to be goals of Iroquois warfare.[43]

The problems with Hunt's work flowed from his assumption that people were all always the same. But the Iroquois of 1640 were similar to Americans in 1940 only in the range and complexity of their emotions, drives, and cultural limitations. Hunt failed to take into account the multiplicity of human motives and cultural differences. Unfortunately for the history of the Iroquois, Hunt was all too successful. His simplistic, monocausal, and economically deterministic explanation seemed to have resolved the question of why the Iroquois engaged in wars against other natives. Historians of the Iroquois, other native groups, and European colonies have come to rely almost exclusively on Hunt's work for their assessments of Iroquois motives.

One of the first important works on French-Iroquois relations to incorporate Hunt's middleman thesis was Léo-Paul Desrosiers's *Iroquoisie, 1534–1645*.[44] Despite the title, *Iroquoisie* was not really a book about the Iroquois. Desrosiers focused mostly on the Mohawks and his concern was the French. Indeed, the first one hundred pages dealt mostly with Champlain. The Iroquois were mentioned because, in establishing the colony, one of Champlain's problems was dealing with them. For Desrosiers, like Hunt, the central goal of all Indian behavior was to control or take advantage of the fur trade. His view of the causes of Iroquois wars against natives and New France reflected that belief. According to Desrosiers, the Mohawks soon came to realize how "a beaver pelt . . . could bring them hatchets" and how, "in the end, the middlemen . . . accumulate profits at the expense of others" to earn their living. The Iroquois desire to assume the middleman role and the pressing need for furs are what led to hostilities with the Hurons and Algonquins.[45]

Desrosiers's explanation of Iroquois hostilities against New France relied on a curious blend of economic determinism and inevitability—that is, the struggle for the fur trade between the Iroquois and the French would have led sooner or later to conflict; the actions of the participants influenced only the timing. For Desrosiers it was obvious that Iroquois enmity toward New France was the product of Champlain siding with the Algonquins in the early years of French settlement. But equally apparent was the fact that "the Franco-Iroquois conflict was inevitable from the beginning, for it was in the nature of things. Nothing could prevent it." As the Mohawks ran out of furs and became "fur pirates," they began to affect the lifeblood of the colony, and this led to conflict. The pressure from the Dutch for furs, the Mohawk need for goods, and the fear of the French trading those wares to their enemies all put pressure on the Mohawks to do this. The Mohawks had to "either obtain furs or revert to their primitive civilisation" in the face of their enemies' access to European goods.[46] The answer was to rob others of furs when the middleman position either did not produce the desired results or could not be maintained.

Like Hunt, Desrosiers placed great emphasis on the role of the fur trade. For him economic motives were at the heart of Mohawk actions, even if he was not as rigid in his interpretation as Hunt had been.[47] But, if he differed in detail, he did not in substance.[48] If in stressing a predestined conflict Desrosiers seemed to hark back to the religious overtones of Faillon and Ferland, in the economic basis of that struggle one can clearly find the influence of McIlwain and Hunt. The historians of New France who wrote after the 1940s, from Abbé Groulx to W. J. Eccles, could refer to Hunt or Desrosiers with equal assurance that there would be support for their claims that it was an Iroquois desire to play the middleman in the fur trade that accounted for their wars against the colony.

Abbé Groulx was the last of the great clericonationalist writers to turn his attention to the history of New France. For him the early history of Quebec was important because it showed the benevolent role of the Church in helping God form a special French and Catholic people.[49] He focused on the Iroquois because of the obstacles they represented to the growth of that unique society. Like Desrosiers he felt that the struggle between the Iroquois and French was inevitable. The Iroquois struggle for hegemony over the tribes in North America, he believed, "could be fatal to New France." The competition between the French and Iroquois for control of the fur trade meant that sooner or later these two powers would clash. The Iroquois needed to control the fur trade because they did not have enough furs to satisfy their appetite for European goods.[50]

Groulx was less precise about Iroquois motivations than Desrosiers, but in the end it remained that Iroquois desires for furs to trade for goods, worthy of attaining for their own sake, were at the heart of Iroquois aggression.

For Gustave Lanctot the Iroquois were of central importance to the history of New France and thus were featured prominently in his work. Major and minor raids against the colony were noted, often in detail. Lanctot's implicit assumption was that the cause of these attacks against the French was really an extension of the reasons for the wars against the Hurons and other French native allies. Lanctot recognized that wars could be caused by infringements on hunting territories, desire to assert political supremacy, and individual aspirations for honor. But the Dutch sale of firearms to the Iroquois for beaver pelts fueled old rivalries. "With an economic pretext for war, the Iroquois now deliberately sought to annihilate the Huron peoples so that they might become the sole middlemen" in the trade between the western Indians and the "Europeans on the Atlantic seaboard." Lanctot did not completely dismiss traditional motives for leading to war, but he subordinated them to this broader economic motive. For example, he recognized that some raids against the Hurons were made solely to capture people. But for him that was part of a broader policy of trying to incorporate all the Hurons into the Iroquois Confederacy to enable the Iroquois to "become the sole intermediaries and beneficiaries in the trade with the Dutch." The Iroquois wars against New France were also tied to Iroquois ambitions in the fur trade. As a result of pressure from the Dutch and later the English, whom the Iroquois needed as suppliers, the Iroquois sought to eliminate French competition from the fur trade. In short, it was the "economic ambitions and atavistic instincts" of the Iroquois that "determined the unflinching hostility" they showed toward New France.[51]

If Lanctot left room for noneconomic motives to account for some Iroquois hostilities, Marcel Trudel did not. In Trudel's work one can find Hunt's thesis accepted without qualification. The wars against native groups were to gain a middleman status, a position made necessary because the Iroquois had run out of furs and were dependent on them for survival.[52] The wars against New France were simply the extension of these motives to the Iroquois' major competitor. Trudel was rebelling against the clericonationalist writers who had preceded him.[53] He focused on the economic development of the colony to show that trade, as much or more so than religious preoccupations, led to its founding and shaped its growth. It was only natural that his conception of the role of the Iroquois would be colored by this approach. Hunt's work, with its emphasis on economic motives and the role of the fur trade, fitted into Trudel's framework.

If New France was shaped by economic rather that religious forces, what better example to cite than the destructive competition waged with the Iroquois over control of the fur trade?

For different reasons but in much the same spirit of rebellion, W. J. Eccles came to rely on Hunt's interpretation. Among the most eminent historians of New France in both French- and English-speaking Canada, Eccles published his critical study of Governor Frontenac in 1959. In it the Iroquois were major players and the success of Frontenac's career was judged, in large part, by his Indian policy. Unfortunately, Eccles did not turn the same critical eye to the contemporary interpretations of Iroquois policy. He accepted Hunt's thesis wholesale and it has formed the basis, until recently, of his interpretation of Iroquois-native and Franco-Iroquois wars. Eccles concluded that the hostilities of the Iroquois were "an attempt to divert the fur trade of the Huron and the Ottawas from New France to Albany" with the Iroquois keeping "the middleman's profit" for themselves. The struggle against New France was part of that fight over control of the fur trade. For Eccles, Hunt served as a "useful corrective to . . . Parkman," who ignored or rejected economic factors.[54] Recently, Eccles has written that he erred in accepting Hunt's economic interpretation.[55] Eccles has now concluded that the Iroquois wars were for power or control over the lands in which they warred, "rather than [for] mere commercial advantage." Iroquois wars against New France proceeded from these same motives.[56] He is the only historian of New France to reject the middleman interpretation in particular, and "economic" or Beaver Wars explanations of Franco-Iroquois relations in general.

Unlike most historians of New France, recent historians of the Iroquois and other native societies have, for the most part, rejected Hunt's specific middleman thesis.[57] They do, however, continue to argue that warfare for "economic" ends was a significant motive for Iroquois hostilities. They contend that the Iroquois warred to obtain furs, either for material profit or because the Iroquois were dependent on European goods, and because they lacked their own, or a sufficient, supply of furs. The furs thus stolen went to trade for those needed goods. The struggle for the furs of others is what led to the wars of the Iroquois.[58] For some of these writers this motive was central to explaining Iroquois wars; for others it was but one of several motives for war. Daniel Richter, for example, while suggesting that economic factors grew to be the most important causes of Iroquois warfare, also recognized the role of cultural factors, such as the need to replace people lost to war and disease, as motives for some warfare.[59] But for all, economic motivations are at the root of Iroquois hostilities.

Recently, three historians of native groups have come to reject economic explanations for understanding the Iroquois wars in the seventeenth century. Conrad Heidenreich and Lucien Campeau, scholars of the Hurons, and Dean Snow, historian of the Iroquois, have played down the role of economic warfare and suggested that the causes of Iroquois hostility can be found in cultural practices related to war and in responses to population losses brought on by new diseases.[60] They have not, however, written detailed critiques nor delineated alternative interpretations of Iroquois-French relations.[61] Thus in the 125 years since Francis Parkman articulated its essential elements, the Beaver Wars interpretation has been fleshed out somewhat, but remains virtually unaltered and dominant.[62]

The Beaver Wars thesis of Iroquois policy has come to dominate how historians of New France account for Iroquois hostilities against that colony. From its origins in works on the history of New France, it has gone on to become the basis of interpreting Iroquois-native relations and has worked its way back to be the foundation for understanding the nature of Franco-Iroquois relations. Parkman's original thesis has been modified and expanded over the years, and it has grown in stature with repeating, but it remains essentially a series of unproven assumptions based on a flawed understanding of Iroquois culture and character. If Hunt's work seemed to give it respectability by cloaking it in apparently rational economic garb, he nonetheless ignored, or misunderstood, Iroquois culture. It may have been undergoing change, but Iroquois culture was very much alive, and its processes and values shaped Iroquois responses to Europeans and their cultural and material baggage. The reasons for the Iroquois wars against the French and others were as complex as their culture and the circumstances the Iroquois faced. Iroquois wars were not the products of ''insensate fury,'' and they were certainly much more than just the upshot of ''intertribal trade relations'' gone sour.

# CHAPTER TWO

# Government and Social Organization among the Iroquois

Few aspects of Iroquois culture are as essential to understanding Iroquois policy and conduct as are the means of group and individual control, the decision-making processes at the various levels of government, and the nature of the government of the Five Nations. Strikingly different from their equivalents in authoritarian New France, decision-making and government among the Iroquois reflected a deep and overriding concern with individualism. Indeed, government among the tribes that made up the Confederacy was not so much a political system as an extension of the individual control process to a more complex level. Another feature of Iroquois culture—the clan system—provided the basic framework for cooperative effort at both the tribal and intertribal levels.

While Europeans knew of the Iroquois by 1603, it was not until the 1650s that detailed analyses of their culture were made, and these did not cover all aspects under study here. This makes it necessary to rely on eighteenth-century data to flesh out the picture. The question of how the Iroquois were governed before the 1650s or whether that process was the same or significantly altered by midcentury remains unresolved. Further, because detailed seventeenth- and eighteenth-century accounts of the same processes are rare, comparisons of changes between the mid-1600s and the early 1700s were also not possible. Indeed, while later sources often provided more detail about matters touched on briefly by earlier authorities, one can rarely be certain whether different informants were revealing a changed process, or if the variant descriptions simply reflect powers of observation and/or degrees of familiarity with the Iroquois. A consequence of using sources from different centuries is that Iroquois society appears static. This was not true of culture in general and probably not of government. But if the sources do not allow for complex comparisons of change over time, they nonetheless yield a clear picture of how the Iroquois governed themselves in the latter half of the seventeenth century. It may only be informed speculation to suggest that the process worked in a similar fashion before the 1650s, but it is unlikely that question will be resolved unless new sources are found.

The Iroquois of the Five Nations were a proud and independent people. As A. F. C. Wallace has written, they held autonomous responsibility to be an ideal, and "self reliance and independence of spirit were sedulously inculcated" in their young.[1] This inclination toward individual freedom and a strong sense of pride and honor were fundamental features of Iroquois society. Frederick Post noted that there was "not a prouder or more high minded people in themselves than the Indians,"[2] while the Jesuit Joseph Lafitau concluded that "it is really honour which forms the mainspring of their actions."[3] This sense of pride and honor was so strong that fear of disgrace was sufficient to keep most Iroquois from behaving in a manner unacceptable to society.[4] Indeed, suffering public disapproval or humiliation often led members of Iroquois society to commit suicide.[5] This practice was compounded by the fact that the Iroquois were very sensitive and "easily affronted."[6] Because of this the Iroquois went so far as to contain visible signs of their anger in order not to offend members of their society.[7] The tendency to avenge insults also played a strong role in keeping personal relations amicable.[8] As a consequence of these values and beliefs, respect for the rights of others served as the underlying principle that guided interpersonal relations. Each Iroquois, wrote Lafitau, regarded "others as masters of their own actions and themselves, lets them conduct themselves as they wish and judges only himself."[9]

This, however, did not mean that individuals, even young ones who had least authority, could not make their desires felt. It simply meant that care had to be taken and imagination used so that protocols were not broken. For example, a young Christianized Iroquois wanted to prevent some of his elder tribesmen from drinking. He could not command an end to this behavior because as a young man he did not have that authority and he had to respect his elders. Instead he got up, pretended to stumble, and deliberately knocked over the kettle with the alcohol. The others, amused at his clumsiness, as it appeared, were not offended. The young man thus had put an end to the drinking without offending his elders by overstepping the bounds his youthful status had assigned him.[10]

All these values were reflected in the Iroquois authority structure and control process. The Iroquois recognized some members of their society as leaders, usually based on generosity, wisdom, and skills as a hunter or warrior.[11] The clan matron was also a recognized leader.[12] Yet these leaders were severely constrained in their exercise of authority because they had to pay deference to the right of the individual to determine his own course of action. Clan matrons, for example, could intercede to prevent a revenge raid, and village elders would appeal to them to do so if the planned action threatened to produce conflict in relations with a tribe with whom they wished to remain at peace. Yet regardless of whether it suited the clan matrons' interest to intervene, they tended not to because they were "not eager to set in motion [their] means of prestige and authority to constrain others against their will."[13] Chiefs were likewise restricted, and as Governor Philippe de Rigaud de Vaudreuil and the Intendant Antoine-Denis Raudot noted in their dispatch to the Minister of the Marine in 1708, "it is true that the Indians have leaders among them, but these leaders do not have absolute authority. They just state what should be done, and afterwards, the others do so if they want. Since there is no punishment among them, one cannot subordinate them."[14]

Further, in order not to infringe on individual rights or to offend someone's honor, a chief phrased his commands as requests, either directly to a person or through an intermediary who was a relative of the person.[15] This point is extremely important and reveals much about the complex nature of social interaction and control among the Iroquois. By making his wishes known in the form of a request, the chief respected the rights of the individual by not directly ordering him to perform a task. He also shifted the onus for compliance to the individual who had been asked because the person asked ran the risk of public disapproval if he did not comply.[16] To deny a favor was looked upon as ungenerous—a quality disapproved of by the Iroquois.[17] The intermediary also assumed responsibility since, by acceding to the chief's request, he had to help persuade the individual to do as the chief had asked.[18] Had the chief phrased his desire as a command, he would have risked public disapproval for his disrespectful manner and might have suffered a loss of prestige if his orders had not been followed.[19] The fear of public defiance was another reason that a clan relation of the individual in question was used as an intermediary to obtain a response. Defiance by the individual asked was a very real possibility since the individual affronted through a command would not likely suffer another blow to his pride by actually carrying out the command. A request, however, was much more likely to be performed since it allowed individuals to persuade themselves (and society) that they obeyed out of generosity rather than because they had been instructed to do so.[20]

Decisions that affected groups of Iroquois were handled in much the same way, but in councils. Invariably, a great deal of skill was required, yet by pursuing the same principles used to reconcile the apparently opposite needs of individual self-determination and the necessity for social control, the political integrity of village and tribe could be respected and intravillage and intratribal cooperation could be affected.[21] Thus, while the views of recognized tribal leaders influenced the decisions reached at public councils, everyone was permitted to voice his or her opinion.[22] Joint decisions were reached by consensus and those villages or tribes that had not agreed to the final outcome were not bound by that decision.[23] While those in favor of a course of action tried to persuade those who voted against it, they could only do so in the same manner as persuading an individual. The councils themselves had no other means to ensure that their decisions were carried out even by those who had voted in favor.[24] It was fortunate that the Iroquois liked to discuss political affairs.[25] While this system was particularly well adapted to Iroquois cultural needs, the complex manner of resolving internal matters, added to external political concerns, meant that a great deal of the time of an Iroquois leader was spent dealing in political matters.[26]

Possibly because so much time was spent in councils, the procedures to be followed were clearly established.[27] When a council was to be held, a messenger was sent to announce the time and place, or an elder called out the announcement.[28] When these councils involved people from outside the village or tribe, the arriving delegates were greeted with ceremonies outside the village and given a pipe to smoke.[29] In meetings with Europeans it was common practice to fire a gun salute to greet arriving delegates.[30] The delegates were then led to a cabin set aside for their use. In this procession,

> one of the notable men walks at the head, and pronounces a long string of words which have been handed down to them by tradition, and which are repeated by the others after him. The ambassador who is to be the spokesman comes last of all, singing in a rather agreeable tone; he continues his song until he has entered his cabin, around which he also walks five or six times, still singing; then he sits down. There the pledges of friendship are

renewed, and presents are given to dispel fatigue; to wipe away tears; to remove scales from their eyes, so that they may easily see one another; and, finally, to open their throats and give freer passage to their voices.

The formalities over, the delegates were fed, news was exchanged, and the actual business of the visit was put off for the next day or later.[31]

Once they were at the meeting, the various delegates sat at assigned places, depending on their position in the confederacy.[32] All propositions were discussed by one tribe, "handed" across the fire to be discussed by another tribe, and eventually returned to the first tribe.[33] At Confederacy councils this procedure was based on the position of the tribe in the Confederacy structure, or, more properly, based on its moiety affiliation; the "elder" moiety of tribes discussed an issue first.[34] After a few speeches, the council was adjourned for the day to give delegates time to prepare answers. As English traveler John Bartram noted, "there is nothing they contem so much as precipitation in publick councils; indeed they esteem it at all times a mark of much levity in anyone to return an immediate answer to a serious question."[35] Speeches at these councils were made by trained speakers well versed in the proper protocol. They could be subtle and evasive enough to give an answer that the other side wished to hear, but without actually committing their tribes to a specific course of action. David Zeisberger observed that, when speakers wished to be obscure, they could "speak so cleverly and with so much circumstance that even Indians must puzzle at the true sense of their allusions."[36] It was probably witnessing one of their conferences that led Bartram to characterize the Iroquois as a "subtile, prudent and judicious people in their councils."[37]

As each proposition was made, the speaker of the tribe being addressed handed out a small stick to one member of his delegation. That person was then responsible for bringing up the proposition at the meeting in which the tribe prepared a response to the earlier speech.[38] By this means the speaker was not under pressure to recall exactly every proposition in the usually long speeches, and this practice ensured that every chief would be able to take an active part in ensuing discussions. After every proposition, the speaker who held the floor handed over a belt or string of wampum to the tribe he was addressing. These served as mnemonic devices to recall the content of the speech and as a material confirmation of the verbal message.[39] The length, width, color, and design of the belts varied with the contents of the speech (the more important the speech, the larger the belt), but as a general rule the belts were about two feet long and six inches wide.[40] When the Iroquois sent a report by messenger unaccompanied by wampum, it meant that the sender could not vouch for the veracity of the message but was passing it along anyway.[41] Any message confirmed by wampum was deemed to be true. The belts and strings were displayed at the councils and conferences in the order in which they would be presented, on a string or rope strung across two poles stuck in the ground.[42] While conference delegates were furnished with extra belts to deal with unexpected proposals, if they ran out, they confirmed a speech with sticks that would later be replaced with belts.[43] The wampum used at Iroquois councils and at Iroquois-European conferences was contributed by individuals in a given village at the request of a chief. At both types of gatherings, when the speaker presented a belt, he announced which village or tribe had sent the belt.[44] While at each level of council belts were presented on behalf of all (either village or tribe), it was still important to identify whom had furnished the belt.

This last point about wampum underscores an important aspect of Iroquois government: the essentially independent spirit of its members. The clearly specified process at decision-making councils was not the result of some government commission that met and decided that this would be the most efficient way to conduct business. Instead, the established protocol represented the accumulation over time of customs that developed as the Iroquois sought to protect the integrity of village and tribe, while still recognizing the need for, and advantages of, cooperative effort.[45] The Iroquois had no permanent governing body constantly in session and directing policy. What they had instead was a framework that allowed for joint action when the member tribes felt the need for it. The rest of the time each village and tribe conducted its affairs as best suited them.[46] Even when all five tribes agreed on a course of action, when it was no longer convenient for a given tribe to adhere to it, the tribe would do what it could to ignore that policy or to negate its effects.[47] The Confederacy had no ruling body to control such groups, and efforts to bring them back into line were made only by those tribes still in favor of the course decided at the Confederacy council.

This problem was compounded by the accepted practice of one tribe negotiating business with other groups on behalf of the whole Confederacy, and often informing their Iroquois confederates after the fact.[48] Sometimes individuals seeking their own ends did this. In 1700, for example, the English learned that the Senecas and Cayugas were treating for peace with the French. It turned out, however, that the Cayugas knew nothing of this and that only two Seneca chiefs, Assicchqua and Awenano, were involved. Even the rest of the Senecas were unaware of their actions.[49] These Iroquois leaders probably calculated that those among the Senecas and Cayugas who favored an end to warring would support their actions once they presented the tribes with a *fait accompli*. Awenano had lost most of his family in raids by the French and their Indian allies, and he simply wanted to speed up the protracted peace talks to prevent further losses. Awenano even went so far as to take his own wampum and not that contributed by the council in order to keep the reasons for his visit to Canada a secret.[50] While behavior of this sort did not always meet with public approval, it was sometimes difficult to negate the effects of such actions because it was only possible to do so by getting the person who had committed the action to agree to change his mind. In 1726, for example, the Onondagas granted the French permission to build a fort in Seneca territory against Seneca wishes. In this case, however, even though the Senecas managed to convince the Onondagas to withdraw their permission, the damage was done because the French fort was by that time established and the French refused to tear it down.[51]

Despite this lack of central authority and the wide range of freedom accorded its members, the Five Nations Confederacy managed its political concerns with such shrewdness that the Iroquois earned the praise of being one of the most subtle and most politic nations in the world.[52] Father Lafitau clearly recognized Iroquois political capacity, and he credited "a most refined policy" on the part of these Indians for making them a dominant power in the region between New York and New France.[53] He wrote further that

> it is affairs of state which carry off the principal attention. Constant distrust of their neighbours keeps the Indians alert to the advantage of all favourable occasions either to cause disorder [in neighboring states] without seeming to do so or to form alliances by making themselves necessary. Their skill in this respect has infinite resources which they keep always active and stirring, and while they humour their allies by frequent visits and all the duties of reciprocal courtesy, they are always occupied and observing and deliberating endlessly the least events.[54]

The need for endless debate over the least matter reflects the consensus approach to government and the daily preoccupation with politics that resulted from having to reconcile the various needs of the villages and tribes of the Confederacy. The dominant role of the Iroquois among the European and native nations of the St. Lawrence and Hudson Valley underscores how successful the Iroquois were in reconciling the strong feelings of personal and collective independence fostered by their culture with the need for unified efforts to keep from being overwhelmed by their Indian and European neighbors. The need for individual, village, and tribal autonomy was not always adequately reconciled, nor were the consequences of that behavior effectively counterbalanced or negated when it contradicted a Confederacy council decision. Nonetheless, the Iroquois Confederacy did, for the most part, resolve these problems. What facilitated such success as they were able to attain, and formed the basis of government among these independent-minded people, was their clan structure.

The Iroquois clan system, at its least complex, can be described as follows: two or more maternal lineages (extended families) composed a clan, several clans constituted a moiety, and two moieties (halves) made up a tribe.[55] Diagrammatically it can be represented thus:

| | | tribe | | | | | |
|---|---|---|---|---|---|---|---|
| | moiety 1 | | | | moiety 2 | | |
| clan 1 | | clan 2 | | clan 1 | | clan 2 | |
| $1^1$ | $1^2$ | $1^1$ | $1^2$ | $1^1$ | $1^2$ | $1^1$ | $1^2$ |

(lineage)

In reality, however, the system was much more complex. Clans could have more than two lineages, while each tribe had at least three clans.[56] In fact, except for the Mohawks and the Oneidas, all the other tribes of the Confederacy had more than three clans—the Onondagas alone had nine.[57] Further, most tribes were divided into two or more villages, and each village had two moieties and at least three clan groups.[58] While moieties were usually made up of two or more clans, among those tribes that had only three clans—the Mohawks and the Oneidas—a single clan (the Bear) comprised a moiety.

The clan system of the Iroquois was one of the most significant features of their culture. The rules and obligations of the clans affected almost every aspect of Iroquois life, from where a person lived in a village to whom he or she could marry, when to wage war, and who would mourn his or her death.[59] Even in their dealings with Europeans, the customs of clans were followed. In 1700, for example, at a meeting requested by Governor Bellomont of New York with two chiefs of each tribe, the Iroquois brought along three, "saying it was their custom to transact all Business of moment by the 3 tribes [clans] or Ensigns that the 5 Nations consisted of viz. the Bear, the Wolf and the Turtle, one from each of these Ensigns in each Nation was to be present."[60] (Only these three clans were present in all five tribes.) Even when the Iroquois made treaties with the French or English, they drew their clan symbol beside their name rather than an *x*.[61] This latter point is extremely important in that it documents the Iroquois tendency to associate themselves more as representatives of clan groups than of tribes.

If the Iroquois felt more of an attachment to their respective clans than to their tribes it was because they defined themselves through their clan affiliations. The clan system established the parameters of relationships and obligations between individuals.[62] Everyone in Iroquois society knew exactly his or her role in relation to others.[63] When no real blood relationships existed, they called each other by kinship terms rather than proper names, "observing exactly the degree of subordination and all proper relationships" that the title conferred.[64] Thus a child who was adopted to fill the place of a grandfather found himself treated with the respect due a grandfather by those who were older than him.[65] This need to establish the boundaries of relationships was so great that the Iroquois extended names of consanguinity to other tribes and to Europeans.[66]

Equally important for the Iroquois, the clan system served to facilitate intertribal activities. Among the Cayugas, the Wolf, Snipe, and Heron clans comprised one moiety, while the Turtle, Bear, Deer, and Ball clans constituted the other. Thus in any Cayuga village two clans from one moiety and at least one from the other would have to be present. This was important for several reasons. First, since clans were exogamous an individual had to marry someone from another clan. Second, it is quite probable that, as nineteenth-century anthropologist Henry Morgan suggested, the moieties were also exogamous, and that the individual not only had to marry outside his clan but also outside his moiety.[67] This would certainly help explain the presence of two moieties even in tribes with just three clans. In both cases this process reinforced relationships between clans and moieties through intermarriage. Third, intergroup relations were further strengthened because, since each village had at least three clans and two moieties, one of these clans would have members of its clan, or a clan in the same moiety, in another village, thereby providing a kinship link with that village. Thus in a simplified example, if one Cayuga village moiety consisted of the Wolf and Snipe clans and the other of the Turtle, the other village would have to include members of the same clans or moieties. In the case of the Turtle clan it would be members of this same clan or members of the Bear, Deer, or Ball clans who were part of the same moiety. The same type of network was found at the tribal level with each tribe having similar clans found among other tribes, but with moiety composition slightly different. These kin relationships and their attendant reciprocal obligations facilitated intervillage and intertribal cooperative action by providing the necessary links between individuals and communities in a society with no "formal" hierarchal political structure.

For example, it was the obligation of one moiety to mourn the death of a leader in the other by bringing presents.[68] It is true, as Fenton has noted, that at this level the obligations were symbolic.[69] But that was all that was needed. At the village level, if someone died, the women of the same clan were responsible for preparing the burial and mourning the deceased.[70] When a tribe in the opposite Confederacy moiety arrived to mourn the same death, they merely reproduced the socially integrating function of the mourning act because all the other aspects had been dealt with by those responsible at the village or tribal level. The very act and costs of traveling long distances provided visible proof to the deceased's family and tribe of the seriousness with which the other tribe viewed its obligations to the Confederacy and its members. Even so, the visiting tribe still provided presents to "cover" the dead. Interestingly, as Father Le Jeune noted, the gifts given to console the bereaved were eventually returned during the distribution of the deceased's effects among the mourners.[71] This, too, reinforced social ties.

Nowhere is the role of the clan system more noticeable, or more important, than in the process by which the Iroquois governed themselves; the clan system was the foundation of their government.[72] Before a matter of concern received the attention of the village or the tribe, it first had to have been dealt with at the household level, that is, within one lineage of a clan.[73] If the clan leaders and matrons decided the matter was of importance to the rest of the village, the other clan leaders were notified. Most likely the lineage that had decided the issue merited more attention first contacted other lineages from the same clan. The clan then informed members of its moiety in the village. Each clan presented their view and furnished wampum, and discussion continued until some consensus was reached. If the topic involved war, a war chief of the clan(s) was asked to participate. If the council decided that the issue merited the involvement of other villages or tribes, the message and wampum to be used were agreed upon, and one or two representatives of each clan were sent to the villages or tribes concerned. Since messengers going to other villages announced information to the whole, it is likely that representatives of each clan were sent in order to make certain that links existed with each clan or moiety in the village. This process was repeated until the matter, if of sufficient import, was raised at the Confederacy council.

Even the ad hoc administration of the Confederacy reflected the impact of the clan system. Village leaders were chosen from clan leaders who, in turn, were selected from candidates picked by the clan matron from her lineage.[74] Tribal leaders were chosen from village leaders, and Confederacy chiefs were selected from among tribal leaders.[75] The Confederacy itself was divided into two moieties, the tribes in each having reciprocal obligations. The Senecas, Onondagas, and Mohawks comprised the "elder brother" moiety, and the Oneidas and Cayugas (later the Tuscaroras and Delawares) made up the "younger brother" one.[76] Further, tribal representation and responsibilities in Confederacy councils were related to clan affiliations and to the number of clans in a tribe rather than to the tribe's population.[77] In short, clan leaders, using a complex system of personal contacts, relationships, and diplomacy, ran "local" and "national" councils. At village, tribe, and Confederacy levels, these councils were the government of the Iroquois.

Daniel Richter has argued recently that while the League of the Iroquois may be old, the Confederacy council was a product of responses to Europeans in the historic period.[78] I have been unable to determine that such a difference existed. The two expressions seem to be used interchangeably in the documents. *League*, from the French word *ligue*, is the older of the two words in the documentary literature. It was the word French observers used to describe what in English is best described as a confederacy. Even in the unlikely prospect that the League and the Confederacy of the Iroquois were two different bodies, there is no evidence that the Iroquois leaders were picked by a different process or that government in either body functioned in a different manner.

All this is not to suggest the Iroquois were one large, homogeneous group. Indeed, archaeological evidence demonstrates that the Iroquois divisions predate European contact by at least eight hundred years.[79] At the same time, the Iroquois must have recognized that on some occasions, all five tribes would have to cooperate and submerge their independence, at least briefly, in order to survive. These pressures probably led to the formation of the Iroquois Confederacy.[80] To be sure, it was difficult for the Iroquois to decide, given their independent nature, what situations called for these actions and the best policy to pursue in each case. But when the occasion arose and a consensus could be reached on a course of action to follow, the network of relationships established through the clan system facilitated the decision-making and the carrying out of the chosen policy. However, when a consensus could not be reached, the tenuous nature of Iroquois government became apparent. The framework that the clan system furnished, important as it was, could not be a substitute for a government with the means to enforce decisions and to carry them out in the face of opposition—a type of government that existed in New France but which the independent nature of the Iroquois did not permit to develop in their tribal areas.

In order to arrive at some assessment of Iroquois policy toward New France, and to show how Iroquois behavior reflected their goals, the complex and fragile nature of Iroquois government must be kept in mind.

# CHAPTER THREE

# Warfare Part One: Functions and Process

War was a fact of everyday life among the Five Nations. In 1701 an Iroquois chief, asked how many tribes the Iroquois were at war with, replied that there "are six nations that make war upon us that wee know besides those that wee do not know."[1] Either that number represented a conservative estimate or the Iroquois had considerably reduced the number of their enemies, because in the years between 1603 and 1701 the Iroquois were attacked by at least twenty different groups or combination of groups. In return, the Iroquois attacked fifty-one groups or combination of groups. In this same period the Iroquois were involved in at least 465 hostile encounters, of which they initiated 354.[2]

Warfare, then, was a central element of seventeenth-century Iroquois culture. Among the Five Nations warfare was at times an extension of the political process, but on other occasions it defied the decisions of the political leaders. Warfare was a means of satisfying personal needs and of fulfilling clan and public duty. Warfare was an expression of the Iroquois worldview and served as a means by which to find release from the constraints and strictures of daily life. In short, warfare was a complex and integral part of Iroquois culture and daily existence. This was reflected in the goals and style of Iroquois warfare.

It is difficult to determine what motivated the Iroquois to war before contact with Europeans or how much contact altered the goals and processes of "traditional" warfare. However, it is not difficult to establish what those goals and processes were in the seventeenth century. Also, many of these goals were central features of eighteenth-century Iroquois warfare. In what follows I have added data from the eighteenth century. I do not seek to make the case that the goals and processes were unaltered for two hundred years. The importance of some objectives grew while that of others diminished. Changes also occurred in the rituals of war. However, the fact that they endured, and that the Iroquois modified rather than abandoned these goals and processes, speaks to their importance in Iroquois culture in the seventeenth and eighteenth centuries.

Among the Iroquois, the decision to wage war was made by a council. Male village elders joined the female clan leaders in the latter's council, called *Houtouissaches*. At this joint assembly the wrongs committed against the Iroquois by the intended target group were enumerated and discussed. Once the council agreed that war was justified or necessary, the war chiefs were asked to join in the deliberation. At the combined council a speaker for the elders and clan matrons spoke to the "war Chiefs and let them know the indispensable necessity they were under to avenge themselves against those that they believed had insulted them."[3] After the speech the war chiefs met apart from the elders to consider what they had heard. When the war chiefs reached a decision, they returned to the main council and informed the elders and clan matrons of their intentions. If war was decided on, each captain sang his war song. When the projected expedition involved more than one village or tribe, the civil and war leaders of the village initiating the action met, decided the merit of the project, and sent emissaries to other villages and tribes to ask them to send their representatives. If the combined group agreed to go to war, a starting date was set and the war captains of the respective tribes returned to their villages to enlist volunteers and to prepare for war. The conduct of the war was left to the war chiefs.

Revenge or adoption raids were initiated in much the same way. A clan matron decided, probably in consultation with other matrons of her clan or lineage, that it was necessary to avenge a death or to replace a lost relative. A warrior or war captain was approached, given a wampum belt, and asked if he would avenge the death of the deceased. The warrior had the right to decide whether he would accept the request. However, given the honor attached to being asked, such requests were rarely turned down.[4] Once the request was accepted, the war leader determined for himself whom to attack and how many other warriors, if any, would be in his party.

In his analysis of warfare, Lafitau distinguished between these small raiding parties, or "private wars," and council-initiated public hostilities. The two styles of war, however, did not necessarily involve different motives. Councils as well as individuals could wage war for revenge. Nor did small raids necessarily conflict with council decisions. The council could decide that the best way to achieve its war aims was through continual harassment of a tribe by small raiding parties. Moreover, as Lafitau himself observed, the elders were "not opposed to [raids] when the interest of the tribe is not itself unfavourably affected. They are, on the contrary, very glad to see their people exercising and enjoying themselves in the warlike spirit."[5] In short, both types of warfare were manifestations of social pressures among the Iroquois. Council-approved hostilities and personal revenge raids differed only insofar as the former were sometimes fought as a means of carrying out a public political decision.

Once the decision to go to war was made, the leader of a war party invited other young men to join him in his expedition. For large intertribal wars, the "war captains" performed this task. Since there was always some injury to avenge and Iroquois seeking to increase their reputation as warriors, there was usually no shortage of recruits.[6] The night before the party set off, the leader invited the warriors to his longhouse to feast on a dog that had been prepared for the occasion.[7] During the evening the men painted for war, sang and danced, and asked for divine intervention to make them successful over their enemies.[8] On the following morning the warriors paraded past the villagers in single file behind the expedition's leader.[9] Some distance from the village the men removed their ceremonial dress and gave it to the women to take back to the village. The women, who had been waiting for the men, gave them the clothes they would use on the trip, as well as their provisions and some cooking utensils.[10]

After the women left, the men stripped some bark off a nearby tree and engraved a pictorial account of the mission they were about to undertake, with canoes facing away from the village to indicate they were leaving. The information left on the tree included the number of warriors in the party, the village or nation of the group, and clan of the war chief.[11] On their return the successes and losses of the journey were added. Here, too, clan symbols were used to designate how many scalps and prisoners were taken by each family.[12] The Iroquois also left pictographs at battle sites to indicate the number of captives taken, the size of their party, and the number of wounded and killed on their side.[13] Unfortunately, while this unique endeavor of a people without a written history to record their exploits is often noted by seventeenth-century European contemporaries of the Iroquois, they do not attempt to explain why the Iroquois did this. If nothing else, pictographs reveal the importance attached to warfare by Iroquois men, and their readiness to leave in a public place the record of their deeds.[14]

In the past the weapons of an Iroquois warrior had been the bow and arrow, ball-headed war club, shield, spear, and wooden armor.[15] With the introduction of the musket the defensive weapons were discarded because they were no longer effective against lead shot and brass or iron spears and arrowheads. The bow and arrow were, however, still used because guns were not always available in large enough quantities for everybody to have one. The war club continued to be used and—along with an iron hatchet, a knife, rope to tie captives with, extra moccasins, a small, light kettle, and a mat—formed part of the "war kit."[16] It is difficult to state whether the musket was the main weapon or simply was added to the arsenal, but it did become an important tool of the Iroquois warrior.[17]

In journeying to a given destination, the Iroquois traveled by the most convenient method possible. When progress could be made quickly by water, "they speadily make a canow of bast [bark]. . . . These canows are fashioned of one piece of bast, both ends sharply pointed and securely sewn with bast, the inside being stretched out by a ribbing of bent wooden rods, which keep the canow in its proper shape."[18] When the waterway became impassable and portaging was not feasible, the canoe was filled with rocks and sunk, to be retrieved on the return trip. Another way to get a canoe, of course, was to find one that had been left behind in this fashion and use it.[19] By these methods Indians were able to travel up to fifty miles a day and to undertake journeys of five or six hundred miles in order to capture a prisoner or two.

During the trip the warriors hunted and, when the weather turned foul, built bark shelters for protection.[20] Once in enemy territory they hunted less because the closer they came to their foes the greater the chance of being caught or of giving away their position to enemy warriors or hunters. For the same reasons, if food was needed, the bow and arrow were used. These weapons did not make the type of noise likely to attract enemy attention, and using them saved ammunition. While the Iroquois were in ambush, however, no one hunted and the warriors lived off the game they had caught along the way and had managed to save.[21] Because food supplies were not replenished just before attacking, food was stored at designated spots along the way to be used when retreating. If it could be spared, ammunition was also stored for later use.[22] The Iroquois also built temporary fortifications to be used as staging areas or to fall back to in case of sustained pursuit by foes.[23]

Surprise was a key element of Iroquois warfare.[24] This was particularly true as a strategy for small raiding parties, but it was also an important consideration when larger groups were involved. If the Iroquois did not think they could surprise their foe, they tended not to attack.[25] When the Iroquois did attack, they initiated the engagement by letting out loud cries, followed by a volley of arrows or musket fire, and then rushed in for hand-to-hand combat or to scalp those who had fallen after the initial round of fire.[26] The abandonment of shields following the advent of metal projectile points may have led to more deaths during this stage of battle than in previous eras.[27] Regardless of whether the Iroquois emerged victorious, they made every effort to remove their dead and wounded from the battlefield.[28]

If the raid were successful, the all-important prisoners were brought back to the warriors' home village.[29] Some captives, of course, were killed because the party brought back only as many as they could safely control without fear of being overpowered. Those captives who were spared made the trip to Iroquoia with their arms tied behind their backs (above the elbows), and were usually subjected to minor torments along the way.[30] At night prisoners were tied to stakes.[31] Another method was to secure prisoners with stakes. Two stakes, one with an area hollowed out to fit a part of the anatomy, were planted in the ground. A captive's arm or leg was then placed between the two stakes, and the stakes were tied together at the top.[32] The stakes used to restrain prisoners were sometimes painted.[33] On the way home, if the group passed villages of allied tribes or those of their own people, runners were sent ahead to inform the villagers. The inhabitants then came to the outskirts of the village and formed a double row through which the prisoners ran while being assailed with blows from all sides. Once the captives were inside the village, the punishment stopped.[34] As a rule, these beatings were not as harsh as the ones the prisoners received at the home village of the war party, where the same process was followed.

About one day before the Iroquois came to their home village, they sent a runner ahead to announce the outcome of the excursion.[35] If an Iroquois in the war party had died, the family of the deceased was consoled and then the community went to the outskirts of the village to "welcome" the warriors and their captives.[36] (This greeting can be viewed as a cruel parody of the traditional welcoming ceremony for guests during which their tears were dried, their throats cleared, and so on.) According to Father Lamberville, as victor and vanquished approached, a member of the war party cried out "*koué, koué, koué*; these are shouts of rejoicing and victory, which denote the coming of as many captives as the number of times they are repeated."[37] The inhabitants then went to the outskirts of the village and formed two lines, down which passed the expedition's leader followed by the warriors and prisoners. The village elders waited at the end of the line closest to the village and the fire.[38] The reception of Father Isaac Jogues in 1642 at the hands (and feet) of the Mohawks was typical of the process:

> The Father, as the most important [captive], was greeted by a quantity of blows from cudgels, feet, and fists, of a sort that he was [left] covered in blood. . . . After that they dispose of the captives; they put them in a row to better see the magnificence of their triumph. Between each prisoner they put an Iroquois in order to keep the captives from walking too fast. . . . At the same time a speech is made to the youth to exhort them to greet the prisoners in the fashion of the country; they do not spare themselves.[39]

Prisoners were not usually killed during this process. If the raid had been undertaken at the request of a clan matron to capture a replacement for a dead clansman or woman, the warrior had some incentive to make sure that the captive was not so abused that he or she would not make a suitable adoptee.[40] The person for whom the captive was intended could also step in front of the prisoner and thus spare him the worst of the abuse.[41] However, the final decision on the prisoner's fate was made by only the village council. French trader and explorer Pierre Radisson, for example, escaped from the Mohawks after he had already been adopted. When he was recaptured, his "parents" recognized him in the reception line to the village and his "mother" quickly led him away. But she did not untie him, and he was not allowed to return to his former family until his "father" pled for his life before the village council.[42]

For the tribes of the Five Nations Confederacy, waging war was an honored pastime. While there could be and often were material rewards for engaging in war, more powerful and enduring reasons for the almost constant warfare by the Iroquois were the pursuit of glory, honor, and the taking of revenge against those who had done them injury or slighted their pride. As Pierre Boucher, a soldier and interpreter for the government of New France, noted, the "war they wage against one another is not to conquer lands, nor to become great Lords, not even for gain, but purely for vengance."[43] In his history of the Iroquois published in 1727, Cadwallader Colden wrote that "it is not for the Sake of Tribute . . . that they make War, but from Notions of Glory which they have ever most strongly imprinted on their Minds; and the farther they go to seek an Enemy, the greater the Glory they think they gain."[44] General Thomas Gage, writing in 1772 to Superintendent of Indian Affairs William Johnson, echoed Boucher and

Colden's observations: "I never heard that Indians made War for the sake of Territory like Europeans, but that Revenge, and eager pursuit of Martial reputation were the motives which prompted one Nation to make War upon another."[45] These inducements to war were instilled in Iroquois youth until the end of the eighteenth century. Both Joseph Brant and John Norton, Iroquois leaders and warriors in the War of 1812 between Canada and the United States, recalled that in their youth they were urged to be "daring and indefatigable in war," and that the "chief thing inculcated into the minds of young men was a principal of honour as a warrior."[46]

Another incentive for war, closely related to honor, was the need to avenge an injury, whether an insult or a death incurred during a previous raid. While presents could be given by an offender to atone for a death, Father Lafitau remarked that "even though these presents are accepted, if the omens are not favourable for taking complete vengeance for the assassination at that time, [the guilty party] should not flatter themselves that the insult is entirely forgotten. The dressing put on this wound only covers, without curing it. . . . The council keeps an exact register of people killed on occasions of this sort [small raids] and the memory of these events is refreshed until conditions are such that the most magnificent satisfaction can be gotten for them."[47] At a conference in Detroit in 1704 a Seneca spokesman summed up the Iroquois philosophy on revenge to a group of Hurons: "You know, my brothers, our customs which are to avenge, or to perish in avenging our dead."[48] One can assume that for the Hurons this was a unnecessary reminder.

Revenge raids were launched either as the result of dreams or, more frequently, at the request of a clan matron.[49] In the latter case, not just anyone was requested to avenge a death in the household, nor indeed anyone from the clan. This obligation belonged "to all those men who have marriage links with that house, or their *Athonni,* as they say; and in that fact, resides the advantage of having men born in it. For these men, although isolated at home . . . marry into different lodges. The Children born of these different marriages became obligated to their fathers' lodge to which they are strangers, and contract the obligation of replacing [those slain in war]."[50] This meant that in the case of the death of a person in one clan, the matron asked the child of a male from her clan, but one who lived with the mother, to avenge that death. The child was a stranger to his "father's lodge" because "marriage did not require of those contracting it that either one pass into the other's lodge, both remaining in their own."[51] Further, since clans were exogamous, the mother of the child was from another clan and, because descent was traced through the mother's line, so was the child.[52] Thus the responsibility to avenge the death of a person belonged to another clan, and prisoners who were brought back for adoption were given by the warriors to "their father's households," and not the one the warrior lived in. This aspect of revenge warfare served as a means to reinforce ties among the clans. In fact, the role of clans was so important that even the prisoners who were rejected for adoption and destined to die were tortured by another clan, not by the one that had refused the captive.[53]

The clan matron could also put an end to a revenge raid. If the raid was planned against a tribe with which the village council was trying to maintain good relations, the chiefs would try "underhanded measures to stop the leaders" of a war party. But the best way to put an end to an expedition was to "reach the matrons of the Lodges, where those who are engaged with the Leader have their *Athonni* [paternity] for these have only to interpose their authority to turn aside all the best devised plans."[54] But much to the displeasure of colonial officials, these small raids were not easily put aside.[55] The clan matrons were not very willing to ignore their obligation (and need) to replace those lost in war.[56]

The impulse for revenge (blood feuding) was so strong that not only individuals but entire tribes at times broke treaties with friendly nations, both Indian and European, in order to fulfill this obligation. In 1712, for example, the Mohawks passed a war belt among the other four tribes of the Confederacy in order to raise an army to attack the English in New York because some English colonials had killed several Mohawks.[57] While nothing came of this (the other tribes recommended against it), it is a good example of the extremes to which some Iroquois were prepared to go in order to avenge deaths. After all, the English were not only allies of the Five Nations but could prove to be powerful foes since they largely controlled the Iroquois gun supply.

Needless to say, the emphasis on blood feuding continually thwarted efforts to effect peace between various Indian tribes.[58] Iroquois leaders had difficulty in making colonial officials understand the reasons for these excursions. They explained that raids were the result of the ungovernable passions of the young or the work of an evil spirit.[59] The strength of "blood revenge" as a motive for hostile actions may be evinced by the fact that as late as the early twentieth century this behavior was still in the process of "giving way to white law enforcement on the reservation."[60] Admittedly, wars were not being waged at this point, but for some Iroquois at least, revenge was still an accepted means of settling disputes.

Revenge could be achieved by several means; bringing back a few prisoners or scalps was one. As one French observer remarked, three or four hundred Iroquois that obtained four or five scalps and an equal number of prisoners "return with as much glory as if they had won an entire battle."[61] In fact, taking prisoners and scalps were in themselves motives for war because they demonstrated a warrior's skill.[62] More than one observer noted that the Iroquois "rarely kill those they can make prisoners because the honour and profit of the victory is to conduct prisoners to the village."[63] There was, of course, no need for these objectives to be mutually exclusive. An Iroquois who set out to avenge a death and brought back prisoners and scalps would thereby furnish proof of his skills as a warrior and that the murder of a fellow Iroquois had been avenged. But the search for scalps and prisoners as proof of martial skill was cause enough for warring even when deaths were not to be avenged. These trophies of martial valor continued to be sought well into the eighteenth century. Baron La Pause noted in 1758 that among French-allied Indians (some of whom were Mohawks from Caughnawaga), a few scalps and prisoners were all they desired, and that they would stop fighting after getting these.[64]

Iroquois warriors gained glory by returning with prisoners because captives served important functions in Iroquois society. Captives, for example, were used for public torture. Despite the significant body of evidence left on Iroquois torture rituals, a definitive study of this practice has not been written.[65] Existing work suggests that the Iroquois administered torture to strike fear into opponents, for emotional release and revenge, and for religious purposes.[66] While these all seem reasonable suggestions, the reality was more complex.

There is no doubt that revenge and emotional release were served by torture, but it was not always so.[67] Certain rules made the Iroquois rein in the very passions that led them to want prisoners for torture. A clan matron may have initiated a raid in order to avenge a previous loss. But if the prisoner given to that clan was rejected for adoption and was given up for torture, "the members of the household to which he has been given do not touch him. It would not be suitable for them to become torturers of one who has been offered to represent some member of their family."[68] Rules of propriety, in this case those of clan obligation, meant that direct venting of grief and rage had to be deferred. Also, intended torture victims were often clothed, given a kin relationship, and even given a going-away feast before being killed.[69] Why did the Iroquois initiate a symbolic tie to the person whom the captive was to replace and then kill him anyway? In what sense did the torture of such victims represent revenge or emotional release for the family that had initiated the raid to replace a lost relative?

Equally unclear is the religious aspect of Iroquois torture. There is some evidence that the torture and/or death of a captive had religious significance. The Iroquois made every effort to prolong torture and to ensure that the victim did not die before dawn.[70] One reference, albeit among the Hurons, suggests that the delay was to allow the sun or war god to witness the process.[71] On the other hand, the dawn death may have had no sacrificial meaning at all. It may have had more to do with the Iroquois belief in the afterlife and killing people at a time when their souls might better see the path to their final destination, rather than at night, when they might lose their way and hover about the Iroquois villages to harm them. The Iroquois fear of retribution from the soul of a deceased torture victim was the purpose of the ceremony, undertaken in the evening after a prisoner's death, in which the villagers shouted and struck the longhouses in a bid to drive out any remaining spirits.[72]

Matters are made more complicated because, even if it is not clear that torture served a religious purpose, it seems evident that aspects of the torture process reflected Iroquois spiritual beliefs. Certainly drinking a brave victim's blood and rubbing it over the heads of children reflected the Iroquois belief that doing so would transfer some of that individual's strength and courage to them.[73] Intended torture victims were also painted before being tortured and killed, again implying some ritual if not spiritual connection.[74] The difficulty with all of this is that it is hard to establish links between these practices and the capture of people. Were people captured specifically to be tortured as fulfillment of some religious rites? Or do the rituals and processes surrounding torture simply reflect the influences that shaped all aspects of Iroquois life, namely, their clan system and their animistic worldview? While the answer is probably the latter, these questions point to the need for a new and detailed study of the role of torture in Iroquois society.[75]

For whatever reasons the Iroquois engaged in this activity, they had certainly refined the process of torture to maximize pain and minimize real harm to the body in order to prolong the torment. Iroquois torturers, wrote Lafitau, had a habit of starting "at the extremities of the feet and hands, going up little by little" to the body.[76] The first phase of torture was also limited to minor abuses (minor only in relation to what would follow), such as ripping off fingernails, cutting or chewing off fingers, and slicing off bits of leg flesh.[77] The victim suffered great pain as a result of these practices, but his body seldom sustained the type of damage that led to a sudden death—unless shock induced a heart attack.

The Iroquois were also shrewd enough to avoid cutting major arteries and veins in order to prevent severe blood loss and "premature" death.[78] They recognized that torture by fire helped to prolong life by cauterizing veins and stemming the flow of blood. This goal seems to have been the purpose behind such practices as putting stubs of fingers in pipes or placing burning ashes on scalped heads. Such tortures had the combined effect of producing excruciating pain and prolonging the victim's period of suffering.[79] However, if a specific type of torture did not stop the bleeding, the Iroquois wrapped the body part in question to ensure that the victim did not die before they were finished with him.[80]

The Iroquois mastered the torture process. They learned how much abuse the body could sustain and refined torture practices that delayed a victim's demise as long as possible. Even if the full role of torture is not clear, it seems reasonable to conclude that it was an essential aspect of Iroquois culture and that taking prisoners to be put to death in this fashion was an important goal of warfare.

Another, more important use of prisoners was to replace those who had died in war or of some other cause.[81] The Iroquois selected those they felt would be suitable for adoption and either killed the others or saved them for torture.[82] Even captives destined for torture were usually given first to some family to replace one who had died but were rejected because they were somehow unsuitable.[83] Those who underwent torture more than likely suffered this fate because the family in question wanted revenge more than they wanted to replenish the strength of the clan.[84] However, a prisoner, once adopted, was treated as if he had always been an Iroquois, and if he replaced someone who had died, he assumed all the rights and privileges of the deceased.[85] This practice enabled the Iroquois to retain a large enough population to remain a powerful political force well into the eighteenth century.[86] In fact, capturing people for adoption grew in importance as a goal of warfare and led to a decrease in the frequency of torture. As Bartram noted, "Now their numbers being very much diminished . . . they very politically strive to Strengthen themselves not only by alliances with their neighbours, but . . . [by] prisoners they take; they are almost always accepted by the relations of a warrior slain. . . . This custom is as antient as our knowledge of them, but when their number of warriors was more than twice as many as now, the relations would more frequently refuse to adopt the prisoners but rather chuse to gratify their thirst of revenge."[87] According to Lafitau, the need to replace lost kin and to shore up clan lineages made war a "necessary exercise for the Iroquois."[88]

Not all prisoners were sought solely for torture or to replace dead kin. Political and military concerns also created pressure to capture people. The Iroquois used captives to add to their ranks in order to ensure that they had enough warriors to provide adequate defense against their enemies. Many able-bodied male captives were spared death in order to bolster Iroquois military strength.

Captives often made up part of predominantly Iroquois war parties. In some cases captives came to identify themselves, and be seen, so thoroughly as Iroquois that raiding parties were entirely composed of former prisoners. In June 1660 one such group of "Iroquoised Huron," as the Jesuits called them, attacked the French in the Quebec area.[89] It was thus, Father Ragueneau wrote, "that the Hiroquois swell their troops."[90] Enemies of the Iroquois knew this was their practice. In 1665 the Hurons advised Sieur de Tracy that the first step to success against the Iroquois was to lure away the captives they held. The strength of the Iroquois lay in these people whom the Iroquois made to fight on their behalf.[91]

Even if the Iroquois were not fighting a losing battle against population decline, they sought to increase the size of their fighting force as a means to carry out military or political objectives (see chapter 6). As the Hurons told the French in the 1650s, the Iroquois may have wanted to incorporate the remaining Hurons because the Iroquois wished to "strengthen themselves with our colony, and compel us, when we are with them, to take up arms against you."[92] In 1681 the Onondagas attacked the Piscataways for a similar dual purpose. The Onondagas hoped to capture some Piscataways because they wanted to "strengthen themselves as much as they could with other Nations" because their relations with the Senecas were strained and they feared an armed confrontation.[93] Military and political considerations, then, even led to war against groups that were not a real threat to the Iroquois as a means to garner captives.

The blood-feud nature of native warfare also made the capture of people an important military strategy. A good way to ensure defeat and demoralization of the enemy was to capture them. The surest way to defeat a foe and prevent reprisal raids was to leave few or none able or willing to engage in revenge raids. Father Lalemant wrote that this was the purpose of the Hurons practice of capture and torture. It served to "ruin and exterminate their enemies by killing them, and to frighten them from coming to war against them."[94] At a conference in June 1711, Onondaga leader Teganissorens recounted to Governor Hunter of New York what he had recently told some French envoys at Onondaga. The Iroquois, said Teganissorens, "are not like you *Christians* for when you have taken Prisoners of one another you send them home, by such means you can never rout one another. We are not of that Nature, When we have war against any nation Wee endeavour to destroy them utterly."[95] A clearer statement of Iroquois military strategy would be difficult to find.

For a wide range of reasons, then, the capture of people was an important goal of Iroquois raids. In fact, if there was one objective of seventeenth-century

Iroquois warring that outweighed all others in significance, it was the capture of people. As early as 1643 Father Jogues, writing from among his Mohawk captors, informed the French that capturing and incorporating the Hurons into the Iroquois tribes accounted for the Iroquois wars against that nation.[96] By 1660 the Iroquois had captured and incorporated so many people into their villages that the Jesuit Lalemant could write that the Iroquois were, "for the most, only aggregations of different tribes whom they have conquered."[97] In some cases, captive groups comprised as much as two-thirds of the overall village population.[98] This Iroquois policy was so well known that, by the end of the seventeenth century, a French observer could generalize about it and the means by which it was accomplished: "They employ all their industry to engage the other nations to give themselves to [the Iroquois]; they send them presents and the most able people of their nation to speak to them [*les haranguer*], and to let them know that if they do not give themselves to [the Iroquois] they cannot avoid being destroyed. . . . but, on the other hand, if they want to give themselves up and disperse themselves among [the Iroquois] longhouses, they will become masters of other men."[99]

In short, there can be little doubt that capturing people was a deliberate and important Iroquois strategy. Indeed, traditional accounts of the founding of the Iroquois League make receiving new people into the Iroquois longhouse a central goal of Iroquois policy toward other natives.[100] Unresolved, however, is the question of whether taking in new people was to be done by peaceful means or by war. Arthur Parker makes it clear that war was to be used to bring peace to those who did not see the light right away. Horatio Hale suggests that war was the natural consequence of not having an effective peace settlement but does not indicate that League "rules" called for war against those who would not join the Iroquois League.[101] The "Traditional Narrative," written in 1900 by a group of Iroquois chiefs at the Six Nations Iroquois settlement in Brantford, Ontario, makes no mention of what to do with those who did not join the League. The issue is further complicated by questions about the origins of the League. Was it created to foster peace or to facilitate war? Matthew Dennis has argued recently that the League was created not only to bring peace to the Five Nations but to others as well. Deganawidah, the League's mythical creator, gave this "mission" to the Iroquois.[102] Unfortunately, this hypothesis overlooks the contradictory traditions of the League's founding and the fact that, as Mohawk John Norton wrote in the early 1800s, "no traditions exist to inform us" as to whether the League was begun to promote defense or aggression.[103] What is certain, however, is that, regardless of the League's original purpose(s) and rules, the Iroquois did war a great deal, and they did bring new peoples into the longhouse once they had defeated them. The Iroquois effectiveness in carrying out this policy can be seen by the number of different peoples found among the Iroquois and by the geographical redistribution that resulted as various native groups sought to put vast distances between themselves and the people-grabbing Iroquois.[104]

Warfare was an essential part of Iroquois culture in the seventeenth century. It was an expression of a political decision and served as a means to obtain military and/or political ends. But it was also an expression of social and cultural imperatives. The need to gain honor, revenge, along with the obligations of the clan system, made warfare almost inevitable. Insofar as warfare was an expression of cultural, political, and military dictates, no goal of warring was as crucial to the Iroquois as the capture of people. Prisoners were central to nearly all the functions served by warfare. Without captives, warriors did not gain as much esteem, victims for torture were lacking, deaths could not be avenged, and grief could not be assuaged. More important, without prisoners to be adopted into Iroquois society to take the place of the deceased and to bolster Iroquois fighting strength, the Iroquois would wither away and die. The decline in population would lead to the fragmentation of their clan system and with it the social and political structures of their society.

# CHAPTER FOUR

# Warfare Part Two: Cultural Change and "Economic" Warfare

Despite evidence that the Iroquois waged war for a variety of reasons, most historians and ethnohistorians have persisted in describing Iroquois warfare as "economically" inspired. Iroquois contact with Europeans, it is claimed, led to wholesale cultural change. The Iroquois became dependent on European trade goods but soon ran out of the furs they needed to purchase those wares. The Iroquois then attacked other tribes to steal their furs, to drive them off fur-bearing lands, or to win control of the fur trade between natives and Europeans in order to use stolen, trapped, or bartered furs to trade for European goods. In support of these assumptions, scholars have pointed to Iroquois attacks against native and European fur brigades and smaller groups of traders. Indeed, the Iroquois wars of the 1600s have come to be known as the Beaver Wars because of this interpretation, which reduces almost all Iroquois warfare to efforts to obtain beaver pelts.

Any monocausal explanation should be suspect, and this one is no exception. The Beaver Wars interpretation is an economically reductionist and simplistic explanation that downplays both Iroquois cultural resilience and other important goals of seventeenth-century Iroquois warfare. A closer look at the central tenets of this economic interpretation reveals several reasons for questioning its validity; the most important is that there is little or no evidence to support it. Wars continued to be fought for a wide variety of reasons, and the Iroquois never became "like Europeans" in their value system. Even if the Iroquois did become dependent on some European goods, a systematic study of seventeenth-century Iroquois hostilities reveals that raids against fur brigades or trading groups did not take place in significant numbers. The evidence requires us to reject the view that economic goals were a major feature of Iroquois warfare.

The issue of cultural change is central to any examination of the Iroquois wars, but it has not been dealt with satisfactorily. It has long been recognized that Iroquois society underwent change as a result of contact with Europeans.[1] Indeed, aspects of Iroquois society were in the process of changing before contact with Europeans, and archaeological work has uncovered some of the changes.[2] However, the ability to document material change has led to the development of a false confidence in our ability to measure changes in value systems. The question that is begged, however, is, changed from what? It is possible to look at material culture and see how things were modified due to contact with Europeans, but we do not know what the Iroquois valued or fought for before contact with Europeans.

Lack of understanding has not prevented speculation about what precontact Iroquois warfare was like, and the result has been a tendency to romanticize the past. Many writers depict precontact warfare as little more than a violent version of "hide and seek" that turned destructive with the introduction of new weapons and "economic" motives.[3] They argue this in the face of archaeological evidence that clearly reveals that large-scale destructive warfare predated European arrival. Palisaded prehistoric villages, and particularly the heavily palisaded village of Hochelaga, with its galleries filled with rocks to throw down at those who tried to breach the walls, all indicate that large-scale warfare, including sieges against fortified villages, antedate European arrival on the St. Lawrence.[4] That these raids were destructive is attested to by the death of close to two hundred Stadaconans in 1533 at the hands of the Toudamans who breached the Stadaconans' temporary fortification.[5]

Adding to the distortion is the tendency to equate possession of European goods with the acceptance of European values, and to view change as equal to displacement—that is, acceptance of something equals the loss of something that existed.[6] This view overstates the power of those goods and represents a simplistic perception of how cultures work. It is possible to add to a culture or to modify aspects of it without losing completely that which existed. As James Axtell has observed,

the mere presence of [European] goods in native society, even on a large scale, did not necessarily denote a significant change in Indian culture.

Material objects, no less than people, receive their cultural status only by being assigned meaning and value by members of a society. The form and the function of an object, therefore, are far more important culturally than the material from which it is made. An artifact may be made of several alternative materials, but if its traditional form and function do not change, neither does its cultural meaning.[7]

Moreover, in any discussion of cultural change it is vital to distinguish between profound and superficial changes. As A. F. C. Wallace has noted, a "culture can undergo drastic modifications while the personality structure of a society yields only slightly, and that in a regressive way."[8]

If those arguing for cultural change have created an idyllic picture of Iroquois society as the starting point from which change took place, that does not mean that one is limited to discussing cultural change or stability within that framework. After all, given that basis, to argue for strong cultural stability is to appear to endorse a vision of Iroquois society that hints at the noble savage myth. Instead we must establish what values existed among the Iroquois in the period under study, and if (and how) they were altered and became like European values. It is crucial to establish that such changes occurred before one can contend that "new" and "economic" warfare took place. Moreover, claims of cultural change must be based on more than simplistic notions that possession of European goods made the Iroquois into Europeans in moccasins.

Among the Iroquois, acceptance of European goods did not always lead to their use as Europeans employed them, nor to changes in Iroquois values. By 1700 many Iroquois used cloth rather than furs for parts of their dress. However, as more than one observer remarked, they "have changed only the material of the clothing, keeping their former style of dressing."[9] Because an Indian wore European clothes did not mean he had adopted European values, in this case, a European sense of clothing style. Swords were also not used as Europeans intended. The Iroquois did not take up swordsmanship; rather, the handles of the swords were broken off and the blades attached to the ends of spears because they were effective projectile points.[10] The new weapon was adopted to improve an ancient tool, not to replace it. Moreover, because an Iroquois used an iron knife to lift a scalp rather than a flint one did not change the intent or the meaning and value of the act, merely the means by which it was accomplished.

Using cloth instead of pelts and iron instead of stone were changes in themselves. It is also true that the fur trade brought much more to the Indians than just goods. But it is clear that the Indians were able to internalize many changes and make them fit into their value systems. Even alcohol, which wreaked havoc on Indian culture, was used to suit Indian values.[11] They drank to get drunk or to carry out some act that society did not normally permit.[12] The Iroquois even incorporated alcohol into their traditional feasts and medicines.[13] But they did not get together for a brandy after work, have a drink before dinner, or sip a glass of wine with their meals.

The Iroquois also adjusted new religions to suit their cosmology. There is no doubt that missionaries had an impact on native religion.[14] But while the Iroquois incorporated what would fit into their cosmology, the vast majority of them did not give up their own views and practices.[15] They tolerated the opinions of the Jesuits and expected theirs to be likewise respected.[16] Indeed, the various French Orders never managed to convert large numbers of Iroquois, and most of those baptized were given the sacrament only on the verge of death. Of the 3,199 Iroquois baptized between 1667 and 1679, almost all were children, and at least 2,002 children and adults died shortly after baptism.[17] The largest obstacle to conversion was not really the religious exactions, but rather the cultural proscriptions that accompanied the switch from "pagan" to "true believer."[18] While the Iroquois resisted the cultural changes, they nonetheless incorporated elements of Christian doctrine, not because they rejected their own but because it made sense to add the powerful European god to their pantheon of gods.

The question, then, is not whether transformations occurred in Iroquois society—they did—but how these changes were handled. Take, for example, the question of trade in Iroquois culture. Before contact with Europeans, the Iroquois engaged in very little trade with non-Iroquois groups, and trade among themselves served mostly to reinforce social and political ties.[19] This situation changed after European contact and the Iroquois carried on trade with the Dutch, French, and English settlers who surrounded their homelands. But if trade took on an economic importance it had not had, there is every indication that trade continued to be used to strengthen social and political ties among the Iroquois and between them and their European neighbors. Iroquois efforts to make peace and establish trade with the French in the 1650s were related to desires to gain the support of the French in their wars with the Neutrals and Eries. Trade with the Dutch was carried on, in part, because the Iroquois recognized that their political alliance with that nation depended on their bringing them furs. Moreover, relations between the Iroquois and various nations, whether economic or political, were based on fictive kinship ties and gift exchanges.[20]

Nor did the increased importance of the economic aspects of trade with Europeans alter the social nature of exchange among the Iroquois. The goods given to Iroquois leaders to cement political and economic ties continued to be distributed among their followers.[21]

It is, of course, quite possible that new products were valued by Indians. A copper kettle may have been a mere reproduction of a clay one, but it was shinier, more durable, more efficient, and came to the Iroquois only through trade.[22] Yet the new goods were not stored up and saved; in fact, the person who had the most goods gained honor and esteem by giving them away, not by keeping them.[23] Reciprocal gift giving was a method of sharing wealth, trade, and cementing social ties that helped unify the Iroquois.[24] The new goods did not undermine the value systems or the redistribution procedures of Iroquois society in the seventeenth century. If anything, European trade goods made these ceremonies more important. Certainly, this was in itself a modification, but the purpose of giving away presents and the reinforcing of social ties did not undergo transformation.

The practice of putting goods in graves provides another example of how the advent of European wares changed an ancient custom but not its underlying significance or the values it reflected. Before European contact, the Indians placed few material artifacts in the graves with the dead.[25] In the postcontact period, more goods were placed in graves. Even Iroquois converts to Christianity who lived in missionary settlements could not be dissuaded from this practice.[26] Buried goods included European wares as well as goods of Iroquois manufacture. It is quite possible that the European goods were included in the burials because the Iroquois valued them in this world and did not want to be without them in the next. But in general, the Iroquois put items in graves because of their utilitarian functions, not their material value. European kettles were buried, as clay ones had been, because they held food for the deceased to use in the afterlife.[27]

As the burial of goods and their continued redistribution indicate, the purpose for which trade objects were used, and not any intrinsic value, made them desirable. The Dutch minister Megapolensis noted that when a Mohawk leader was told how much a "rix-dollar" was worth, the Iroquois laughed and suggested that the Dutch "were fools to value a piece of iron so highly."[28] The Jesuit Father Le Jeune remarked on a similar attitude among French Indian allies. The Indians were amused at the Europeans' willingness to exchange such a wide range of goods for furs.[29] The Iroquois, however, were not fools. They understood well enough how the Dutch economy worked. The Iroquois simply did not believe that the European approach to goods and their exchange was superior to theirs.

The Iroquois did not want more than they could use, and they placed no value on having goods simply for the sake of amassing wealth.[30] The Iroquois shared all among themselves. As Father Le Jeune wrote after his first visit among them, a "whole village must be without corn, before any individual can be obliged to endure privation."[31] Their willingness to share was extended to other groups—native and European—and continued to be a feature of their culture throughout the seventeenth century.[32] Proximity to Europeans, who took advantage of their generosity but failed to reciprocate when called upon, led to some modification in this aspect of Iroquois culture.[33] But generosity continued to be a major characteristic of Iroquois tribal society well into the eighteenth century.[34] In short, acceptance of European goods did not make the Iroquois like Europeans in their value system.

Nor did the Iroquois accept everything. For example, Father Lafitau, who lived among the Iroquois for years, remarked that "since their first contact with Europeans, the use which they have been able to make of such improvements [European goods, etc.] has not inspired them to alter their ancient folkways."[35] Indeed, both Lafitau and David Zeisberger asserted that in one of the most demanding tasks, that of forest clearing, the Iroquois had not given up their traditional method; "the Europeans brought them sharpened steel and set the example of felling trees and sawing them. Nonetheless they did not make much use of this method and went on using their former one which was to girdle the trees, strip them of their bark so that they die and let them dry standing."[36]

The Iroquois saw that along with acceptance of European goods, the newcomers wanted them to adopt European values, and they resisted. They considered themselves superior to other peoples, Europeans included, and saw no reason to change.[37] This was a common view among natives in the Northeast. Well into the eighteenth century they told colonists that they had no desire to be like them: "We are Indians and don't wish to be transformed into white men. The English are our Brethren, but we never promised to become what they are."[38] As David Zeisberger, the Moravian missionary, was told, "each creature, bear, deer, or other animal continues to live its own way and it has never been observed that an animal had adopted the habits of another. The same principle, . . . applies to Indians and Europeans."[39]

At the end of the seventeenth century a French observer remarked that it was possible to find French influences in native religions and in the fact that Indians used French arms and other trade goods. However, not one native group, the Iroquois included, had adopted the French form of government or way of life. He concluded that it would be the work of "many centuries" to "reduce" the Indians to "take up our habits and customs."[40] Contact with Dutch, English, and French cultures during the seventeenth century did not transform the Iroquois into a predominantly Christian, patriarchal, and hierarchial society. Despite the examples and efforts of Europeans, the Iroquois did not abandon their way of life. They did not change how or by whom they were governed, how they maintained cultural stability, nor what they considered important. Iroquois society was not the same in 1700 as it was in 1600, but then again, it was not in 1600 what it had been in 1500. Cultural evolution took place, but the nature of change was conditioned by existing cultural values. Iroquois culture underwent some changes and adapted some new material goods, but Iroquois society remained governed by its own people, principles, and values, not those of Europeans.

Even if the Iroquois did not "cherish" goods for their own sake and did not value them beyond their utilitarian function, could they not have become dependent on them? The term *dependent* has a variety of meanings, but they usually refer to essentially the same thing: a dependent person is someone who *needs* something, as opposed to merely desiring it. The question of cultural dependency, at least as it relates to the causes of Iroquois wars, revolves around how much the Iroquois *needed* those new goods.[41] Did Iroquois survival as a people depend on kettles, knives, guns, and other trade items?[42] Dependency of this nature is hard to prove—certainly, no one has. One would have to demonstrate that certain goods were essential for Iroquois *survival*, and to establish that the Iroquois could not make those goods they needed to survive. It is difficult to imagine a culture falling apart because it did not get enough kettles. After all, they could always have made clay ones again. Guns and ammunition may have been more important, but even here the Iroquois showed independence of mind. In the 1690s Governor Fletcher of New York wrote to London to ask that "light Fuzees" be sent to give to the Iroquois as presents because "they will not carry the heavy firelocks I did bring over with me."[43] Dependent people would hardly refuse to use a product because they preferred a different brand.

Nonetheless, it may be conceded that even if the Iroquois were not dependent on the products of European technology, they wanted them. But did they want them enough to destroy other groups in order to get at their furs in order to trade for those goods? Suggestions in the literature that this was the case are based on several interconnecting assumptions: the Iroquois ran out of furs to trade for goods or could not get enough to meet their needs; the Iroquois were a unified people capable of long-term strategic planning and had the means to ensure that plans were carried out; other goals of warfare were displaced by this new "economic" motive; and the Iroquois warred to steal furs.[44] The first two assumptions are debatable and will be taken up in the next chapter. However, even if they were correct, as we have already seen, other important motives for war did not disappear. The question that remains is whether there is any proof that "economic" warfare was significant.

Warfare may be defined as economic when the goal of specific raids or systematic raiding against various groups was to gain goods, furs, and/or to drive groups out of certain areas so that the Iroquois could gain access to the fur-bearing animals of those groups. This, of course, is my definition. No Iroquoianist has defined the term, but these are the types of activities most scholars allude to when they refer to the "economic" nature of Iroquois war. Without direct evidence from the Iroquois that such was their intent, historians must ascertain their goals from the results of their actions. Some might contend that Iroquois intent may be gleaned from what they said at conferences with Europeans. This is true. Unfortunately, most scholars who use this type of evidence view it through lenses distorted by Beaver Wars ideology and make the data fit into that interpretative framework. The most glaring example of this is the constant misreading of Iroquois efforts to lure French native allies to trade at Albany. Despite the fact that the evidence shows the Iroquois were trying to weaken the French alliance system by providing French trading partners *direct* access to traders at Albany, writers continue to cite this behavior as evidence that the Iroquois wanted to act as middlemen.[45]

An important piece of "evidence" used to support claims of the economic nature of Iroquois warfare is that of raids against fur brigades or smaller trading parties. Because these groups carried furs or goods, historians have assumed that the Iroquois attacked them to steal the items they carried.[46] Since raiding to steal goods or furs produces a material benefit, it is therefore considered an economically motivated activity. These raids are also made to serve as evidence of cultural change and as proof that economic concerns were central to Iroquois policy. Furthermore, this line of reasoning allows writers to argue that raids for which little detailed evidence remains were economic raids. Even if a given foray did not produce furs or goods, and even if the benefits to the Iroquois remain unclear, scholars have assumed that the raid reflected overall Iroquois policy, which was to derive some economic advantage.[47] Surely this is poor historical method. One cannot assume on the basis of some well-documented raids that other raids, for which little data exists, were carried out for the same or similar reasons. Instead, the results of each raid must be taken into account, and if the outcome of the foray is unknown, one must concede that the motives could well have been diverse.

Nonetheless, more information is available about the outcome of Iroquois raids than past writers have assumed. A careful reading of the standard sources of Iroquois history yields a surprising wealth of details and numerical data about seventeenth-century Iroquois warfare.[48] The results cast doubt on the view that such warfare was carried out for economic ends.

A comprehensive data bank listing all Iroquois raids up to 1701 reveals that raids for the purpose of economic gain (or theft raids) did not take place in significant numbers. The Iroquois were involved in 465 recorded hostile encounters before 1701; they initiated 354. In these attacks against natives, Europeans, men, women, traders, hunters, warriors, soldiers, farmers, and fishermen, theft of goods or furs was reported in only 20 of them. This represents only 5.6 percent of all Iroquois-initiated raids. If one includes Iroquois raids against trading parties, possible trading parties, and fur brigades, where theft of furs or goods are not recorded but may have been intended, 14 more raids are added to the total. In all, then, there were 34 raids, or 9.6 percent of the total, for which economic gain—capture of goods or furs—could be ascribed as the goal or sole motive for the attack.[49]

Theft raids, then, were hardly a significant feature of Iroquois warfare. This becomes all the more obvious when the results of these raids are compared with the results of other Iroquois raids. For example, at least 25 percent of *all* Iroquois-initiated raids resulted only in people, not goods, being taken. Since Indians and Europeans resisted capture and such opposition might lead to unintended deaths, this is a significant percentage. If raids in which some people were captured and some were killed (30 percent) are added to those in which people only were captured, that produces a figure of 55 percent of all Iroquois-initiated raids in which at least some people were taken captive. Indeed, the Iroquois captured well over six thousand people between 1600 and 1701 (table F.1).

A closer examination of the 34 theft-motivated raids supports a case for diminishing the role of economic warfare and specifically calls into question both the notion of widespread attacks against fur brigades and trading parties and the assumption that those raids produced large quantities of furs or goods for the Iroquois. Of those 34 raids, 14 raids in which goods were reported taken were not against native fur brigades or trading parties: 4 attacks were against missionaries and/or their escorts taking supplies to various missions; 3 were incursions against enemy villages; and 7 were against the homes of French or English settlers. Of the 20 attacks against native fur brigades or trading groups, in only 9 instances (2.5 percent of all raids) was the group carrying furs. On the other 11 occasions the groups were returning with European goods after trading their furs. More significant in light of claims that these attacks were important sources of furs and/or goods for the Iroquois is that materials were actually stolen only 6 times.[50] That is, successful attacks against native or European fur brigades or groups of traders (assuming theft was the initial goal) represent only 1.7 percent of all Iroquois-initiated raids. In only 3 of those 6 raids were the traders carrying furs. Thus raids against fur brigades that resulted in furs for the Iroquois represent only 0.8 percent of all Iroquois raids.

Of course, it may be argued that the Iroquois did not attack more fur brigades in order not to cut off completely the flow of furs coming down to the French— that is, they did not want to kill the golden goose. Given how few attacks netted them furs, this is not a persuasive argument. (More to the point, most scholars argue the opposite—that is, attacks against fur brigades took place often.) Moreover, general blockades of the main river routes, a tactic the Iroquois often used, also kept native traders and their furs at home.[51] That the Iroquois began using this tactic on the St. Lawrence River long before it became a regular route for upriver native fur brigades would seem to suggest that blockades were undertaken for reasons other than bushwhacking fur brigades.[52] Nor should the low figure of 0.8 percent really come as a surprise. Dutch and later English trading partners of the Iroquois repeatedly lamented that the wars and raids of the Iroquois led to a decline—not an increase—in the number of furs traded.[53] In short, both statistical evidence and that from seventeenth-century contemporaries of the Iroquois suggest that attacking fur brigades to steal furs simply was not an important Iroquois strategy.

The insignificance of raiding for economic gain can be demonstrated in other ways as well. If results are to be the only basis of determining intent, then those raids against brigades and trading parties in which theft did not take place (14 raids) should not be included as part of the 34 economic-gain raids. Theft may have been the objective, but it did not take place. It is entirely possible that other concerns motivated the Iroquois. Indeed, in 11 of those 14 instances, only deaths or captures were reported. Some attacks against fur brigades seem to have been unintentional.[54] One must also consider that in these 34 raids there were a variety of results. In 26 of the 34, people were also captured or killed. Of the 20 raids in which goods or furs were reported stolen, 16 of them resulted in captives being taken and/or people being killed. Given the importance of prisoners and revenge, one cannot deny that capture of individuals or taking of scalps were equally likely motives for these raids. That leaves only 4 instances where theft can be said to have been the sole motive.

The particular circumstances of a given raid may, of course, indicate a primary motive. But a closer examination of the available evidence for many of these raids indicates that economic gain was seldom the principal motive for these hostilities—even when goods and furs were taken.

Of the twenty raids in which goods were taken, seven were against the homes of settlers in New France and in the English colonies. Throughout the late summer and early fall of 1681, the Iroquois were accused of a wide range of attacks against Marylanders, especially in Charles County.[55] It is not clear how many of these attacks were actually carried out by the Iroquois. In the past they had been accused, and later exonerated, of similar behavior.[56] It appears likely that the Iroquois were participants in at least two of these attacks in which they stole some belongings and freed Indians held as servants by the colonists. However, it seems clear that the Iroquois were as intent on wreaking havoc as they were in taking linen.[57] Moreover, as the colonial authorities recognized, these raids were by-products of the Iroquois war against the Piscataways.[58]

Two other incidents of theft can also be described as offshoots of Iroquois-native tensions. In June 1687 a party of three hundred Iroquois attacked the Weanocks at the head of the James River.[59] After taking prisoners, the Iroquois broke off their attack and ransacked several English homes in the vicinity of the Weanocks' fort. Similar circumstances account for a May 1656 incident in which the Mohawks "pillaged" some abandoned French homes on Île d'Orleans.[60] The Mohawks had come to take by force the Hurons living on the island. The Hurons had agreed to relocate to Iroquoia but were not making the move quickly enough to suit the Mohawks. In the process of taking the Hurons, the Mohawks broke into the French homes.

While it seems clear that in all the above cases ransacking the settler's homes was for the purpose of robbery, it is important to note that the Iroquois had traveled to the areas in question for other reasons. The thefts were offshoots of their expeditions, not the reasons for them.[61]

Of the four attacks against Jesuit missionaries and their escorts, unqualified desire for goods rarely accounted for the theft that took place. On 2 August 1642 Father Isaac Jogues and his Huron escorts were attacked and robbed as they headed to Huronia with supplies.[62] The Iroquois had planned an attack against the new French fort being built on the Richelieu River.[63] The group that attacked Jogues may have come up for this purpose. In any event, the raid against the Jesuit proved fortuitous since the Iroquois managed to capture eight thousand livres (money value) worth of goods. Among them, according to Marie de l'Incarnation, the Iroquois found "everything they [had] lacked to make war upon us."[64] It is obvious she was alluding to firearms.[65] The attack she was referring to was against the fort on the Richelieu, and there the Iroquois used guns against the French. Whether the Mohawks knew that Father Jogue's group was carrying firearms is open to question. Certainly they knew the French had them because they had approached the French the previous year in order to trade for them.[66] Also in 1641, Governor Montmagny had authorized the sale of guns to new Christians.[67] The Iroquois probably knew that much.[68] If the Mohawks suspected that firearms were being taken to the Hurons and attacked to steal them, then the motive was theft, but with strategic overtones. Not only would the Mohawks get guns, but equally important, they would keep guns out of the hands of their enemies.

This double-edged motive for theft may also have accounted for at least one other raid against Jesuits and their native escorts. However, little is known of the raid that took place on 15 September 1643 other than that nine Hurons were killed and the supplies were "lost."[69] If theft was the main motive for this raid, it appears not to have been a particularly significant motive for the raid in April 1644 against Father Bressani and his escorts.[70] It is unlikely that the Iroquois anticipated meeting this group. The Jesuits had deliberately sent Father Bressani off early in the spring in the hopes of getting him past the Iroquois before they could set up their ambushes.[71] The Iroquois who attacked him were most likely part of a larger group that had raided the Montreal region earlier in the year.[72] In fact, the group that captured Father Bressani was said to be attacking in reprisal for an earlier loss at Montreal, and the Jesuit was given to an Iroquois family to replace a relative lost in war.[73]

Theft was even less a motive for the May 1656 attack against the Jesuits and their escorts.[74] Indeed, the Jesuits were being escorted by the Onondagas when they were attacked by the Mohawks. The Mohawks ill treated all and "pillaged" the canoes. The real reason for the attack was that the Jesuits were going to establish a mission among the Onondagas and the Mohawks were upset about this. They feared that a mission might lead the Hurons under Jesuit guidance to relocate to Onondaga rather than moving to Mohawk villages.[75] It was to prevent that from happening that the Mohawks attacked the Hurons at Île d'Orleans a few nights later.[76]

Theft appears to have been a motive in all six attacks against native traders.

However, in all but two cases the evidence suggests that theft was not the only, or even most important, reason for the attack.[77] In a raid of 9 June 1643, forty to sixty Hurons were attacked by forty Iroquois.[78] In all, eleven canoes and twenty-three Hurons on their way to Montreal to trade were captured as they passed a spot where the Iroquois lay in ambush not far from the town. However, the Iroquois were waiting to capture Frenchmen and the Huron trading party just wandered into the trap. Shortly after they attacked the Hurons, the Iroquois attacked some Frenchmen, killed three of them, and carried away two more as captives.[79] The Iroquois then killed some thirteen Hurons and left behind over thirty beaver robes because they needed room in the canoes for the prisoners.[80] If the raid had been solely to gain furs, they would not have left so many behind. There also would have been no need to risk capture or death by feigning an attack on the French fort while other Iroquois captured the Frenchmen working a few hundred paces from the fort. An attack against the French seems to have been the major reason for the Iroquois presence on Montreal Island.

Theft and revenge against an old enemy also appear to have been the motives in the June 1647 attack against Algonquin traders.[81] The Algonquins were preparing to come to trade with the French when the Iroquois struck. The Iroquois took their furs but also brought along forty captives. At one point the Iroquois supposedly refrained from chasing escaping Algonquins to ensure hanging onto the furs they had taken from the latter. It is much more likely that the Iroquois, only five canoes of them, felt that forty captives were more than enough.

Even when theft was a prime objective of a raid, it often served as a means to other ends.[82] This was true in the case of the two attacks against French traders and their allies during which goods were taken. In 1684, while en route to a planned attack against Fort St. Louis, the Iroquois came across some French traders taking supplies to the *pay d' en haut*. They attacked the convoy and plundered 15,000–16,000 livres (money value) worth of goods.[83] Given the value of the cargo and the fact that only seven canoes were going up, the goods must have included firearms.[84] The Senecas who initiated the attack justified their hostility on just those grounds. They were going to attack the fort because the French were trading arms to their enemies, and, when they spotted the supply convoy, attacked it for that reason. The Senecas were angry that the governor of New France forbade the Iroquois from making war "on any of the Nations with whom he trades; and at the same Time furnishes them with all sorts of Ammunition, to enable them to destroy us."[85]

A similar motive explains the attack against Algonquin traders and their French escort in 1692.[86] The Iroquois were at war with the French and their allies in the 1690s.[87] A group of Iroquois had set themselves up on the Ottawa River and from that position launched a series of raids against the French colony during the summer of 1692. The Iroquois were also there to block the route to the upper country and to keep the French from supplying their Indian allies. When a group of Algonquins carrying weapons and ammunition tried to ascend the river, they were attacked. As Intendant Champigny observed, this defeat of French Indian allies served to make the Iroquois insolent and at the same time gave them the means to carry on their war against the French.[88] Of course, it also kept the weapons out of their enemies' hands. In sum, if theft was the primary goal of either of these attacks, it was once again because of broader strategic military concerns.

Attacks against villages, where looting took place, also were not undertaken simply to steal the wares of their inhabitants. There is no clear evidence why the Iroquois attacked and decimated the villages of certain tribes. The view that this was to steal the goods or furs accumulated in them is not based on evidence but rather on assumptions about the role of economic warfare. However, based on the known goals of warfare, and on the results of these attacks, it is certainly possible to suggest that capture of people was a major motive. In two of the three attacks against villages where goods were reported taken, the Iroquois removed between thirteen hundred and eighteen hundred people.[89]

Even if theft was not a primary goal of Iroquois attacks, what of broader notions of economic warfare? It seems difficult—even ludicrous, some would argue—to deny economic motives for war. In reality it is not. Hunt's middleman interpretation was to serve as support for his contention that the Iroquois were motivated by economic concerns. That is, since the Iroquois acted as middlemen, which qualifies under most definitions as an economic activity, and they fought to protect that position, it was obviously economic warfare. In rejecting Hunt's theory, most historians of native groups also reject the one serious effort to establish economic motivation for Iroquois warfare. They seem to realize this and now point to Iroquois efforts to attack fur brigades as proof of economic motivation, that is, theft. As we have seen, that simply was not the case: these raids represented a tiny fraction of all Iroquois hostilities.

Economic warfare, of course, can refer to something more than raiding for immediate material gain. But determining what that may be can be difficult. In the Iroquoian literature, *economic motive* and *economic warfare* are rarely if ever defined, and the actions alluded to by these phrases have a very broad range indeed. Most writers seem to have adopted the view of Marshall Sahlins, who suggests that anything that "provisions" a society can be an economic activity.[90] That definition means that practically everything the Iroquois did can be labeled an economic action. Writers who accept this view see no problem in contending that postcontact Iroquois warfare became more violent due to the introduction of economic motives. However, if almost anything is an economic activity, precontact warfare must also have been fought for economic reasons.

Such an amorphous definition also means that the terms *economic motive* and *economic warfare* serve no explanatory purpose and have little descriptive value. For example, if the Iroquois robbed others for furs to trade for guns, this can be said to fall within the category of an economic activity. But if the guns were then used to exact revenge on some nation for a perceived wrong, the final motive for the robbery had little to do with economic warfare or economic gain. One has come no closer to knowing the reason for the attack against the fur brigade simply by recognizing that it fit the vague criteria of an economic action and labeling it as such. Similarly, fighting to protect a territory can be considered an economic action, but automatically describing such behavior as economic does not end the obligation to try to discover the ultimate purposes for the territorial wars. A description of an action cannot serve as a substitute for explaining why the action occurred. In this sense, then, to reject the notion of economic warfare is merely to abandon a label that has served more to obscure than to clarify explanations of Iroquois actions.

But even if such raids are not defined as economic, can one reasonably exclude material gain—which is clearly an "economic motive"—as an objective of raiding? Some writers of native history have been reluctant to accept the idea that material gain was a minor aspect of Iroquois warfare or that other motives can account for Iroquois hostilities against various groups. Indeed, Bruce Trigger has labeled romantic those who assert that native responses to the fur trade were conditioned by cultural imperatives.[91] According to Trigger, in the early contact period, cultural precepts informed natives' responses, but as they came to understand Europeans, "rational" self-interest modified their original responses. Unfortunately, Trigger has a limited definition of *self-interest* and no definition of *rational*. As an example of a cultural response that was eventually replaced by one based on rational self-interest, Trigger cited the case of Montezuma not resisting Cortés's invasion because the Spaniard was thought to be a god. As natives learned the truth and came to resent being exploited, they rebeled against the Spanish.[92] What is not clear is why leaving Cortés unharmed was not a rational decision that reflected Montezuma's self-interest. Surely angering or killing a god (if the latter was possible) would bring harm to Montezuma and his people. Montezuma's perception of Cortés was wrong, but he acted rationally based on what he did believe. What Trigger has done is to define self-interest in strictly economic or materialistic terms and to ignore the cultural values that continued to shape native strategies toward Europeans.[93] A raid undertaken to avenge a death or to prove martial valor was no less a product of rational native self-interest.

Historians, it seems, are eager to attribute a variety of motives to Europeans, but not to the Iroquois. It is impossible to deny that Iroquois raids produced some material rewards. There can also be little doubt that goods or furs were taken in some raids and went unrecorded. But why should these all be classified as economic raids and be made to serve as evidence of the economic orientation of Iroquois policy? After all, looting was a normal part of native and European warfare.[94] For Europeans, the spoils of war were an incentive to enlist in armies and were often given to soldiers in lieu of pay. To the Iroquois, goods and furs were important for many of the same reasons as were scalps and prisoners: they were symbols of a successful raid. Thus to say that theft—or looting—when it took place was the only motive for a raid is to misjudge the purpose of looting.

To use such reasoning to support claims that Iroquois policy was dominated by economic concerns is even more specious. This is an ethnocentric view that is based on applying criteria to the Iroquois that are not used when assessing their European counterparts. For example, there are several instances of French attacks undertaken deliberately to steal furs. The most famous (albeit unsuccessful) of the French thieves was Dollard des Ormeaux.[95] But even French governors filled up their loot bags. In 1666 the French, under Governor De Tracy, attacked the Mohawks. He destroyed and looted some of their villages and returned to New France with the spoils of war, including some four hundred kettles.[96] Applying the same "logic" to these incidents as is used in the Beaver Wars interpretation of Iroquois actions, one can contend that French wars against the Iroquois were waged solely to steal their furs and that De Tracy attacked the Mohawks to steal their kettles. The latter's theft is particularly revealing. Since De Tracy had no personal use for four hundred kettles, he probably stole them in order to profit from their sale. This behavior can only be viewed as a sign of significant cultural change among the French in Canada since, as a general rule, aristocratic French military leaders rarely performed the office of kitchenware merchants. The patent absurdity of such an explanation of French policy will escape few. Yet the equally specious and superficial reasoning and "evidence" used to support existing interpretations of the economic orientation of Iroquois warfare and policy go unchallenged.

All the evidence points to the fact that warfare served a wide range of functions among the seventeenth-century Iroquois. It is difficult to determine the goals of specific raids, and lack of data often makes it impossible. However, little is gained by ignoring a complex reality in favor of simplistic interpretive solutions, or by assuming what is convenient to make those interpretations work. The reality is that theft of furs or goods was the least important of all the goals of Iroquois warfare. Theft did not represent a primary goal of a significant percentage of Iroquois raids. When theft did occur, it was almost always a by-product of raiding or a means to other ends. Without other evidence to support the idea that economic concerns dominated Iroquois policy, and without theft-inspired raids to support such a claim, one is left to ask what caused the Iroquois wars.

# CHAPTER FIVE

# The Early Wars

The Iroquois had warred against the Hurons and the St. Lawrence and Ottawa Valley Algonquins before the establishment of French settlements in Canada. Their hostilities may even have predated France's first contacts in the St. Lawrence interior. The arrival of the French and their alliances with the Hurons and Algonquins may have complicated matters for the Iroquois, but they did not alter Iroquois enmity toward their native foes. The Hurons and Algonquins became New France's most important allies in the first half of the seventeenth century, but they remained enemies of the Iroquois until their respective nations were defeated, driven from their lands, and incorporated into Iroquois villages.

Before outlining Iroquois policy, some important points need to be addressed. Assessing Iroquois policy is a difficult task because often one has to rely on European accounts of Iroquois actions rather than on records left by the Iroquois of their council decisions and policy objectives. This dearth of direct evidence and the complexity of Iroquois society, especially the diverse aims of warfare and the diffuse nature of government, make it difficult to determine just how those actions reflect Iroquois Confederacy policy. To further complicate matters, even if one is certain what objective any given action reveals, one must often guess as to whether the actions of one tribe represent the position of other Confederacy members. While tribal councils often appeared to share similar views and the Confederacy was apparently consistent in its policies toward certain groups, it is not at all clear if the continuity in Iroquois policy was the product of well-thought-out, long-term Iroquois planning, the result of the constant nature of the perceived threat posed by given groups, the outcome of lack of Iroquois options, or the consequence of the process of historical inquiry. In what follows, then, despite the apparent coherence of Iroquois policy, it is best to think of Iroquois policy as referring to the immediate decisions of a tribal or Confederacy council on a given issue.

Warfare, of course, was an important indicator of Iroquois policy. However, vital as military actions are to revealing Iroquois objectives against various groups, care must be exercised when interpreting that data. Because the Iroquois fought for many reasons, and because a full range of data does not exist for every Iroquois raid, one cannot assume that every raid was a reflection of a policy decision. A raid could have been the result of any number of political and cultural imperatives. Indeed, it is not clear why Iroquois warriors fought even when they participated in raids initiated for political ends. Warriors may have known of the political purpose of a raid but went along to take a captive, to avenge a loss, or to gain honor. These were not mutually exclusive objectives. Nor should every war against every native group be viewed as one deliberately provoked as part of some "master" policy. A raid to gain honor may have led to reprisal raids, which, in turn, led to more protracted and significant warfare between two groups. In such instances, any "policy" would have been a response to circumstances, not part of some preconceived plan.

It is also worth stressing that for all the above reasons, and because the Iroquois fought so many peoples, it is not possible to discern Iroquois policy toward every group in the Northeast. The Iroquois fought against fifty-one groups or combinations of groups. The reasons for hostilities against some of these peoples will remain unknown—in some cases there simply is no evidence upon which to base a reasonable explanation of Iroquois behavior.[1] In suggesting reasons for wars against certain groups there is no intent to imply that those reasons were equally valid for all groups. Where evidence is lacking to account for Iroquois actions toward a given tribe, historians must accept those limitations. Certain native groups receive attention here because there is some evidence to help account for Iroquois policy toward those tribes, and because Iroquois interaction with those groups had a bearing on Iroquois-French relations and policy.

The Hurons and Algonquins were the most important native allies of New France in the first half of the seventeenth century. Iroquois relations with and policy toward these tribes seem to have centered on access to the St. Lawrence River Valley. The origins of that dispute may date back to the early 1500s and to the disappearance of the Hochelagans and Stadaconans who lived along the St.

Lawrence when Jacques Cartier traveled there in 1534 but who had disappeared by the time Samuel de Champlain first began exploring the area in the 1600s. Both the scant historical evidence and early recorded oral traditions point to possible Iroquois involvement in these events.

It is difficult to explain the disappearance of the St. Lawrence Iroquoians because the evidence is fragmentary and often contradictory. In 1642, for example, the Jesuit Vimont recorded the accounts of two Algonquins who claimed that they were descendants of the inhabitants of Montreal Island and that their people had been driven from their home by the Hurons. In 1645–46 the Jesuit Lalemant recorded a similar story by another Algonquin. In all three accounts the time of the dispersion can be dated to 1560–80.[2] In 1615, however, the Recollet Denis Jamet recorded that wars destroyed the early inhabitants of Montreal Island but cited a Huron who claimed that the Iroquois were the attackers. This too can be dated to the latter half of the sixteenth century.[3] Marc Lescarbot, writing in 1610 and referring to Iroquois-Algonquin and Huron wars, suggested that theirs was a long-standing enmity and that the Iroquois were determined to exterminate the present inhabitants of the St. Lawrence much as, it is believed, they once destroyed the St. Lawrence's inhabitants of Cartier's time.[4] Champlain suggested that warfare in general produced the displacement of St. Lawrence groups, but he was not specific about which tribes were involved.[5] None of the accounts identifies who started the wars.[6]

At best all that can be said is that some type of warfare probably caused the dispersal of the St. Lawrence Iroquoians. Whether one group was responsible for this devastation or whether the Hochelagans were destroyed by one native foe and the Stadaconans by another is difficult to determine. There is evidence to suggest that this was the case, but it is hardly conclusive. For example, in support of the Algonquins' version of events is Cartier's observation that the people of Hochelaga were at war with the Agojudas, a "bad people" who lived somewhere up a river (usually thought to be the Ottawa) and who wore armor made of sticks. This description of the armor fits well with the description of that later observed to be common among the Hurons, as does the indication that these people came from somewhere up the Ottawa. Cartier admitted to not understanding whether the Agojudas were at war with the Hochelagans or warred among themselves.[7] However, even if one accepts the testimony of the Algonquins and Cartier's evidence as conclusive proof that the Hochelagans were at war with the Hurons (they certainly were at odds with someone or else they would not have bothered to go to the trouble of palisading their village), there is still the testimony of the Huron recorded by Jamet. Even if this is dismissed as an attempt of a "guilty" party trying to exculpate himself, which is highly unlikely given the prestige attached to victorious raids, the fact remains that existing evidence about the Hochelagans has most experts convinced that they were of Iroquoian, not Algonquian, linguistic stock.[8]

One way to reconcile the Algonquin and Huron versions of events is to suggest that they were referring to different time periods. The Hochelagans, an Iroquoian group, were destroyed first by the Five Nations Iroquois or other Iroquoian groups. If Cartier was wrong about, or if historians have misinterpreted, the direction in which the Agojudas were located, this is a possible scenario. The Agojudas may have been other St. Lawrence Iroquoians living up the St. Lawrence, or the historic Five Nations group.[9] The Algonquins may then have moved into the area abandoned by the Hochelagans and were in turn driven out by the Hurons. This makes more sense than at first appears. Traditionally, the large amount of St. Lawrence Iroquoian pottery found on Huron sites has led archaeologists to suggest that the Hurons attacked the St. Lawrence Iroquois and captured the women who made the pottery.[10] This view tends to support Cartier's account and dismisses the Algonquin claims that they lived on Montreal Island. However, archaeologists cannot determine conclusively how the St. Lawrence material got to Huron sites. The Hurons might have captured the St. Lawrence Iroquois, or they may have fled to the Hurons to escape the attacks of some other group. If the latter were the case, these refugees then may have pushed the Hurons to attack those that had taken up their lands.

Evidence that the Stadaconans were destroyed by the Iroquois is less contradictory because there is less of it, but it is no more conclusive. Lescarbot is the only observer to suggest that they were destroyed by war. The only other reference to the Stadaconans being at war was Cartier's relation of a story told him by Donnacona, a Stadaconan headman, of a continual war between the Stadaconans and the Toudamans.[11] This group is usually identified as the Micmac, but there are grounds for questioning this view.[12] Donnacona seems to indicate that he knew of the existence of the Iroquois and their location. He described a hostile people who lived one month's journey up the [Richelieu] river and who wore furs as they did. Once again Cartier stated that the groups there fought one another, but Donnacona could have meant that his people fought them. These stories were, after all, told by signs, pointing, and drawing because neither group could speak the language of the other. Making a distinction between "they fight each other" and "we fight each other" could not have been easy by such means. Moreover, the Toudamans were clearly identified as a group who lived to the south. Since the Stadaconans traveled to the Gaspe to fish and had met Cartier there, it is hardly likely that they would be confused about the habitat of the Micmac, if that was who they meant by Toudamans. Moreover, when Cartier first met the Stadaconans they were fishing in the Gaspe region not too far from a Micmac group and there were no signs of hostility between the two. Nor does it seem likely that the Micmac could amass an army to destroy two hundred Stadaconans since they were themselves composed of a number of small independent bands.

The only reason for suggesting the Toudamans who attacked the Stadaconans were Micmac is a confused passage in the translation of Cartier's journal in which the Stadaconans recounted a story about a Toudamans attack as they were resting overnight while en route to the Gaspe. Both the French and English texts suggest that it was a war trip—although why there would be women and children on such an excursion is not clear—and that it was toward the Gaspe. However, only the English translation states that the raid was against the Toudamans, thus implying that they were located in the Gaspe.[13] The French text simply states that the Stadaconans were going to war in the Gaspe area when they were attacked by the Toudamans on an island opposite the Saguenay. Since the Toudamans were the traditional foes of the Stadaconans, and lived to the south, and not to the northeast, it is unlikely the attackers were the Micmacs. Thus it is possible that the Iroquois were the Toudamans who attacked and maybe even destroyed the Stadaconans. Whether they were also responsible for removing the tribes who lived between Hochelaga and Stadacona is even more conjectural.

In the end, however, all the above scenarios are, at best, informed speculation and, at worst, conjecture. And, as Major John Norton, the nineteenth-century Mohawk warrior wrote, "it is useless to say much on conjectures, which have no demonstrative certainty to support them, and which, though to one person may appear probable, another perhaps will hardly allow them to be possible."[14]

Even if the Iroquois played no role in the destruction of the St. Lawrence Iroquoian groups, it is clear from the testimony of the Algonquins and Hurons that Iroquois hostility toward them dates from an early period and that the St. Lawrence River Valley was a main theater of war. Several other recorded versions of native oral traditions also bear this out. What is consistent in all the accounts is that the Iroquois lived somewhere on the St. Lawrence, either at Quebec or Montreal, and were driven out by the Hurons or Algonquins.[15] These traditions accord well with the pattern of warfare evident in the early 1600s, when the Iroquois were on the run from the Hurons and Algonquins.[16] However, the traditions of Iroquois flight from the St. Lawrence contradict archaeologists' contentions that the Five Nation Iroquois developed *in situ*, or came from the south, and that they were culturally distinct from the St. Lawrence Iroquoians.[17] On the other hand, theories derived from archaeological evidence are often based on assumptions and hypotheses. The evidence uncovered is real, but how it got to the site and what that means is informed guesswork. Different assumptions often lead to different interpretations, and archaeologists are continually reevaluating data and reformulating hypotheses.[18] It may yet be possible to reconcile the historical, oral, and archaeological data, but for now John Norton's advice seems best.

If establishing the earliest date the Iroquois became involved in the St. Lawrence is difficult, native oral traditions hint at and are in accord about the reasons for the warfare evident by 1600. The wars were fought to avenge previous wrongs committed by one side against the other. Either jealousy, a dream, or a misunderstanding caused the initial confrontation.[19] The retributive nature of Indian warfare accounts for the escalation and enduring consequences of the initial encounters. If these appear to be vague explanations, they nonetheless fit well with what is known of native warfare in the seventeenth century. It may be contended that these traditions are vague because the real cause is unknown. That, however, is an ethnocentric assessment based on modern writers' willingness to accept as legitimate only causes that appear rational by modern standards. Oral histories served to account for and justify aspects of a group's past. In the sources cited above, different tribes were blamed for initiating the wars. Thus if more important or, to be cynical, more self-serving reasons could be found or invented, they would have been. The fact that the Iroquois, Hurons, and Algonquins felt that their traditions provided adequate explanation for the devastating wars they were engaged in should be reason enough to accept them as the causes of the wars as they understood them. More importantly, the hostilities persisted, in part, because those reasons continued to be valid ones for war.

Despite this, some writers claim that a desire for economic gain from the fur trade caused the Iroquois to war in the St. Lawrence Valley sometime after 1535 and that the pattern that emerges around 1600 is a concrete manifestation of a new type of warfare: one produced by the new goal for warring—economic gain.[20] This view is based on an unsupported and illogical interpretation of one incident between the Stadaconans and Jacques Cartier. It is contended that Donnacona, the Stadaconan headman, opposed Cartier's visit to Hochelaga because he wanted to keep the position of middleman and somehow profit economically from the fur trade.[21] This incident then serves as proof of a new motive introduced into Indian culture. All patterns of warfare that emerge afterward such as the Iroquois presence on the St. Lawrence, are said to have been produced by this motive. That this motive for Iroquois warfare was not particularly significant in the later settlement period might be reason enough to dismiss it as an important motive in the early contact period.[22] However, there are more compelling reasons to do so. The most significant reason is that there are no grounds to substantiate such a view of Donnacona's actions.

Donnacona could not want to keep a middleman status, nor to profit from the fur trade, because he never occupied such a position and because there was no "fur trade." Cartier gave a few axes, but mostly trinkets, to the Indians. Cartier himself put no great value on furs and traded for them as a means of maintaining the friendship of the Indians. Indeed, most of the groups he met on the St. Lawrence offered and traded him food, not furs.[23] In 1542 Spanish sailors questioned about what they knew of Cartier recalled the ships he had and what the Indians had told him, but made no mention of a fur trade.[24] Indeed, Cartier was commissioned to return to Canada to find (what turned out to be) a mythical kingdom, not to establish a fur trade.[25] Moreover, no serious efforts were made to exploit the upper St. Lawrence fur trade until the 1580s.[26] Native opposition kept the French and any potential fur trade at bay until then.[27]

There is little data on the fur trade in the sixteenth century, and what little there is comes, not surprisingly, from the latter decades. By the 1580s furs began to arrive in Europe in sufficient numbers to attract attention. Richard Hakluyt, a promoter of English colonization, noted that he saw in Paris furs to the value of five thousand crowns in 1584. The furs came, he wrote, from "the most nether parts of those countries whereunto our voyage of inhabiting is intended."[28] One assumes this meant the northeast coast of North America. What five thousand crowns represented in pelts is difficult to say. A silver crown was worth five shillings, and during the 1600s a beaver pelt was worth about one pound sterling.[29] That means five thousand crowns represented about 1,250 furs. If furs were more valuable in this early period, then even fewer furs would be required to produce the same value.[30]

Furs were an attraction and were valued probably because so few arrived. Even by the 1600s, large fur shipments seem to have been rare.[31] If they arrived, they have so far escaped historical scrutiny. Indeed, evidence suggests that the volume of the early fur trade was not high. In 1607 Saint Malo merchants were granted the right to trade freely in Canadian furs. In 1609 they were ordered to pay six thousand livres (about one thousand furs) for this privilege.[32] The

French Crown can hardly be said to have reached an advantageous decison in this matter if the number of furs traded annually was in the tens of thousands. However, it appears that the Crown decision was not that one-sided. The few references to lots of furs put up for sale in France reveal that the number of pelts offered was in the low hundreds.[33] Further, Sieur de Monts, in asking for compensation for furs shipped without his permission while he still held the monopoly on the fur trade, put in a claim for just over seventeen hundred beaver pelts.[34]

That the fur trade was profitable seems obvious, but that it required a large volume of fur is not. The price of trade goods was low, the Indians provided the labor, and ships could fill out their holds with fish to ensure a full return cargo. There is no need to assume that eyewitness accounts of profitable journeys necessarily involved a large number of furs. In 1583, for example, a voyage by the French merchant Étienne Bellenger produced four hundred crowns' worth of furs in return for forty crowns' worth of trade items.[35] This tenfold return on investment obviously represents a significant profit margin and must have been a good incentive to engage in the fur trade again. But, based on the same calculations as above, this represents only one hundred pelts.

In short, there is little evidence that even by 1600 the fur trade was of such volume and significance to Indians that they refocused their lives, seasonal patterns, and cultures to provide furs to Europeans in order to obtain European trade goods. It is too much to credit that Donnacona foresaw the French desire to develop a vast and rewarding fur trade (that would keep the French interested in Canada) before the French figured it out. Even by 1618 Champlain felt that while the fur trade was valuable to New France, other resources held a greater potential benefit.[36] However, the almost complete lack of European trade goods on any of the pre-1600 St. Lawrence sites serves as clear evidence that what furs were reaching Europe were not from the St. Lawrence interior.[37] (Either that or the Europeans were trapping their own furs or the natives were giving away their fur catches.) Moreover, if keeping a middleman position or profiting from the fur trade was all important to Donnacona and his people, the Stadaconans would hardly have harassed their main supplier to the point that Cartier was forced to abandon his stay in Canada.

Donnacona did not refuse to escort Cartier to Hochelaga because he wanted to protect some nonexistent economic arrangement; fear appears to be a more reasonable explanation for his behavior. According to Cartier, the Stadaconans were subjects of Hochelaga. Regardless of whether this was the case, Donnacona apparently objected to the visit upriver for fear that Cartier would either strengthen the Hochelagans' grip or form an alliance with them. When he first objected to Cartier's visit, one of his complaints was that Cartier "and his people carried so many weapons when they on their side carried none." Later Donnacona sought to establish an alliance with Cartier and formalized it by giving the Frenchmen some children, a traditional practice, as a "sign of alliance." The preoccupation with the weapons, however, continued unabated, and Donnacona asked Cartier to fire off the ship's cannons since he had never heard the like. After this, when Cartier insisted on going upriver, he was asked to leave a hostage behind, indicating a continued distrust of Cartier. Uncertainty over Cartier's motives was probably due to the fact that when Donnacona gave Cartier a few of his people, Cartier did not give Donnacona any of his in return as native custom required.[38]

Cartier suspected that the two Indians he had taken with him to France were leading the opposition, and he was possibly right. Donnacona's concerns may have been fueled by Domagaya and Taignoagny. In Indian society, however, all individuals have input into the decision-making process. Moreover, if anyone could tell Donnacona of the power of French arms, it would have been those two since they had observed them firsthand in France during welcoming ceremonies and other functions designed to impress them with French power and wealth.[39] Throughout all this, the behavior of Donnacona is consistent with that of a cautious leader. He sought to establish peaceful relations with Cartier as he might have with any Indian leader. When Cartier failed to do things in the manner he was accustomed to, Donnacona tried to prod him into doing so. Donnacona's actions reveal that his goals were simply to establish sure bonds between himself and the powerful and potentially dangerous stranger who wanted to go to a group who either had defeated his people or could do so with the weapons that stranger possessed. There is nothing in Donnacona's behavior to indicate that he was motivated by desires of economic gain.

It is true that the Indians were eager for the trinkets Cartier provided, but to suggest that desire for these few trifles produced war of sufficient magnitude to destroy an entire people is far-fetched. There are other reasons that help explain this early eagerness for goods. Cartier was regarded as something of a god and people sought to touch him and have him touch and "lay hands" on their young.[40] Given the Indians' animistic worldview, the trinkets Cartier gave out were probably seen to be charms either because of people's perceptions of Cartier or because of their novelty. In any case, Indians were not so attached to them that they acted irrationally or out of character. While the Stadaconans were willing to trade for trinkets, if they did not get a good deal for their provisions they did not trade. By 1541, when his presence was proving to be undesirable, the Indians forced Cartier to abandon his stay among them. This type of behavior was hardly to be expected from a people so dedicated to profiting from a fur trade that one can suggest they exterminated others to attain that end.[41]

But even if there had been a fur trade in the 1530s, and had Donnacona sought to take advantage of it, there still remain several problems with this "economic" interpretation. To begin with, there is no conclusive evidence that the Iroquois preoccupation with the St. Lawrence was new; in fact, it may have predated Cartier's arrival. More to the point, there is absolutely no evidence that the Five Nations Iroquois were motivated by the same concerns as Donnacona. He was not a headman of any of the Five Nations Iroquois. Using Donnacona's concerns, even if known, to account for the actions of peoples living hundreds of miles away and who may have been his enemies, not his followers, is, to say the least, weak historical reasoning.

It is impossible to accurately assess the time when, the extent to which, or the reasons why the Iroquois became involved in the St. Lawrence theater of war. What can be affirmed is that by 1600 they had claimed the St. Lawrence as their own and had established themselves as foes of the Hurons, Algonquins, and Montagnais. By the time Champlain arrived, most areas along the St. Lawrence (the Richelieu River, Lake Champlain, and Lake Ontario) were recognized as belonging to or claimed by the Iroquois.[42] By 1603 the Iroquois had already made passage along the St. Lawrence a risky endeavor for native groups. Champlain even suggested building a settlement at Three Rivers because it "would be a boon for the freedom of some tribes who dare not come that way for fear of their enemies, the said Iroquois, who infest the bank all along the said river of Canada."[43] A settlement was built at Three Rivers, but it did not stop Iroquois attacks on New France's native allies. Not even after most of them had been driven from their homelands did the Iroquois relent in their wars against the Hurons and Algonquins.

# CHAPTER SIX

## *"But one people"*

If establishing the causes of Iroquois hostilities toward some French native allies before 1600 is difficult, the reasons for Iroquois warfare seem clearer for the period after 1600. Regardless of who started their wars, the evidence suggests that their hostility toward each other was ancient. After 1600 the revenge cycle continued to give impetus to raiding, as did the Iroquois military strategy of capturing people to weaken their foes and to strengthen their own forces. The importance of capturing people even led to intensified and new wars because of the Iroquois' need to replace populations decimated by warfare and disease. Nor can one discount native traditions explaining these wars because buried in these accounts is an implicit cause for war. In their focus on the St. Lawrence and in the consistency with which the wars were said to have started as a result of murders that occurred as groups hunted near each other is the suggestion that the wars were in part fought over territory—either to gain it or protect it. As the fur trade grew in importance for the Iroquois tribes, defending their territories must have taken on new significance. Land was needed to hunt for furs for clothing and trade, it was a source of food, and it served as a buffer between the Iroquois and their enemies.

There is little direct evidence about the importance of revenge, honor, and capture of people as specific causes of the Iroquois wars against the Hurons and the Algonquins. That is, no Iroquois council record has been found in which Confederacy leaders are reported to have agreed to "attack the Hurons and Al-

Table 6.1. Population Losses to the Iroquois to 1701

| Type of loss | Captured | Killed | Lost | Total |
|---|---|---|---|---|
| Due to Iroquois raids | 3,791–4,157 | 1,738–2,065 | 2,150–2,667 | 7,679–8,889 |
| Due to own raids | 19 | 278–293 | 127–128 | 424–440 |
| Total | 3,810–4,176 | 2,016–2,358 | 2,277–2,795 | 8,103–9,329 |

*Source*: Table F.1.

gonquins to avenge ourselves on them, and to capture their people in order to replenish our dwindling numbers." But, as we have already seen, the evidence left by European observers and the Iroquois confirm the importance of revenge, honor, and the need to capture people as objectives of raiding. Reason alone dictates that these general causes of war must have been operative and can serve to explain hostilities against, or policy toward, specific groups such as the Hurons and Algonquins.

Nonetheless, in the case of capturing people, one need not rely solely on persuasive logic. The data on the numbers of people captured and killed by the Iroquois confirms the significance of the capture of people as a goal of Iroquois warfare in the seventeenth century. By 1701 the Iroquois had captured 3,810 to 4,176 people. If one adds to this total people said to have been "lost" to the Iroquois (2,277–2,795) but who were almost all captured rather than killed, this puts the total number of people captured by the Iroquois at 6,087 to 6,971. During this same period they killed between 2,016 and 2,358 people. Thus the Iroquois captured two, probably three times as many people as they killed. Given this type of data, it would not appear unduly sanguine to suggest that capture of people was an important policy of the Iroquois.

At first glance the suggested numbers of people captured might appear high. But, depending on what one accepts as the overall Iroquois population, the above figures are either fairly accurate or they underestimate the number of captives among the Iroquois. If the Iroquois population is placed at 10,000 to 12,000, as first suggested by Parkman, and one accepts the various assertions of the Jesuits that half to two-thirds of the population of Iroquois villages were made up of captives, then the total of 6,087 to 6,971 seems an accurate reflection of the number of prisoners taken by the Iroquois.[1] If the Iroquois population is placed at 20,000 to 25,000, then the above total of captives appears to be conservative.[2] If one applies the Jesuit observation on the percentage of villagers who were not Iroquois to this higher population figure, then the number of captives should be 12,000 to 15,000.

Table 6.2. Iroquois Population Losses to 1701

| Type of loss | Captured | Killed | Lost | Total |
|---|---|---|---|---|
| Due to raids by others | 855–892 | 1,270–1,378 | 724–839 | 2,849–3,109 |
| Due to own raids | 108 | 486–509 | 414–425 | 1,008–1,042 |
| Other causes | | 3,905 | | 3,905 |
| Total | 963–1,000 | 5,661–5,792 | 1,138–1,264 | 7,762–8,056 |

*Source*: Table E.1.

But where were all these people going? After all, there were limits to how many captives could be tortured and how many dead kin the Iroquois needed to replace. The answer is, quite simply, that high as the number of captives may have been, they were still not enough to offset Iroquois population losses. The Iroquois were continually losing people due to the onslaughts of their enemies and disease. They also lost many people, mostly males, as a result of their own raids.[3] Epidemic disease may have meant a more dramatic and tragic death toll, but slow and gradual depopulation seems to have been the rule in the intervening periods.[4]

Indeed, it can be argued that Iroquois population losses were greater even than those listed in table 6.2. For example, "other causes" include nonwar-related deaths—mostly deaths due to illness and disease, both foreign and native to the Iroquois.[5] Of the total of 3,905, a large portion, 2,002, represent only the number of baptized Iroquois who died between 1667 and 1679 (tables A.2, B.1). The total number of unbaptized Iroquois that died in those twelve years went unrecorded. Also, the figure of 3,905 includes deaths from only seven, possibly eight separate epidemics (appendix B; table B.1). There is no evidence concerning the number of lives lost in the other seven or eight outbreaks of epidemic disease that struck the Iroquois during the 1600s. However, if loss of life was no more severe during those epidemics for which no death records exist, and if the annual death rates in nonepidemic years was similar in other years to the rate for the period 1667 to 1679, then one can postulate a like number of dead per year—that is, 2,002 deaths over twelve years, or 167 deaths per year.[6] If one multiplies that figure by the remaining years in the century, that would put the number of nonwar-related Iroquois deaths at 14,863. In short, there was no need to be concerned with where to put those who came to replace the dead. It was Iroquois cemeteries, not their longhouses, that were crowded.

Be all that as it may, is there evidence that raids to capture people were related to these population losses? Reason, if nothing else, should indicate that this was indeed the case. Since raiding to capture people was, according to both European contemporaries and the statistical analysis of Iroquois hostilities, an important goal of warfare, one may assume that population losses heightened pressure to capture people and led to increased raiding for this end. There are two other compelling pieces of evidence to support this conclusion. Figure 6.1 charts the number of Iroquois raids against all groups by year. Also marked on this graph are the years during which serious disease or epidemic struck the Iroquois. With few exceptions, the years during which epidemics struck, or shortly after, are followed by an increase in raiding.

The exceptions are the years 1646–47, the early 1660s, 1676, and 1682. But it is easy enough to account for the lack of increased raiding in these years. The years after 1647 saw the destruction of the Hurons and the capture of a large portion of their population via a small number of large-scale raids. This was true for the period after 1682. Then the Miami and Illinois were the targets. After 1676 the Iroquois incorporated the Susquehannocks into their villages, and that probably offset the population losses caused by the epidemic. In the early 1660s the number of raids increased after the first and second epidemic, but they soon dropped off. This decline can be explained by the severity of the epidemics, the instability in New York caused by Dutch and English struggles to control the colony, thus creating uncertainty in Iroquois gun and ammunition supplies, and by the news of the impending arrival of French troops to be used against the Iroquois. The combined effect of all these events may have caused Iroquois warriors to stay at home to conserve ammunition and protect their villages.

There does not seem to be a direct relationship between the number of raids and the number of captives taken (table F.1). This, of course, can be the result of the vagaries of war. It also suggests that the increase in warfare was the result of many small raiding parties that did not necessarily capture large numbers of people (see table D.1). There is no evidence to confirm that such attacks against specific groups were part of overall Confederacy policy. On the other hand, there is a clear relationship between large-scale attacks and the number of captives taken. For example, the Iroquois armies sent against the Hurons, Neutrals, Susquehannocks, Eries, Illinois, and Miamis all returned with large numbers of captives.[7] Perhaps not so surprisingly, all followed shortly on the heels of years when disease struck the Iroquois.[8]

In short, increased hostilities against a variety of foes after periods of epidemic or disease reflected, at the least, the response of individuals who sought to assuage their grief by capturing people for torture or to replace those recently

Figure 6.1. Iroquois Hostilities to 1701

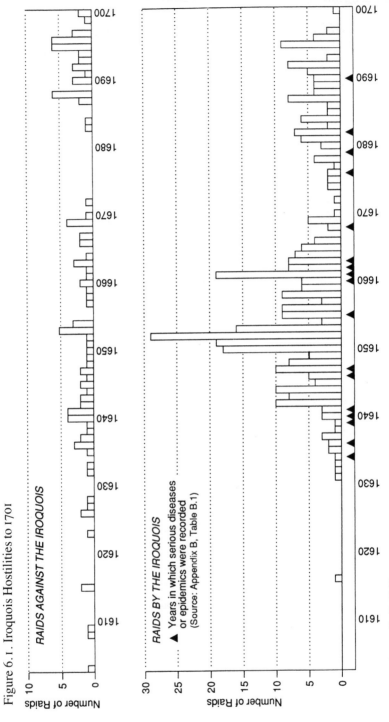

Source: Appendix D, Table D.1.

deceased. At times, population decline seems to have been a factor in Confederacy decisions to war against certain groups in order to capture people. A closer look at the results of Iroquois aggressions against some of these groups, especially against the Hurons, their linguistic cousins, reinforces the importance of capturing people as a goal of Iroquois warfare against them.

The first clearly recorded Iroquois attack against a group composed solely of Hurons took place in 1631; the last took place in 1663. During these years the Iroquois attacked the Hurons seventy-three times.[9] In this same period the Hurons were also attacked nine times when they were part of other groups targeted by the Iroquois. The results of the seventy-three raids against the Hurons were 300–304 Hurons captured, 523–531 killed, and 1,241–1,255 lost to the Iroquois (table F.3). In all, the Iroquois were responsible for the removal of just over 2,000 Hurons from a post-1630 population estimated to have been as high as 10,000.[10] This represents between one-fifth and one-fourth of the total Huron population. If the Iroquois goal was to capture and kill Hurons to exact revenge on them or to deplete the Hurons' population in order to exterminate them, the above totals suggest that Iroquois policy achieved considerable success.

However, it seems that Iroquois policy toward the Hurons was geared toward capturing rather than exterminating them. At first glance the data on the human toll exacted on the Hurons by the Iroquois may not appear to support the contention that capturing people was an important reason for Iroquois raids against the Hurons. After all, only 300 out of 2,000 Hurons taken by the Iroquois were clearly recorded as having been captured. However, the number of Hurons "lost" to the Iroquois should be considered as people captured, not killed. The Jesuits, who left the most detailed accounts of the raids during which Huronia was destroyed, use the word *lost* to convey the sense of living people who have been taken from the reach of their ministrations by the Iroquois. This is, admittedly, an impression derived from reading the sources, and one favorable to the thesis being advanced here. However, if true, it puts the number of Hurons captured at about 1,550—or three times more captured than killed.

Nonetheless, whether one accepts 300 or 1,550 as the total number of Hurons captured by the Iroquois, it may be contended that both figures are far too low. For example, in 1651 the Jesuits reported that the Hurons from St. Michel and St. Jean-Baptiste had given themselves freely to the Senecas. By 1657 one whole village among the Senecas was made up of these Hurons.[11] It seems clear that they should be included among the total of captured Hurons. The fact that they relocated before being attacked reveals they understood that their capture was a goal of Iroquois raiding against them. By voluntarily moving to Iroquoia they avoided the unpleasantness that would follow a defeat and a forced resettlement. It is not clear how much of the estimated (pre-epidemic) Huron population of 3,600 in these two villages relocated to Iroquoia.[12] But it seems certain that the Huron refugee village referred to in 1657 was that of Gandougaraé. In 1669 Father Frémin reported that this village was comprised entirely of people from captured nations.[13] Gandougaraé was one of the smaller Seneca villages that observers stated was made up of about thirty longhouses.[14] Based on an average of three or four central fires per longhouse and two families (ten people) per hearth, the estimated population of this village alone was 900 to 1,200, mostly if not entirely Huron refugees.[15] Also, in 1667 the Jesuits reported that one Mohawk village, where Father Jogues had been killed, was made up of only one-third Mohawks. Hurons and Algonquins made up the other two-thirds of the population.[16] This village was known by several names, but by the 1660s was called Caughnawaga.[17] The village contained about twenty-four houses in 1677.[18] If the refugee population of that village was evenly divided, which is by no means certain since the Hurons were attacked and captured in greater numbers than the Algonquins, then one could surmise that the Hurons occupied approximately eight longhouses. Based on the same calculations as above, this puts the Huron population of Caughnawaga at 240 to 320.

Thus the number of captive Hurons found in just two Iroquois villages (1,140 to 1,520) exceeds the number of Hurons clearly said to have been captured by the Iroquois (300). Indeed, the number of Hurons in these two Seneca and Mohawk villages equals even the most optimistic estimates derived from records of raids (1,550). Moreover, this figure does not even begin to take into account the numbers of Hurons scattered among the other Seneca and Mohawk villages, and among the villages of the Cayugas, Onondagas, and Oneidas.[19]

Even if no data existed on the number of Hurons the Iroquois captured, one could still contend that the capture of Hurons was a major goal of Iroquois warfare against them. The Iroquois certainly made no secret that this was their policy. As early as 1642 Father Isaac Jogues, writing from among his Mohawk captors, informed his superiors at Quebec that "the design of the Iroquois, as far as I can see, is to take, if they can, all the Hurons; and, having put to death the most considerable ones and a good part of the other, to make of them but one people and only one land."[20] Indeed, some Hurons, recognizing this to be the aim of Iroquois attacks against them, chose to join the Iroquois rather than suffer at their hands.[21] An incident in the spring of 1650 serves to reveal how clearly the

Hurons recognized Iroquois policy. That year a Huron who was on his way to raid the Iroquois ran into a band of Iroquois warriors. To save himself he said, "I am going to my country, to seek out my relatives and friends. The country of the Hurons is no longer where it was,—you have transported it into your own: it is there that I was going, to join my relatives and compatriots, who are now but one people with yourselves: I have escaped the phantoms of a people who are no more."[22] Doubtless the circumstances in which this Huron found himself influenced his eloquence, but in what he chose to say to his potential captors he revealed what he understood was Iroquois policy toward his people, as well as what he hoped would appease the Iroquois and save his skin.

The Iroquois policy of incorporating the Hurons into their tribes did not end with the destruction of Huronia. In the summer of 1650 the starving Hurons on Christian Island were told by some Iroquois that they had come in peace and were entreated to "take refuge" among the Iroquois so that "in future they might be but one people."[23] The Jesuits, who recorded this exchange, suggest that the Iroquois offer was not sincere. This is a natural enough reaction considering the destruction wrought by the Iroquois. The good Fathers may also have cast doubt on the Iroquois offer in order to make the Hurons attack against this possibly peaceful group look better. However, given Iroquois desire to incorporate the Hurons, it seems plausible to suggest that the Iroquois were sincere in their offer, if somewhat undiplomatic in suggesting refuge from destruction among those who had brought it on. Even if the Iroquois offer was not made in good faith, the fact that they used it as a strategy suggests they expected it to have some appeal to the Hurons—again, because this goal of their warring against the Hurons was so well known.

Throughout the rest of the 1650s various Iroquois tribes even competed among themselves to attract to their respective villages the remnants of the Huron nation. In August 1653 an army of five hundred Mohawks besieged the French town of Trois Rivières. During the ensuing peace negotiations, which were conducted at Montreal and dragged on until November, the Mohawks sent a secret offer to the Hurons settled on Île d'Orléans *"in order to attract the hurons* into their country."[24] A condition of the final peace settlement was that the Hurons live among the Mohawks and "inhabit but one land, and be but one people with them."[25] In January 1654 the Onondagas came to New France seeking an arrangement similar to the one the Mohawks had made in November of the previous year.[26] And in the fall of 1656 the Oneidas made their bid to attract some Hurons to their villages. The Hurons, claimed the Oneidas, should relocate to their villages because formerly the two groups had "comprised but one

Cabin and one Country."[27] It is tempting to take the Oneidas' statement at face value. If true, Iroquois desires to incorporate the Hurons could be explained as efforts to reunite lost kin and add to the Iroqouis Confederacy. However, the Oneida claim contradicts current archaeological knowledge about the Hurons and the Iroquois. But even if the Oneidas' contention is little more than a rhetorical flourish, it does emphasize the consistency of Iroquois policy to make the Hurons and themselves "one people." In short, regardless of the origins of the Iroquois-Huron war, it seems clear that by the early 1600s, capture of people was a major, if not the most important, goal of Iroquois warfare against the Hurons.

Nor, it seems, should this objective of Iroquois policy be excluded as a factor in explaining Iroquois wars against other native groups. Indeed, even if tribes other than the Hurons had no convenient historical or mythical link to the Iroquois, the evidence points to capture of people as a possible explanation for Iroquois wars against many of them. For example, between 1631 and 1695 the Iroquois launched twenty-seven raids against Algonquin groups living near the St. Lawrence between the Ottawa River and the town of Quebec.[28] Of these attacks, twenty-five took place between 1631 and 1660. In all, the Iroquois captured 220 to 246 people and killed 69—or about three times as many captives as people killed. Further, as noted above, the large-scale invasions against the Eries, Neutrals, Susquehannocks, Miamis, and Illinois all led to significant numbers of captives. Given that relationship, it would seem reasonable to conclude that those armies were sent, at least in part, to obtain captives.

Moreover, despite the fact that capture of people was not a novel part of Iroquois policy by the latter half of the seventeenth century, it continued to draw comment from French observers. In 1682, after learning of the arrival among the Iroquois of six hundred Eries from Virginia who had given themselves up rather than be taken by force, Father Lamberville observed that the Iroquois "bring prisoners from all parts and thereby increase their numbers."[29] This indicates the enduring nature of this aspect of Iroquois policy.

Doubtless there were other factors that led the Iroquois to war with these and other groups. As far as one can determine, the Iroquois war against the Neutrals began as an effort to avenge an insult against the Senecas.[30] The war against the Eries started when the Iroquois attempted to avenge a Seneca death. The Eries, urged on by refugee Hurons among them, chose to engage in war rather than try to appease the Senecas with the usual tokens of condolence.[31] Captives among the Iroquois also put pressure on them to war. The Hurons from St. Michel who relocated to the Iroquois tried, unsuccessfully, to convince the Senecas to ally themselves with the French and war against the Mohawks.[32] In the late 1670s and early 1680s the Susquehannocks among the Iroquois were more successful. Once established in Iroquois villages, they managed to convince their new partners to help them exact revenge on their former foes the Piscataways.[33] Yet for whatever reasons any given war may have started, and whether or not the need to capture people was a cause, the numbers of captives taken in these wars clearly indicate that capture of people became important if for no other reason than it was a key military strategy.

But what of the Beaver Wars explanation for Iroquois wars in the first half of the seventeenth century? Even if one rejects the broad sweeping assumptions that inform this interpretation, what of the suggestion that the Iroquois fought to obtain fur-bearing lands to trap furs to use in trade for European goods? This question can best be answered by a discussion of the role of land and the fur trade among the Iroquois.

The Iroquois did not "own" land the way Europeans did. They expressed their relationship to land more in terms of their belonging to, and sharing an identity with, a specific region.[34] The Iroquois had, nonetheless, a clear idea of who belonged to which land and who could hunt on it. One group or nation gained the right to hunt in certain areas based on precedent and continued use of the area. A river, lake, or meadow served to demarcate each tribe's hunting lands.[35] Thus even if the Iroquois did not own their lands, they might still have fought to preserve their right to their use of, or to prevent encroachments upon, their hunting lands.

Iroquois and Huron traditions of warfare suggest that control or use of the St. Lawrence area lands was important to them and may have been a cause of their early wars. There is some evidence that it was a factor in their hostilities in the seventeenth century. In early 1641 the Mohawks captured two Frenchmen as a means of initiating peace talks with the French. On their return, one of the freed captives informed colonial authorities that he had learned that Mohawk desires for peace were designed to isolate the French from their native allies. The Mohawks, he said, wanted to eliminate French support "in order that they might take all the savages, our confederates, ruin the whole country, and make themselves masters of the great river."[36] Along with emphasizing the goal of capturing people as a means to their destruction, this assessment of Iroquois policy also suggests that the removal of the native groups allied to the French was to give the Mohawks access to the St. Lawrence lands. The wording of this statement further suggests that one reason for capturing French native allies was to help facilitate that conquest.

However, present inability to determine who encroached on whose territory presents a problem when trying to make a connection between the Iroquois wanting access to fur-bearing lands and warfare to secure them. French authorities, of course, had no problem stating that it was the Iroquois who were trespassing on the lands of the king and of France's native allies along the St. Lawrence and toward the north shore of Lake Ontario.[37] French claims to these lands were based on the view that they had once belonged to the colony's native allies, a dubious but convenient assertion. This claim reflected French preoccupation with the fur trade and their fears of losing access to or control over fur-bearing lands. It also helped justify their own hostilities toward the Iroquois and their support of natives who were at war with the Iroquois. However, the reports of Governors Courcelles and Frontenac and that of the Intendant Talon were meant to draw attention to the vast profits that New France's economic rivals, for many years the Dutch and, after 1664, the English, were reaping from land that the colony believed to be its own. At the same time, these men sought to stress the illegitimate nature and cost of the Iroquois presence in order to overcome the misgivings of Jean Colbert, the minister at Versailles responsible for the colony. Colbert was opposed to any further westward expansion of the colony, while Talon and Frontenac hoped to increase the fur trade by building forts on Lake Ontario.[38]

The Iroquois, on the other hand, had a different perception of whose land it was and who the trespassers were. The Iroquois and Hurons and Algonquins had been fighting in and possibly about the St. Lawrence River Valley for some time before French settlement in these areas. Who claimed it first, and who was defending it from whom, is not clear. But the Iroquois obviously considered it theirs. At a meeting with the French in 1700 they asserted that the land north of the lake, especially that around Fort Frontenac, "was the place where we do our hunting since the beginning of the world."[39] The French may have supported their allies' claims to certain areas because it suited their needs, but that did not make those claims valid or acceptable to the Iroquois, nor can it serve as evidence that the Iroquois encroached on these lands.

Also in question is why the Iroquois, Hurons, and Algonquins sought access to or control over these areas. The French—again, because of the importance of the fur trade to them—assumed that the Iroquois were hunting along the St. Lawrence primarily to obtain furs in order to participate in the fur trade and had fought to get at this land for that reason. However, not all trips into enemy territory that produced furs were launched solely to obtain furs. In the spring of 1653, for example, the Mohawks took the recently adopted French trader Pierre Radisson on an extended trip toward Lake Erie. The reason for the trip was to avenge a Mohawk death, but the group hunted people and game with equal determination and success.[40] Whether these tribes were fighting to protect or regain ancestral lands, it is likely that they did so because they needed the resources in these areas. Certainly from the 1660s onward there is ample evidence of the Iroquois using the St. Lawrence from Montreal to present-day Kingston and the north shore of Lake Ontario as hunting areas.[41] In the 1640s and 1650s more than one observer commented on the abundance of game in the St. Lawrence around Montreal.[42] Whether game was abundant in these areas before 1600, and whether the Iroquois, Hurons, and Algonquins fought to get at this abundant game, can only be guessed at.

Even if the Iroquois wanted the areas for hunting in the postcontact period, one should not make the mistake the French did and assume that the desire for land was geared exclusively, or even primarily, to obtain furs to trade. Land, after all, was important for a variety of reasons and not just because it contained fur-bearing animals. While the Iroquois were agriculturalists, they depended to a large degree on hunting for food.[43] If their population was anywhere near twenty-five thousand, one can reasonably postulate that demand for meat made hunting land of prime significance to the Iroquois. As the deer populations fluctuated due to humans, animal predators, and environmental factors, the land required for hunting a sufficient number of animals expanded and contracted.[44] Moreover, whatever their population, the evidence shows that game for food was needed in large quantities. Thousands of deer were required annually for each tribe.[45] Iroquois agricultural and land-use practices also made land important to them. The "slash and burn" method of agriculture, failure to use fertilizers, depletion of usable wood around villages, and insect and rodent infestations made it necessary for the Iroquois to relocate their villages every ten to twenty years.[46] All of these factors must have created pressure on the Iroquois to maintain a large land base. Even if the Iroquois did not need to expand their land base, they may have fought to keep others from using up the resources of their land.

Obviously, furs were also a resource that the Iroquois took from their lands. But how important was this goal in wars that may have been fought over land? Historians from Parkman on have contended that lack of furs drove the Iroquois to war to get furs to trade for European goods, and that this was a central goal of all of their warfare, not just wars fought over land. Yet only George Hunt ever sought to establish that the Iroquois ran out of furs. Unfortunately, Hunt's evidence was either edited or invented to help him make his case, and thus his claims about the Iroquois exhausting their fur supply by 1640 remain unproven.

As evidence of Iroquois fur depletion, Hunt cited a May 1640 letter by Killiaen van Rensselaer, the patroon of the Fort Orange region, in which van Rensselaer defended himself against charges that he was outbidding the West India Company and diverting the fur trade to himself.[47] Hunt quoted this letter and ended his quotation of van Rensselaer thus: "Now, as far as I can see, the trouble is not with the price of skins but with the quantity, which is a great paradox to me that I can not understand." Hunt then accused van Rensselaer of having ulterior motives, and that he understood the "paradox of high prices and no beavers."[48] Why van Renesslaer would want to cover up the Mohawks' lack of furs is not clear, but as proof that van Rensselaer knew that the Iroquois had run out of furs, Hunt cited a 1633 document in which the patroon claimed that Indians in New France had more furs than the Mohawks but that the Mohawks would not allow those groups to trade with the Dutch.[49]

Unfortunately, Hunt edited both documents to make them fit his conclusions. In the 1640 letter, Hunt omitted the part of the letter in which van Rensselaer clearly stated that there was no lack of furs, and left out the rest of the sentence in which van Rensselaer explained the "paradox." He was being charged with diverting the fur trade, he wrote, because the company had few furs. The resolution to this quandary, van Rensselaer suggested, was to be found in the company's low prices for furs and lack of merchandise, which probably drove the Mohawks to trade with the English.[50] As early as 1634 the Mohawks had threatened to take their furs to New France because of low Dutch prices for their furs.[51] Van Rensselaer might further have suggested that deliberate efforts by the English to divert the trade, illegal trade by the company's own employees, and the opening up of the fur trade to colonists could also account for any downturn in their fur take.[52] That van Rensselaer increased the quantity of trade merchandise he was sending to be used for the fur trade, and increased the insurance on his reported fur take threefold, suggests that furs continued to be available even if the West India Company was not getting all it wanted.[53]

As for the 1633 document, it is not clear how van Rensselaer's claims that more furs could be garnered from New France serve as proof of anything other than the fact that the patroon wanted access to that trade. Hunt seemed to want to leave the impression that the Mohawks opposed Dutch trade with New France's Indians because they had no furs of their own and did not want to lose their ties to the Dutch. To this end, Hunt omitted van Rensselaer's explanation that Mohawk opposition to Dutch trade with New France's Indian allies was due to the fact that the Mohawks and those tribes were "hostile" to each other.[54] Twenty years later, Mohawk hostility toward the Canadian tribes was again blamed for the Dutch inability to gain access to the furs of those tribes.[55]

The supposed lack of furs among the Iroquois, of course, stemmed from their overhunting in order to trade animal pelts for ever more European wares. As an indication of the extent of Iroquois overtrapping, Hunt speculated that by 1633 the Iroquois brought in as many as thirty thousand pelts. Unfortunately for his thesis, this claim is also false. Dutch figures for the late 1620s and early 1630s do not indicate who brought in furs, but they reveal that the Dutch fur take averaged around sixty-six hundred pelts per year. Indeed, a document Hunt lists in a footnote, but either chose to ignore or did not read, clearly puts the Dutch beaver trade for 1633 at just under nine thousand pelts.[56] In short, there is no evidence that the Iroquois overtrapped and ran out of furs before 1640.

It seems incredible that the question of whether the Iroquois had furs or not, so crucial to the Beaver Wars interpretation, rests on such spurious reasoning and "evidence." Admittedly, the wealth of the Iroquois fur supply is difficult to establish. The Iroquois kept no records, and detailed statistics on the early Dutch fur trade do not exist. However, that no Dutch authority on record complained about lack of Iroquois furs, and that the French made this claim only after 1670—and even then it is suspect—speaks volumes about the inadequacy of this as a goal of Iroquois warfare before 1670.

Indeed, in the early 1620s and again in 1645 the Mohawks tried to use access to their lands as bargaining tools in peace talks with the French and their allies.[57] Admittedly, a goal of the 1645 peace effort was to isolate the Algonquins from their French allies, but the Mohawks' offer of hunting on lands they claimed were full of beaver would not have been much of a incentive if everyone knew that they were bereft of game.[58] In any case, the Algonquins seemed to accept the Mohawks offer. In February 1646 the Algonquins asked the French not to leave them out of peace negotiations and that the "chase be everywhere free; that the landmarks and the boundaries of all those great countries be raised; and that each one should find himself everywhere in his own country."[59] It might be claimed that the Mohawks had asked to use the Algonquin land in 1645 and in 1646 the Algonquins agreed to the request. This is not likely. If the Mohawks had run out of furs in 1640, why would they wait five years to make a move to gain more fur-bearing lands? They certainly did not seem to be trying to accomplish this through warfare. Of the thirty-eight Iroquois initiated raids be-

Table 6.3. Dutch Fur Take, 1624–1635

| Year | Beaver Pelts | Otter Pelts | Value (Guilders) |
|------|------|------|------|
| 1624 | 4,000 | 700 | 27,125 |
| 1625 | 5,295 | 463 | 35,825 |
| 1626 | 7,258 | 857 | 45,050 |
| 1627 | 7,520 | 370 | 12,730 |
| 1628 | 6,951 | 734 | 61,075 |
| 1629 | 5,913 | 681 | 62,185 |
| 1630 | 6,041 | 1,085 | 68,012 |
| 1632 | 13,513 | 1,661 | 143,125 |
| 1633 | 8,800 | 1,383 | 91,375 |
| 1635 | 14,891 | 1,413 | 134,925 |

*Source*: Extract from De Laet, "History of the West India Company," in *New York Historical Society Collections*, 1:385.

tween 1640 and 1645, only eight were against the Algonquins (table D. 1). Moreover, it was the French who initiated these peace talks, not the Mohawks.[60] It is extremely unlikely that the French would agree to sell out the Algonquins and lose their lands as well. They had no assurance that the Mohawks would trade any furs they trapped on Algonquin lands to the French. The French would have gained nothing and lost much by such an arrangement.

Even after 1670, French claims about the lack of Iroquois furs rest on assumptions that Iroquois hunters on the north shore of Lake Ontario were there primarily because they had no furs and that those were not Iroquois lands.[61] However, as noted above, the circumstances under which these assertions were made mean they are of questionable value as evidence about the status of the source and extent of the Iroquois fur supply. But even if the land never belonged to the Iroquois, the search for food and pursuit of martial objectives, including the capture of old enemies, were equally likely explanations for the Iroquois presence in these areas. The Dutch may have dreamed, as did the French, of controlling the entire North American beaver trade, but that is not proof that the Iroquois ran out of furs.

If the Iroquois did not run out of furs, did they have enough to meet their needs? If they did not, they may have warred to obtain land primarily to get at fur-bearing animals. Unfortunately, this question is almost impossible to answer. The data on the volume of furs the Iroquois traded do not exist, nor has anyone ever found a list indicating the Iroquois monthly or annual requirement of European goods. What little data exists about the Dutch and English fur trade in the seventeenth century is suggestive, but it raises more questions than it answers.

According to Killiaen van Rensselaer, the West India Company had a "good" year in 1636 and took in 8,000 skins.[62] The 1636 fur take was, in fact, above average. Based on the data in table 6.3, the average number of pelts taken from 1624 to 1635 was roughly 6,600.[63] This fits nicely with van Rensselaer's estimate that 5,000 to 6,000 pelts were taken every year in the Fort Orange area in the fifteen years before 1640.[64] The only anomalies in these averages are the totals for 1632 and 1635. But in both cases the data for the preceding year is missing, and the totals for 1632 and 1635 are just about double the yearly take. Further, after each of the abnormally high yield years, the figures return to the level of the twelve-year average. Thus it appears reasonable to conclude that the higher numbers are the result of combining the fur take for two years rather than astronomically good years of trading. This was, apparently, not unheard of. In the 1650s the directors of the West India Company threatened to delay supplies to New Netherland unless the annual supply ships brought back beaver as return cargo.[65]

There is some evidence of Dutch fur trading in the 1640s, but it makes the data for the late 1620s and early 1630s, incomplete as it is, look remarkably comprehensive. In 1688 Symon Groot gave evidence that he came to New Netherland in 1638 and lived and worked at Fort Orange for seven years. The Dutch, he claimed, carried on a "great Trade with the Sinnekes" and other westward Indians during that period. In one year he helped trade and pack up 37,000 furs for the West India Company.[66] The other reference to the Dutch fur trade in the 1640s hints at an even higher volume of trade. Adrian van der Donck claimed that 80,000 beaver furs were traded annually during this decade.[67] One, of course, may question the accuracy of these figures. Groot, after all, was only twelve years old in 1638. Moreover, his deposition was made to try to establish English claims to sovereignty over the Iroquois. He also may have confused the trade for 1657, when he would have been about thirty-one, which was 37,000 beavers, for that of the earlier period. Van der Donck's figure is even more dubious.[68] Certainly if the trade volume had been this high, Symon Groot would have used this as his example of a peak year. At the end of the century some English officials bemoaned the poor beaver trade and, looking on the past through rose-colored glasses, imagined a vast fur trade volume during the Dutch occupation of New York, but none ever claimed it was that high.[69] In the end, even if Groot's recollection is accurate, 37,000 was, by his own admission, not representative of the annual fur trade. If it was, it suggests a significant fur trade in the 1640s and is clear proof that the Iroquois had not run out of furs.

The records for the 1650s and 1660s are equally scanty but appear more reliable. A list of furs shipped from 20 June to 20 September 1657, probably from Fort Orange, reveals that 37,640 beaver pelts were sent down the Hudson that year.[70] There is no comparable list for 1660, but the trade for that year was estimated at 25,000 to 30,000 beaver pelts.[71] A year later an anonymous writer reported that the beaver skins shipped out of New Netherland annually exceeded the value of twenty thousand pounds sterling. At approximately six guilders to one pound sterling, and beaver selling for seven guilders each, that comes to just over 17,000 beaver pelts annually.[72]

These data about the Dutch fur trade shed little light on the question of whether the Iroquois fur supply was adequate to their needs. There is no way to determine how many of the furs were brought in by the Iroquois. One may assume that before 1670, and the establishment of a clandestine trade between New France and Albany, most of these furs came from the Iroquois.[73] But how much is not certain, and the proportion must have changed from year to year, especially during periods when the Iroquois were at war. Even if the bulk were brought in by the Iroquois, was it enough to satisfy their demands? The answer to that question depends on estimating Iroquois demand and the prices of the goods they wanted. Unfortunately, the evidence is again too spotty to allow for firm conclusions.

Weapons, for example were highly sought after by the Iroquois and, despite their relatively low cost to the Dutch, the Iroquois were charged exorbitant prices for them. In the 1630s and 1640s firelocks could be had for about 12 Guilders, muskets for as little as 3 guilders, and powder for 2 guilders a pound.[74] Yet the Iroquois paid as much as 120 Guilders (about twenty beaver pelts) for a musket and 10 to 12 Guilders for a pound of powder.[75] Despite the cost, three hundred to four hundred Mohawks had muskets by 1648. Assuming they were all charged 120 guilders per musket, it would require about six thousand to eight thousand beaver pelts to purchase the muskets. Supplying the estimated two thousand warriors of the Confederacy would, at these same prices, require forty thousand beaver pelts. That certainly does not seem to exceed the Iroquois' trapping capabilities. A hunter could trap forty to eighty beavers in one season.[76] Moreover, the Iroquois certainly did not all pay the same price, nor did they all purchase their weapons in one year. The cost of arming themselves would thus be lower and spread across many years.[77] On the other hand, the dearth of information about Iroquois demand for and prices of "household" goods means that one cannot estimate the overall Iroquois ability to meet their demand with the furs they could trap.

The Dutch fur trade data also does not help clarify the relationship between fur supply and warfare for fur-bearing lands. For example, the increase in the volume of Dutch trade appears to have taken place in the 1640s. This was at the time of the Iroquois's heaviest wars, and wars, Dutch authorities stated, resulted in fewer furs being traded. However, if one considers as reliable only the data from 1657 to 1660, then part of the problem is solved. These were peaceful years for the Iroquois, and men were free to devote themselves to hunting. But this raises several more questions. Was the higher volume of Iroquois trade due to increased time to pursue hunting, or was it because the Iroquois had gained access to more lands? If it was the latter, had the Iroquois fought to reclaim or claim that land primarily to exploit its fur resources? Or was the increased volume of furs to the Dutch the result of the western Iroquois tribes finally participating in the fur trade after the 1640s? In the end, it simply does not appear possible to prove or disprove that the Iroquois ran out of furs or did not have enough to meet their needs.

Despite ambiguity about the extent of the Iroquois fur supply, there is evidence to suggest that the Iroquois fought over land. One reason, possibly even the most important reason, for land wars was to exploit the fur resources of the area. As the century wore on, this objective of Iroquois policy probably grew in significance. But the Iroquois wanted furs and participated in the fur trade for their own reasons. It is not enough to say that the Iroquois needed furs to trade for Europeans goods because the Iroquois had become acquisitive like Europeans, or dependent in various vague and unspecified ways on weapons and European luxury and household goods. There is no doubt that the Iroquois wanted these items and sought to obtain good value for their furs when they exchanged them for European wares.[78] They may not have had the habits of modern economic men, but they were not fools and did not like to think they were being cheated.[79] But while obtaining household goods was part of the reason for Iroquois participation in the fur trade, a more important reason was to establish political and trade links to European suppliers. That relationship was needed in order for the Iroquois to gain access to weapons so that they could carry out their political and military policies against their native foes.

At a conference with the Dutch at Fort Orange in 1659 a Mohawk spokesman summed up the tenuous nature of their relationship. The Dutch, he caustically remarked, "say we are brothers and joined together with chains, but that lasts only as long as we have beavers, after that no attention is paid to us."[80] If the

Iroquois had been looking for military allies when they first established their relationship with the Dutch, the Dutch made it clear that all they wanted was an economic arrangement and that the Iroquois had to pay in full for what they desired. But while the Iroquois complained about Dutch parsimony, they too seemed content with an economic link to the Dutch and later with the English of New York.[81] And what they wanted from both were weapons and ammunition to help them in their wars. The Iroquois made no bones about their goal: it was trade "which induce[d] us at first to make the Covenant Chain together."[82] They also made no secret that the trade they wanted most was in arms, and that it was because of those weapons that they "conquered their Enemies and rooted them out so that where they then inhabited is now become a Wilderness."[83]

All this is not to suggest that every Iroquois tribe had the same policy and adhered to it throughout the century. Different tribes surely developed different strategies in response to the time and circumstances in which they found themselves. A closer examination of Iroquois relations with individual tribes would show what those strategies were. But it seems obvious that at the heart of Iroquois policy was their desire to survive as a people. Ensuring that survival underlay the actions and policy of the Iroquois toward various native groups. Indeed, according to their traditions, it was the threat to their survival that had led them to end their internecine feuding and to form the now famous League of the Iroquois sometime before Europeans came to settle in North America. The arrival of Europeans led to changes in political relations and presented the Iroquois with new challenges, as well as with new opportunities. But even if the Iroquois added new foes to their list of enemies, they also continued to fight the same tribes with whom they had long been warring. Regardless of their origins, by 1600 the Iroquois had decided that their survival depended on winning those wars. An important strategy to accomplish that end was to capture their foes and incorporate them into Iroquois society—to make "but one people, and but one land" with their foes, as they had done among themselves. The depopulation brought on by new epidemic diseases increased the importance of this strategy and probably led to more wars.

The fur trade came to play an important part in overall Iroquois military and diplomatic policy. Furs were needed to purchase the weapons the Iroquois wanted to carry on their warfare. Whether war was waged to gain honor, exact revenge, or to capture people for torture or adoption, whether war represented the decision of an individual or of a council of elders, European weapons were sought to help facilitate the outcome of the raid. This meant that land, already vital to the Iroquois because of its food resources, grew in importance. Protecting their land against the encroachments of others, or expanding their land base, thus also led to wars against native groups. But in the end, access to land was still only a means to social and political survival for the Iroquois. After all, they had been fighting long before there was a fur trade.

# CHAPTER SEVEN

# The Failure of Peace

The statistical results of Iroquois warfare against the French in Canada reveal what historians of New France have long claimed: if the English in the thirteen colonies represented the largest obstacle to the expansion of the French empire in the eighteenth century, the Iroquois were New France's most serious obstacle to growth and development in the seventeenth.[1] The Iroquois were the colony's major foe, and warfare with the Iroquois cost the French more lives (and money) than warfare with any other group in that century.[2] After 1640 New France was rarely free of either Iroquois attacks or of the fear of impending war. Between 1633 and 1697—the first and last attacks against groups comprised solely of French—the Iroquois launched 123 raids against the French.[3] The result of these direct attacks by the Iroquois was the removal of 675–94 people from the French colony. If one includes French losses incurred in raids against groups of which the French formed a part, the figure rises to 756–75 French taken by the Iroquois.[4] This breaks down as 343–56 people captured and 404–10 people killed.[5]

John Dickinson, in his study of Iroquois hostilities against New France, puts French losses due to war with the Iroquois up to 1666 at 153 killed and 143 captured for a total of 296 lost to the Iroquois.[6] My figures for the period up to 1666 are: 133–34 captured, 125–28 killed, and 9 lost, for a total of 267–71 French lost to the Iroquois. That separate studies should arrive at not too dissimilar totals is reassuring. The different totals are partly the result of the methods of inclusion we each used. Probably a more significant cause of the different totals is that Dickinson was able to determine the outcome of raids that my sources noted as "some more raids" during which "some people were lost." Because of the vagueness of my sources, such references could not be included in my calculations. François de Belmont de Vachon estimated that 600 French were killed or captured in the years between 1680 and 1700.[7] My figures for this period are 564–81 captured or killed by the Iroquois.

The data on Iroquois raids against the French also reflect some interesting aspects of Iroquois policy toward New France. The distribution of raids against the French (figure 7.1) shows clearly that almost all raiding against the French occurred in two distinct periods: 1641–66 and 1687–97. If revenge raiding was a factor in wars against the French, the Iroquois were quite capable of controling that impulse. The Iroquois forgave Champlain his transgressions against them in 1609, 1610, and in 1615, and were prepared to bide their time to avenge Sieur De Tracy's insolence in 1666. Writing about the period up to 1666, John Dickinson has suggested, based on the results of raids, a periodization of Iroquois hostilities that he says reflects Iroquois policy toward New France. Open hostility toward the French only began in 1642. From then until 1649, warfare was sporadic. The period from 1650 to 1653 marked open war, and 1654 to 1659 was one of uncertain truce. The years 1660–61 signaled a renewed intensity to Iroquois hostility, while 1662–66 reflected raiding, the goal of which was to keep pressure on New France until a durable peace could be negotiated.[8] Based, however, on the number of Iroquois attacks, not on their unpredictable outcome, another periodization is possible. The year 1642 does seem to augur the start of Iroquois hostilities. But the periods of intense warfare are clearly 1650–55 and 1658–62. While the years 1653–56 also marked a period of active Iroquois-French peace talks, the continued raiding against the French reveals clearly that not all Iroquois agreed with that course of action.

Equally revealing are the numbers of French captured and killed and when those losses occurred. Unlike the case in attacks against native foes where the Iroquois captured two, often three times as many people as they killed, the Iroquois killed more French than they captured. This suggests that capture of French was not a primary goal of Iroquois attacks against them, or it might reflect an ambivalence in Iroquois policy toward New France. However, the fact that twice as many French were killed in the period 1687–1701 than in the much longer period ending in 1666 and that fewer than half the number of raids were required to do this indicates that any Iroquois ambivalence about attacking the French was overcome by the mid-1680s.[9]

The size of Iroquois raiding parties in these two periods also shows the

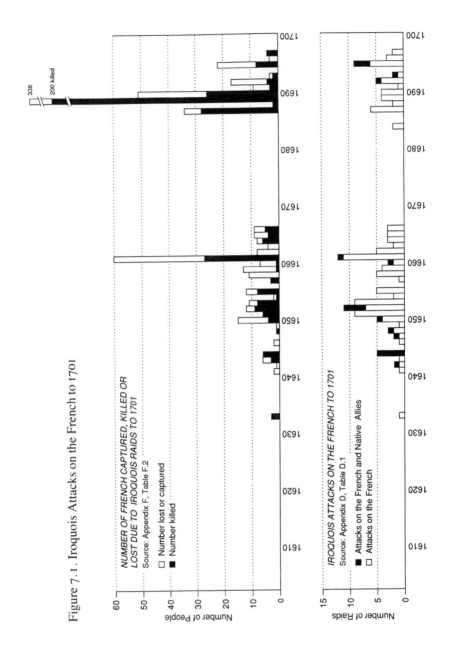

Figure 7.1. Iroquois Attacks on the French to 1701

changing nature of Iroquois policy. Most attacks against the French before 1666 were by either small (3–12 men) or medium-sized (30–60 men) groups of Iroquois.[10] On only two occasions did the Iroquois send armies of over 500 men against the French. In each instance they were comprised mostly of Mohawks.[11] In the years after 1684, raiding parties averaged 200 men and the Iroquois sent armies of over 1,000 men against the colony on three separate occasions. Because no Iroquois tribe alone could field an army that large, groups of this size reflected the joint effort of all Five Nations and the intent of the Iroquois to conquer the French.

But Iroquois hostility toward New France was neither inevitable nor constant throughout the seventeenth century. After Champlain's initial attacks against the Iroquois, both the Iroquois and French tried to establish peace with one another. Unfortunately, neither side was prepared to accept the other's terms. The failure of peace efforts led to war.

Despite, and possibly because of, Champlain's attacks against the Mohawks and Onondagas or Oneidas, none of these groups, nor the Confederacy as a whole, was eager to wage war against the new French settlers and their native allies. Instead, the Iroquois tried to make peace with their native foes. In the early 1620s and again in the early 1630s the Mohawks sought to conclude truces with the Algonquins and Montagnais who lived along the St. Lawrence, and the Senecas made a short-lived peace with the Hurons. The goals of the Senecas remain a mystery, as do those of the other tribes who were also said to be ready to make peace with the Hurons; but the Mohawks clearly wanted access to the French and some sort of trading arrangement.[12] In the end, none of these negotiations led to a lasting peace. Sooner or later, one side or the other jeopardized the peace process, or the tentative truce, by a raid on their ancient foes.

As the French native allies continued to press the attack against the Iroquois, the Mohawks decided to take another tack.[13] In early 1641 they tried to negotiate a peace directly with the French. The Mohawks were willing to conclude a peace with New France but not with the Hurons, and especially not with the Algonquins. In return for peace, and a present of guns, the Mohawks offered to bring their pelts to the French and said they were prepared to accept a French trading post nearer to them. Governor Montmagny refused this offer because he did not trust the Mohawks. He thought their offer was made only to keep the French out of their wars as a means to destroy French native allies. Moreover, even if French allies were spared, granting the Iroquois unhindered access to French posts might discourage other tribes from coming to trade with the

French for fear of running into the Iroquois.[14] The French were not prepared to abandon their allies and jeopardize their fur trade. The talks ended in gunfire.

The French refusal of the Mohawk offer is interesting because it reflects an attitude toward the Iroquois which dominated Franco-Iroquois relations throughout the seventeenth century. Despite the fact that they first attacked the Iroquois, the French did not trust the Iroquois. The French seem to have accepted the claims for, or legitimacy of, the wars waged against the Iroquois by groups that came to be French allies. Without objective proof and because it suited their political, economic, and missionary needs, the French concluded that the Iroquois were the aggressors in these wars. Since the belligerent party is often assumed to be in the wrong, that belief led to a concomitant view that deprived Iroquois actions of moral legitimacy. Opposing the Iroquois became justified.

The French, of course, did not support war against the Iroquois merely because they thought their allies more virtuous, but rather because they believed it was to their own advantage. This policy developed gradually, and not all French officials adhered strictly to it, but its inception can be dated back to Champlain. Even though he had aided the Algonquins, Hurons, and Montagnais against the Iroquois, Champlain did not appear to rule out the hope of peace among these groups. Indeed, at first Champlain had looked favorably on peace efforts between the Iroquois and his native allies because he thought it would lead to an increase in the fur trade.[15] But by 1633 he had changed his mind. If not a threat to the French directly, the Iroquois were, nonetheless, enemies of French allies, and the constant warring endangered the fur trade. Rather than try to establish a lasting peace, Champlain became convinced that the interests of the French and their fur trade would be better served by conquering the Iroquois. A combined French and native force should be sent to destroy the Iroquois and make the countryside safe for trade. According to Champlain, an added advantage of such a move would have been to show their allies that the French were powerful and could protect them. That knowledge, and the fact that once the Iroquois were gone the French would be left as the most powerful force in the region, would help bring French native allies more firmly under French control.[16] By 1642 even the Jesuits had come to accept that New France was not safe unless the Iroquois were "won over or exterminated," and Father Le Jeune was sent to France to plead with the Crown to send help against the Iroquois.[17] By the end of the century, the French had decided that peace with the Iroquois was desirable because it would save French lives, but that peace between the Iroquois and French native allies was to be discouraged to prevent their native trading partners from taking their furs to the English.[18] The French

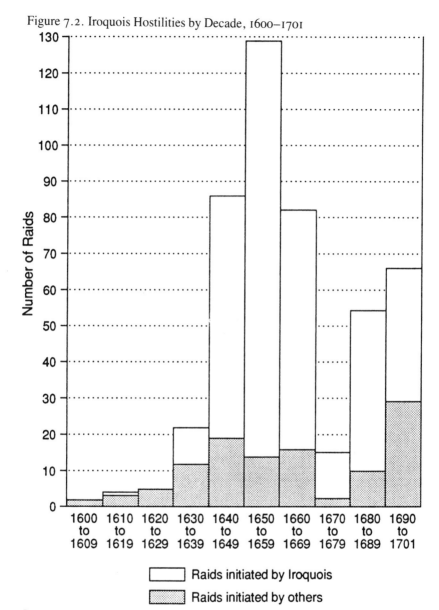

Figure 7.2. Iroquois Hostilities by Decade, 1600–1701

Legend:
- Raids initiated by Iroquois
- Raids initiated by others

Source: Appendix D, Table D.1.

did not want to engage in competition with other European traders, and the hostile Iroquois would ensure this.[19] The possibility that, with effort, peace could be maintained and that the French could attract the Iroquois fur trade did not seem worth the challenge.

But in 1641 Champlain's plan had come to nothing, the idea of balancing war between the Iroquois and French native allies had yet to take shape, and Governor Montmagny was prepared to entertain thoughts of peace with the Iroquois, if not exactly on the terms they presented. He simply could not see the advantages of the Mohawk proposal. For Montmagny, the Iroquois did not appear to be a serious threat to the colony or to the fur trade. The number of pelts traded to the French continued to grow, and French native allies more than held their own against the Iroquois in the years up to 1640.[20] Moreover, amicable relations between the French and the Five Nations would not guarantee peace with French native fur suppliers, and might facilitate their destruction. Worse, if the Iroquois destroyed French fur suppliers, the French could not be sure the Iroquois would bring their furs to French forts.[21]

For the Iroquois, however, this rejection and other French actions in the early 1640s seemed to present them both with clear evidence of New France's hostile intent and with few options. It is doubtful if the Mohawks saw the logic in New France's refusal of their peace offer. The advantages to the French of an alliance with the Algonquins rather than with them were not readily apparent to the Mohawks, and they were angered by the rejection. Father Jogues, who was captured and tortured by the Mohawks a year after the failed peace effort, concluded that the Mohawks had attacked the French because they were "enraged against the French because . . . [they] had not been willing to accept the peace" on the Mohawks' terms.[22] Whether the Mohawks most wanted an alliance or guns is not clear, but years later French explorer Pierre Radisson was told by an old Iroquois that the French "should have given us [guns to] kill the Algonquins." If they had, he was assured, the Iroquois would not have warred against the French and would have traded their furs to them.[23] In any case, Montmagny's rejection of the Mohawks peace offer meant that they were free to attack New France.

Hard on the heels of this snub in 1641 and as further evidence of New France's stubborn position came two bold French moves into land claimed by the Iroquois. In 1642 Fort Richelieu was started at the mouth of the Richelieu River and Chomedey de Maisonneuve planted a colony on Montreal Island. The fort was set up to hinder Iroquois access to the St. Lawrence, and Ville

Marie was created to further the missionary effort of converting the Indians to Christianity.[24] The Iroquois, however, were unaware of Maisonneuve's beneficent intent, and both enterprises were viewed as threats to the Iroquois and immediately attacked. It is not clear if the Iroquois attacked because these places were on Iroquois lands or because they felt the forts were an attempt to circumscribe their mobility—probably a little of both. These types of concerns were expressed later in the century, and there is no reason to believe that they were not factors in the 1640s.[25] The fact that both places were attacked so soon after they were established—Fort Richelieu as it was being built—indicates that the Iroquois opposed their existence in those areas. Both continued to be favorite targets of Iroquois aggression throughout the century (table D.1). The French should have expected as much and should have been aware that fortifications in these areas would not be well received by the Iroquois. In the peace efforts of the 1620s, questions of hunting in these areas had been a topic of negotiations.[26] Indeed, the Richelieu River was known to the French as the Rivière des Iroquois and continued under that designation on French maps until the 1650s.[27] This suggests that even if the French were not prepared to concede Iroquois rights to the area, they recognized that the Iroquois used that route on their travels. They should not have been surprised that a fort there would be unwelcome.

Added to French expansion into Iroquois lands was their apparent arming and aiding of Iroquois foes. The extent of the French gun trade to their native allies and thus to the foes of the Iroquois is not clear, but there is some evidence that the French did sell or give guns to their native allies.[28] Almost all historians acknowledge that, in general, the French prohibited the sale of guns to natives in the 1640s. But some guns sales were permitted to native converts to Christianity, and no one knows whether any or how many were traded illegally. Certainly the Mohawks knew that the French had guns and tried to obtain some as a price for peace with them in early 1641.[29] Knowledge of French guns sales went even further abroad. In 1644 the English at New Haven passed an ordinance prohibiting the sale of guns and ammunition to the French and Dutch because they "doe sell and trade to the Indians, guns, pistolls and warlike instruments."[30] The Dutch appear to have been the worst offenders in these years, but the fact that the French were also mentioned suggests that the French traded guns and that knowledge of this practice was not a secret.

References to French gun sales, of course, could have been to those sold to native converts. This type of trade was legalized by Montmagny in 1641.[31] Indeed, the Mohawks' attack against a convoy taking supplies to Huronia in August 1642 netted them guns.[32] The guns could have been the property of Huron converts, or they could have been for the use of Jesuit *donnés* who were allowed to carry weapons. By 1641 there were seven such servants working in the Huron mission.[33] But even if the reality of French gun sales to their native allies, and the military support that a few *donnés* could provide the Hurons was far less than it appeared, the Mohawks had no real way to determine this in 1641. All they knew was that the French had refused to trade guns to them and appeared to be trading them to one of their enemies and sending armed Frenchmen to live among them.

Unfortunately for the French, others were willing to sell guns to the Mohawks. Although the sale of guns in New Netherland was legalized only in 1648, the consequence of opening up the fur trade in 1639 was the widespread sale of guns to the Mohawks.[34] From that year until the gun trade was condoned, ordinances prohibiting the sale of guns were issued almost annually.[35] That they had to be issued so often is proof that they were of little effect and that gun sales continued unabated. Indeed, gun smuggling in New Netherland was widespread and well organized. Some gunrunning ships put in at New Haven and Dutch smugglers went there to pick up their supplies. Others placed guns in sealed casks and dropped them off the ships near shore before they could be boarded or reached port for inspection. Waiting accomplices rowed out from shore to snag the profitable catch.[36] However the guns got to the natives, by 1641 the Mohawks had at least thirty-six and boasted that they would "go well armed" to meet the French.[37] It was not an idle boast; by 1643 they were reported to have three hundred guns, and had increased that total to four hundred by 1644.[38] That means that more than half the Mohawk warrior population had guns.[39]

In short, the French refusal to trade or give the Mohawks guns to use against their native foes, their apparent military support of the Hurons, and their attempt to circumscribe Iroquois movements by building a military fortification, possibly on Mohawk land, all seemed to confirm New France's hostile intent toward the Iroquois. Since the French had already refused peace, the Mohawks decided to declare war against New France. Had the Mohawks not had access to guns from the Dutch, they would not have had the technological wherewithal needed to take on the French directly and might have tried to make a peace more suitable to the French. As it was, they did not have to do that. In the end, a unique combination of events and misunderstandings, all of which took place in the span of about one year starting in 1641, led to the Iroquois decision to war against New France. Not so surprisingly, it was about this time that Iroquois attacks directly upon the French began.

Some attacks against New France in this period, of course, may have been the result of accident. As one Iroquois spokesman explained, "the French hold the Hurons and Algonquins in their arms; so it is not to be wondered at if, when we wish to strike those of one Nation, the blows sometimes fall upon the others."[40] Most likely, however, this was the Iroquois' metaphorical way of telling the French that one reason for Iroquois anger against them was that had chosen to make alliances with Iroquois foes. In any event, by the end of 1641 it was obvious that the Mohawks, at least, had had enough and were prepared to declare themselves enemies of New France. In that year, French authorities recognized that, at last, the Iroquois were at war with New France, not just with their native allies.[41]

Nonetheless, although the Iroquois attacked New France, the colony did not immediately become a major target of their aggression. If the Iroquois, especially the Mohawks, were prepared to fight the French, the Mohawks were either unwilling or unable to persuade the rest of the Confederacy to pursue all-out war. The Iroquois had yet to resolve their wars with the Hurons and other native foes, and attacks against those groups continued to account for the largest percentage of raids in the early 1640s (see table D.1, entries for the 1640s). It is possible that the Iroquois even stepped up their raids against these groups in order to capture natives to bolster their armies in preparation for war against New France.[42] Still, if the French did not become the Iroquois' most hated foe, they became regular targets as the Iroquois increased their raiding against the French and their native allies.[43]

Montmagny probably had not anticipated this type of Iroquois response to his policies. New France's native allies had more than held their own against the Iroquois until 1641, and the Iroquois had never seriously attacked the French. It is possible that the French even assumed that Fort Richelieu, located on a main Iroquois war route, would be sufficient to deter further incursions. But, if anything, the new fort seems to have angered the Mohawks and led to raids directly against the French. This, and the noticeably increased number of attacks against French native allies after 1641, must have worried the French. As early as 1643 Montmagny was trying to encourage peace between his native allies and the Iroquois. Those efforts may have taken on greater urgency when he learned that the Hurons were undertaking such a course on their own.[44] In any case, whether for fear of continued Iroquois incursions, of damage to the trade, or of being left out of talks between the Iroquois and Hurons, Montmagny again tried to initiate talks between the Mohawks and his allies in 1645 and sent an envoy to the Mohawks.

The Mohawks accepted Montmagny's offer to negotiate a peace. The Mohawks may have concluded that their attacks had frightened the French, or that they had finally come to their senses. The Mohawks certainly acted as if they had the upper hand and tried again to negotiate a peace with the French that excluded the Algonquins.[45] Montmagny, while unprepared to abandon Algonquin converts, was willing to give the Mohawks tacit approval to continue their war against the non-Christian Algonquins.[46] During these negotiations the Mohawks also pressed the Hurons to resume the negotiations they had begun sometime in 1643. The Hurons were encouraged to bypass the French and come directly to the Mohawks to negotiate.[47] The Mohawks were obviously trying to work out a separate arrangement with the Hurons. This and the attempt to exclude the Algonquins from the peace with the French suggests that the Mohawks were trying to separate the French from their allies. The French may have assumed, as they had in 1641, that this was a means to destroy their native allies, but the Mohawks also may have pursued this policy in order to isolate the French and to attack them. In any case, a peace was concluded between the Mohawks and the French.[48]

Like other peace efforts before it, this one was short-lived. Less than one year after it was concluded, the Mohawks killed Father Isaac Jogues and relations between the French and the Mohawks resumed their hostile footing. Despite the historiographic debate over what impelled the Mohawks to take this action, the evidence seems fairly clear.[49] To begin with, the Mohawks still did not seem to trust the French, nor had they any reason to. The French had not razed Fort Richelieu and Montreal—in fact, both places had been strengthened since their inception—and they continued to sell or give guns to the Hurons and Algonquins.[50] Moreover, the peace was initiated by the French, not the Mohawks. The latter agreed to meet with the French in hopes of fulfilling their own agenda, but it is not clear that the French met all the Mohawks demands. Added to this was the fact that during early negotiations, the Mohawks were warned by a Huron not to trust the French.[51]

Even if the Mohawks did not mistrust the French, two events served to raise doubts about the sincerity of French motives. In the fall of 1645 Father Jogues, while working out the details of peace between the French and Mohawks, had tried to include the Onondagas in the discussions. He had, however, suggested that the French go directly to the Onondagas rather than through the Mohawks.[52] To the Mohawks this could only seem an attempt to conclude a separate peace, possibly one detrimental to their interests. They certainly were familiar with this type of tactic, having just tried the same thing with the Hurons a few weeks earlier. Since the Mohawks' efforts to conclude a separate peace with the Hurons was probably not for pacific reasons, they may have concluded that the French goal in concluding a peace with the Onondagas was for equally warlike ends. This may have both angered and worried them. The events that followed must have served only to confirm Mohawk suspicions of French duplicity. When Father Jogues returned to New France in the fall of 1645, he had left behind a small black box among the Mohawks. Shortly after that, disease and pestilence struck the Mohawks and their crops. Already warned by Huron captives about the Jesuit's destructive powers, the Mohawks concluded that Father Jogues left the box to destroy them. For this reason he was killed in the manner usually reserved for sorcerers rather than tortured to death.[53] As far as the Mohawks were concerned, Jogues's death did not mark the renewal of the war against New France; the French had started that when they had sent the priest to work his witchcraft on them.[54]

If the French had started the war, the Mohawks were prepared to continue it. Even before they killed Father Jogues, in October 1646, they had sent presents to the other tribes in the Confederacy in order to try to persuade them to war against the French and their allies.[55] The results of this effort are not clear, but it appears that the rest of the Confederacy was prepared to continue to war against their native foes, and possibly against the French, but they did not want all-out war with New France—at least they did not launch a full-scale attack against the French.[56] Unfortunately, the Iroquois left no records of their decisions or why they made them. It is, however, possible to suggest reasons for their reluctance to fight. The loose nature of government among the Iroquois, based as it was on their clan system, meant that each tribe pursued policies that best suited them. If one or more tribes could not convince the others in the Confederacy of the efficacy of their plan, each tribe did as it thought best. The Mohawks simply may have been unable to convince the Onondagas, Oneidas, Cayugas, and Senecas that their interests would be served by fighting the French. Rivalry among the tribes may also have been a factor.[57]

On the other hand, the Confederacy may have agreed to war against New France and was simply waiting for a more propitious moment. They may have wanted to bolster the size of their fighting force by gaining more captives. They may have wanted to attack French native allies to weaken the French power base, or they may have wanted to augment their gun supply. It appears to be more than mere coincidence that the French came to be major targets of the Iroquois after 1649 and the destruction of the Hurons (see fig. 7.1 and tables F.2 and F.3). However, since the attacking tribe is often not clearly identified in the historical record, this may have been just the Mohawks pursuing the French because they now had more time and resources after the defeat and capture of the Hurons. Although it is highly likely that warriors from the other tribes struck the French and joined Mohawk war parties, Iroquois other than the Mohawks are not regularly identified as attacking the French until after 1656.

The Confederacy's political machinations from the early 1650s to the mid-1660s, however, suggest that whatever decision the Five Nations had arrived at in 1646, it had not fully resolved to destroy New France. If it had, some tribes, at least, were prepared to reconsider that position and to pursue other options in light of new circumstances.

# CHAPTER EIGHT

## Conflict and Uncertainty

After the defeat of the Hurons and the Neutrals, and as New France was reeling from Iroquois attacks, came news in the summer of 1653 that some members of the Iroquois Confederacy were interested in peace with the French. The Onondagas—and, shortly after, the Oneidas—wanted to conclude a formal first peace with the French. The Onondagas in particular wanted priests and a French post among them.[1] The French, of course, were delighted, and the Jesuits credited God for this miraculous change in Iroquois policy and for their willingness to partake of Christianity.[2] The joy, however, was to be short-lived. If in 1653 the talk was of peace, the next decade was filled with conflict and uncertainty. The Confederacy as a whole could not agree on a policy toward New France, and within a few years the Onondagas, too, were at war with the colony.

Regardless of God's role, the Onondagas sought peace with New France in 1653 for decidedly secular reasons. They were being pressed by the Eries and they might have heard that a large army of Iroquois foes and French allies were amassing to strike against the Iroquois.[3] The Onondagas may have wanted ties to the French and Frenchmen among them in the hopes that the French would help defend them against this large group, or even to prevent them from attacking the Onondagas if they became French allies as well. In any event, the Onondagas clearly wanted French aid against the Eries. What they seem to have wanted most was guns; the French obliged and traded guns to the Iroquois shortly after peace was concluded in 1653.[4] By 1655 the Onondagas were openly asking for both guns and French soldiers to help them against the Eries.[5]

Another reason for the Onondaga desire for peace was, the Jesuits suggested, that rivalry had developed between the Onondagas and the Mohawks and that the Onondagas sought to open trade links to the French to bypass the increasingly arrogant Mohawks. The Mohawks were said to have resented this because it would hurt their trade. This implies that the Mohawks exacted toll charges from their Confederacy partners and that the dispute between the Mohawks and Onondagas was over trade.[6] Both views seem unlikely. It was customary among native societies in the Northeast that the group that first made contact with another had the right to that trade.[7] The Mohawks may have wanted to uphold that right with the Dutch since they had made the first contact with them,[8] but other members of the Confederacy traded directly with the Dutch.[9] Having allowed this, it is unlikely they charged tolls or exacted tribute for right of passage. Given the importance of ceremony and reciprocal gift exchange among the Iroquois, it seems more reasonable that the Mohawks expected that those who traveled through their lands would meet with them, ask for permission to pass by, and exchange gifts. While to some observers this may have appeared a toll, the Iroquois were merely following the protocol required when tribes met each other. That possibly four large trade convoys passed almost annually probably meant that the Mohawks received quite a few gifts. However, the reciprocal nature of gift exchanges meant that the Mohawks had to give gifts in return.

There is, of course, evidence that the Onondagas desired a closer relationship with the French; if they sought military aid from New France, they also wanted peace in order to gain access to French weapons. While trading for guns is still trading, it is not evidence that the Onondagas wanted to trade with New France because of trade problems with the Mohawks. A more likely reason for the Onondagas desire to establish trade links to the French was the fact that the Dutch had little to trade and were charging high prices for what they did have.[10] The shortage was probably caused by the outbreak of the Dutch-English war (1652–54), which had an adverse effect on shipping. More significant, the Dutch, apparently due to this same war, had prohibited the sale of ammunition to natives. In 1654 a special resolution was passed in New Netherland to allow sales to the Mohawks only.[11] Thus even if the Onondagas wanted to trade with the Dutch, they could not get the supplies they wanted most—those they needed to carry out their defense against the Eries.

The Mohawks' anger at the Onondagas can best be accounted for by their policy disagreements about what to do with New France. The Onondagas were making direct contact with the French, the Mohawks' enemies, and they had not followed the proper route through the eastern door of the Confederacy, thus slighting the Mohawks' position in the Confederacy.[12] Moreover, while it is not clear if the Onondaga peace offer to the French was a break with Confederacy policy, it appears that the Onondagas acted on their own initiative and in obvious contradiction of Mohawk policy. The Oneidas, for example, were asked to participate in the peace talks only after the Onondagas had confirmed that the French were willing to consider peace with the Onondagas.[13] While the Jesuits reported that the Senecas and the Cayugas had also been prepared to discuss peace, there are no references to these groups' presence at the peace talks.[14] In fact, the Senecas came to New France to talk of peace only in 1655, and then just to say they were interested and would send a larger delegation the following year to confirm a peace with the French and the Algonquins and Hurons.[15] It is unlikely that the Senecas, at least, had seriously consented to peace in 1653. They had promised to aid the Mohawks against the French if the Mohawks helped them against the Neutrals, and the Mohawks had done this.[16] The Mohawks certainly had not agreed to peace. In August 1653 the Mohawks sent an army, comprised mostly of their warriors, against Trois Rivières and ravaged the countryside.[17]

Thus whether the Onondagas had contravened Confederacy policy or merely had not consulted the other members, it is obvious that their peace overtures to the French in 1653 caught the Mohawks by surprise, and that the Mohawks did not like it. At first the Mohawks even intercepted the Onondaga ambassadors and took their peace presents.[18] At last the Mohawks seemed to have New France ready to crumble, they had apparently garnered the support of the powerful Senecas, and then the Onondagas offered the French a respite.

But the Mohawks were nothing if not adaptable. Despite having an army at the French doorstep, the Mohawks agreed to discuss peace with the French. They did so for several reasons. Some Mohawks had been captured during the most recent skirmishing and at first they may have wanted an opportunity to recover them.[19] But this was not the motive for continuing the peace talks since the Mohawks managed to recover most of their people in a raid before negotiations with the French were seriously under way.[20] Several more likely motives account for the Mohawks' continued participation in the talks. While unwilling to see the Onondagas and Oneidas become allies of their worst enemies, the Mohawks did not want them to strike some arrangement with the French that would be to their detriment. They might have felt they could better monitor events if they took part in the negotiations. As well, while the Onondagas sought French aid, which the Mohawks must have known that the French would never extend to the Mohawks, the latter used the opportunity presented by the peace talks to try to lure the remnants of the Huron population to their villages. During the siege of Trois Rivières some Hurons in the area made contact with the Mohawks in the hopes of learning about their captured relatives.[21] Whether or not this event inspired the Mohawks, they clearly sought to take advantage of the peace talks secretly to convince the other Hurons in the colony to relocate among the Mohawks.[22]

Finally, the Mohawks agreed to peace with the French and their native allies because they had no intention of keeping it. The continued raiding against the French and their allies in the years following the supposed peace of 1653 is clear proof of that duplicity. The Mohawks were identified as the attackers in ten of the eighteen raids launched by the Iroquois against the French and their allies from 1654 to the end of 1657. Of the eight attacks solely against the French, the Mohawks were clearly responsible for at least five of those (see table D.1, entries for 1654 to 1657). Indeed, no sooner had the Mohawks supposedly agreed to peace than they went to the Dutch at Fort Orange to tell them to write to the French to ask them to stay out of any war that might develop between the Mohawks and French allies.[23] This continued hostility toward New France's native allies should not be surprising. The Mohawks had apparently tried again to isolate the French from their native allies and refused to include the Algonquins and Hurons in the truce. The French had agreed to exclude from the peace talks French allies not living in the colony proper, and the Iroquois were free to attack those tribes.[24] However, the French continued their efforts to have the Hurons and Algonquins included in the peace treaty.[25]

The last of the Iroquois nations to join in the truce were the Senecas. In September 1655 they came to New France to indicate their willingness to be included in the treaty reached between the Onondagas and the French, and in January 1656 a delegation of ten Senecas confirmed their nation's adherence to peace with the French.[26] Possibly, as the Jesuits suggested, because of their wars with the Eries, they wanted to limit the number of enemies they faced. The Senecas may also have wanted access to French guns, as the Onondagas had. They may even have sought peace in order to get in on the partition of the Hurons in New France.[27] In 1657 the Senecas accompanied a group of Onondagas who came to escort some Hurons to Iroquois villages.[28] Whatever their reasons, the French were happy to include the Senecas on their list of friendly Iroquois.

Yet for all the talk of Iroquois peace with New France, it was not a Confederacy policy. Peace with the French seems to have been an ad hoc policy that developed as individual tribes pursued their respective self-interests. Indeed, the events of the mid-1650s reveal if not a rift in the Iroquois Confederacy, at least a lack of consensus among the tribes about the best policy to pursue toward the French, and that which would most benefit each tribe as they sought to deal with their respective problems. The Onondagas, or at least a leading group of them, seemed convinced that peace with New France was in their best interest, while the Mohawks were obviously committed to war. The Oneidas, Senecas, and possibly the Cayugas—the latter do not appear in the records for these years—were also prepared to maintain peace with New France. Yet neither the Onondagas nor the Mohawks were able to convince each other of the merits of their respective positions, and each continued to pursue their opposite policies. And if they did not actively try to thwart each other's plans, their endeavors to carry their policies to fruition certainly interfered with their respective efforts. Indeed, the disagreements between the Mohawks and other tribes in the Confederacy about peace versus war with the French and the competition over the remnants of the Hurons created serious rifts among the tribes and even led to some killings.[29] The Mohawks admitted to killing an Onondaga chief in 1654, were accused of killing two Senecas in 1655, and admitted to shooting accidentally a Seneca negotiator in 1656.[30] Since each of these events took place as either the Onondagas or Senecas tried to solidify their peaceful relations with the French, one may assume that Mohawk actions reflected their displeasure and were efforts to thwart the peace process.

Needless to say, these killings and the continued pursuit of the Hurons kept tension and mistrust at a high level among some of the Confederacy tribes; the extent of that distrust can be seen in Mohawk efforts to turn the French against the Onondagas. In the spring of 1656 the Mohawks asked the French "to close the doors of his houses and of his forts against the Onnontageronnon, who wishes to be my enemy, and who is hatching some plot of war against me."[31] The Mohawks even tried to have the French join them in an alliance with the Dutch. By June 1656 French authorities apparently believed that the various Iroquois tribes had reconciled their differences.[32] But if so, the Mohawks were not certain that all had been forgiven, and one year later they went to Fort Orange to ask the Dutch for shelter for their women and children and to request a cannon for their villages in case they should go to war with the "Sinnekes."[33] As late as 1660, Dutch authorities still seemed to accept that relations between the Mohawks and the some of the other tribes of the Confederacy (they used the term *Sennekes* to refer to all the tribes but the Mohawks) were tense. At a conference that year they asked the "Sinnekes" not to use the gift of powder they were given against the Mohawks.[34]

In 1658, just as it seemed that the Onondagas had brought most of the Confederacy around to their point of view, and as conflict with the Mohawks threatened to lead to internal war among the Confederacy, their differences were put aside and the Onondagas and Oneidas joined with the Mohawks and renewed their war against the French.[35] Beginning in the spring of 1658, these three tribes were repeatedly identified as those attacking the French, and they continued to lead the war against New France for the next few years.[36] Of course, one cannot be certain that renewed war was any less an ad hoc process than peace had been. In fact, it seems reasonable to suggest that either Mohawk pressure on the other tribes or continued Mohawk raiding in the years before 1658 encouraged some tribes, or factions of some tribes, to pursue war.

Factional strife certainly appears to have been a factor in the Onondaga decision to war. While the Onondaga headman Garakontié consistently and sincerely sought peace with New France and even with some of her allies, others in his tribe did not. In 1656 a member of his own delegation jeopardized Garakontié's plans and the nascent French mission and post in Onondaga by attacking the very Hurons Garakontié had managed to lure to his tribe.[37] In 1658, despite his continued desire for peace, a group of his own tribe agreed to renew war against the French. Garakontié was forced to warn the French among the Onondagas of this in order to save their lives.[38] Nor did this problem disappear. A few years later, as Garakontié tried to patch up damaged Onondaga-French relations, another Onondaga headman, Otreouti, was engaged in attacking the French.[39] By 1664 the Jesuits despaired that factionalism would stymie Garakontié's peace efforts. They knew that there were other clans in his tribe "too envious and too much opposed to him" to allow Garakontié to conclude a "general peace with the French."[40]

By 1658 Mohawk pressure and action led to renewed war with New France. If before 1660 the raids had been conducted by small groups of Iroquois and did not reflect tribal consensus, the Mohawks still had not given up hopes of larger-scale incursions. In the spring of 1660 an army of five hundred Mohawks set off to attack New France. In May they met up with two hundred Onondagas and defeated a small group of French and Hurons.[41] It is not clear if the Onondagas had gone up to the colony to join with the larger Mohawk army. The French at Trois Rivières had left their fort because they expected some returning Iroquois hunters and hoped to steal their furs. Given the size of the Onondaga and Mohawk forces, it seems likely that the Onondagas had gone to New France to join the Mohawks and had done some hunting while awaiting the Mohawks' arrival. A more telling indicator that the Onondagas had gone to the colony to war was that in June 1660 the Mohawks went to the Onondagas and invited them to "once more" join their forces. The Mohawks obviously hoped to follow up the recent success and this time "sweep away the French Colony of Three Rivers." The French also learned that the following year, 1661, the entire Confederacy was going to meet at Onondaga to develop a joint plan of attack against the French.[42] The Confederacy did, in fact, meet in 1661, but most of the tribes decided to renew peace with the French.[43] Yet if no more major invasions of New France were launched and some members of the Confederacy looked for a peaceful resolution of their problems with the French, others did not, and the Mohawks and some Oneidas and Onondagas continued to press the French (see fig. 7.1 and table D.1, entries for 1660 to 1662). Indeed, the Mohawks did not stop raiding against the French until 1666 (see table D.1, entries for 1662 to 1666).

Why were the Mohawks prepared to continue fighting and some factions, or other tribes, willing to listen to them and also pursue war? Certainly, revenge may have had something to do with the Mohawks' position. Over the years they had lost a number of kinsmen to the French, and the Mohawks sought to kill and capture French people to avenge those losses or to replace dead Mohawks.[44] Possibly the motivation for the Mohawks' hostile policy in these years is best summed up by that shrewd observer of life in New France, Marie de l'Incarnation. She had no doubt that the "design of the Iroquois" was to drive the French out of Canada. The reason was, she wrote, that they desired to be "alone in all these lands, in order to live without fear, and to have all the game to live off, and to give the pelts to the Dutch." The French, she implied, were obviously a threat to this future; otherwise, there was no need to remove them. It was not, she added, that the Iroquois necessarily liked the Dutch better than the French, but that they had to make use of someone to trade with, and the Dutch were closer.[45] She might have added that the Iroquois, the Mohawks in particular, had stuck with the Dutch because Mohawk attempts to deal with the French on Mohawk terms had been rebuffed and because the Mohawks still did not trust the French.

Indeed, the French had done little to alter their apparently hostile posture toward the Mohawks. In 1655, for example, the Mohawks told the Dutch that they suspected the French were opposed to their peace with French allies, and said that "their promises . . . [are] mingled with many lies."[46] They most likely blamed the French for the reluctance of the Hurons to relocate to Mohawk villages, and they were partly correct. In 1654, when the French learned of the various Iroquois offers to the Hurons, they counseled the Hurons to agree to them in order to prevent more attacks against the Hurons, and to buy time so that the French could help stop such a move.[47] But if protecting the Hurons and keeping a goodly number of native warriors in the colony to bolster its fighting strength was a reasonable policy for New France to follow, to the Mohawks it must have seemed that the French were interfering in their plans. When the French sent Jesuits and Hurons to Onondaga, thereby helping to thwart the Mohawks efforts to gain the Hurons for themselves and, at the same time, bolstering the strength of the Onondagas, it could only have confirmed New France's hostile intent toward the Mohawks.

New France's continued arming of their native allies can only have reinforced Iroquois doubts about the sincerity of French professions of peace with the Iroquois. The extent of the French gun trade in this period is not clear, but selling guns to natives appears to have been a fairly common practice. In 1656, a returning Ottawa fur brigade gave away their position to the Iroquois because they fired their newly acquired weapons.[48] In 1660 the French trader Radisson chastised the Ottawas for not taking better care of their guns and for fearing to go with their furs to New France. After all, he said, his partner Groseilliers had more to fear from the Iroquois because he had "long since" been the one who had furnished the enemies of the Iroquois "with arms."[49] By 1662 the Ojibwas had guns, and the Jesuits reported in their journals that "powder and firearms" were what groups such as the Ottawas sought in their trade with the French.[50] While the French sale of guns to their allies was logical, it must have seemed the height of duplicity to some Iroquois. They may even have harbored fears that the French were encouraging native wars in order to kill off the Iroquois.

All of these reasons, then, help explain the continued hostility of some Iroquois toward New France. Indeed, these reasons may have provided those who wished to pursue war against the French colony with the ammunition to dissuade groups considering a more peaceful path. French actions may also have weakened the position of those Iroquois who advocated peace with the French. The credibility of those Iroquois who sought closer ties to New France in order to obtain military help must have been diminished by the French response. Not only did the French continue to arm Iroquois foes, but the French had not provided men for Iroquois wars. Instead, they sent priests who told them their view of the world and their customs needed to be changed.[51] The altered political and military situation of the late 1650s may also have meant that calls for war fell on more receptive ears. By 1658 the Eries and the Neutrals had been defeated, and the Iroquois appeared to be holding their own against their remaining foes.

Still, if some Iroquois wanted to wage war against New France, others did not. Between 1660 and 1664 all of the Iroquois tribes tried to renew peace with the French.[52] The reasons for these peace overtures varied with each tribe and time. Some Onondagas, of course, had never wanted to breach the peace. Garakontié had tried to patch up Onondaga-French relations as soon as other members of his tribe and of the Confederacy had harmed them.[53] Thus his efforts to establish a firm Onondaga-French peace were merely the continuation of a process he had begun years earlier. As for the Senecas and Cayugas, they had not actively raided the colony of New France after they had agreed to peace in 1655, as had the Mohawks, Oneidas, and some of the Onondagas.

But peace with New France took on added urgency in the early to mid-1660s, even for the Mohawks. The optimistic military situation of the late 1650s had quickly altered. The renewal of war between the Senecas and the Susquehannocks in 1660 did not go quite as well as the Senecas had hoped. The Susquehannocks received military support and weapons from the English government of Maryland, and this thwarted Seneca war efforts.[54] The Mohawks, on the other hand, met with costly losses against eastern Algonquians in 1663 and 1664.[55] These military setbacks, added to famine and disease, led the various tribes of the Confederacy to seek peace with New France in the hopes of obtaining weapons, military aid, or a reduction in the number of those actively at war with them.[56]

Political and trade uncertainty, the result of English-Dutch conflict over what came to be New York, may also have played a part in Iroquois desires to seek a peaceful relationship with the French. In 1663 Connecticut took parts of New Netherland, and in the summer of 1664 the whole colony fell to the English. In these same years the Dutch were also engaged in war against the Esopus Indians. The latter event may even have led to restrictions of gun and ammunition sales to the Iroquois. Indeed, the lack of ammunition to carry out a defense was one reason for New Netherland's capitulation to the English.[57] Given all of this, it does not seem unreasonable to suggest that the supply to the Iroquois for their own wars was affected. In any case, these events could not have failed to cause some concern among the Iroquois about the security of their supply sources. This may have led some to want peace with the French as a means to gain access to a more stable supplier or because war against the colony would be difficult to sustain without the guns and ammunition supplied by the Dutch.

Yet if the diplomatic and military events of the 1650s and early 1660s reveal anything, it is the complexity of Iroquois policy—due, in part, to their decentralized government—and the enduring hostility of the Mohawks toward the French. As the Jesuit [Lalemant] remarked, referring to the Indians he observed, "one cannot assume any other standard than that of their own self interests. . . . Nothing but the terror and fear of our arms, or the hope of some considerable profit in their trading, or the aid to be obtained from us against their enemies, can hold them in check; and even that will not prevent some from separating from the rest and coming by stealth to slay us."[58] Thus in 1664, even as most of the Confederacy appeared to want peace, some Iroquois—most likely the Mohawks—conceiving their self-interest differently from the rest of the Confederacy, again renewed the war against the French. Between 1664 and 1666 the French were attacked nine times by the Iroquois.[59]

But by 1666 French government officials had had enough. They either did not understand the complex and diffuse nature of Iroquois government and politics, did not care, or thought that repeated offers of peace in the face of continued raiding were part of some Machiavellian scheme on the part of the Iroquois Confederacy. In any case, New France had passed under direct royal control in 1663 and the colony now had greater resources.[60] One of the first changes made was to provide it with coordinated military leadership and a small professional army for its defense. The result was that in 1666 two expeditions were launched against the Mohawks (table D.1, entries dated 9 Jan. to 8 Mar. 1666; 28 Sept. to 5 Nov. 1666). The aftermath of these attacks was, at last, a firm peace between all of the Iroquois and the French.[61]

It is an accepted view that the French attacks against the Mohawks finally instilled the fear of French military strength necessary to keep the Confederacy loyal to a peace treaty.[62] This may be partly true; after all, the Mohawks could not help but be convinced of the French ability to strike a serious blow against them after De Tracy's destruction of their villages in 1666. But while this view helps to account for the Mohawks' readiness to come to terms with the French in 1666, it overlooks other, equally important reasons for the Mohawks' and the Confederacy's decision to make peace and to keep it for almost two decades. This interpretation, for example, overlooks the fact that part of the Confederacy had not been interested in war with New France since at least 1655. They did not need the threat of French arms to convince them that peace was desirable; they already felt that way. Also, the strength of their foes' resistance helps explain why most of the Confederacy still sought peace and why the Mohawks were ready to consider peace in 1666–67. The western Iroquois, especially the Senecas, were still being pressed by the Susquehannocks, while the Mohawks continued to have difficulties to the east.[63] Indeed, their wars against other groups were an important reason why peace with New France was kept for so many years. It was not until 1677 that the Susquehannocks were finally defeated.

Other reasons also played important roles in persuading some Confederacy members that peace with New France had long been a good course to follow, and in convincing the Mohawks to make and keep peace for a while. One of the most significant was that time was needed to establish political and trade relations with the new English rulers of New York, formerly New Netherland. In September 1664, the year the English captured New Netherland from the Dutch, the English agreed to furnish the Mohawks and the "Synicks" with the same goods as had the Dutch.[64] However, one must wonder at the English ability to establish traders, supply lines, and native trust quickly enough not to disrupt the flow of goods, especially weapons, to the Iroquois. Indeed, it is questionable just how willing the English were to continue arming tribes that had been allied to those they had just conquered. The Dutch traders at Albany (formerly Fort Orange) eventually held on to the trade, but they too must have struggled at first to establish new suppliers, and to overcome English reluctance to allow their newly conquered subjects to engage in arms trading.[65] In any case, until the English could prove themselves reliable trade partners, or possibly political allies, it was not wise to renew war against New France.

Disease, new wars, and the influence of the Jesuits may also have contributed to Iroquois reluctance to renew war against New France. While some of their foes were providing strong resistance, and their own access to guns and ammunition was less than certain, the Iroquois were also suffering from epidemics. Between 1668 and 1682 the Confederacy was struck by epidemic disease on five separate occasions (table B.1). If the widespread illness and death did not sap the Iroquois will to fight, it certainly impaired their ability to do so as the Confederacy lost well over twenty-two hundred people in these years (table A.2). Efforts to gain new peoples to replace those lost to disease and new wars begun at the instigation of newly adopted peoples also kept the Iroquois preoccupied enough that they could forget about wars with New France.[66] Nor should one discount the influence of the Jesuits among the Iroquois tribes during the years 1667 to 1682; they worked assiduously to keep French-Iroquois relations harmonious.[67]

Despite all the reasons for wanting and maintaining peace, and although the peace of 1666–67 lasted longer than any other before it, it too finally broke down. If the years before 1666–67 had been marked by constant Mohawk hostility and peaceful overtones tinged with hostile ambivalence on the part of the rest of the Confederacy, the wars of the 1680s and 1690s reflected no such doubts or divisions. This time the Iroquois were united in their determination to extinguish the French "fyres" in North America.

# CHAPTER NINE

## *"Your fyre shall burn no more"*

Despite all the reasons for peace and almost twenty years of relatively amicable relations between the Iroquois and the French, the Iroquois decided to renew war against New France in the early 1680s. French authorities, even if they did not all arrive at the same conclusion, were not at a loss for explanations. For some French officials, Iroquois desires to be feared and dreams of continental mastery explained why they sought the destruction of New France.[1] Others, such as Governor La Barre, saw the destruction of New France as part of an Iroquois plan to control the fur trade.[2] Needless to say, since the 1680s marked the beginning of Anglo-French commercial and imperial struggles in North America, these types of assessments reflected the political and economic aspirations of French officials more than they did the goals of the Iroquois.[3]

Yet if French officials projected their concerns onto the Iroquois and found in Iroquois actions and policy the type of goals they were themselves motivated by, the causes of renewed Iroquois hostility against New France were not hidden. The simple answer is that French actions and policy conflicted with and threatened the security and survival of the Iroquois. True, some warfare, such as the attack on the French village of Lachine, represented Iroquois efforts to exact revenge for previous losses at the hands of the French.[4] But in the long run, Iroquois hostility was the product of the threats they felt were posed by New France's expansionist policy.

Among the French actions that threatened and angered the Iroquois was the continual French expansion of their network of Indian allies. The Iroquois thought it suspicious that the French allied themselves with tribes with whom the Iroquois were at odds, and that the French asked the Iroquois to give up warring against these French native allies who, meanwhile, continued to strike against the Iroquois. As one Seneca asked Governor Courcelle,

> For whom does Onnontio take us? . . . He is vexed because we go to war, and wishes us to lower our hatchets and leave his allies undisturbed. Who are his allies? How would he have us recognize them when he claims to take under his protection all the peoples discovered by the bearers of God's word through all these regions; and when everyday, as we learn from our people who escape from the cruelty of the stake, they make new discoveries, and enter nations which have ever been hostile to us,— which, even while receiving notification of peace from Onnontio, set out from their own country to make war upon us, and to come and slay us under our very palisades?[5]

It is clear that the Iroquois suspected the French of building up this network of native allies to help them destroy the Five Nations.

That their foes and new French allies were armed with guns when they attacked the Iroquois and encroached on Iroquois lands must have confirmed Iroquois misgivings about French policy toward them. In the years up to 1680 French gun sales to natives had been sporadic and, possibly, unauthorized (and this is by no means certain; the lack of data leaves this impression), but by the 1680s the French had finally overcome their reluctance to arm their allies. Both French traders and government authorities traded and gave guns to French native allies. In January 1680 La Salle journeyed to the Illinois and agreed to sell them arms and "munitions."[6] The extent of the arms sold is unknown, but in 1684 one French trade convoy on its way to resupply a fort in Miami and Illinois territory, carrying goods valued at 15,000 livres, was attacked because guns were part of the shipment.[7] Indeed, arms and ammunition probably accounted for the high value of the trade cargo. In 1697 the trade list for Fort Bourbon showed that 620 guns, 10,000 livres weight of powder, and 12,000 livres weight of lead for making balls were valued at 15,330 livres.[8] If the gun trade at other forts matched that at Fort Bourbon, one can suggest that the French were trading guns to natives in large quantities.[9] Nor did French allies obtain guns just by trade. A significant number of guns were given to French native allies during conferences to cement their allegiance and to encourage them to war against the Iroquois. In 1686 the Illinois were given 150 guns to this end, and at a conference in 1693 some 158 guns were distributed as presents among the tribes in attendance.[10] The Iroquois did not fail to complain of the deleterious effects that the French gun trade had on their ability to war and hunt.[11]

More annoying and threatening to the Iroquois were French expansion into and building of military posts on lands claimed and used by the Iroquois. Between 1666 and 1701 the French built almost thirty forts and fortified posts in the St. Lawrence-Great Lakes basin.[12] Of these, at least seven were located around Lakes Ontario and Erie, lands claimed by the Iroquois and used by them for hunting. The French built most of their forts in order to secure the fur trade, their religious missions, and militarily important areas against the encroachments of the Iroquois and the English in the thirteen colonies. Indeed, by the eighteenth century it became official French policy to use these forts to hem the English in along the eastern seaboard and not let them into the western interior.[13] The policy of containing the English, however, was first considered for and used on the Iroquois. Fort Richelieu, built in 1642 at the mouth of the Richelieu River, was erected to impede Iroquois access to New France. In 1666 three more forts were built farther up that river for a similar purpose, and in 1673 Fort Frontenac was established, among other things, to monitor Iroquois movements at the eastern end of Lake Ontario.[14] By the early 1690s officials in New France were giving serious consideration to a plan to build a series of forts to keep the Iroquois from going much beyond the western end of Lake Ontario and to confine them to the areas south of the lake.[15]

The Iroquois objected to these incursions into their lands for several reasons. First, they opposed them on principle. To the French claim that such lands were theirs by right of conquest, by which the French meant the destruction of Iroquois villages in 1666 and 1687, the Iroquois replied that they had never been conquered.[16] For the Iroquois, conquest meant the total destruction of an enemy and the incorporation of the defeated foe into the victor's society. The French had certainly not accomplished this in their raids against them. Moreover, if conquest of a tribe was grounds for claiming their lands, then, the Iroquois responded, "We can claim all Canida, for we not only did soe [that is, they conquered it], but subdued whole nations of Indians that liv'd there, and demolished there castles in so much, that now great oake trees grow where they were built, and afterwards we plyed the French home in the wars with them, that they were not able to go over a door to pisse."[17]

The Iroquois also opposed French expansion onto their lands because they saw French expansion in general and the building of French forts and posts on Iroquois land in particular as threats to their control over their hunting areas.[18]

Encouraged by the French presence, their enemies might also start hunting more freely on lands claimed by the Iroquois and use up their food and fur resources. Certainly the Iroquois complained that increased hunting by others was depleting their fur supply. In 1683, when asked why they brought so few furs to trade, the Mohawks replied that when they were at war with "other Indians, those Indians would not dare to come on [Iroquois] hunting places; but now they are all in peace; the Indians catch away the Beaver so fast that there be but a very few left."[19] Tribes hunting on Iroquois lands may have felt it was safe to do so because of the general peace, but French forts in these areas undoubtedly helped bolster their confidence.

Worse still for the Iroquois, the presence of French forts on their lands and along their borders were a threat to their security. The forts might draw their foes closer to the Iroquois, serve as staging areas for raids against the Iroquois, and as havens for their enemies when pursued by the Five Nations—as happened after the start of Iroquois hostilities against New France. This would threaten the Iroquois as they hunted on their own land. Indeed, the Iroquois often complained that their foes, now armed by the French, attacked their hunters.[20]

In short, the Iroquois saw French expansion for what it was: an attempt to encircle them and to circumscribe their hunting and military endeavors. Time and again, the Iroquois expressed their concerns about the threats posed to their lands, livelihood, and security by the string of French forts. The French, they said, "build forts around us and penn us up." They felt enslaved, as if they were "in prison so long as they are standing," and saw the forts as the first step to the eventual French usurpation of all their lands.[21]

No French establishment in the latter half of the seventeenth century raised Iroquois ire as much as did Fort Frontenac, located in modern day Kingston, Ontario. It seems to have symbolized all that the Iroquois feared the other posts could be: a direct invasion of their territory, a precursor of further encroachments, a threat to their hunting grounds, and a constant military menace. In 1673, when Governor Frontenac began building the fort, the Iroquois had little choice but to accept it. The Dutch and English were once again struggling over control of New York, and the Albany merchants had little to offer in the way of war goods.[22] Still fighting against the Susquehannocks and the Mahicans, the Iroquois could not afford to turn down French arms supplies (table D.1, entries for 1670 to 1677). Indeed, at the meeting during which the Iroquois resigned themselves to let the French build the fort, they asked the French for aid against the Susquehannocks.[23] However, by 1675 the circumstances changed. The English were firmly in control of New York, the war with the Susquehannocks had concluded, and some Iroquois were prepared to renew war against New France by destroying Fort Frontenac.[24] At a meeting with the Iroquois in 1676, Governor Frontenac managed to convince the Iroquois to leave the fort alone, but it was eventually razed by the French in 1689 as they withdrew their troops closer to the heart of the colony in response to an all-out Iroquois attack against New France.[25]

French efforts to reestablish Fort Frontenac in the 1690s elicited vivid expressions of Iroquois opposition. They resented the danger the fort had posed in the past and might pose again to their travel to and from hunting and warfare, and because it encroached on their lands.[26] When Governor Frontenac asked the Iroquois to meet with him at the site of the fort in 1690, they refused and asked him, "Don't you know that your Fire[27] there is extinguished? It is extinguished with Blood."[28] A few years later, in an eloquent and impassioned speech, Kaqueendara, an Iroquois spokesman, made their opposition to the fort (called Cadaracqui by the Iroquois and the English) even clearer:

> Onnontio your fyre shall' burn' no' more at Cadracqui it shall never be kindled again. You did steale that place from us and wee quenched the fyre with the blood of our [your?] children[.] You thinke yourselves the ancient inhabitants of this countrey and longest in possession yea all the Christian Inhabitants of New York and Cayenquiragué[29] thinke the same of themselves[.] Wee warriors are the firste and the ancient people and the greatest of You all, these parts and country's were inhabited and trodd upon by us the warrior's before any Christian. . . . Wee shall note suffer Cadaracqui to be inhabited again. Onontio we Canossoené[30] do' say we shall never suffer you to kindle your fire at Cadaracqui; I repeat this again and again.[31]

Unfortunately for the Iroquois, they could not stop the French from reoccupying the site without English help, and, despite promises of such aid, the English did not send men to help the Iroquois drive out the French.[32] Kaqueendara's speech, however, makes it clear that the Iroquois considered the land around Cadracqui theirs and the building of the French fort there a usurpation of their lands.[33]

To add insult to injury, as if arming Iroquois foes and invading their lands were not bad enough, the French also angered the Iroquois by encouraging Iroquois converts to Christianity to leave Iroquoia and settle in New France. By 1676 there were three hundred Iroquois living at Prairie-de-la-Madeleine and an unspecified number at Lorette.[34] In all, by 1700, as many as one thousand Iroquois may have settled in New France.[35] The Iroquois saw this French-inspired population drain as a deliberate effort to weaken them in order to destroy them.[36]

In all these actions by the French there was little to persuade the Iroquois that the French did not have some evil design up their sleeves and much to convince them that French intentions were less than friendly. Still, the Iroquois did not launch a war against New France. In fact, the Confederacy only decided that the French "fyres" in Canada should be extinguished in 1687, and then only after the French had already attacked them. Until then, the only raids the Iroquois launched against the French were against traders supplying arms to their foes (table D. 1, entries dated 1680 to 1687). In 1684 the French sent an army against the Iroquois in reprisal for those two raids. The French forces never reached their target and the French were obliged to conclude a peace with the Iroquois.[37] After that treaty, no French groups or settlements were attacked until Governor Denonville attacked the Senecas in the summer of 1687. Thus if one is searching for the reason as to why the Iroquois decided to war against New France in the 1680s, it was because, as far as the Iroquois were concerned, they had been provoked beyond endurance.

Although the Iroquois did not attack the French before 1687, they did war against French native allies, and the French saw this as a threat. But even if the Iroquois did not have grounds to be suspicious of this increasing network of armed French allies, the Five Nations had their own reasons for carrying on wars against native groups in the latter half of the seventeenth century. The traditional goals of warfare did not disappear; martial honor and revenge continued to be important motives for warfare and help to account for raids by both individuals and tribes. Pursuit of one enemy led to encounters with, and deaths at the hands of, new tribes who were then added to the roster of those from whom revenge had to be exacted. As the Mohawks' spokesman Sindachsegie put it, "It is our Custome amongst Indians to warr with one another" if they killed one of their people.[38] It was apparently such a scenario that accounted for the Iroquois wars against the Illinois and the Miamis. The Illinois were encountered as part of the Iroquois war against the Ottawas, and the Miamis seem to have become foes as a result of events that arose from the wars against the Illinois.[39] Once the feuding process had begun, revenge and the tactical practice of eliminating a foe as a means of terminating the war took over as an impetus to raiding.[40]

Hunting lands were also a factor in Iroquois wars against some native groups allied to New France. The Iroquois frequently reported that the murderous incidents that required revenge began as one tribe—according to the Iroquois, always the other native group—knocked their hunters over the head during some nonhostile hunting trip.[41] This suggests that wars against some native groups were fought as the Iroquois sought to protect their land against the encroachments of others. This should not come as a surprise. The Iroquois sought to protect their land against French encroachments, so it is natural that they sought to hold it against the advances of New France's armed native allies. As New France's native allies became better armed, the Iroquois must have placed greater emphasis on preserving the fur resources of their lands in order to use them to purchase even more weapons to use in their defense. Certainly, the Iroquois complained often enough that other groups hunted in their lands, and at least one source puts the cause of the Iroquois war against the Illinois and Miamis as being due to these tribes hunting in Iroquois lands.[42]

Iroquois self-justification and hyperbole aside, there is evidence that it was, indeed, other groups who invaded Iroquois territory. The Iroquois hunted primarily along the St. Lawrence from the Ottawa River to Lake Ontario and from present-day Kingston toward the falls at Niagara. These continued to be their hunting grounds.[43] It was because these areas were their major hunting grounds that they so vehemently opposed the building of Fort Frontenac and later that of Detroit, and it was, in part, because these areas were excellent hunting and fur-bearing lands that the French wanted to build forts there in the first place.[44] It is not surprising that other native groups wanted to, and did, hunt there as well. Indeed, it was access to hunting lands in these areas that French officials used to encourage Hurons and Miamis to relocate their villages to the vicinities of Forts Frontenac and Detroit. By 1700 some tribes may have needed to use these areas because they had overtrapped their own and run out of beaver. In 1701 an Ottawa chief apologized for his small gift of beaver to the French and excused himself by saying that they had stripped the beaver from their lands. Deputies from other nations echoed his plaint.[45] Doubtless the Iroquois hunted in other areas, and hunted in the lands of other tribes as they went to those areas to war. But in the end, it seems clear that they hunted in their own areas and fought to preserve the food and fur resources of those areas against the depredations of others.

As in past wars against native groups, the Iroquois also fought to capture people. Between 1680 and 1698 the Iroquois captured 2,384–2,608 people.[46] Some of the captives may have been needed to offset population declines brought on by epidemic disease. In 1672, 1676, 1679, and 1682 the Iroquois were struck by disease (table B.1). Military considerations also created a demand for large numbers of captives. Not only was depopulation of an enemy a way to destroy him, it also served to bolster the Iroquois armies. The French were convinced that much of the Iroquois warfare against the colony's native allies was geared to this end. The Iroquois, they believed, wanted to destroy New France's allies in order to leave the colony without adequate numbers of men to draw from for its defense. Worse, they suspected, the Iroquois were using the captives to strengthen their own forces for a large-scale attack against the French. The Iroquois did little to dissuade them from this line of thinking. A 1682 letter to Governor Frontenac from Father Jean de Lamberville, stationed at Onondaga, is typical of French thinking on this issue: "Every year they profit by our losses; they annihilate our allies, of whom they make Iroquois; and have not the least scruple in saying that after enriching themselves with our spoils, and strengthening themselves with those who might have aided us to make war against them, they will all together fall upon Canada, to overwhelm it in a single Campaign. They have strengthened themselves, in this and the preceding years, with more than nine hundred men armed with muskets."[47] The expected attack did not materialize. It may have been because the Iroquois were still unsure of the timing, or possibly the favorable treaty they exacted from the French in 1684 put a halt to war plans. In any event, the French seem to have discovered one important reason for Iroquois attacks against their native allies.

Nor did the Iroquois try to isolate the French from their allies strictly by military means. Throughout the latter part of the century, the Iroquois tried diplomacy to wean French native allies away from the French.[48] The Iroquois even used the English and their trade as a means to break up the French network of native alliances. They actively encouraged French native allies to come through Iroquois lands to trade with the English and Dutch at Albany and cautioned those traders and officials to keep the prices of their goods low in order to show French allies the advantages of trade with Albany over that at Montreal.[49] Some French officials thought that the Iroquois undertook the latter policy at the urging and for the benefit of the English trade.[50] Doubtless the traders at Albany were interested in the economic aspects of this Iroquois policy and encouraged them to pursue it because of the profits they hoped to reap. However, it was the political and military advantages of this policy that interested the Iroquois. As the Iroquois remarked on the occasion of one anticipated relocation, luring to Iroquoia natives who were "in allyance with the French of Canida . . . will strengthen us and weaken the enemij."[51]

The policy of capturing people and getting them to relocate peacefully among the Iroquois was, of course, an old practice of the Iroquois. And the Iroquois had reasons other than mistrust of the French for undertaking such a policy. However, the threatening actions of the French, and later, New France's attacks against the Five Nations, could only have added new urgency to this Iroquois policy. Moreover, whether the French liked it or not, and whether or not they believed these wars against their native allies were interference in their affairs, the Iroquois were equally convinced of their right to pursue their objectives as they saw fit. Indeed, in their opinion it was the Europeans who were meddling in their affairs. As Sindachsegie, an Iroquois spokesman, put it, "But what has the Christians to do with . . . [joining] one side or [the] other" in their wars?[52]

Once the French attacked the Iroquois in 1687, the Confederacy seemed determined not only to extinguish the French "fyres" in North America but to remove every sign that they had ever been lit. From 1687 to 1697 the Iroquois launched thirty-three raids against the French alone, sent armies of a thousand men or more against the colony three times, and captured or killed close to six hundred people (figure 7.1; table D.1, entries for 1687 to 1697; table F.2).

The Iroquois, however, recognized that they were outmanned by the French and their native allies, and that the French held a technological edge.[53] Luckily for them the English in New York, impelled by the imperialist desires of England, were prepared to abet the Iroquois war with New France, and even, on occasion, to help them fight. Thus the Iroquois tried to use their European allies to further their military plans, just as the French used their native allies for those ends. The Iroquois rarely missed an opportunity to encourage the English to pursue the war against New France more vigorously, and even gave them advice on the methods best suited to bring about a victory over the French in Canada. Time and again the English were told that a combined land and sea attack was necessary to destroy the French. Time and again the Iroquois advised the English in the various colonies to join their forces and to go in large numbers to attack and besiege the French towns.[54]

Unfortunately for the Iroquois, the English were not particularly useful allies. They provided the weapons the Iroquois needed, but at a price.[55] Worse still, intercolonial bickering and disunity, not to mention incompetence, meant that the combined military might of New France's foes was never brought to bear on the colony. The Iroquois did not fail to castigate their partners for their lack of unity, incompetence, and laxness.[56] Indeed, authorities in New York recognized that English disunity and military weakness were responsible for Iroquois desires to consider peace with the French.[57] However, New York officials were able to do little to correct these problems and the Iroquois were left feeling that they bore the brunt of the war effort. The Mohawk spokesman Rode, when asked to continue to harass the French responded, "You Sett us on dayly to fight and destroy your Enemies and bidd us goe on with Courage, but wee see not that you doe anything to it yourSelfe."[58] The Iroquois frustration at the lack of English aid is evident here.

The inconstant help of the English, not to mention their separate peace with the French, played no small part in the Iroquois decision to conclude a truce with the French in 1701. There were, however, other reasons as well. The Iroquois sustained tremendous losses to their warrior population in the years between 1687 and 1698. One English estimate suggests that the Confederacy's male population (mostly or exclusively warriors) dropped from 2,550 to 1,230.[59] This represents a loss of 1,320 people and a 51 percent decrease in the size of the Iroquois fighting force. While the 1689 figure of 2,550 warriors may be somewhat high, the number of people lost compares favorably with that obtained from other records.[60] A tally of the number of Iroquois captured, killed, or lost due to warfare reveals that the Confederacy lost 1,144 to 1,346 people between 1689 and 1698 (table E.1).[61] Since most of these losses were sustained in attacks against Iroquois war and hunting parties and during Iroquois-initiated attacks, most of those captured or killed were males.

These Iroquois losses were the product of the raids of the French and their Indian allies. Governor Frontenac and other French officials had finally learned that the best way to war against the Iroquois was to wage the same style of "petite guerre." It was a lesson born of necessity, but it worked.[62] Between 1687 and 1698 the French and their native allies launched thirty-three raids against the Iroquois (fig. 7.2; table D.1, entries for 1687 to 1698). This represented 36 percent of all the hostilities launched against the Iroquois in the seventeenth century. Of those thirty-three raids, seventeen (more than half) were joint enterprises of the French and their allies, and three were by the French alone.

There can be little doubt that these losses were important factors in inducing the Iroquois to make peace with the French and their allies. But one should not be left with the impression that the Iroquois were cowering in fear at the sound of approaching French war parties. They gave as good as they got. In those years the Iroquois launched forty-nine attacks against the French and their native allies and captured or killed 648–673 of their foes (table D.1, entries for 1687 to 1698). Moreover, it was the French who, as early as 1690, began offering the Iroquois peace and who almost annually continued to offer them the olive branch.[63] Nor did considering the French peace offers stop the Iroquois from raiding. Indeed, the French were convinced that the Iroquois were agreeing to truces in order to stop French raiding in order that they could hunt to get the furs they needed to purchase weapons and ammunition to continue the fight.[64]

In fact, weakened though they were by the war, the Iroquois were prepared to continue the fight against New France. As late as 1696 the Iroquois were still urging the English to pursue the French:

> We are not able of ourselves to destroy them. We are become a small people and much lessened by the warr. If all the people of Virginia, Maryland, Pensilvania, the Jerseys, Conneciticutt and New England who have put their hand to the Covenant Chain will joyne with the inhabitants of this place [New York], we are ready to go and root out the French and all our enemies out of Canida. . . . We are now down upon one knee, but we are not quite down upon the ground; lett the Great King of England send the great canoes with seaventy gunns each, and let the brethren of Virginia, Maryland, Pensilvania, the Jerseys, Conneciticutt and New England awake, and we will stand up straight againe upon our feet; our heart is yet stout and good; we doubt not but to destroy the enemy.[65]

Unfortunately for the Iroquois, the English soon made peace with the French who were to remain firmly rooted in Canada.

After the English made this peace with the French, the Iroquois had little choice but to come to terms with their old foes as well. Weakened by war and disease, they could not hope to defeat New France and her allies unaided. The Iroquois were even in danger of losing their hunting lands to the French and their allies. It was the Iroquois fear that they could no longer hold their lands by force that induced them to cede their hunting lands to the English. They might have hoped that if the English had a direct stake in these areas they would work to protect them.[66] Indeed, when the Iroquois learned that the French were planning to build a fort at Detroit, they expected the English to be "busy" in their "books and mapps" to prevent such a disaster.[67] Also, part of the peace with the French included some establishment or, more likely, recognition of hunting area boundaries.[68] The Iroquois, it seems, also wanted the French to help them keep French native allies out of Confederacy territory.

The decision to accept the French peace offer was not easily reached. Individualism and the loose structure of government among the Iroquois made it difficult to arrive at a decision. Some groups wanted to accept peace while others were reluctant to give up the war.[69] As one group was pursuing peace talks with the French, other Iroquois were encouraging the English to renew their military efforts.[70] Some tribes went so far as to deliberately exclude others from their negotiations if they knew that they would oppose the course they had chosen.[71] If some Iroquois distrusted the French and wanted to continue warring, others clearly did not want to carry on fighting.[72] Some Iroquois may even have begun to distrust the English. Even if the Iroquois did not know that the leader of their allies had been instructed to take whatever opportunity that arose to buy "great tracts of land . . . for small sums," the land swindles perpetrated against some of them must have given them pause about how safe their lands were from the English.[73] Possibly some Iroquois had even begun to think that both the French and the English were a threat to them.[74] In short, peace with New France seems not so much to have been a Confederacy policy decision but rather an acceptable compromise until a unified solution could be attained. As the Iroquois knew from past experiences, no decision of peace or war need be permanent.

In the end, then, the Iroquois fought against New France because their respective policies conflicted. The French chose and supported as allies native groups with whom the Iroquois were at war. Iroquois efforts to make peace with the French early in the century did not fit with the ambitions the French had for controlling the fur trade and fur-bearing regions. The result was a threat to Iroquois relations with their native adversaries, a threat to their lands and their survival, and eventually war with New France.

After peace was established between the Iroquois and New France, in 1666, the French pursued their own policies as if the Iroquois were no longer of consequence, which, once again, threatened the security of the Confederacy. If the French failed to recognize, or chose to ignore, that in their own actions lay most of the causes of Iroquois fears and hostility, it was because of an ethnocentric myopia that allowed them to see only French behavior and policy as legitimate. But the views and goals of the Iroquois were no less valid and no less ethnocentric. The Five Nations had every right to protect themselves and their interests as best they could. When the French threatened Iroquois plans and survival, the Five Nations went to war again. Better armed than in the first half of century, and with the encouragement and munitions of the English at New York, the Iroquois determined to rid themselves of the French menace.

In the end, the Iroquois failed. The English proved to be unreliable as allies. They encouraged the Iroquois to pursue war, but when called on to hold up their end of the fight, colonial disunity or imperial considerations in London almost always prevented striking the decisive blow. The French, too, turned out to be a more resilient foe than the Iroquois had anticipated. They had changed, adapted their style of war, and, with the help of native allies eager to exact revenge on the Iroquois for past injuries, proved themselves a match for the warriors of the Confederacy.

Also, Iroquois government was not cohesive enough to bring Iroquois plans, even when unity of purpose was attained, to fruition. Their loose form of government was adequate to the task of handling their policy toward native groups because that policy better incorporated the various goals of Iroquois society and its warfare. However, the policy toward New France required a greater degree of cohesion and unified action than the Confederacy could muster. By 1701 not all the Iroquois agreed that eliminating New France was the best policy to pursue, and in that year the Iroquois agreed to peace. The peace of 1701 marked another cease-fire in their almost century-long feud with New France. It was once again time for the Iroquois to rethink their policy toward their foes and allies. The Iroquois had survived in spite of their failure to extinguish the French "fyres." The challenge that remained was how to keep their own fires from being smothered by foes and allies alike.

# Conclusion

Iroquois policy toward New France in the seventeenth century was essentially hostile. At times different considerations influenced Iroquois actions toward the French, but in the end the French in New France came to be enemies of the Iroquois because French policy in North America put them in conflict with the Iroquois and threatened their survival. As part of the French desire to exploit the fur trade, to spread Catholicism, and later to further Versailles's imperial ambitions, the French leagued themselves with native groups that were foes of the Iroquois. As the French pursued their various interests and increasingly supported and armed their native allies, they came into conflict with Iroquois policy toward their enemies.

Iroquois attempts to reach a peace with the French failed because the terms offered by the Iroquois were unsuited to French needs. These rejections, French expansion into lands claimed by the Iroquois, and continued alliances with groups that were foes of the Iroquois seemed to confirm New France's hostile intent. The result was that the French went from being a threat by association and incidental target of Iroquois military policy to a direct threat and thus the focus of Iroquois hostilities.

Iroquois warfare against, and policy toward, New France's native allies in the latter half of the seventeenth century reflected some of the same causes and goals of warfare as in the years up to 1666. Some hostilities were the result of revenge raids; some started as the Iroquois and various tribes with whom they had no established peaceful relations hunted near each other, others as the Iroquois pursued old enemies into new lands. The Iroquois also fought to protect their land against the encroachment of others, often native allies of New France who were armed and encouraged by the French in their eager pursuit of furs. And whether begun as a means to capture people or not, military strategy and the need to replace those lost to disease and war meant that warfare to obtain captives continued to account for attacks against native allies of New France.

The fur trade played an important part in Iroquois policy. The French worried that the Iroquois would take over the fur trade. However, the Iroquois did not want to control the fur trade; they sought only to use it. The fur trade provided the Iroquois with a way to obtain the goods they desired for domestic use. It also furnished them with those items they wanted to help them carry out their political, military, and cultural objectives against their native foes and the French. The Iroquois even used the fur trade to get at the French. Supported by colonial authorities in New York, the Iroquois tried to lure French Indian allies away from the French trade network. While the English would have welcomed the furs brought by the northern tribes, the benefit to the Iroquois of such a trade pattern was that it might isolate the French from their allies and leave the French more susceptible to Iroquois military efforts to extinguish the French "fires" in North America.

Iroquois policy failed. They did not drive the French out of North America—French fires still burn bright. But contrary to the Beaver Wars interpretation, the Iroquois failed precisely because they did not change enough. Had the Iroquois adopted European materialist values—that is, had they sought to accumulate wealth and fought to control the fur trade—they might have gained enough economic clout to withstand the pressures put on them by their European neighbors. Instead they sought to preserve their values and way of life. War continued to be fought for a variety of reasons, and it never became merely an instrument for carrying out political and economic goals. Government continued to be based on a social system where the rights of the constituent parts seemed to prevail over that of the whole.

There is no doubt that contact and interaction with Europeans brought changes to Iroquois society. The introduction of new diseases threatened to wipe out their population. Guns, on the other hand, seemed to provide them with the means to recoup their losses by conquering other natives to replace those taken by disease. Europeans and their cultural baggage complicated and threatened Iroquois society, but the Iroquois responded to life's struggles informed and constrained by values and processes that were uniquely Iroquois. In short, they fought to live, not for furs.

# Abbreviations Used in the Notes and Appendixes

AN, CI IA
: Archives Nationales, Paris, Archives des Colonies, series CI IA, Correspondance Général, Canada

ASJCF
: Archives de la Compagnie de Jésus au Canada français, Maison des Jésuites, Saint-Jérôme, Quebec

Colden, *Five Indian Nations*
: Cadwallader Colden. *The History of the Five Indian Nations* of Canada Which are dependant on the Province of New-York in America and are a Barrier between the English and the French in that Part of the World

*Correspondance*
: [Marie Guyart], *Marie de L'Incarnation, Ursuline (1599–1672), Correspondance*, ed. Guy Oury

CSP
: Calendar of State Papers, Colonial Series, America and the West Indies, ed. W. Sainsbury et al.

Galinée, "Voyage de Dollier et Galinée"
: [René Bréhant de Galinée], "Ce qui s'est passé de plus remarquable dans le voyage de M.M. Dollier et Galinée (1669–1670)"

JR
: R. G. Thwaites, ed. *The Jesuit Relations and Allied Documents, 1610–1791*

*Md. Archives*
: Archives of Maryland, ed. W. H. Browne et al.

MNF
: Lucien Campeau, ed., *Monumenta Novae Franciae*

"Nation Iroquoise"
: "Abregé des vies et moeurs et autres Particularitez de La Nation Irokoise laquelle est diviseé en Cinq villages. Sçavoir

Agnez, Onney8t, Nontagué, Goyog8an et Sonnont8ans,''
Bibliothèque Mazarine, Paris, ms 1964.

| | |
|---|---|
| *NNN* | J. F. Jameson, ed. *Narratives of New Netherland, 1609–1664* |
| *NYCD* | E. B. O'Callaghan, ed., *Documents Relative to the Colonial History of the State of New York* |
| *RAPQ* | Rapport de l'archiviste de la province de Québec. |
| Wraxall, *Indian Affairs* | Peter Wraxall, *An Abridgement of the Indian Affairs Contained in Four Folio Volumes, Transacted in the Colony of New York from the Year 1678 to the Year 1751* |

# Rebirth and Death: Iroquois Baptisms and Mortality, 1667–1679

In order to assess the impact Iroquois population decline may have had on their policy toward various native and European groups, it is essential to determine just how many Iroquois died yearly. The purpose of tables A.1 and A.2 is to provide some sense of the number of Iroquois who died annually in the Iroquois villages. Table B.1 will present data on when epidemics struck the Iroquois in order to provide a sense of how representative the annual death rate might be. Table D.1 will show, among other things, how many Iroquois died as a result of hostilities undertaken by and against the Iroquois. This data, joined with that of tables A.1 and A.2 here, should provide a relatively clear picture of Iroquois annual mortality. Table C.1 will introduce Iroquois population estimates so that one can attempt to assess what impact these annual death rates may have had on Iroquois society and their policy.

The Jesuits, who left us the most detailed records on the Iroquois, did not list deaths among the Iroquois in general, but did note the number of Iroquois who received baptism and, sometimes, the number of baptized who eventually died. From these various letters and reports of individual missionaries it is possible to arrive at an estimate of total deaths, and what portion of those were adults or children (table A.2). Unfortunately, the number of years for which data is available is limited. But even if we do not have complete data for a prolonged period, at least we have this twelve-year period in which we can gain a sense of how many Iroquois died in the villages.

One of the difficulties of trying to do a quantitative study based on the *Jesuit Relations* is that they had no idea that their work would be put to such use and, in general, were not very exact in their accounting. Moreover, even were it possible to be precise, the *Relations* were intended for a general readership, and it was the moral lessons to be derived from them that were important, not statistics about population numbers and death rates. The number of baptized was important because it reflected the success of the missions, but even here precise numbers were not necessary and therefore not always given.[1] Thus, even though the letters and reports of the various priests noted how many baptisms they had performed, the *Relations* provide few yearly totals for the different Iroquois tribes. Even the one overall total for the Iroquois confederacy lists no tribal breakdown, nor to what time period that total applies. Writing in the *Relation* of 1679, Father Dablon claimed that "more than 4 thousand iroquois" had been baptized, and a "goodly part" of them had died.[2] That figure of four thousand, however, cannot be arrived at by adding up the few yearly totals provided in the *Relations,* nor by adding up the numbers of baptisms individual priests reported for their missions (table A.1). One must conclude that Father Dablon either had more precise data at his disposal, or that he may have been referring to a longer time frame than that being considered here—probably a combination of both.

The data in table A.1 was derived from the *Jesuit Relations* for the relevant years. The editors of the *Relations* rarely provided yearly totals, and when they did they never coincided with the totals that can be derived by compiling the data found in the various mission reports. When such annual totals provided by the editors of the *Relations* were available, they were included in the totals column in braces: { }. Furthermore, the totals in the table include only hard data. That is, when the sources indicate that "half," "some," or "most died," no attempt was made to attach a quantifiable number to such expressions. Thus the tabular totals reflect only the actual numbers provided in the sources. (Table A.2 will provide totals based on estimates arrived at by attaching number values to such imprecise expressions, as well as providing the reasons and methods by which those estimates were obtained.) It will be noted that often the number of adults and children said to have been baptized or to have died does not equal the total numbers of baptized or dead for the year or the period. This is because often there was no specific breakdown in the sources of how many of the baptized or dead were children or adults. When such information was provided, it was noted.

It should be pointed out that in table A.1 the annual totals, and the total for the twelve-year period, do not include the few yearly aggregates provided by the Jesuit editors, except for the years 1678 and 1679. No other figures of dead or baptized were available for those years, and it seemed unwise to exclude such large numbers even if they could not be verified by checking against the accounts for the individual missions. If the annual totals provided by the editors of the *Relations* are taken into consideration, the number of baptized Iroquois from each tribe that I arrived at remain unaltered because the data is not precise enough. However, inclusion of the *Relations'* editors few yearly totals would produce different Confederacy totals for several years and for the twelve-year period. In some years the editors' totals are higher than mine, but in others they are lower (see totals for 1669–70 and 1670–71, for example). If the years 1678 and 1679, which were used in calculating the overall total, are excluded, then the number of Iroquois baptized according to Jesuit editors is 1,201, while figures for the same years (based on adding up accounts from individual priests) produce a total of 1,142 baptized—a difference of 59. Since the Jesuits did not consistently provide annual totals, and the difference is slight, I thought it best to stick to my annual totals in calculating the period totals to avoid complicating the tables any further. Moreover, as table A.2 indicates, the actual number of Iroquois who were baptized and died is greater still.

If we cannot come close to Father Dablon's total of baptized, can we at least determine what that "goodly" part who died represents in real numbers? As table A.1 shows, 917 of those baptized died (28 percent). But while that may be a "goodly" number, when the sources list both those who were baptized and how many of those died (31 instances), the percentage of baptized who died is 71 percent. In the case of children, the percentage of baptized who died is 82 percent. This is certainly in keeping with the observation made by Father Le Mercier that the "children who die after Baptism being the surest fruit of Evangelical labours, especial pains are taken not to let a single one die without conferring" baptism upon them.[3] Indeed, Father Dablon noted that the Iroquois resisted baptism because they believed it caused death. He added that he did not find it strange that they thought this since baptism was "administered only to children at the point of death; and, in fact, nearly all who are baptized die immediately afterward."[4]

In his study of all natives baptized between 1632 and 1672, Pouliot arrived at totals of 16,014 baptized and 1,948 dead according to the figures in the *Relations*. However, he estimated that two-thirds of the baptized actually died (about 10,600), and that 265 of the baptized died annually. Indeed, as the various entries in table A.1 show, most of those baptized were children, and most of those who were baptized, children or adult, died. The question then becomes how to reconcile these differences. Is it possible to arrive at a total number of dead that reflects the Jesuit observation—confirmed by the little hard data that exists—that most who were baptized died? The answer is, I think, yes. As table A.1 shows, the *Relations* often state that "some," "half," or even "most" of the baptized of a tribe died. If we can put numeric equivalents to such imprecise expressions we might attain a better understanding of how many of the baptized were adults, how many were children, and how many from both groups died.

It is possible to come to some fairly precise and not too speculative numerical values for these nonnumerical expressions. Some are quite easy to resolve. "Half" is, of course, no problem. If the number is not one given to equal division (say 27), then the number can be divided in half, and the resultant number (in this case, 13.5) will be rounded down to the nearest whole number (13). Others phrases proved more difficult to translate into numbers. For example, it is impossible to state just what could be meant by "over," "majority," or "most." If "over 30 were baptized," it could be 31 or 39. It is equally difficult to formulate a numerical value when the expression "the majority" is used. If 100 were baptized a majority could be from 51 to 99. There is no way to determine which could be meant. In the first example the solution was to accept the number given and make no attempt to speculate how much beyond the given number was intended by "over." For the second example one can accept half plus 1 as a simple majority. The same rule was used if the "majority" of a given number were said to be either adults or children. It also follows that if the majority of a given number were of one group, the remainder must be of another. If 50 people were baptized, the "majority" children (26 children), then the remainder must have been adults (24 adults). In the case of "most," it seems to be used interchangeably with "majority," and so the same rule of thumb was used for it. I recognize that in following the above procedures I am accepting lower estimates, but it is best to err toward understatement.

The most serious problem is presented when trying to determine child:adult ratios for baptisms and deaths, or how many died when all the sources reveal is that a given number were baptized. While it is true that children outnumber adults in totals baptized, this was not always the case in every tribe, and one can never be sure if one is dealing with an exception in a particular instance. Since there seemed to be no way to resolve this, it was thought best not to attempt to attach any specific adult:child ratio to numbers in those instances. As for determining how many died when all that was given was the total baptized, it is clear from both the precise numbers and the expressions employed by the Jesuits (table A.1) that most of those baptized died. As noted above, when precise figures are available the data reveals that 71 percent of the baptized died. It does not appear unreasonable to accept this figure. Again, no attempt was made to assign a child:adult ratio to the dead.

Several results in table A.2 bear comment. The number of baptized who died based on this table is approximately 63 percent. This is close to the figure Pouliot arrived at for his study.[5] In terms of the test of accuracy, it should be remarked that the ratio of dead children to dead adults is still roughly 2:1, just as it was in table A.1 where no estimates were used. If one uses the ratio of 2 dead children for every dead adult, then we can estimate that of this total of 2,002, roughly 1,200 were children. If we add to this total of dead baptized Iroquois that number of unbaptized Iroquois who died in the villages of disease (213), then the total number of Iroquois who died is 2,215. One should consider that this total does not include those Iroquois lost through warfare (either captured or killed as a result of raids by or against the Iroquois),[6] or those who died in the villages but whom the Jesuits could not baptize (mostly adults). It is impossible to state whether this death rate is constant over any other period. No data exists to compare with it. Also, there were several recorded outbreaks of disease among the Iroquois during this period. On the other hand, no period has as complete a record as this one, so it is impossible to know if disease was equally prevalent in other epochs but simply went unrecorded. What does seem relatively clear is that during this period the Iroquois experienced a serious population drain.[7]

Annual Iroquois Baptism/Death Rates

| Year | Mohawk | Oneida | Onondaga | Cayuga | Seneca | Total - All Tribes |
|---|---|---|---|---|---|---|
| 1667 (f/w) | | 56 c b; 4 a b | | | | 60 b(56 c, 4 a) |
| 1668 | | | | | 120 b most a, more than 90 a d; 150 other [a unbapt.] d | 120 b most a, more than 90 a d; 150 others d |
| 1668-69 | 251 b; over half d | 30 b, more than half d | over 30 b, most d | 28 b; half d | 60 b, 33 d | 399 b; 33 d |
| 1669-70 | | 32 [b] c d | 40 b, most c or dying a, of these 16 [b] [c] d | 25 c b; 12 a b; large part d | | 109 b(73 c, 12 a); 48 d(48 c) {50 c b, most d; 3 a b} |
| 1670-71 | 84 b, 74 d, most c under 7 | | | 62 b, 35 d, most dead c | 110 b | 256 b; 109 d {318-20 b, over half d} |
| 1671-72 | | 30 b, most c, and d | 39 b, of these 16 [b] c d, 4 [b] a d | 30 c & a b, most d | 40 b, 33 d, nearly all c | 139 b(16 c. 4 a); 53 d(16 c, 4 a) {200 b} |
| 1672-73 | 36 b & d | 34 b, of these, 16 [b] d | over 30 b & d, 19 were c, [11 a?] | 44 c b, 18 d; 11 a b & d | 43 c b, 29 d; 12 a b, 9 d; 38 b, of these, 7 a d, 8 c d at least | 248 b(114 c, 41 a); 164 d(74 c, 38 a) {80 a & 200 c b, majority d} |
| 1673-74 | | 45 b | 18 a b, 12 d; 27 c b, 24 d | 22 c b; 5 a b & d | 10 a b & d; 14 c b & d | 141 b(63 c, 33 a); 65 d(38 c, 27 a) |
| 1675 | 80 b | | 72 [c] b, 40 [c] d | 21 c b & d; 11 a b & d | 100 b; 50 d annually after b | 284 b(93 c, 11 a); 72 d(61 c, 11 a) |

a = adults    b = baptized    c = children    d = died

Continued on next page

Table A.1 continued

| Year | Mohawk | Oneida | Onondaga | Cayuga | Seneca | Total - All Tribes |
|---|---|---|---|---|---|---|
| 1676 | 50 b, half d; 50 b, 9-10 d; 3 un-bapt. also d | | 7 a b & [d]; 45 c b, 40 d | 38 [c] b, 33 d; 6 a b, 3 d | 90 b, most c, 50 of those [b] c d; 40 c b & d; 14 a b & d; 60 c [unbapt.] d | 340 b(173 c, 27 a); 196 d(163 c, 24 a); 63 [unbapt.] d(60 c) {350 b; 27 a & 171 c d |
| 1677 | 40 b, most d | 52 b | 36 & 23 a b, all but 12 d | over 50 b; over 40 [b] c d | 212 b, 70 were c, portion d | 453 b(110 c, 59 a); 87 d(40 c, 47 a) |
| 1678 | | | | | | {350 b} |
| 1679 | | | | | | {over 300 b} |
| TOTAL | 591 b; 119 d; 3 unbapt. d | 283 b(88 c, 4 a); 48 d(32 c) | 367 b(195 c, 99 a); 236 d(155 c,81 a) | 405 b(190 c, 45 a); 177 d(112 c, 30 a) | 903 b(225 c, 133 a); 337 d(141 c, 130 a); 210 [unbapt.] d (60 c) | 3,199 b(698 c, 281 a); 917 d(440 c, 241 a); 213 [unbapt.] d(60 c, 150 [a]) |

Source: JR

a = adults    b = baptized    c = children    d = died

Annual Baptized Iroquois Death Rates

| Year | Mohawk | Oneida | Onondaga | Cayuga | Seneca | Total for all Tribes |
|---|---|---|---|---|---|---|
| 1667 | | 40 c d; 3 a d | | | | 43 d(40 c, 3 a) |
| 1668 | | | | | 90 a d; 150 other [a unbapt.] d | 90 a d; 150 other [a unbapt.] d |
| 1668-69 | 126 d | 16 d | 16 d | 14 d | 33 d | 205 d |
| 1669-70 | | 32 [b] c d | 16 [b] [c] d | 18 c d; 8 a d | | 74 d(66 c, 8 a) |
| 1670-71 | 74 d, (38 c, 36 a) | | | 35 d(18 c, 17 a) | 78 d | 187 d(56 c, 53 a) |
| 1671-72 | | 16 c d | 16 [b] c d; 4 [b] a d | 16 d | 33 d, 23 were c | 85 d(55 c, 4 a) |
| 1672-73 | 36 d | 16 d | 19 c d; [11 a d] | 18 c d; 11 a d | 37 c d; 16 a d | 164 d(74 c, 38 a) |
| 1673-74 | | 32 d | 24 c d; 12 a d | 16 c d; 5 a d | 14 c d; 10 a d | 113 d(54 c, 27 a) |
| 1675 | 57 d | | 40 [c] d | 21 c d; 11 a d | 50 d | 179 d(61 c, 11 a) |
| 1676 | 34 d; 3 unbapt. d | | 40 c d; 7 a d | 33 c d; 3 a d | 90 c d; 14 a d; 60 c [unbapt.] d | 221 d(163 c, 24 a) |
| 1677 | 21 d | 37 d | 47 a d | 75 d, 40 were c | | 180 d(40 c, 47 a) |

a = adults   b = baptized   c = children   d = died

Continued on next page

| Year | Mohawk | Oneida | Onondaga | Cayuga | Seneca | Total for all Tribes |
|------|--------|--------|----------|--------|--------|---------------------|
| 1678 | | | | | | 248 d |
| 1679 | | | | | | 213 d |
| TOTAL | 348 d(38 c, 36a); 3 unbapt. d | 192 d(88 c, 3 a) | 252 d(155 c, 34 a) | 284 d(164 c, 55 a) | 465 d(164 c, 130 a); 210 unbapt. d (60 c, 150a) | 2,002 d(609 c, 305 a); 213 [unbapt.] d(60 c, 150 [a]) |

*Source:* Table A.1
*Note:* Only the total number of dead are listed.
*a = adults   b = baptized   c = children   d = died*

# Epidemics and Disease among the Iroquois to 1701

When did the Iroquois suffer from disease and what impact did it have on their population? Did the advent of new, deadlier diseases affect Iroquois relations with native and European groups, and if so, how? In order to address these queries, a reliable chronology of when epidemic diseases struck the Iroquois is needed. Despite the central importance of these questions, no such list can be found in the secondary literature. Karl Schlesier, for example, tried to show a direct cause-and-effect relationship between Iroquois epidemics and their relations with the French in Canada. Yet he overlooked one or two possible epidemics and misdated the one most crucial to his thesis.[1] In brief discussions of the impact of epidemics on the Iroquois and Iroquoians, Daniel Richter and Bruce Trigger have provided more reliable but still partial lists of epidemics, and they stop at 1662. In "Sixteenth-Century Depopulation," Dean Snow and William Starna provide the fullest chronology to date, focusing mainly on the Mohawks, but they also omit several epidemics.[2]

If one is to be left with an accurate view of when disease hit the Iroquois, and if such a chronology is to be of use to other scholars, vague and questionable sources must be explained and distinctions made, whenever possible, about the groups that were affected. What follows then, is a discussion of what various historical sources reveal about when epidemic disease hit the Iroquois in the years covered by this study. The results will then be presented in table format. It should be noted that the groups listed below are those that can be clearly confirmed to have suffered from epidemics. Because a group is not listed does not mean that the epidemic did not reach them, only that the sources do not indicate that such was the case.

In his 1983 book *"Their Number Become Thinned,"* Henry Dobyns argued that pandemic disease seriously diminished native populations before the seventeenth century. His critics have argued that his claims are sustained by distorting evidence or by ignoring it altogether. In short, no real support exists for his claims of widespread pandemic disease in North America, and none at all for disease hitting the Iroquois before 1600.[3] Dobyns has responded to his critics, but he has failed to establish his case any more firmly.[4] Until archaeologists uncover new evidence, one must conclude with Snow and Lamphear that the first epidemic to hit the Iroquois was in 1634.

The first mention of disease among the Iroquois was an outbreak of smallpox among the Mohawks recorded on 13 December 1634.[5] Harmen Meyndertsz Van den Bogaert, the Dutch surgeon who traveled among the Mohawks and Oneidas briefly, does not give the impression that it was current. In fact, one Mohawk chief had already relocated and set up a house away from the village where smallpox was said to have hit. At another village the Dutch noted a "good many" graves. Van den Bogaert does not mention anyone actively suffering from the disease, thus indicating its passage. Throughout the rest of his account, no further mention was made of disease, nor were the Onondagas noted to be suffering from anything when they came to meet with the Oneidas in January 1635. In short, the first recorded evidence of smallpox among the Iroquois was December 1634, but the evidence suggests that the disease struck earlier. It would also seem that by this time it was no longer active among the Mohawks and either did not spread to the other tribes or had worked its way through them as well.

The next recorded outbreak was also among the Mohawks. Writing on 20 February 1637 the Jesuit Le Mercier noted that the Hurons believed that the disease afflicting them came from the Mohawks, who in turn had picked it up from the Susquehannocks. Le Mercier went on to explain that the Hurons believed these groups had been infected with disease by Aataentsic as punishment for their evil ways.[6] It is not clear how the Mohawks had picked up the disease from the Susquehannocks, how the intervening Iroquois groups were spared, nor how the Mohawks passed it on to the Hurons. It could have reached the Hurons easily enough through prisoners captured during raids, but the one raid in 1636 in which the Hurons captured Iroquois was against the Onondagas.[7] The Hurons were reported to have arrived with their prisoners on 2 September 1636, and they were afflicted by disease in the autumn of 1636, before mid-September. Bruce Trigger has suggested that blaming the disease on the Mohawks was an effort by Huron traders to take pressure off the Jesuits who were really thought to be to blame for the disease.[8] However, the timing of the disease and its spread, as described by Trigger, tends to coincide with the arrival and distribution of the Onondaga prisoners among the Huron. If the Onondagas did bring the disease, why blame the Mohawks? Or could Father Le Mercier have been wrong about the origins of the Hurons' captives? Since there is no clear evidence of how the disease got to the Hurons, all that can be said is that it is possible, even probable, that some Iroquois tribe was suffering from some contagious disease in 1636 and passed it on to the Hurons.

In the winter of 1639–40, recorded the *Annales de l'Hôtel-Dieu de Québec*, disease swept through native groups in New France.[9] The disease started out as smallpox but then became something that "took them by the throat" [*les prenoit a la gorge*] and killed the natives within twenty-four hours. Among the groups listed as affected were the Iroquois. It is not clear which of these maladies they suffered from, nor how the good sisters at Sillery knew of the contagion in Iroquoia. They might have received the news from some of their Algonquin charges, or they might have been confusing this outbreak with the one of the following year. The chroniclers of the *Annales* were not always very accurate with dates. Be that as it may, they do clearly list the Iroquois among the groups suffering from disease in the winter of 1639–40.

One of the most commonly noted outbreaks of disease among the Iroquois was that in the winter of 1640–41. While visiting the Neutrals, Fathers Brébeuf and Chaumonot reported that an epidemic was ravaging the enemy.[10] Since the Iroquois were the most obvious enemy of the Hurons, and the closest Iroquois tribe to the Neutrals was the Senecas, that is how this reference is usually interpreted. However, there is no real reason to suppose that the Jesuits were referring to any one group to the exclusion of others. The Jesuits were fully cognizant of the fact that the Mohawks were also implacable foes of the Hurons. The term *enemy* could refer to the whole Confederacy.

A few years later, disease was once again noted among the Mohawks. Some time after June 1646 until at least March 1647 the Mohawks were afflicted by disease. It began sometime after Father Jogues left in June of 1646. It was believed that he caused the malady and the crop failure of that year and it led to his death. An Algonquin prisoner who was captured in March 1647 and escaped a short time later reported that the Mohawks were "afflicted with a general malady."[11]

In 1655 disease was first clearly noted among the Onondagas. But the source reveals little more than that.[12] In 1660 the Mohawks were again struck by disease. The reference, however, is open to question. In the *Annales de l'Hôtel-Dieu de Québec* Catherine Tekawitha was said to have been orphaned at the age of four when both her parents' died of the smallpox that hit their Mohawk village.[13] Since she was born in 1656, this would place the epidemic in 1660.[14] The question is, how sure can we be of the record of her birth, and her age when her parents died? Indians did not issue birth certificates, and all the information about her early life was gathered much later. If the record is off by one year that would place her parents' death in the clearly recorded epidemic of 1661–62. However, the sources do not specifically note that the Mohawks were struck in that one. Unless evidence to the contrary appears, it seem unreasonable to exclude the 1660 reference from the chronology, but it is by no means a certainty that an epidemic struck that year.

Sometime between the fall of 1661 and the summer of 1663, the Iroquois suffered one long epidemic or were hit by two separate ones. The Jesuit Simon Le Moyne was among the Onondagas from July 1661 to August 1662. In a letter from Onondaga dated 11 September 1661 he made no mention of disease.[15] Writing a year later, after Le Moyne's return, Father Lalemant noted that Le Moyne was busy during his stay because the smallpox was prevalent among the Onondagas. If it had struck before Le Moyne wrote his letter it is probable that he would have mentioned it. In any case, during his stay, Le Moyne baptized over 200 children, of whom more than 120 died. He also baptized 60 more children from a passing Seneca "caravan." They, too, were afflicted with smallpox.[16] It is not clear if they had it before arriving among the Onondagas, picked it up while there, or even if they were the ones that carried the disease to the Onondagas.

It is tempting to postulate that the Senecas brought the disease to the rest of the Confederacy as the result of their trip. There is evidence that smallpox hit the Iroquois (the Oneidas were clearly mentioned) at least between August 1662 and sometime in 1663. But there is no record of when the Senecas passed by the other tribes, probably in winter of 1661–62, and no clear idea of when the Oneidas got the disease, except that it came to French attention sometime after August 1662. That was plenty of time for the virus to arrive from a number of other places.

What the sources reveal is that a Frenchman who was captured 25 August 1662, and who was among the Oneidas for nineteen months, suffered from a variety of adventures including surviving a smallpox epidemic that carried off more than one thousand souls.[17] Writing in 1663, just after describing an attack by the Susquehannocks in the spring of that year, Lalemant noted that these defeats, added to the smallpox that has "wrought havoc in their villages," kept the Iroquois on the defensive.[18] Since Lalemant implied that the disease had passed by the time of his writing the *Relation,* usually in the fall, if not earlier, of 1663, and the French witness was caught in August of the previous year, the disease probably struck sometime between August 1662 and the spring of 1663. It may even have lasted that long.

The evidence is not strong enough to conclude that the epidemics of 1661–62 and 1662–63 were continuous, but if the figure of one thousand dead is accurate, this seems more reasonable for the longer, almost two-year period than for the less than one-year span. Certainly the mortality rate a few years later does not indicate the same drastic death rate in such a short time frame (table A.2). It is unlikely that immunities acquired in such a brief period could account for such vastly different mortality rates.

As the Jesuits established firmer contact with the Iroquois, the record of epidemics and illnesses among that people became more detailed. At the end of 1668 Father Fremin found a contagious disease ravaging the Senecas. He baptized 120 people, nearly all adults, more than 90 of whom died. He noted that 150 others, presumably unbaptized, also died.[19] From June to September 1672 a pestilence marked by severe headaches and fever struck the Mohawks.[20] In 1676 influenza struck one Seneca village, and more than 60 children died in one month.[21] From the number of baptisms and projected deaths among the other Senecas, it seems safe to conclude that more than one village was hit (table A.2).

Three years later the Onondagas and Oneidas were struck by smallpox. They failed to attend conferences with the English in the fall because of the "Sicknesse of feavor and Small Pox Reigning soo violently" in their lands.[22] In a letter to the king, Governor Frontenac of New France gloated over the unfortunate circumstances of the Five Nations and left the impression that the malady was fairly widespread and devastating.[23]

Between 1680 and 1701 the records note only two more epidemics among the Iroquois. Sometime before August 1682 the "bloody flux" hit the Onondagas and the Cayugas. Ten people died at Onondaga after the Jesuits ran out of medicine, and sixty at Cayuga of the same disease. Intriguingly, Father Lamberville also noted that three Senecas were killed because they were believed to be "the authors of the Present ills."[24] This may imply that the disease came via the Senecas. On the other hand, it could be that the three Senecas were thought to have used magic to cause the disease. It is, nonetheless, a hint that the Senecas might also have been afflicted. In the spring of 1690 smallpox was reported among the Mohawks gathering to attack New France. It had yet to spread to the rest of the tribes (with the army or in Iroquoia?) because they were out hunting. By the fall of that year the French reported that one hundred Iroquois with the army had died of smallpox, and four hundred others had died in their villages.[25]

Knowledge of European diseases among the Iroquois required the presence of those who would record the diseases—just as that contact with Europeans brought the diseases. This relationship presents several problems when assessing the extent of Iroquois suffering from epidemics. The tribes that had most contact with Europeans were most likely to catch diseases, and also most likely to have Europeans record such. Does lack of information about disease among the interior tribes reflect inadequate historical record, or does it mean that distance from large European settlements made them less prone to catch these diseases? Not having eyewitnesses among all tribes makes it impossible to know if they suffered diseases at the same time as those that the sources indicate were afflicted by contagious illnesses, or if these other groups were struck at other times.

Certainly we cannot assume that every time one Iroquois tribe was hit, every other tribe also suffered. By the late 1660s the Jesuits were among the Iroquois. In some villages they reported contagious disease while in others no mention was made of any malady. Does this reflect spotty reporting on the part of the Jesuits, or active avoidance of afflicted groups by uninfected tribes?[26] If it was the latter, how widespread was this practice? Unfortunately, this question of how to interpret the data available is no more easily resolved than that of how representative of reality those data are. Like so many other aspects of Iroquois history and culture, no resolution to these questions seems forthcoming. The best that can be said is that the available data at least reflect the timing of major outbreaks of disease and their tribal victims.

Disease among the Iroquois to 1701

| Year | Group | Disease/Symptoms |
|---|---|---|
| 1634, Dec. | Mohawk | Smallpox |
| 1636 | Mohawk or Onondaga? | No details |
| 1639-40, winter | Iroquois [not specified] | Smallpox and/or unspecified throat ailment |
| 1640-41, winter | Iroquois [not specified] | No details |
| 1646-47, summer to spring | Mohawk | No details |
| 1655 | Onondaga | No details |
| 1660 | Mohawk | Smallpox |
| 1661-62, [winter?] | Onondaga and Seneca | Smallpox |
| 1662-63, [winter?] | Iroquois | Smallpox |
| 1668, [fall to winter?] | Seneca | No details |
| 1672, June to Sept. | Mohawk | Severe headache and fever |
| 1676 | Seneca | Influenza |
| 1679, [winter] | Onondaga, Oneida and possibly all Iroquois tribes | Smallpox and fever |
| 1682 | Onondaga and Cayuga and possibly Seneca | Bloody flux |
| 1690, spring [to fall] | Mohawk and possibly rest of Iroquois tribes | Smallpox |

# Iroquois Population Estimates to 1701

Estimating the size of the Iroquois population is difficult. A variety of methods can be pursued, but the two most common are the so-called historical and archaeological approaches. Neither method is flawless. Historians tend to accept the population figures of European contemporaries. This leaves us at the mercy of the widely varying powers of observation of these witnesses. One can never be certain if shifts in population figures represent real trends or reflect the eyesight and judgment of the chroniclers. This approach is made even more difficult because these estimates are usually given in terms of Iroquois fighting strength and to arrive at a total population one must multiply those warrior totals by a constant that represents the proportion of warriors in the society. Arriving at that constant usually involves even more speculation.

More scientific is the archaeologist's approach.[1] Using data from excavated village sites that reveal size of villages, longhouses, storage structures, and numbers of hearths per longhouse, archaeologists speculate about the number of people per house based on the size of the dwelling and the number of its hearths. However, it is difficult to date village occupation precisely and to establish which villages were occupied at the same time. In order to do this one has to use archaeological material in conjunction with historical sources. An almost insurmountable problem with this process is that excavations take a great deal of time and in the end the data is never complete or even at comparable levels for all tribes. Moreover, unless all sites are found that were occupied during the historical period under study, it is extremely difficult to discuss changing population sizes over time. These strike me as major reasons to continue to use evidence from documentary sources such as contemporary warrior population estimates.

In order to approximate Iroquois populations, two approaches will be used. The first is to make population estimates based on house totals, hearths:house, and people:hearth ratios. This will be followed by a discussion of population size based on warrior:general population ratios. Finally, some attempt will be made to check population figures arrived at by these two different means. While this involves one speculative method used to verify another equally speculative process, it seems worth the effort.

Determining the number of hearths per longhouse and the size of an Iroquois family is central to using the hearth count approach. The number of people per family is difficult to ascertain, but the consensus is that among Iroquoian groups there were about four to eight people per family, and that two families shared one hearth.[2] Establishing the number of hearths per longhouse involves less speculation because the historical record can be augmented by archaeological findings. Most sources concur that Iroquoian longhouses had an average of three to four central hearths, often augmented by small fires.[3] Since these smaller fires were used by members of the same groups that shared the central hearths, one need not take them into account when determining the number of hearths in a house.

Tables C.1 and C.2 present data used to arrive at Iroquois population estimates for the years 1634, 1669, and 1677. Table C.3 presents population estimates for these same years. These were the only years for which the historical record provided evidence about how many houses were in Iroquois villages. Since we do not have archaeological data on longhouses among all the Iroquois tribes, it was decided to use only the house totals provided by seventeenth-century contemporaries of the Iroquois. Table C.1 lists the various sources that remarked on house numbers among the Iroquois, and their estimates. Table C.2 shows estimates of how many hearths per tribe this would represent at three and four hearths per longhouse. Finally, table C.3 presents Iroquois population estimates derived from people:hearth ratios. The estimates are based on averages of three and four hearths per longhouse. It was assumed that two families shared a hearth and that this represented ten people per hearth.

The population estimates in the documentary sources are almost all given in terms of fighting men. To come to a total population for each of the five tribes and for the Confederacy, such figures are usually multiplied by numbers of three to five. These two numbers represent the upper and lower estimates within the accepted range of possible children and wives an Iroquois warrior could have. The assumption among those that write about the Iroquois is that when the sources refer to warriors, they mean married adult males. No real attempt has been made to see if something other than this was intended. Thus if one accepts that each warrior had one wife, and an average of two to three children, one multiplies the total number of warriors by five to determine the overall tribal population.

The problem is that there is no proof that "warrior" simply equates with married adult male. Moreover, even if this was the case, the multiple of five would be too high. One would have to assume that each warrior was indeed married, and had been long enough to have produced his full complement of children at the time of the estimate, that his wife was still alive, and that fathers never lived long enough to fight alongside unmarried sons.[4] But these assumptions beg too many questions, and they rest on no evidence. For example, on what grounds can one claim that all warriors were married and had the exact quota of children? Two to three surviving children seems to be what the primary sources suggest was common in the postepidemic period from which the statistics below were culled, and the Iroquois were monogamous. But some could, and some certainly did, have more children than that. On the other hand, some warriors must certainly have been widowed or abandoned by wives who would not appreciate the lack of food, support, and affection that sustained warring inevitably produced.[5] Given these types of variables it seems more in keeping with the historical record to multiply the warrior totals by three than by five to arrive at overall population estimates.

Yet historical sources suggest a need for a multiple higher than five. In 1669 the Cayugas were said to be capable of fielding over 300 warriors out of a population of over 2,000 people.[6] If one deducts the number of warriors from 2,000 and divides by 300, that produces a figure of 6.6 people for every warrior. (The source makes clear that the warrior total was part of the 2,000.) In the same year the Senecas were said to have about 1,000 to 1,200 warriors.[7] Three years later the tribe was estimated at 12,000 to 13,000 people.[8] If we accept the lowest estimates in each case and deduct the warrior figure from the population total, that produces a ratio of 11 people for every warrior. One year later the Seneca warrior total was estimated at 800.[9] This estimate seems too low. No epidemic hit the Senecas between 1669 and 1672, nor were there any major war losses in this period (table B.1; table D.1, entries for 1669–72). However, if this figure is correct and the population estimate is still valid, this produces a ratio of 1 warrior for every 14 people.

These scraps of data present several problems in assessing warrior:population ratios. Are these cases representative? Is this ratio consistent for these tribes over time? Do the ratios for the other tribes fall within this range? The answers are, however, fewer than the questions. We can assume that the same ratio could apply to the other three Iroquois tribes, but we cannot be sure. However, it is possible to check the validity of this assumption. If we take the estimated tribal populations for 1677 (table c.3), divide those by the estimated warrior strength of each tribe for that same year (table c.4), and deduct the warrior total from the population total, then we get the following range of ratios for the five tribes: Mohawk, 1:8 and 1:12; Oneida, 1:14 and 1:19; Onondaga, 1:13 and 1:17; Cayuga, 1:9 and 1:12; Seneca, 1:9 and 1:12.

The fact that the Cayugas' and Senecas' ratios are so close to those derived from documentary sources indicates that Iroquois population estimates based on hearth totals and those derived via the warrior:general population ratios produce similar population totals. If this is the case, the warrior:population ratios for the other tribes can be deemed equally valid. This may seem farfetched, especially in the case of the Oneidas and Onondagas. But it is possible to suggest that it is not. If we take the ratio of 1:14 and multiply that by the number of warriors estimated in each tribe in 1677 (table c.4), we get an Oneida population of 3,000 living in 100 houses, or 30 people per house. The Onondaga population comes to 5,250 people living in 164 houses, or 32 people per house. This is the low end of the range of people who could live in a longhouse.[10] In the case of the Mohawks, if the 1:8 ratio is used, that produces a population of 2,700 living in 96 houses, or 28 people per house. While this does not serve as conclusive proof that the ratios are valid across time and for all tribes, it does suggest that they are not as farfetched as they at first might appear and that different tribes had different warrior:population ratios. It also suggests that there might be some value to deriving population estimates based on those ratios. All the caveats mentioned above for not ascribing a large family to each warrior still seem to hold true. What seems equally true, and what the evidence indicates, is that the missionaries and other chroniclers of seventeenth-century native society had more in mind than simply a married adult male when they spoke of warriors, and that Iroquois society consisted of more than an aggregate of nuclear families.

In table c.4 the warrior strength estimates are presented as recorded by various observers. In table c.5 tribal and Confederacy population estimates are presented based on multiplying those figures by the lowest applicable ratio: Mohawks by 8, Oneidas and Onondagas by 14, Cayugas by 7, and Senecas by 11. In the case of the Senecas and the Cayugas these figures were the ones derived from the figures provided in documentary sources. In instances where the sources provide only warrior estimates for the whole confederacy, the multiple of 11 was used. It was close to the average of the five, and in any case the tribes with the higher ratios were the most populous. It was felt this would more accurately reflect the overall population trend. These general Confederacy warrior totals are more often than not lower than those arrived at when individual tribal warrior strengths are added up. The result is that when these confederacy warrior estimates are used, they produce lower population estimates. In table c.5 the total tribal population is arrived at by multiplying the warrior total by the ratio numbers and then adding the warrior population estimate to that figure. As noted above, the warrior total was deducted from the overall population in order to obtain the ratio of warrior to population. To obtain the overall tribal and confederacy population, the warrior total must be factored back in.

As a comparison of tables c.3 and c.5 indicates, the total population of the Iroquois in 1677, arrived at by different means, reveals a remarkable degree of compatibility (23,520 and 25,350 respectively). And as noted above, the warrior:people ratios that could be compared also produce similar numbers.

As for the precontact population, that is even more problematic. By the time we have a complete confederacy population estimate, the Iroquois had already been hit by epidemics. We do not know mortality rates among the Iroquois, nor data precise enough to indicate which tribes had been hit. The best that can be done is some guessing in the face of contradictory evidence. For example, the house totals for the Mohawks indicate a population decrease of 50 percent. But by the time that second house total was recorded in 1677, major wars had been undertaken, and population figures based on warrior totals show an increase in population from 1634 to 1643, then a drop again by 1659–60. In the case of the Oneidas, house totals and population estimates based on warrior ratios indicate an increase in population over time—not a decrease.

Table A.2 indicates that at least 2,215 people died in the period from 1667 to 1679, although the figures in table c.5 barely reflect any population decline. If we assume the population estimate for 1677 to be correct, then the total of Iroquois who died in the villages represents 8.7 percent of the whole population, and thus an 8.7 percent population decline over a twelve-year period during which epidemics struck the Iroquois four separate times (table B.1). In 1663 the Iroquois may have lost as many as 1,000 people in an epidemic. This represents

3.8 percent of the population estimated to be 26,100 in 1665. Even if twice as many died as were noted in the *Jesuit Relations,* this would indicate a significant but gradual mortality rate/depopulation.[11] Moreover, even if the Mohawks, the tribe most often struck by disease, did suffer a 50 percent mortality rate, is it wise to assume that all the others did as well?[12] Until archaeologists uncover a historic village and a cemetery with thousands of skeletons, little more than conjecture is possible. Surely if the Iroquois were dying off in such massive numbers, the physical remains of such devastation will eventually be found.

Based on this study it seems possible to conclude that if the Iroquois population was halved as a result of disease, it was a gradual process. Either that or the Iroquois capture and adoption of over six thousand people was enough to offset much of the population drain brought on by disease (table D.1). The above discussion and tables also indicate that Iroquois population was much higher than most experts have in the past estimated. Despite a series of epidemics, the Iroquois managed to maintain relatively stable population levels, at least insofar as the rather insensitive methods used here could reflect such things. The significant drop in the size of the Iroquois Confederacy during the historic period seems to have been confined to the latter part of the seventeenth century and does not appear to be attributable to any one single factor. Moreover, this observed population decline could be the result of method. The wars of the 1680s and 1690s took a heavy toll on Iroquois warrior populations.[13] Because overall population figures are based on warrior totals, the rapid decline in warrior strength during this latter period may not reflect as rapid a decline in the overall population. Since at present there does not seem to be any more reliable way to obtain population figures for all the Iroquois, it would seem reasonable to conclude that the above population totals reflect to the best of our knowledge Iroquois population during most of the seventeenth century.

Total Houses among the Iroquois

Table C.1

| Year | Tribe | # of Houses | Source |
|------|-------|-------------|--------|
| 1634 | Mohawk | 180 | [van den Bogaert], *Journey*, 4, 7, 13 |
|      | Oneida | 66 | |
| 1669 | Seneca | 360 | Galinée, "Voyage de Dollier et Galinée," 24 |
| 1677 | Mohawk | 96 | "Wentworth Greenhalgh's Journal . . . 1677," *NYCD* 3:250-52 |
|      | Oneida | 100 | |
|      | Onondaga | 164 | |
|      | Cayuga | 100 | |
|      | Seneca | 324 | |

Total Hearths per Tribe

Table C.2

| Year | Tribe | at 3 per house | at 4 per house |
|------|-------|----------------|----------------|
| 1634 | Mohawk | 540 | 720 |
| | Oneida | 198 | 264 |
| 1669 | Seneca | 1,080 | 1,440 |
| 1677 | Mohawk | 288 | 384 |
| | Oneida | 300 | 400 |
| | Onondaga | 492 | 656 |
| | Cayuga | 300 | 400 |
| | Seneca | 972 | 1,296 |

Population Estimates Based on People per Hearth

Table C.3

| Year | Tribe | 3 Hearths per Longhouse | 4 Hearths per Longhouse |
|------|-------|------------------------|-------------------------|
| 1634 | Mohawk | 5,400 | 7,200 |
|      | Oneida | 1,980 | 2,640 |
| 1669 | Seneca | 10,800 | 14,400 |
| 1677 | Mohawk | 2,880 | 3,840 |
|      | Oneida | 3,000 | 4,000 |
|      | Onondaga | 4,920 | 6,560 |
|      | Cayuga | 3,000 | 4,000 |
|      | Seneca | 9,720 | 12,960 |
| Total for 1677 | All Tribes | 23,520 | 31,360 |

Table C.4

Iroquois Warrior Strength Estimates, 1643-1712

| Year | Group | # of Warriors | Sources |
|------|-------|---------------|---------|
| 1643 | Mohawk | 700-800 | JR 24:271 |
| 1659-60 | Mohawk | 500 | JR 45:207 |
| | Oneida | 100 | |
| | Onondaga | 300 | |
| | Cayuga | 300 | |
| | Seneca | 1,000 | |
| 1661 | All Iroquois | 2,000 | JR 47:105 |
| 1665 | Mohawk | 300-400 | JR 49:257-59 |
| | Oneida | 140 | |
| | Onondaga | 300 | |
| | Cayuga | 300 | |
| | Seneca | 1,200 | |
| 1668 | All Iroquois | 2,000 | JR 51:139 |
| 1669 | Oneida | 160 | JR 53:247 |
| | Cayuga | 300 | JR 52:193 |

Continued on next page

Table C.4 continued

| Year | Group | # of Warriors | Sources |
|---|---|---|---|
| | Seneca | 1,000-1,200 | Galinée, "Voyage du Dollier et Galinée," 24 |
| 1672 | Cayuga | 300 | JR 56:51 |
| 1673 | Seneca | 800 | JR 57:27 |
| 1677 | Mohawk | 300 | NYCD 3:250-52 |
| | Oneida | 200 | |
| | Onondaga | 350 | |
| | Cayuga | 300 | |
| | Seneca | 1,000 | |
| 1681 | All Iroquois | 2,000 | AN, C11A 5:309 |
| 1682 | Seneca | 1,500 | JR 62:163 |
| 1689 | Mohawk | 270 | NYCD 4:337 |
| | Oneida | 180 | |
| | Onondaga | 500 | |
| | Cayuga | 300 | |
| | Seneca | 1,300 | |

Continued on next page

Table C.4 continued

| Year | Group | # of Warriors | Sources |
|---|---|---|---|
| 1691 | Mohawk | 130 | *NYCD* 3:815 |
| 1698 | Mohawk | 110 | *NYCD* 4:337 |
|  | Oneida | 70 |  |
|  | Onondaga | 250 |  |
|  | Cayuga | 200 |  |
|  | Seneca | 600 |  |
| 1710 | All Iroquois | 1,000-1,100 | [Raudot], *Relation*, 189 |
| 1712 | All Iroquois | 1,200 | "Memoire sur les coutumes," 445 |

Iroquois Population Estimates Based on Warrior to People Ratios

Table C.5

| Year | Group | Tribal Totals | Confederacy Totals |
|---|---|---|---|
| 1643 | Mohawk | 6,300 | |
| 1659-60 | Mohawk | 4,500 | 24,900 |
| | Oneida | 1,500 | |
| | Onondaga | 4,500 | |
| | Cayuga | 2,400 | |
| | Seneca | 12,000 | |
| 1661 | Confederacy | | 23,000 |
| 1665 | Mohawk | 2,700 | 26,100 |
| | Oneida | 2,100 | |
| | Onondaga | 4,500 | |
| | Cayuga | 2,400 | |
| | Seneca | 14,400 | |
| 1668 | Confederacy | | 23,000 |
| 1669 | Oneida | 2,400 | |

Continued on next page

Table C.5 continued

| Year | Group | Tribal Totals | Confederacy Totals |
|---|---|---|---|
| | Cayuga | 2,400 | |
| | Seneca | 12,000 | |
| 1672 | Cayuga | 2,400 | |
| 1673 | Seneca | 9,600 | |
| 1677 | Mohawk | 2,700 | 25,350 |
| | Oneida | 3,000 | |
| | Onondaga | 5,250 | |
| | Cayuga | 2,400 | |
| | Seneca | 12,000 | |
| 1681 | Confederacy | | 23,000 |
| 1682 | Seneca | 18,000* | |
| 1689 | Mohawk | 2,430 | 30,630* |
| | Oneida | 2,700 | |
| | Onondaga | 7,500* | |

Continued on next page

*Table C.5 continued*

| Year | Group | Tribal Totals | Confederacy Totals |
|---|---|---|---|
| | Cayuga | 2,400 | |
| | Seneca | 15,600* | |
| 1691 | Mohawk | 1,170 | |
| 1698 | Mohawk | 990 | 14,590 |
| | Oneida | 1,050 | |
| | Onondaga | 3,750 | |
| | Cayuga | 1,600 | |
| | Seneca | 7,200 | |
| 1710 | Confederacy | | 12,000-13,200 |
| 1712 | Confederacy | | 14,400 |

*These population totals are too high. The number of warriors may have gone up as a result of captives gained in warring and the latter may have led to increased total population, but nothing in the historical record provides justification for such massive overall population increases

# The Statistics of War: Iroquois Hostilities to 1701

Central to the study of the Iroquois wars have been the questions of whom the Iroquois attacked and why. The following table was created in an attempt to answer these and several other questions: who initiated a raid, against whom was it intended, when was it launched, where did the attack take place, and what were the results of these aggressions? In each case, could the cause of the raid be determined, and was it possible to ascertain any relationship between a given raid and Iroquois policy? It was possible to chart answers to all but the last two questions. Nonetheless, it was hoped these more specific questions could help answer the general queries more precisely, while the data generated from the recorded answers to these questions might then allow for a critical assessment of past interpretations of the causes of the wars. The latter have often been based on imprecise answers to the broader questions of whom the Iroquois attacked and why.

### SOURCES

The bulk of information used in compiling the table was taken from the writings of French observers and other French sources. Few colonies in North America, especially in the early period of contact, had as much interaction with Indians as did the French, and fewer still left such detailed records. (That the best sources for writing a history of the Iroquois come from their enemies, and not their allies, is an irony not to be overlooked.) Among the most important documentary sources were the *Jesuit Relations.* While every effort was made to find other sources to corroborate and supply information lacking in the *Relations,* this was not always possible, and the work of the French Jesuits headed the list of primary sources, especially up to 1666. Before this date records of New France's history consist primarily of the *Jesuit Relations* and other—mostly published—memoirs. Many of the latter are wholly or partially based on the *Relations.* Even the French Crown had to rely on published memoirs of French explorers when referring to the early period of New France's history. To bolster some claims of sovereignty over the Iroquois by right of conquest, the Crown had no other reference than Champlain's published journals.[1]

It might be expected that the historical record on the Iroquois would be somewhat more diversified. The area that is now New York State was occupied by the Dutch and later by the English. These two European colonizers came to be, each in their turn, allies of the Iroquois. It would be natural enough to turn to their records for information about the Iroquois and to compensate for the biases present in the French sources. And, indeed, the Dutch colony along the Hudson River at one time had a full documentary record. A fair quantity of data was also left from the period of English occupation. However, the bulk of the material from the period of Dutch occupation, in the form of the Dutch West India Company records, was sold off in the 1850s, possibly even as early as 1674.[2] Many of the documents from both the Dutch and English periods of occupation were also destroyed or damaged by fire. Moreover, much of the Dutch and English material was not based on close personal contacts with, or direct observations of, the Iroquois in their tribal lands. This is the type of material required to answer the questions raised by the patterns present in the *Relations* evidence. In short, there is no Dutch or English equivalent to the *Relations* of the French Jesuits.[3]

The problems presented by this bias in the sources should not be overlooked. It meant that it was possible to formulate a view of Iroquois relations with the French and their allies, but much less so of Iroquois relations with other European and Indian groups—the latter could only be approximated. A reliance on European observers for information also meant that I was confined to examining Iroquois relations with groups that had dealings with some colonial power. Otherwise, records of Iroquois relations with these groups did not survive. Because information was so scarce it was almost impossible to cross-check accounts of events and properly evaluate any emerging patterns. For example, because one could not go much beyond the *Jesuit Relations* as a source before 1666, it was difficult to assess whether a shift in a developing trend was the result of changing Iroquois tactics, or if the authors and editors of the *Relations* simply felt other matters were of greater concern for a given year. Was the noticeable increase in Iroquois raiding in the 1640s a real increase, or were that many raids occurring before that time but only in the 1640s did the Jesuits decide to publicize the fearful impact of the Iroquois? Without independent sources against which to check the *Relations* data, it is impossible to answer these questions. After 1666, the slightly wider range of sources available mitigated this problem somewhat.

Another problem with the sources is their representativeness. The question of representation revolves around two main concerns: how accurately do the historical sources reflect the actual number and range of hostilities engaged in by the Iroquois, and how well does the resulting table reflect the number of raids recorded in those sources? It seems to me next to impossible to fully resolve questions of how well the sources reflect the reality of the period. As noted above, the sources used for this study were limited in terms of origins, and this led to some readily noticeable coloring of results in terms of working out Iroquois relations with some native and European groups. And the problems with the records did not end with bias: years passed without activities being recorded, at times groups appeared and disappeared from the historical record without any indication as to why or how the Iroquois became involved with them, nor how matters were resolved. Even in years for which data were available, it was impossible to conclude that the surviving records had captured the full extent of Iroquois activities for that period. But meager and incomplete as they are, they are all that we have to work with. Unless some huge cache of documents covering the seventeenth century is unearthed, it appears unlikely that these lacunae can be filled, or that we will ever know how well or how poorly the sources presently relied on have served us.

As the preceding implies, I do feel I have been comprehensive in my research. As to how well the table reflects the sources available, I suppose only time and critics will tell. I have tried to read all the sources that might have some bearing on the questions listed at the outset of this section. I have no doubt that some sources were overlooked and that local archival deposits that I was not able to consult may contain material that could serve to illuminate aspects of raids listed here, and may provide evidence of raids that the sources I have consulted omitted deliberately or failed to record. The range of data available from these sources and the extent to which it can alter the information and patterns that this table reveals is, at present, a moot point.

Equally uncertain is the degree of error in the table.[4] Aside from raids that may have been overlooked, how accurately have those entered in the table been recorded? It would be only natural to wonder if some events have been mis-dated. Have accounts that actually refer to two separate raids been mistakenly lumped together to make one raid, or vice versa? The vagueness of some sources make such errors almost inevitable, and some have been detected and corrected. How many more remain uncorrected is anyone's guess. However, I do not consider this table to be a complete and finished product, nor do I intend that it be viewed as such. It is merely in the development stage and it, as well as the conclusions derived from it, can be modified as more research is under-taken.

METHOD

In constructing the table, many subjective decisions had to be made. The first and most obvious was what to include as a raid. Should rumors of raids be noted? What of accounts of raids that were from questionable sources—that is, sources that were known not to have been eyewitnesses to events? It was de-cided not to list passing references to groups going to raid unless it could be con-firmed that the raid was carried out. A band of warriors may have decided to go to war and some omen put a stop to the expedition long before the intended tar-get group was reached. A record of a war party setting off to raid was not suffi-cient evidence that the action was carried out. Since most raids were recorded by other than the actual participants, it would be self-defeating to eliminate all but eyewitness accounts. This did not mean that efforts to corroborate as many accounts as possible could be forsaken, but one would still have to assume that unless the accounts could be proven to be false, they reflected what the observer who left the written record believed to have happened. However, a few known raids were omitted from the table because it was impossible to date their occur-rence and there were not enough other details about the raid. Without a date, sufficient clues to arrive at a probable date, or adequate particulars to match or distinguish one raid from another, it was futile to try to determine whether that raid had already been entered in the table. Rather than run the risk of thus pad-ding the table, it was deemed best not to list such raids. In no instance was a raid rejected for inclusion in the table because the source or the account seemed "unreliable." When the source or the account appeared dubious, for whatever reason, the raid was recorded in the table, and any reservations about the events or the source were noted in the comments.

For those who might wish to check the veracity of the interpretation of the raid, it was decided to list the sources on which the decisions were made. The sources listed after each raid refer to the actual accounts of the raid and to where evidence can be found to justify aspects of my interpretation of the raid—either the time, place, who should be designated aggressor, why a particular group is clearly designated as the target when the actual account does not make it apparent, and so on. If more than one account of a raid was found, it was included in the list of sources. Often the various accounts did not differ in substance, but equally often they provided some significant detail that helped clarify the course of events.

At times it was difficult to determine who the initiating tribe was in accounts of a particular raid. If the Hurons decided to go to war and while en route were attacked by the Iroquois in Huronia, several points are clear: both groups were set on an offensive policy, but the Iroquois deserve aggressor status because to arrive in Huronia they had to have implemented their decision to go to war before the Hurons; at the same time, the Hurons' offensive role should be noted. This type of information, necessary to minimize the distortion that mere listing can produce, is found in the comments. In the Groups Involved column, the group listed first was deemed the aggressor, or more properly, the group initiating the encounter.

The vagueness of some of the sources about dates, locations, target groups, and results of raids meant that far too often it became necessary to determine where raids took place, when, and just what groups were involved. If the sources provided some clues, or logical reasons could be adduced for arriving at some conclusion concerning one or more of these matters, an estimate was made. The reasons for that assessment were then noted in the comments, and whatever clues the estimates were based on were listed with the sources.[5] At times the dates given in the sources reflected when the news of the raid reached the group or observer that left the record of the event, and not when it took place. If grounds existed for estimating when the raid took place, the estimated date was used, and the time the raid was brought to an observer's attention and the reasons for the estimate were noted in the comments. If estimating the actual date of the raid was not possible or proved to be too conjectural, the time that the raid was recorded was used, and this fact was noted in the column.

All numbers of killed, wounded, captured, and the size of groups involved are as given in the sources. Those numbers range from wild speculation to informed estimates. Where numbers differed in various accounts, the range of numbers was used. If the sources were clear about how many people were in the target group, that number was used. It was not assumed that the number reported as captured or killed during any encounter reflected the total size of the target group. Because two Hurons were caught was not reason enough to conclude that only two were targeted. There may have been forty Hurons in the group, only two caught, while the rest escaped.

Wherever my estimates are included in the table, they are enclosed in brackets. This included any part of a date that was not clearly specified in the account of a raid and/or tribal names. If the sources used an obscure form of a tribal name, the modern name was used and placed in brackets. Where a tribal name used in a document did not correspond clearly to any known tribe, the original name, as spelled in the source, was used and the possible modern corollary was put in brackets. Any blank spaces in any column mean that more details were not available.

The purpose of creating this table was to see if by listing all Iroquois raids data could be generated that would help explain aspects of Iroquois-native and Iroquois-European relations. In arriving at some of that numerical data—used throughout the book—certain decisions were made when faced with vague terms. Expressions such as "some" or "several" were taken to mean at least two people. Thus "some killed" would add two deaths to the total number of people killed by the Iroquois. At times the size of the attacked group was recorded but the source did not provide precise numbers of captured or killed. In such instances the source might have indicated that "half," "most," or "almost all" were killed. If this was the case the numerical equivalent could be determined. Thus if the group was 100 strong and "half" were killed, that would equal 50 deaths. If the record indicated "most" were killed, half plus one was used and the figure was put at 51 dead. If "almost" all were said to have been captured, a range was used; in this same example that would mean 90–100 captured. When assessing the number of raids undertaken in a year or decade by the Iroquois, raids that may have occurred in the winter of one year or the spring of the next were attributed to the first year in which they might have happened. A raid recorded as having taken place in the winter of 1663 or spring of 1664 was counted as a 1663 raid.

ABBREVIATIONS

| C | child |
| capt. | captured |

| F | female |
| fc | female child |
| FIA | French Indian allies |
| Fr | French |
| Ft Rich | Fort Richelieu |
| K | killed |
| L | league |
| lost | lost (either captured or killed) |
| LSP | Lac Ste. Pierre |
| M | male |
| mc | male child |
| Mont | Montreal Island |
| Mont Ft | Montreal Fort, Ville Marie |
| Ott R. | Ottawa River |
| Que | Quebec (area) |
| Rich R. | Richelieu River |
| Sag | Saguenay River |
| St. Law | St. Lawrence River |
| Tad | Tadoussac (area) |
| TR | Trois Rivières (area) |
| TR Ft | Trois Rivières, fort |

*Native Groups*

| Abnk | Abenakis, unspecified tribe |
| Algk | Algonquins, unspecified tribe |
| Cay | Cayugas |
| Huron | Hurons, unspecified tribe |
| Ill | Illinois, unspecified tribe |
| Iroq | Iroquois, unspecified tribe of Confederacy |
| Mah | Mahicans |
| Moh | Mohawks |
| Mt | Montagnais, unspecified tribe |
| Nip | Nipissings |
| On | Oneidas |
| Onon | Onondagas |
| Ot | Ottawas, unspecified tribe |
| Pisct | Piscataways |

Sen      Senecas

Shaw     Shawnee

Susq     Susquehannocks

For a full listing of the tribes in the Northeast, their linguistic affiliations, and their geographic locations over time, see Heidenreich, in Harris, ed., *Historical Atlas of Canada,* plates 18, 37, 38, 39.

Iroquois Hostilities to 1701

| Date | Groups Involved | Results | Location | Comments | Sources |
|---|---|---|---|---|---|
| 27 May 1603 | 1,000 Mt, Algk, & Etechemins vs. Iroq [Moh?] | 100 Iroq scalped [K?] | Mouth of Rich R. | Raid was earlier. This was the celebration of success. Champlain gives impression raid was recent. | Champlain, *Works* 1:103 |
| 29 July 1609 | 60-100 Huron, Algk, & Champlain vs. 200 Iroq [Moh] | 10-12 Iroq capt., 50 beheaded [scalped or K?] | Lake Champlain | | Champlain, *Works* 2:67-101; *MNF* 1:91 |
| June 1610 | Algk, Mt, & Champlain vs. 100 Iroq | 15 Iroq capt. | [Mouth of Rich R.] | Champlain was awaiting Huron with Mt to attack Iroq when news arrived that Algk had surprised Iroq. Champlain and Mt proceeded to battle. Huron arrived too late. | Champlain, *Works* 2:125-38 |
| 9-16 Oct 1615 | Champlain, at least 200 Huron vs. Iroq [On or Onon] | 4 Iroq M, 3 F, 1 mc, 3 fc capt., unspec. no. K; 20 Fr & Huron wounded, one of whom died | Iroquoia, at village of target group | Capt. Iroq were on way to fishing spot, one of captives was Algk captured previously. Much killing took place, but no numbers given, nor which side suffered most. Susq were to be part of raid but did not arrive in time. | Champlain, *Works* 3:64-78; *JR* 18:219 |
| [Oct to Nov] 1615 | Fr & Huron vs. Iroq | 4 Iroq [M] K, 2 capt | | Étienne Brulé and some Huron on way to Susq to ask for aid in Fr & Huron raid vs. Iroq when ran into Iroq. | Champlain, *Works* 3:53-54, 58, 78, 215-17 |

Continued on next page

| Date | Groups Involved | Results | Location | Comments | Sources |
|---|---|---|---|---|---|
| [Spring] 1616 | Iroq vs. ? | É. Brulé capt. | | Brulé was returning from wintering amongst Susq when he ran into Iroq war party. Iroq target group unknown. Brulé escaped first group, but in escape efforts ran into other Iroq. Suffered minor tortures & released. | Champlain, *Works* 3:217-24 |
| [Fall 1623] | Huron [Bear tribe] vs. [Iroq] | 60 Iroq K | Frontiers of enemy | Some killed on spot, others brought back to Huronia, tortured and K. Sources speak of enemy and Neutral are mentioned, but gives clear impression that war had yet to break out. | Sagard, *Long Journey,* 151, 152, 157 |
| July 1626 | Mah & Dutch vs. Moh | 4 Dutch M & 24 Mah M K | 1 L from Ft Orange | Mah asked for Dutch help. Group was surprised by Moh who apparently anticipated the attack or spotted the approaching attackers. | *NNN,* 84; Champlain, *Works* 5:208-9, 214 |
| 1626 | Mah vs. Moh | Moh abandon village | | Writing in 1635 Bogaert reported that his Moh guide pointed out a village site abandoned 9 years previously when the Mah forced them out. This would put the attack(s) in 1626. It may have been revenge for the above incident. The village seems to have been located close to the Hudson. | *NNN,* 157 |

Continued on next page

| Date | Groups Involved | Results | Location | Comments | Sources |
|---|---|---|---|---|---|
| June 1627 | Mt vs. Iroq [Moh] | 3 Iroq capt. | Mouth of Rich R. | Mt envoys to apologize for errors of youth. Envoys were K. | Champlain, *Works* 5:224, 229-31 |
| [Spring] 1628 | Mah vs. Moh | Mah defeated and abandon lands | Albany area | Sources imply the Mah are the aggressors. | *NNN*, 89; *Van Rensselaer-Bowier Manuscripts*, 306 |
| Fall 1631 | Iroq [Moh] vs. Algk | 1 Algk [M] K, several F & C capt. | | Captives were later returned. | Champlain, *Works* 6:3 |
| [Mid-May] 1632 | Que Algk & Mt of Tad vs. Moh | 9 Iroq capt., 1 Iroq M, & 7 F K | Moh village | News of raid rec'd 6 June. Raid probably carried out in May. Prisoners tortured to death–6 at Que, 2 at Tad. One child was spared by Tad area Mt. | Champlain, *Works* 6:4; *JR* 5:21, 27, 29, 45, 49 |
| 2 June 1633 | 28-40 Moh vs. Fr | 2-3 Fr. M K | St. Law, near TR | Iroq surprised Fr towing a boat against the current. Iroq scalped dead and fled at sight of armed Fr reinforcements. | *JR* 5:213-15, 251; *JR* 21:21; Sagard, *Long Journey*, 262 |
| 24 Oct 1633 | Algk vs. Iroq | 1 Algk [M] K, & 1 capt. | | | *JR* 5:93 |
| [Spring] 1634 | 1,500 Sen vs. 500 Huron | 200 Huron [M] K, 100 capt. | [South of Huronia] | Huron had planned to attack, but Sen learned of it and struck first as Huron traveled south. | *JR* 6:145; 7:213-15; 8:69, 115, 149 |

Continued on next page

| Date | Groups Involved | Results | Location | Comments | Sources |
|---|---|---|---|---|---|
| [July] 1635 | Iroq vs. Algk (Petite Nation) | 7 canoes[ful]] of Petite Nation destroyed [21 K ?] | | News was rec'd 10 Aug from TR. Raid must have taken place earlier, but not clear when. | JR 8:59; 9:227 |
| [Early Oct] 1635 | 20 Indians of TR [Mt] vs. Iroq | 1 Iroq capt. | | Group returned 23 Oct. Raid took place earlier in month. | JR 8:23 |
| [1634-35] | Iroq vs. Algk [of Allumette Island] | 23 Algk K | | 28 March Algk are reported among Huron seeking aid vs. Iroq for the massacre of 23 of their people since the peace [of 1634?] | JR 10:75-77 |
| 13 June 1636 | Iroq vs. Huron | 12 Huron [M] K | Near village of Contarea | Group of Huron warriors heading south to attack the Iroq were surprised in their camp outside the village. Not clear if they were of that village. Rest of Huron escaped. | JR 10:83, 95 |
| [late July] 1636 | 100 Mt of Tad vs. Iroq | 28 Iroq M, F, C, capt. & K | Fishing spot near Iroq village | Mt caught 2 Iroq who led warriors to fishing spot to spare their own lives. Mt surprised group of Iroq, K some on spot, others on return trip. Indians above TR [Mt] got 2 Iroq M & 1 fc to torture. Indians of Que [Mt] got 1 Iroq M & 1 F. | JR 9:235-37, 251-55 |
| 14 Aug 1636 | Petite Nation Algk vs. Moh | 1 Moh capt. and tortured [to death] | | Jesuits passing via village note the torture. | JR 9:65; 13:83 |

Continued on next page

| Date | Groups Involved | Results | Location | Comments | Sources |
|------|----------------|---------|----------|----------|---------|
| 24 Aug 1636 | Moh vs. English | Some English K | Connecticut | | *Winthrop Papers* 3:318 |
| 2 Sept 1636 | Huron (Rock, Cord, & Bear) vs. Onon | 7 Onon capt., 1 K | Fishing spot, [S. Shore] Lake Ontario | Huron attacked 25-30 fishing Onon. Prisoners were divided among tribes that had participated in raid. The victors arrived 2 Sept. Raid was likely in mid-August. | *JR* 13:37, 45 |
| [Early May] 1637 | Mt & Algk vs. Iroq [Moh] | Mt & Algk captains K, unspec. others capt. & K | Field outside Iroq village | Left to raid 24 April, so raid must have been in May. Route was down Rich R. and Lake Champlain area, so probably vs. Moh. Attackers chased 1 Iroq into a group clearing fields & were overwhelmed. | *JR* 12:153, 155-59 |
| 27 June 1637 | Iroquet vs. Iroq | 13 Iroq capt. | | News rec'd 27 June. Algk outnumbered Iroq. Iroq were all tortured [to death?]. One Iroq captive was sent TR to [Mt]. Those who had lost relatives to Iroq in Mt raid of April 24 were particularly vicious. | *JR* 12:181-83 |
| 1 July 1637 | Moh & Pequot vs. English & Indians | Some K | Connecticut | Moh are also said to "trouble" the Narragansett Indians. | *Winthrop Papers* 3:438 |

Continued on next page

| Date | Groups Involved | Results | Location | Comments | Sources |
|------|----------------|---------|----------|----------|---------|
| 6-11 Aug 1637 | 500 Iroq vs. Huron [& Fr ?] | 30 Huron capt., 1 K | TR & LSP | Iroq appeared before fort and tried to lure Fr and Indians out to fight. Had blockaded western end of LSP. Caught Huron, mostly traders, as returned to Huronia. Some were youths headed for the Que seminary. Huron goods probably taken. Either because met objectives or because of fear of Fr reinforcements, Iroq withdrew. | *JR* 12:99, 101, 199-215 |
| [1637? to] before fall 1638 | Iroq vs. Wenro | 600 Wenro abandon lands and relocate to Huronia | | Wenro arrive among Huron of Ossossane around fall 1638. Withdrawal of Neutral support left them vulnerable to Iroq attacks. Not clear when Iroq began attacking, but probably by 1637. | *JR* 15:159; 16:253; 17:25-29 |
| [Fall 1638 to spring 1639] | Iroq vs. Algk | Algk were defeated | TR | Very confused chronology of events because dating is speculative and all information is very vague. | *JR* 16:41, 51, 65, 213 |

Continued on next page

| Date | Groups Involved | Results | Location | Comments | Sources |
|---|---|---|---|---|---|
| [Fall 1638 to before] 4-5 Dec | 300 Huron & Algk vs. 100 Iroq [On?] | 80 Iroq capt. | [Iroquoia] | Huron and Algk scouts capt. by Iroq lied about size of their force, led Iroq to fight. Iroq were outnumbered. 17-18 K, some escaped, at least 3 were tortured to death at Huron (Deer) village. Raid may have been against the Oneida; at least one prisoner was said to be of that tribe. But raid was clearly against one of "upper" Iroq. | *JR* 15:171, 173; 17:63, 65, 71-77 |
| 27 May 1639 | Huron (Bear) vs. [Seneca] | 12 Sen capt., most K | | Prisoners arrived in village this day, raid was earlier. In 1638 a Huron had killed a Sen [during above raid?]. Rather than atone for this, a general war had been decided on. | *JR* 15:185, 187; 17:105, 111 |
| [Summer] 1639 | [Iroq] vs. Huron | 4-5 Huron K | Huronia, fishing spot, near Bear village of St. Xavier | Were attacked as fished. 3-4 Huron K on the spot, one died of wounds later. | *JR* 18:27; 19:223-27 |
| [Late April] 1640 | Huron [Bear] vs. [Iroq] | 1 Iroq capt., tortured & K | | Date is of arrival of prisoner at the Huron village. | *JR* 18:29 |
| [Summer] 1640 | Huron vs. Iroq | Huron defeated, unspecified number K | | Huron on way to attack Iroq were ambushed by Iroq. Some Huron stayed to cover retreat of others and were K. | *JR* 18:43-45 |

*Continued on next page*

| Date | Groups Involved | Results | Location | Comments | Sources |
|------|-----------------|---------|----------|----------|---------|
| [Summer] 1640 | Huron [Cord] vs. Iroq | 1 Iroq capt. & tortured [to death] | | | JR 21:169 |
| 2 Aug 1640 | [Sen] Iroq vs. Huron | 1 Huron scalped & K | Huronia, 3 L from St. Marie | One of Jesuits most faithful converts was attacked by Iroq as he was working in his fields. | JR 20:79, 81; 21:211 |
| Late 1640 | [Iroq] vs. [Petun] | Village of Ehwae destroyed, many taken capt. | [Perth County Ont.] | Greater part of cabins burned. Many also died of smallpox. | JR 21:181 |
| [Late fall 1640 to spring 1641] | Algk [Allumette], Petite Nat., & Mt vs. Iroq | Defeated by Iroq | LSP | Attacking group was discovered and ambushed by Iroq who were on the lake. | JR 20:167-69 |
| [Late winter 1640 to early spring] 1641 | [Iroq] vs. Huron | 1 Huron mc K | Huronia | Huron boy K while in his mother's arms. | JR 21:235 |
| 20 Feb 1641 | [60] Iroq (Moh) vs. Fr | 2 Fr M capt. | TR | 90 Iroq had set out, 30 went to Mont area, rest to Tr. The 2 Fr M were returned 5 June 1641 by Moh and were apparently capt. as means to initiate talks with the Fr. | JR 21:23, 25, 27, 35, 37, 45 |

Continued on next page

| Date | Groups Involved | Results | Location | Comments | Sources |
|------|-----------------|---------|----------|----------|---------|
| [Early June] 1641 | Iroq [Moh] vs. 3 Algk | 1 Algk F & 1 M K, 1 Algk M escaped | TR | Iroq were part of a group of 350 mostly or all Moh that had arrived June 5 to return Fr capt. Attacked 3 Algk in their canoe as awaited Fr governor to begin talks. | JR 21:41 |
| [Mid-June to mid-Sept] 1641 | Algk vs. Iroq [Moh] | Many Iroq F & C K; 5-6 Algk [M] capt. or K | Iroq village | Algk set out to avenge above loss. Moh as target based on this. Gained Iroq village, lost 5-6 (must have been males) during retreat and pursuit by Iroq. Date based on time of initial Iroq attack (June) and date news reported (Sept. 16). | Correspondance, 143-44 |
| Summer [1641] | Huron (Arrendaronnon) vs. Iroq | Huron defeated, one war captain K | | Huron raid was led by Atironta and his brother Aeotahon. Atironta was K, and Aeotahon took his name. | JR 23:159, 167 |
| Summer [1641] | Huron (Cord) vs. Iroq | At least 1 Iroq K, unspecified number also K, some capt. | [Lake Ontario] | Huron led by Ahatsiscari. Both groups were warriors, but Huron get initiating status because to arrive at "great lake which separates the Hurons from their Enemies" they had to have undertaken their journey first. | JR 23:25, 27, 33 |
| [Late summer to fall 1641] | 50 Huron (Cord) vs. 300 Iroq | Some Iroq capt. | | The 50 Huron were again being led by Ahatsiscari when encountered Iroq on way to attack. Ahatsiscari attacked Iroq. Boldness of this move put Iroq to flight. | JR 23:25 |

Continued on next page

| Date | Groups Involved | Results | Location | Comments | Sources |
|---|---|---|---|---|---|
| [Winter 1641 to 1642] | Iroq [Moh] vs. Algk | Many M & older F K, 30 younger F spared | "Island" far into Algk lands [Manitoulin?] | Iroq were part of a group 200 strong that had split up. Started out in fall, followed Algk that had abandoned TR area to avoid Iroq attacks. After raid questioned captives about results of raid "last year" with Fr at TR. This would indicate that this raid was carried out very close to start of 1642. Moh identified based on reference to skirmishing between themselves and Fr at TR. Moh were clearly the group at TR in June 1641. | *JR* 22:43, 51, 129, 249, 251, 253, 265 |
| Spring 1642 | Iroq [Moh] vs. Iroquet | Some Iroquet K, 2 families capt. | | Moh designated because prisoners made by Moh in above raid were brought along by this group, part of 300 who had set off in spring to war, as baggage carriers. That would indicate these Iroq were Moh as well. | *JR* 22:267, 269 |
| Spring 1642 | Iroquet vs. Iroq [Moh] | Some Iroq K, their baggage taken | [Iroq territory] | A "score" of Iroquet and some converts from TR set off to avenge above raid. Some of the attackers returned, but those that carried on found some Iroq and attacked them. Moh identified because it was assumed Iroquet were attacking those that had attacked them. | *JR* 22:53, 55; 24:249, 253 |

Continued on next page

| Date | Groups Involved | Results | Location | Comments | Sources |
|------|-----------------|---------|----------|----------|---------|
| [June 1641 to June 1642] | | | | Apparently many raids between the Iroq and the Huron were carried out between June 1641 and June 1642, but went unrecorded. Writing around 10 June, 1642, when he finished the Huron Report, Father Lalemant informed Father Vimont that several expeditions were raised to go fight the Iroq, but disunity, defeat in battles, and ambushes have meant that "nearly all...have ended only in disaster." The Iroq, meanwhile, "have everywhere and at almost all seasons of the Year committed massacres." The available data for this time frame did not reflect that activity. | JR 22:305 |
| [Summer, after 10 June, 1642] | Iroq vs. Huron village | All Huron destroyed [capt. or K], except a "score" [20] | Huron "Frontier" village [Arendaronnon?] | Date is based on Lalemant's June 1643 observation that raid took place shortly after he finished previous year's relation 10 June 1642. | JR 26:175 |
| [Summer, after 10 June, 1642] | Huron vs. Iroq | Huron defeated | | Raid said to have occurred about same time as above one. Huron outnumbered Iroq 6 to 1. | JR 26:175, 179 |

Continued on next page

| Date | Groups Involved | Results | Location | Comments | Sources |
|------|-----------------|---------|----------|----------|---------|
| Summer [1642] | 2 Iroq vs. 2 Huron F | Huron F scalped and later died | Field outside village | Of all the small attacks that took place this summer, this was the only one recorded. | JR 26:225 |
| Summer [1642] | | | | Throughout this summer the Iroq continued to attack the Huron. The only one of these small raids recorded was that noted above. The toll exacted by the Iroq in these raids went unremarked. The Huron, however, managed to capt. 2 Iroq. | JR 26:179 |
| 2 Aug 1642 | 30 Iroq vs. 3 Fr & 40 Huron | 3 Fr M capt., 19 Huron capt. & 3 K; 1 Iroq M K | 15 L from TR [St. Law, past LSP] | This was the raid in which Father Jogues was capt. The Iroq was K by one of the French who in turn was capt. The Iroq took the supplies being carried up to the Jesuits in Huronia. The rest of the Huron escaped. | JR 22:269; 31:21, 23, 31-37; Correspondance, 167; NNN, 175; Van Rensselaer Bowier Manuscripts, 625 |
| [2 Aug 1642] | Iroq [Moh] vs. 11 canoes of Huron traders | 4 Huron capt. | Island, 50-60 L above Mont [Alumettes or Calumet Islands, Ott R.?] | This raid was said to have occurred at the same time as above one. Moh identified based on Jogues meeting these 4 capt. among the Moh. The Huron were attacked while stopped to hunt on the Island. Iroq capt. some who were hunting. No mention of furs being taken. | JR 22:273; 26:195 |

Continued on next page

| Date | Groups Involved | Results | Location | Comments | Sources |
|------|-----------------|---------|----------|----------|---------|
| 20 Aug 1642 | 200-300 Iroq [Moh] vs. Fr | 1 Fr M K, 4 wounded; 5 Iroq [M] K, some wounded | Ft Rich | The Iroq attacked as Fr were building the fort. Jogues, who met the attacking group as he was being taken to the Moh, put the size of army at 200. Others at the fort made it out to be 300 strong. The Iroq may have picked up more people between the time Jogues saw them and the actual attack. | JR 22:277, 279; 24:23, 281; 25:69; 28:123; 31:31 |
| Fall [1642] | 20 Iroq vs. 40 Huron (Cord) | Several Huron K, at least 1 was M | Near village of Teanaustaye | Huron gathering hemp at night were attacked by Iroq. | JR 23:241; 26:203, 205 |
| [Oct 1642 to Mar 1643] | Moh vs. Abnk | 20 Abnk capt., unspecified number tortured & K | | Date based on arrival of group in Mar, 6 months after they had left to war | JR 31:85, 87 |
| [March] 1643 | 24 Algk (some Alumette & Petite Nation) vs. Iroq [Moh] | 4 Algk capt. or K, some wounded; 1 Iroq K | Up Rich R. [Iroq territory] | Moh identified based on fact that raiders went down the Rich R. to attack. Date based on late Feb gathering to start and return of Algk in Apr. The Algk split up into two groups, one of 15 and the other of 9. Losses are for larger group. No details for group of 9, except that it was one of their number that K Iroq. | JR 24:205, 207, 231, 233, 255, 259, 261 |

Continued on next page

| Date | Groups Involved | Results | Location | Comments | Sources |
|---|---|---|---|---|---|
| 9 May 1643 | 19 Iroq vs. 8 Algk traders | 2 Algk K, 6 capt. & 2 pelt-laden canoes taken | 4 L from TR | Algk were returning from Huronia. | JR 24:273, 275 |
| 9 June 1643 | 40 Iroq [Moh] vs. 60 Huron traders (11-13 canoes) | 23 Huron capt., 13 later K, Iroq took furs | Mont, half a L from Ft | Moh identified because Iroq bragged they had other Fr captives. Only Iroq group known to have Fr prisoners were Moh. The Iroq were on the Island waiting for Fr or Huron. (See raid below.) Iroq left over 30 beaver robes behind. When Maisonneuve learned of this, he sent his men out to claim them as booty. | JR 23:247, 249, 267; 24:275, 277, 279; Dollier, Histoire, 109, 111 |
| 9 June 1643 | 30 Iroq [Moh] vs. 5-6 Fr | 3 Fr K, 2-3 capt. | Mont Ft | Iroq were part of above group & attack took place same day. 10 Iroq stayed with Huron capt. 20 Iroq went to front of fort to draw Fr attention while 10 Iroq attacked those Fr working in nearby fields. It was from the escaped Fr that Maisonneuve learned about abandoned furs. (See above.) | JR 23:247, 249, 267; 24:275, 277, 279; Dollier, Histoire, 109, 111 |
| 30 July 1643 | 2 canoes of Iroq (one with 12 M) vs. 7 Algk | 2 Iroq fatally wounded; 1 Algk wounded | Near Mont | Algk setting out to hunt. Both sides exchanged fire and Iroq withdrew. | JR 24:289, 291 |

Continued on next page

| Date | Groups Involved | Results | Location | Comments | Sources |
|---|---|---|---|---|---|
| [Late July to early Aug] 1643 | Iroq vs. 120 Huron | Over 20 Huron capt. or K | After a journey of 100 L, near huge waterfall [Rideau Falls?] | The date is based on arrival of survivors in Huronia in early Aug. The group of Huron, if not traders, were carrying supplies. In eagerness to escape they left them behind and Iroq took them. The same group of Huron was attacked twice on this trip; once at the falls, and few days previous. It seems the attacks were by same Iroq. | JR 26:183, 235, 237 |
| Summer [1643] | Over 100 Huron vs. 700-800 Iroq | Over 100 Huron capt. or K | Frontiers of Iroquoia | The Huron, 100 Christian converts and some "pagan" Huron, went to lay ambushes against Iroq. Not clear which group attacked nor how battle started, but after a long fight, the Huron were defeated. | JR 28:45 |
| 15 Aug 1643 | 20 Iroq vs. 12 Algk | 3 Algk & 1 Huron capt., 1 tortured to death, 2 escaped; K & wounded on both sides | St. François River | Algk were hunting. Both sides had guns. | JR 24:291 |

Continued on next page

| Date | Groups Involved | Results | Location | Comments | Sources |
|---|---|---|---|---|---|
| [15 Sept] 1643 | Iroq vs. Huron | 9 Huron K, many more wounded | | Writing 30 Sept, Marie de l'Incarnation stated the raid had taken place 15 days prior. The Huron were carrying supplies to the Jesuits in Huronia. Brébeuf claimed that the supplies were lost. It is assumed that means the Iroq took them. | JR 23:251, 269; Correspondance, 201 |
| [1643] | | | | Writing in March 1644, and summing up the impact of the Iroq on the Hurons in 1643, Father Lalemant noted that they had closed up the route to the French and defeated those who had attempted passage of it. Huron efforts to pursue Iroq attackers in Huronia had also ended in defeat. The data for this year seems to reflect accurately that general assessment. What is not reflected is information to flesh out his observation that "Nearly everyday, unfortunate women were killed in their fields," and that "captives were taken by [the] hundreds" from Huronia. | JR 27:63-65 |

Continued on next page

| Date | Groups Involved | Results | Location | Comments | Sources |
|------|-----------------|---------|----------|----------|---------|
| 30 March 1644 | 80 Iroq vs. 30 Fr | Some Iroq K, some wounded; 3 Fr K, 2 capt. & later tortured to death | Mont Ft | Fr attacked what they thought was small group of Iroq that had come to raid in area. Dollier claims Iroq group was 200 strong, but he was writing years after. The Jesuit data was used here. | JR 26:35-37; Dollier, Histoire, 117-21 |
| [March to April 1644] | 40 Iroq vs. Algk | All the Algk capt., most later K at Iroq village | Rivière-des-Prairies | News reported by Huron who escaped from Iroq that capt. Father Bressani. This raid, then, must have occurred before the end of April. | JR 26:37 |
| [28-30] Apr 1644 | 30 Iroq vs. 1 Fr M, 1 Fr mc, 6 Huron converts | 1 Fr M, 1 Fr mc & 5 Huron capt, 1 later escaped, 1 Huron K | Marguerie River | Father Bressani, a young boy going to serve as an assistant, and the Huron converts were returning to Huronia when attacked. The Iroq took the goods that were being carried up to the Jesuits in Huronia. | JR 25:193; 26:21, 29, 31, 33 |
| June 1644 | Iroq vs. 16-18 Huron | 16-18 Huron capt. | | Some or all of these Huron were released or escaped as a result of a Huron raid. See raid below. | JR 26:37; ASJCF, No. 826-8 |

Continued on next page

| Date | Groups Involved | Results | Location | Comments | Sources |
|------|----------------|---------|----------|----------|---------|
| [July] 1644 | Huron & Algk vs. Iroq [Moh] | 3 Iroq capt. | Ft Rich area | Group returned from raid 26 July 1644. 60 Huron had come to attack Iroq. Did not meet any before they got to TR. They learned of Iroq in area and, accompanied by some Algk, went to raid. An offshoot of this group struck against 10 Iroq that had set out to ambush Fr near the Ft. As a result of either this attack or of the general movements of the larger Huron and Algk group, some Hurons capt. in June were released, or escaped to this group, probably the latter. The Algk gave their prisoner to Fr. In 1645 he was sent to Moh to intiate peace talks. Iroq identified as Moh based on this. | JR 26:53-57; 27:245; ASJCF, No. 826-8 |
| Summer [1644] | Iroq vs. 2 canoes of Huron converts | 2 Huron K | | Most of the Huron escaped. Of those capt., two were K when arrived at Iroq villages. | ASJCF, Recueil du lettres du P. Charles Garnier, No. 95 |
| End of summer [1644] | Iroq vs. Huron | 1 Huron K | La Conception | The Huron was a Christian convert. | ASJCF, Recueil du lettres du P. Charles Garnier, No. 95 |

Continued on next page

| Date | Groups Involved | Results | Location | Comments | Sources |
|------|-----------------|---------|----------|----------|---------|
| 14 Sept 1644 | 4-5 Iroq vs. 1 Fr M | 1 Fr M wounded | Ft Rich | Soldier was attacked as he worked in a field near the fort. | JR 27:221 |
| [Mid to late Sept] 1644 | Iroq vs. Huron | 10-12 Huron capt. | Rich R. | The raid was said to have taken place shortly after that of Sept 14. | JR 27:223 |
| 7 Nov 1644 | Iroq vs. 1 Fr M | 1 Fr M K | Ft Rich | The soldier was K after having strayed ahead of his small hunting party. | JR 27:223-25 |
| 12 Dec 1644 | Iroq vs. 7 Fr M | 1 Fr M scalped, but he lived | Ft Rich | Soldiers were attacked when went out to gather hemp. | JR 27:225 |
| Beginning of spring [1645] | Iroq vs. Huron F | Huron F all capt. | Near Huron frontier village | The women were going to work in the fields when were attacked by unspecified number of Iroq. 200 Huron gave chase to no avail. | JR 29:240 |
| April 1645 | 7 Algk vs. 14 Iroq [Moh] | 9-11 Iroq K, 1 drowned, 1-2 escaped, 2 capt. | Island, Lake Champlain | Algk also took the Iroq guns. Iroq are identified as Moh because these captives were used to bring Moh to peace talks later that year. Marie de Incarnation stated that 9 Iroq were K, 1 drowned, 2 escaped & 2 were capt. | JR 27:229-31, 237; Correspondance, 250 |

Continued on next page

| Date | Groups Involved | Results | Location | Comments | Sources |
|------|----------------|---------|----------|----------|---------|
| End of summer [1645] | Iroq vs. Huron | Huron defeated, some K | | Iroq & Huron ran into each other in woods. Iroq managed to convince Huron that they wanted a peaceful resolution. When most Huron had withdrawn, the Iroq attacked. Unspecified number of Huron K. It seems clear both groups were war parties, but Iroq initiated the attack. | JR 29:249-51 |
| 29 Oct 1645 | 7 Oneida vs. Algk | Some Algk K | Mont | The news was received this day. At first Moh were suspected, but it was later confirmed to have been the On. | JR 27:99-101; 28:281; Correspondance, 280 |
| [1645] | Iroq vs. 2 Huron M | 2 Huron M K | St. Joseph [Cord village] | Iroq attacked two guards of the village. The Huron avenged this raid by an attack vs. the Sen, which may indicate that the Iroq were Sen. See raid below. This and the raid below took place some time in 1645. Both were noted as among the more memorable raids of the year. Others occurred, but went unrecorded. | JR 29:253, 255 |
| [1645] | Huron (Cord) vs. Sen | 2 Sen M K | Sen village | In reprisal for the above attack the Huron attacked 2 Sen M while they slept in their longhouse and set the house on fire before making a successful escape. | JR 29:253, 255 |

Continued on next page

| Date | Groups Involved | Results | Location | Comments | Sources |
|---|---|---|---|---|---|
| Spring [after May] 1646 | Iroq [Onon & On] vs. Huron | Huron village nearly destroyed | Huron village | The attack must have been after May because the Huron Relation for 1645-46 was sent in May and made no mention of this event. Two separate references point to the Onon and On as the attackers, but neither is conclusive. | JR 29:59, 147, 149 |
| 15 Aug 1646 | 17 On vs. Algk | 1 Algk M K, 2 F capt. | Above "Long Sault" [Ott R.] | News received about this date. The capt. were released as a result of the raid below. | JR 28:225; 29:149 |
| [After 15 Aug 1646] | 30 Huron vs. 17 On | 1 On M capt. | | As On returned with their two capt. they ran into Huron warriors. Both groups resolved to fight, but fled after war shouts convinced each that the other group was larger. Algk F were let go. One of them met and explained to Huron the size of On group. Huron then set out to round up On. Managed to capt 1 M. | JR 28:225; 29:229, 231, 233 |
| [After 22 Sept 1646] | Iroq vs. Huron | At least 1 Huron M capt. | "great lake" | Canoe of Hurons, part of returning fur brigade, broke off from main group to go via the "great lake" and were attacked. 2 Huron escaped. | JR 28:231 |

Continued on next page

| Date | Groups Involved | Results | Location | Comments | Sources |
|---|---|---|---|---|---|
| Around 17 Nov 1646 | Iroq vs. Huron | 4 Huron capt. | Mont area | Three Huron reported 17 Nov that one of their group had been capt. They were capt. a few days after when they went in search of their capt. companion. | JR 30:229-31; Correspondance, 325; Dollier, Histoire, 135 |
| 30 Nov 1646 | Iroq vs. Fr | 2 Fr M capt. | Mont | Fr were capt. not far from the settlement. | JR 30:231; Correspondance, 325; Dollier, Histoire, 135 |
| Beginning of winter [Jan-Feb] 1647 | Onon vs. Huron | Some Iroq K, some capt. | Huron frontiers | The Onon were spotted, pursued, and defeated. The saving of one Onon leader led to peace talks between the two groups. | JR 33:117 |
| 5 Mar 1647 | Moh vs. Algk (Petite Nation) | 2 Iroq M K; 80-100 Algk M, F, & C capt., at least 3 Algk M K along with old and weak of both sexes | TR | Moh, accompanied by some On, capt. 2 Algk M and 2 F. From these they learned the locations of the larger band that was hunting on the north & south shores of St Law around TR and attacked them. Most older M were later distributed to other Iroq tribes to be tortured and K. | JR 30:161, 231-45; Correspondance, 325-27; Dollier, Histoire, 135 |
| 6 March 1647 | Iroq vs. Fr | 2 Fr houses robbed of clothing, blankets, powder, lead, & guns | Near TR | The houses were robbed as inhabitants attended Ash Wednesday services. | JR 30:161; Correspondance, 325; Dollier, Histoire, 135 |

Continued on next page

| Date | Groups Involved | Results | Location | Comments | Sources |
|---|---|---|---|---|---|
| [Around 20 May 1647] | FIA & 5-6 Fr vs Iroq | 2 Huron capt. & 1 K | "faverel" River LSP | FIA, Christian converts from St. Joseph mission, and Fr set out to prowl St. Law for Iroq. The 2 Huron were in a canoe too far ahead of main body, and were attacked. Iroq later retreated in the face of superior odds, but not before shooting a Huron who had gone to scout their camp. | JR 30:173; 31:173, 175 |
| [Spring-summer 1647] | Iroq vs. Algk | 40 Algk capt., 3 K & furs taken | "Island" [Manitoulin] | Algk from various tribes were capt. on an island as they awaited the Huron to go with them to trade. Iroq were led to spot by former Huron. One eyewitness said Iroq did not pursue more captives because they were greedy to take the furs. But 40 capt. may have been enough; besides, more captives would have meant more carriers for the furs. | JR 30:287-89 |
| June 1647 | 7-8 Algk (some of Petite Nation) vs. Iroq | 10 Iroq K; 10 Algk capt. released | | Algk heading to "Island" to warn others of the major defeat of Algk at TR spotted above Iroq group. He returned at night with more men and K 10 Iroq and freed 10 Algk captives. Algk, being unable to carry away furs abandoned by Iroq, threw them into the water. | JR 30:283-89, Correspondance, 330-31 |

Continued on next page

| Date | Groups Involved | Results | Location | Comments | Sources |
|------|----------------|---------|----------|----------|---------|
| Summer [1647] | 300 Sen vs. Neutral (Aondironnon) | Many Neutral K & many more capt. | Neutral village near Huronia | | JR 33:81 |
| End of summer [1647] | Iroq vs. Christian Huron | 4-5 Huron K, 7 Huron M, F, & C capt.; 2 Iroq capt. | "lonely island" [L Huron] | The Huron had gone to fish. An escapee went for help. The Iroq were pursued, 2 capt., and Huron captives released. | JR 33:91, 93 |
| 17 Aug 1647 | Iroq vs. Algk | 6-7 Algk capt. | "La Poterie" [Que] | News received this day. | JR 30:191-93 |
| [Early] Sept 1647 | [20] Iroq [Moh] vs. Fr & FIA | 6 Fr wounded, 1 later died, 2 FIA K; 7 Iroq wounded, 2 K, & 1 Iroq capt. and later K | [Que?] | News of returning party noted this time. Moh identified because next Spring Moh ask for Iroq capt. during this raid. Iroq attacked Fr or FIA canoes. Fr and FIA pursue Iroq. Fr took guns abandoned by Iroq. | JR 30:193-95; 32:19-21, 145 |
| [Sometime before 20 Oct 1647] | Moh vs. 6 Huron | 3 Huron capt., 2 escaped | | Jesuits note that only 6 Huron came to Mont this year. This was their fate. They may have been traders, converts come to get supplies, etc. Neither the date of the attack nor the nature of the group is clear. | JR 32:29 |
| 4 Nov 1647 | Iroq vs. Huron | 2 Huron capt. | TR | | JR 30:195 |

Continued on next page

| Date | Groups Involved | Results | Location | Comments | Sources |
|---|---|---|---|---|---|
| End of winter [Feb to Mar 1648] | Sen vs. Huron (Cord tribe of St. Ignace) | 7 Huron K & 24 Huron M & F capt. | "2 days journey" [southwest of village] | 300 people from the tribe had gone hunting. Sen fell upon one cabin of the group. | JR 33:83 |
| End of winter [Feb to Mar 1648] | 100 Moh vs. Huron (Cord tribe of St. Ignace) | 40 Huron K or capt. | 4-5 L from village | Date is based on the observation that this raid took place a few days after above one. The 300 Huron had returned to gather meat left after first attack. Were struck by Moh as returned to village. | JR 33:89 |
| April 1648 | 100 Mohr vs. 6 Huron | 4 Huron K | | The Huron were envoys in peace talks under way between the Huron & the Onon. This is most likely the same group of Moh as above. | JR 33:125 |
| 30 May 1648 | FIA (2 Alk & 1 Huron) vs. 3 Iroq [Moh] | 2 Iroq capt., 1 K | TR | 2 Iroq hunting in area gave themselves up to Fr—not clear why. When Fr and FIA went back to convince 3 other Iroq to come to Fr, they ran. Were pursued by FIA. | JR 32:151 |
| 20 June 1648 | 29 Iroq [Moh] vs. Fr | 2 Iroq capt. | TR | 29 Iroq came to raid. Did not seem to know Fr had prisoners, but when did discover this, tried to dupe Fr into freeing prisoners. Fr instead kept two envoys as captives. | JR 32:155-57 |

Continued on next page

| Date | Groups Involved | Results | Location | Comments | Sources |
|------|-----------------|---------|----------|----------|---------|
| 4 July 1648 | 80 Iroq [Moh] vs. Fr & Huron | 1 Fr M K, 2 capt.; 1 Huron [M] K, 2 capt.; 2 Iroq [M] K, 2 wounded | TR | Fr attacked while tending cattle; Huron had come to their aid. The Iroq attacked because were told by one of the prisoners capt. 30 May, and since released, that rest of prisoners were being badly treated. One of the Fr was eventually returned. The Moh are identified as participants in all three raids because one of those capt. 30 May was clearly a Moh, and the sources make clear that the other groups were of his countrymen. | JR 32:95-99, 151, 157-59 |

Continued on next page

| Date | Groups Involved | Results | Location | Comments | Sources |
|---|---|---|---|---|---|
| [17 or 18 July] 1648 | 100 Iroq vs. 250 Huron [Traders] | 17-20 Iroq [M] capt., [15-17 K] | 3 L below TR, on St. Law | 100 Iroq said to have been involved. A band had come up to try to free the prisoners, so were probably Moh. Were dissuaded from attacking. Not clear how they came to set up on St. Law, but that total of 100 is probably a combination of the above two groups and this band. In any case they saw a few canoes of Huron and, not realizing they were followed by many more Huron, they attacked and ran right into the incoming Huron fur brigade. It is assumed the canoes attacked were carrying traders and furs. They may, however, have been scouts for the larger group. The Iroq were defeated and plundered of their possesions. | JR 32:97, 163–83; Correspondance, 352-53 |
| 28 July 1648 | 12-13 Iroq vs. Fr [M] | 1 Fr [M] K, 1-2 Iroq K or wounded | Mont | Iroq shot at some Fr as they were gathering hay in a meadow. Fr returned fire. | JR 32:169 |
| July 1648 | Iroq vs. Huron [Cord] | 700 Huron capt. & K. Mostly F. & C. 1 Fr M K. | Huronia, Teanaustaye | 2 Huron villages attacked and destroyed in a dawn raid. Teanaustaye was central village, had about 400 families. Jesuit Antoine Daniel K. | JR 33:259-61; 34:87-91, 99; Correspondance, 364 |

Continued on next page

| Date | Groups Involved | Results | Location | Comments | Sources |
|---|---|---|---|---|---|
| 16-19 Mar 1649 | 1,000-1,200 Iroq vs. Huron, the Cord, & Ataronchronnon | 630 Huron capt. & K, at least 230 of whom were M, and were K. 2 Fr M K. 140 Iroq M K, 30 capt. | Huronia, villages of St. Louis & St Ignace | The Iroq losses came at St. Louis where the Huron put up a valiant defence. The Iroq had plans to attack St. Marie, but the offensive of the Bear tribe warriors, mostly Christians from Ossossane, and the ensuing losses put an end to that. On 19 March the Iroq left with their captives and their spoils of war. 700 Deer tribe warriors gave chase but abandoned pursuit after 2 days. The Jesuits Brébeuf and Lalemant were K. | *JR* 34:27, 123-37, 213, 217 |
| 30 May 1649 | Iroq vs. Fr | 1 Fr M capt. | Mont | | *JR* 34:53 |
| 30 May 1649 | Iroq vs. [FIA] | Some Indians capt. & K | Mont | | *JR* 34:53 |
| 12 June 1649 | Iroq vs. Algk [Petite Nation?] | 14 Algk capt. | Third rapid above TR [Ott R.] | Learned of raid this date. | *JR* 34:55 |
| [June] 1649 | Petite Nation vs. Iroq | 7 Iroq K | | Shortly after news of above raid came this news. Above raid could have been against Petite Nation and this one against Iroq as they were fleeing with captives. Identification of Algk group as Petite Nation in raid above is based on this reasoning. | *JR* 34:55 |

*Continued on next page*

| Date | Groups Involved | Results | Location | Comments | Sources |
|------|-----------------|---------|----------|----------|---------|
| [15] June 1649 | Iroq vs. Huron | Some Huron capt. & K | Huronia, mainland near [Christian Island] | Father Ragueneau wrote that "massacres" continued to take place throughout the summer against the Huron. | JR 35:83, 91 |
| 7 Dec 1649 | Iroq [some Onon] vs. Petun | Many capt. & K, 1 Fr Jesuit K | Village of St. Jean, [south of Nottawasaga Bay] | Petun warriors had gone out to ambush Iroq who they learned were coming to attack. Iroq came via another route, capt. 2 Petun, learned of defenseless state of village, and attacked in midafternoon. Some of the Jesuits' effects were later found among Onon. Village was said to hold 500-600 families. | JR 35:107-13; 41:121 |
| 25 Mar [1650] | Iroq vs. Huron | 150 Huron capt. & K | [Huronia, mainland, oppposite Christian Island] | Huron were fishing group, had split up into several bands. | JR 35:187 |
| [18 Apr 1650] | Iroq vs. Huron | Group capt. & K | [Huronia, mainland, oppposite Christian Island] | Group had gone out to hunt, were starving on island. Group left day after Easter. A few days later news arrived of their fate. Easter Sunday was April 17 this year. | JR 35:37-41, 189 |
| [Late Apr 1650] | Iroq vs. Huron | Group capt. & K | [Probably same as above] | This group too had gone out to hunt. News arrived 8 days after above news. | JR 35:191 |

Continued on next page

| Date | Groups Involved | Results | Location | Comments | Sources |
|---|---|---|---|---|---|
| [Late Apr to early May] 1650 | Algk from TR & St. Joseph vs. Iroq | 1 Iroq [M] capt. Many Algk K, some capt. | [Iroquoia?] | Algk set off to attack Iroq. Capt. 1 but decided to push on to village. A scout of their group was caught, divulged size of party to Iroq, and Algk were routed. News arrived around 13 May, probably via escaped Algk. Raid must have been earlier. | JR 35:43, 217-21 |
| [Before 9 May] 1650 | Iroq vs. Fr | At least 1 Iroq M capt. | TR | News arrived at Que that day. Raid was probably very late in April or in first days of May. | JR 35:41; Correspondance, 389 |
| [2 May] 1650 | Iroq vs. Fr | 2 Fr [M] K, 1 house burned | Que [Cap Rouge?] | Iroq attacked one house, K 2 servants, sacked the house, and set fire to another house not too far away. | JR 35:41; Correspondance, 389; Annales de L'Hôtel-Dieu, 76-77 |
| Shortly before 13 May 1650 | [Iroq vs. FIA?] | 2 Indians K, 2 wounded | Lake Champlain | Not clear what happened. Sources note 2 Indians K and 2 wounded. Since the Jesuits usually only note attacks by Iroq, it is assumed this reference is to that. Since Indians are not said to be enemies, it is further assumed they were allies of Fr or at least enemies of Iroq. | JR 35:43 |
| Spring [1650] | Iroq vs. Nipissing | Many capt. & K | [Lake Nipissing] | Iroq wintered nearby to attack in spring. | JR 35:181, 201 |

Continued on next page

| Date | Groups Involved | Results | Location | Comments | Sources |
|---|---|---|---|---|---|
| [Mid-June 1650] | 10 Iroq vs. 25-40 Fr traders & 20-30 Indians [mostly Huron], 60 in all | 7 Huron K, Father Bressani wounded. 6 Iroq K, 2 capt., 2 escaped | [Ott R.] 60 L above TR | Iroq had wintered in area. Snuck into camp and murdered Huron before others awoke and retaliated. The group was going up to Huronia to aid Hurons. They left TR 7 June 1650. | JR 35:45, 201-3 |
| Summer [June to July 1650] | 300 Iroq vs. Huron | Huron group "defeated" | 12 L from Christian Island [Georgian Bay?] | The Huron from the above group had proceeded to Huronia. Were defeated on the Great Lake. | JR 35:203-5; 36:119-21, 181 |
| Summer [June to July 1650] | 300 Iroq vs. 50 Petun men [traders or warriors?] | Petun "defeated" | [Either in Huronia or on Ott R. on way south to TR] | This group of Petun had been following the trail of fleeing Huron led by Ragueneau to Que. Were attacked by same group of Iroq that took part in above raid. Ragueneau leaves impression raid was soon after he left Huronia in June. | JR 36:181 |
| Summer [1650] | 30 Iroq vs. Huron | Many Huron K | [Christian Island, at fort] | Iroq set up fortified position in front of Huron fort to trap Huron as they left. Huron attacked Iroq, sustain losses, and Iroq escaped. | JR 36:181 |
| Toward end of summer [1650] | Iroq vs. Huron | 8 Huron capt. | Little Island opposite [Christian Island] | | JR 36:119 |
| 10 Aug 1650 | Iroq vs. Fr | 9 Fr capt. and/or K | At TR | News arrived at Que this day. Attack was a few days earlier. | JR 35:51 |

Continued on next page

| Date | Groups Involved | Results | Location | Comments | Sources |
|------|----------------|---------|----------|----------|---------|
| 22 Aug 1650 | 25-30 Iroq [Moh] vs. 60 Fr | Some Fr M K, others greviously wounded | Near TR | News arrived at Que this day. Attack was a few days prior. Fr had gone out to try and recapture those taken in raid above. Iroq were in ambush. Fired at Fr and ran. Continued this approach until Fr gave up chase. Fr K were soldiers. Iroq were led by "Flemish Bastard," a Moh. | *JR* 35:53, 211-13; *Correspondance*, 394 |
| Autumn [1650] | 7 Iroq vs. Huron | 3 Huron K | [Huronia?] | The Huron had returned or were returning to Huronia. | *JR* 36:121 |
| Autumn [prior to 30 Aug 1650] | 600 [Sen?] Iroq vs. Neutral | Neutral village taken [many capt.?]. 200 Iroq capt. or K | Neutral Frontier | News rec'd around 30 Aug. The Iroq were K and capt. during a reprisal raid by Neutral and Huron among Neutral. The sources seem to suggest that it was as Iroq were returning. Because of this, it is not listed as a seperate raid. The Iroq vowed to avenge this loss. One source reveals a severe loss by Sen in a raid vs. Neutral. | *JR* 36:119, 121, 177; 37:97; *Correspondance*, 399 |
| Toward end of Autumn [1650] | 100 Iroq [Onon] vs. Huron | 30 Iroq M K | Village, Christian Island | Iroq tried to dupe Huron. Huron did not fall for it. Once Iroq were inside the village the Huron attacked them. Rest of Iroq left. | *JR* 36:123, 181-89 |

*Continued on next page*

| Date | Groups Involved | Results | Location | Comments | Sources |
|---|---|---|---|---|---|
| 22 Nov 1650 | 17-18 Moh vs. Huron | 7 Huron capt. | Mont | News rec'd this day. Were capt. within sight of 10 other canoes of Huron who fled at the capture of these. The capt. Huron may have been a group that had left Que for war 15 Oct. | JR 35:55, 59 |
| 1 Mar 1651 | 40 Iroq vs. [Fr?] | Shots exchanged | Mont | The Iroq appeared before Mont, were discovered, and shots were exchanged. | JR 36:119 |
| Spring [1651] | 1,000-1,200 Iroq vs. Neutral | Neutral village of Teoto'ntdiaton capt., many K, huge number capt. | Neutral frontier | Young and old were K, women kept to be adopted. Jesuits stated that this disaster, added to earlier fall attack, has meant the destruction of the Neutral nation. | JR 36:141, 177; Correspondance, 395 |
| Spring [1651] | Iroq [Moh] vs. Huron | 2 Huron M capt. | | Capt. as were hunting. One later escaped from Moh. | JR 36:123, 133 |
| 27 Apr 1651 | Iroq vs. 2 Fr | 1 Fr died of wounds | [Que?] | Iroq tried to take 2 Fr alive, a third fired on Iroq and drove them off. Iroq joined some others and fired at house of another Fr. | JR 36:121, 246 |
| End of Apr 1651 | 3 Iroq vs. [Huron?] | 1 F K & her 6-year-old son capt. | | The name of K F is of Huron origin. | JR 36:123 |

Continued on next page

| Date | Groups Involved | Results | Location | Comments | Sources |
|---|---|---|---|---|---|
| [End of Apr 1651?] | Iroq vs. Fr | | | 2 Iroq were spotted about to attack house of Fr. 2 others, with same intent, were spotted at home of other Fr. [Were driven off?] | *JR* 36:123 |
| 6 May 1651 | 8-10 Iroq vs. 2 Fr | 1 Fr M K, 1 Fr F K, 1 Fr M scalped | Mont, near fort | Iroq attack house of Fr, behead M, brutally butcher his wife, and scalp another Fr M. This latter lived 14 more years. Home of the above Fr was robbed as was the miller's. Iroq part of a group of 40-50. | *JR* 36:125, 165; Dollier, *Histoire*, 155-57 |
| 14 May 1651 | 6 Algk vs. Iroq | 2 Iroq K | | News rec'd this day. 1 Iroq was K on spot. The other, a captain, was tortured and K at Mont. | *JR* 36:123-25 |
| 24 May 1651 | 10 Iroq vs. 2 Fr | 1 Fr fatally wounded, 1 wounded | TR in sight of fort | Attack had taken place shortly before this date. Fr had gone to take in fishing line. | *JR* 36:125-27 |
| 24 May 1651 | 4 Iroq vs. Huron | 1 Huron K | TR | Same time as above attack. 4 Iroq from above group of 10 then went into nearby fields and K 1 Huron. | *JR* 36:127 |

Continued on next page

| Date | Groups Involved | Results | Location | Comments | Sources |
|------|-----------------|---------|----------|----------|---------|
| 18 June 1651 | 50-60 Iroq vs. Fr | 1 Iroq captain was K, several Iroq wounded. 1 Fr fatally wounded, 3 others wounded | Pointe St. Charles, Mont | Dollier says 25-30 Iroq were K. It is unlikely that many were K and the Jesuits would fail to note it. Dollier was writing some years after the event, and the Jesuits at the time it took place. Their estimates were used. | *JR* 36:133; Dollier, *Histoire*, 157-59 |
| 29 June 1651 | 5 Iroq vs. Algk | 2 Algk [M] capt. | La Chaudière Falls, [Que] | Capt. at a fishing spot. 1 later escaped. | *JR* 36:131 |
| 30 June 1651 | 5 Iroq vs. Algk | 1 Algk [M] capt. | "la Poterie" [Que] | 1 Algk escaped. The capt. Algk later escaped also. This raid and above raid, by same Iroq. | *JR* 36:131 |
| 4 July 1651 | 50 Iroq vs. Tangwaonron- nons [Algk] | Tang. were defeated & massacred. F & C taken capt. | Lake Nipissing | News rec'd this day. Were fishing. Some escaped. | *JR* 36:131, 189 |
| 1 July 1651 | Iroq vs. 6 Huron | 1 Huron [M] K, 1 capt. | Opposite TR | Had gone to get hay. 4 other Huron escaped. Iroq also K several cattle in area. | *JR* 36:135 |
| 26 July 1651 | 60 Iroq vs. [Fr] | | Mont Ft. | Only casualty was a gunner who died when the cannon he was firing blew up. | *JR* 36:137 |

Continued on next page

| Date | Groups Involved | Results | Location | Comments | Sources |
|---|---|---|---|---|---|
| 7 Aug 1651 | Iroq vs. 1 Fr M | 1 Fr M K | [TR] | Fr was shot twice, and had hatchet buried in his head. Was alone, had gone out to hunt. | JR 36:135 |
| 18 Sept 1651 | 3 Iroq vs. Fr. | 1 [Fr] F K | [Sillery] | K in her house. | JR 36:139 |
| [Between end of June & 25 Oct 1651] | Iroq vs. Attikamek | 19-20 Att. capt. 3 M K. | Lake Kisakami | Iroq attacked a cabin at night. Most M were off hunting. Occupants of nearby cabin fled. | JR 36:147; 37:69-71 |
| 15 Nov 1651 | Iroq vs. Huron | 1 Huron M capt. | Mont | | JR 36:149 |
| 17 Feb 1652 | 4 FIA vs. 8 Moh | 3 Huron M capt., 1 Algk M escaped | 1 day's journey from [Moh villages] | FIA set off to attack. Moh picked up their trail shortly after they left Mont. Attacked when caught up with them. | JR 37:97 |
| 2 or 3 Mar 1652 | Iroq vs. 12 Huron M, 6 Algk M, & 10 Algk F | 7 Algk F capt., 3 escaped, as did 5 Algk M & 2 Huron M. [1 Algk M K?], 4 Huron M K, 6 capt. | LSP | Were heading for Mont. 1 Huron M later escaped. | JR 37:93, 101 |
| 6 Mar 1652 | Iroq vs. Huron | 1 Huron M K, at least | Rivière de-la-Madeleine, TR | Huron were going out vs. Iroq when were ambushed. Huron leader was K. Other attack survivors were spared. 1 Huron escaped. | JR 38:49, 51 |

Continued on next page

| Date | Groups Involved | Results | Location | Comments | Sources |
|---|---|---|---|---|---|
| [Winter 1652] | 1,000 Iroq vs. Susq | 130 Iroq lost [K]; 500-600 Susq capt., mostly M | Susq village | | *JR* 37:97, 103-5, 111 |
| Toward end of winter [1652] | Iroq vs. Attikamek | | Attikamek [lands] | Vague details. Sources refer to Iroq striking a considerable blow and to large number K. | *JR* 37:103, 203; 38:53 |
| End of winter [1652] | Iroq vs. Algk | 25 Algk capt. | | Sources say Iroq went toward "Paisans" and capt. 25 Algk. Not clear if Paisans is place or group. Could be a corruption of Poisson Blanc, Attikamek, but group capt. is clearly noted as Algk. | *JR* 37:103-5 |
| [Late Mar or early Apr 1652] | 75 Iroq [Moh] vs. 3 Fr M | 2 Fr M K & beheaded, 1 Fr M capt.; 1 Iroq M wounded | Ouvamsis R. [LSP near TR] | This was the raid in which Radisson was capt. The dating is difficult to explain, but about 6 weeks after he was capt. he escaped and was recaptured. At that time the group that got him was carrying 11 Algk scalps. That particular raid was on 16 May 1652. See below, this date. | [Radisson], *Explorations*, 1-16 |
| 10 May 1652 | 14 Iroq vs. 2 Fr M & 1 Huron M | 2 Fr M K, 1 Huron capt. | [St. Maurice R], Third rapid above TR Ft | Jesuit Buteux and Fr M were K on way up to Attikamek. The Huron later escaped. | *JR* 37:99, 141-43 |
| 13 May 1652 | 14 Iroq vs. Algk of TR | 1 Iroq M K, 1 Algk M K | [St. Maurice R], Third rapids above TR Ft | Same group of Iroq as above. Algk were going to Attikamek to trade. | *JR* 37:99; 38:51 |

*Continued on next page*

| Date | Groups Involved | Results | Location | Comments | Sources |
|---|---|---|---|---|---|
| 15 May 1652 | 50-60 Iroq vs. 2 Huron F & 1 mc | 2 Huron F & 1 mc capt. | Mont | Women had gone to get meat. | JR 37:101 |
| 15 May 1652 | Iroq vs. Huron | 1 Huron F and her 2 C capt. | Mont | She was in field with her children when were attacked. Probably by part of group above. | JR 38:51 |
| 16 May 1652 | [20] Iroq vs. 11 Algk of TR | Algk cut to pieces for most part, some escaped | LSP | Had set out to ambush Iroq in revenge for attack vs. their people 13 May. Ran into Iroq already on LSP. These Iroq may have been part of a party 150 strong. | JR 37:101; 38:51; [Radisson], Explorations, 16 |
| 21 May 1652 | Iroq vs. 1 Fr & 1 Algk M | 1 Algk M died of wounds, 1 Fr M wounded | St. Law opposite TR | The 2 had gone to work on a fish line. Iroq retreated in face of pursuit by forces from TR. | JR 37:101; 38:51 |
| 26 May 1652 | 50 Iroq vs. 1 Fr M | 1 Fr M K | Mont | The Fr was a cowherd. It is assumed he was alone when K. | JR 37:101-3 |
| 26 May 1652 | Iroq vs. 1 Fr. F | 1 Fr F wounded | Mont, in sight of Ft | She survived her 5-6 wounds. | JR 37:113; 38:51-53; Dollier, Histoire, 165-67 |
| 8 June 1652 | Iroq vs. 2 Huron M | 2 Huron M K & scalped | TR | Iroq were pursued so quickly that left behind baggage and scalps. | JR 37:105; 38:53 |

Continued on next page

| Date | Groups Involved | Results | Location | Comments | Sources |
|---|---|---|---|---|---|
| [Before mid-June 1652] | Iroq vs. Ekaetouton [Petun?] | A "capture" was made | | News rec'd this day. Raids were probably in spring. | JR 37:111 |
| [Before mid-June 1652] | Iroq vs. Askikwannhe [Nip.] | Made a "capture" | [Lake Nipissing?] | See above for date. | JR 37:111 |
| 2 July 1652 | 80 Iroq [Moh] vs. Fr & FIA | 2 Iroq K | TR | 8 Iroq attack two canoes of Hurons going to fish. They escape. During protracted maneuvering 2 Iroq M capt. 1, Aontarisati, was leader of the group. He was Moh. Both Iroq tortured to death. | JR 37:107-9; 38:53-55, 57 |
| 7 Aug 1652 | 100 Iroq vs. 80-100 Algk & Huron [FIA] | 1 Algk M K, 1 Huron M K, 3 Iroq M K | Mont | FIA had set out 25 July to attack Iroq. Iroq attacked them as they were returning to Mont. | JR 37:111-13; 38:55-57 |
| 18 Aug 1652 | Iroq vs. 4 Fr M | 2 Fr M K, 2 capt. | Between TR and the "Cap" [Cap-de-la-Madeleine] | 8 Iroq canoes. Two Fr were K on the spot. | JR 37:113; 38:57 |
| 19 Aug 1652 | 120 On & Moh vs. 40-50 Fr & 10-12 Indians [FIA] | 15 Fr M capt., at least 5 K | TR | Fr went to regain some Fr capt. as they had gone to round up some cattle scattered by Iroq. Attacked entrenched Iroq group that had come up to avenge death of Aontarisati at hands of TR FIA. | JR 37:113-15; 38:57-59; 40:97 |

Continued on next page

| Date | Groups Involved | Results | Location | Comments | Sources |
|------|-----------------|---------|----------|----------|---------|
| 19 Aug 1652 | Iroq vs. 1 Huron M & F | 1 Huron M & F K | TR, not far from Ft. | Iroq were part of above group. | JR 37:115; 38:57 |
| 30 Aug 1652 | Iroq vs. Huron | 1 Huron M capt. | TR | | JR 37:115; 38:61 |
| 16 Sept 1652 | Iroq vs. Fr | 1 Fr M K | Mont, near Ft. | | JR 37:119 |
| 14 Oct 1652 | Iroq vs. Fr | 1 Iroq M K, 1 Fr M K. Wounded on both sides. | Mont | Iroq came to attack, 24 Fr went out to meet them. Fr were outnumbered and retreated. Dollier notes 37 Iroq wounded. This would appear to be speculation. | JR 37:117; Dollier, Histoire, 171-75 |
| 25 Oct 1652 | Iroq vs. Huron | 1 Huron F K | TR | | JR 37:117 |
| 26 Oct 1652 | Iroq vs. Fr | 2 Fr M K, 1-2 Fr M wounded | Cap [de-la-Madeleine] | | JR 37:117; 38:61 |
| [End of Oct 1652] | Iroq vs. Algk | 1 Algk M & 2 Algk F capt. | St. Croix [Que] | News rec'd Nov. 1, and raid was recent. | JR 38:61 |
| 17 Dec 1652 | Iroq vs. Huron | 2 Huron capt. | 1 L from TR | | JR 38:169 |
| 29 Mar 1653 | Iroq vs. Huron | 1 Huron M capt. | Cap [de-la-Madeleine] | He was bringing mail from TR to Que. | JR 38:171 |

Continued on next page

| Date | Groups Involved | Results | Location | Comments | Sources |
|---|---|---|---|---|---|
| Spring [1653] | 11 Iroq (Radisson, 9 Moh, & 1 On) vs. ? [Probably Petun or Neutral] | 22 of enemy K [5-7 F, 1 C, 5-10 M, rest undetermined]; 1 Iroq M K | [North shore Lake Erie & Lake Ontario?] | This group set out to raid to avenge the death of one of Radisson's adopted brothers. They traveled around hunting and raiding for some time. The fatalities were inflicted in several small raids vs. unidentified groups. All that is said about one is that they had some Huron words in their language. Given this clue and the probable location, it is conjectured that at least one of the attacked groups was Petun. | [Radisson], *Explorations*, 27-35 |
| [Before 21 Apr 1653] | Iroq vs. Huron | 2 Huron M capt. | | News rec'd this day. Were going from Que to TR. | *JR* 38:171 |
| [Before 21 Apr 1653] | Iroq vs. Huron | 1 Huron M capt. | TR | News rec'd this day. Was hunting around TR. | *JR* 38:171 |
| 13 May 1653 | Iroq vs. 5 Fr | 2 Fr K | TR | Fr were working in field. Retreating Iroq abandoned their baggage. | *JR* 40:101 |
| 28 May 1653 | Iroq vs. Fr | 1 Fr C K | Near TR Ft | | *JR* 40:101 |
| 28 May 1653 | 20 Iroq vs. Fr | 1 Fr M K | TR, at the Commons | | *JR* 38:177 |
| 30 May 1653 | 20 Iroq vs. Nipissing | 1 Nip. M capt. | Lake Nipissing, [Sturgeon Falls] | This M later escaped. | *JR* 38:177 |

Continued on next page

| Date | Groups Involved | Results | Location | Comments | Sources |
|------|-----------------|---------|----------|----------|---------|
| 30 May 1653 | Iroq (1 Sen & 3 former Huron captives) vs. Fr | 1 Huron M capt., 1 Sen K, 3 former Huron capt., 2 tortured to death | TR | The Huron capt. was a sentry for Fr farmers that the Iroq intended to attack. 12 Huron and Algk from TR set out to free their compatriot (and did). Sen was K on spot, 2 former Huron tortured to death, the third was allowed to live. | JR 38:177; 40:101-3 |
| 2 June 1653 | Iroq vs. Fr | 1 Fr M K | Cap de-la-Madeleine | | JR 38:177 |
| 9 June 1653 | Huron vs. 20-30 Iroq | Iroq were "plundered" | [TR] | | JR 38:177 |
| 10 June 1653 | Iroq vs. Fr | 1 Fr M K, 2 Fr M & 1 mc capt. | Cap Rouge | 5 canoes of Iroq. | JR 38:175 |
| 21 June 1653 | Iroq vs. 2 Indians [Huron] | 2 Indians capt. | TR | | JR 38:179 |
| 20 July 1653 | Iroq vs. Fr | 1 Fr [M] K | Mont | | JR 38:183 |
| 16 Aug 1653 | 8 Iroq vs. Huron | 2 Huron capt. | Island, at TR | | JR 38:191 |
| 20 Aug 1653 | 10 Iroq vs. Fr | 2 Fr M capt., 1 later K, 1 released | Cap Rouge | Father Poncet was later released. Attackers were 4 Moh and 6 former Huron. | JR 38:191; 40:121, 139-41, 155 |

Continued on next page

| Date | Groups Involved | Results | Location | Comments | Sources |
|------|-----------------|---------|----------|----------|---------|
| 21 Aug 1653 | 30 Huron vs. 17 Moh | 1 Iroq K, 5 capt. 2 Huron K, 2 wounded | île St. Hélène | News rec'd this day. Iroq were going to ambush some Fr when Huron fell on them. The Iroq prisoners & the victorious Huron fell into the hands of the Moh army besieging TR a few days later. | *JR*, 38:189, 195; Dollier, *Histoire*, 179-83 |
| 22 Aug 1653 | 500 Moh vs. Fr | 1 Huron wounded, 2 Iroq M K | TR Ft | Army of Moh besieged TR Ft. The shooting and skirmishing before the siege led to the deaths. Nothing came of this and peace talks were intiated with the Moh. | *JR* 38;193-99; 40:103-17, 171-93 |

Continued on next page

| Date | Groups Involved | Results | Location | Comments | Sources |
|---|---|---|---|---|---|
| [Winter 1652? to spring 1654] | Erie vs. Sen | Sen village taken & burned | Sen village | The dating on these three is very problematic. The Onon informed the French of these events, the consequence of a "fresh" war against the upper Iroq, and suggested that this led them to think of peace with Fr and their allies. If this is the case, these raids may have begun as early as the winter of 1652, because by spring to summer of 1653 the Onon had come to Fr to talk of peace. What is certain is that the raids occurred prior to summer of 1654. The capt. of the Onon M, one a famous warrior, appears to have been between the summer of 1653 and spring of 1654. Another M capt. with him escaped. | *JR* 40:89; 41:77-81, 111-13; 42:177-79 |
| | Erie vs. Onon | 80 Onon "cut to pieces" | On return from [Lake Huron] | | |
| | Erie vs. Onon | 2 Onon M capt., 1 escaped | Near Onon village | | |
| Apr 1654 | 12 On vs. Fr | 1 Fr M capt. | Mont | Was beaver hunting. Later released. | *JR* 41:67, 69 |

*Continued on next page*

| Date | Groups Involved | Results | Location | Comments | Sources |
|---|---|---|---|---|---|
| [Apr to June 1654] | [120] Petun & Ott vs. 8 Sen & 5 Mah | 8 Sen capt. | | Petun and Ott group of traders ran into this group. Sen released later. No mention of what happened to Mah. | JR 41:79, 111 |
| 9 Aug 1654 | Erie vs. Onon | 3 Onon [M] K | Near Onon central village | | JR 41:107 |
| Fall 1654 | Iroq vs. 1 Fr M | 1 Fr M K, 1 Iroq M wounded & capt. | Mont | A sentry was K. Fr caught 1 Iroq and nursed him back to health as a means to arrange peace. | Dollier, Histoire, 197-99 |
| [Fall 1654] | [Huron] vs. Iroq | 8 Iroq K, 3 capt. & later K | [Mackinac Island] | [Grosilliers and some Huron] Indians went out to ambush some Iroq that were thought to be in area. Found them and attacked. | [Radisson], Explorations, 88 |

Continued on next page

| Date | Groups Involved | Results | Location | Comments | Sources |
|------|-----------------|---------|----------|----------|---------|
| [Fall 1654 to winter 1655] | 1,200-1,800 Iroq vs. 3,000-4,000 Erie | Erie villages destroyed, great massacre of Erie. Heavy Iroq losses. | Erie villages [southeast shore Lake Erie] | Dating is difficult. Writing in 1656 Jesuits note raid as "last year"--so in 1655. In August 1654 a Jesuit among Onon noted an army of 1,800 to set out "as soon as possible." If it did, the raid was in the Fall of 1654. The army could have been delayed and the actual attack might have occurred in 1655. Despite references to only the Onon, the other Iroq must have participated--the Onon could not field an army of that size alone. The Moh, at least, were part of this army. | JR 41:121; 42:113, 177-83; 45:209 |
| [Early May? 1655] | Iroq [Moh] vs. Fr | 1 Fr M & 1 Fr F K, [4 fc] capt. | île-aux-[Noix] | Husband and wife K, 2 daughters capt. 2 other Fr fc capt. All later released. | Dollier, Histoire, 199-201; Correspondance, 563 |
| 29 May 1655 | Moh vs. Fr | 1 Fr M K | Sillery | He was a Jesuit layman. K as went to investigate shots he'd heard. | JR 41:213, 215, 217; 42:263; Correspondance, 563 |
| [Spring, maybe 29 May, 1655] | 5 Iroq [Moh] vs. Algk | 2 Iroq M K | [Sillery?] | Iroq attack and capt. 1 Algk M. His wife attacked and K 2 Iroq, released husband. | JR 41:215; Correspondance, 563 |

Continued on next page

| Date | Groups Involved | Results | Location | Comments | Sources |
|------|----------------|---------|----------|----------|---------|
| [31 May 1655] | Iroq [Moh] vs. Fr | 1 Fr M K | [Mont] | | Dollier, *Histoire*, 201 |
| [Late May? 1655] | Iroq vs. Fr | 4 Fr [M?] K | [Que] | | *Correspondance*, 563 |
| [Late May to early June 1655] | Iroq [Moh] vs. Fr | At least 5 Iroq M capt. | Mont | Raid took place after that of 31 May above. Iroq came to attack, were capt. as tried to land. Another group was capt. when they came to negotiate. Led to Moh peace talks with Fr and release of fc capt. at Île-aux-Noix. | Dollier, *Histoire*, 201-5 |
| 12 Feb 1656 | Onon vs. Erie & ? | 3 scalps from unidentified group & 2 Erie capt. | | Unidentified group spoke a language different from Iroq. | *JR* 42:191-93 |
| 25 Apr 1656 | 2 Moh vs. 2 Huron | 1 Huron [M] K, 1 Iroq M K | Que | The escaped Huron got news to 20 other Huron who pursued the Moh. Moh had split up & Huron capt. 1 Iroq who was tortured to death. | *JR* 43:105-7 |
| 18 May 1656 | 300 Moh vs. Fr, Onon, & Huron | Wound some Fr, ill-treat all, pillage canoes | 12 L above Que | This was rear guard of group of Onon and Jesuits going to set up mission among Onon. All released. This group of Moh had come up to carry off the rest of the Hurons to their villages. | *JR* 43:135 |

Continued on next page

| Date | Groups Involved | Results | Location | Comments | Sources |
|------|-----------------|---------|----------|----------|---------|
| 19-20 May 1656 | 400 Moh vs. Huron | Some Huron K, 71-85 lost or capt. | île d' Orleans | Moh snuck past Mont and attacked Christian Hurons. The Huron had agreed to relocate and Moh came to make sure the promise was fulfilled. Moh pillaged abandonded Fr houses. No harm was done to Fr. | JR 43:117, 119, 187-89; Correspondance, 583-84 |
| 29 June 1656 | Moh vs. Amikwa | 4 Amikwa [M] scalped, 1 F & 2 C capt. | | Moh were seen returning this day. There were 3 canoes of Moh. At the end of Oct 1655, 60 On had set out to attack the Amikwa as well. | JR 42:75, 77-79; 43:145 |
| 30 Aug 1656 | [120] Moh vs. 250 Ot & Huron | 1 Fr M K, unspec. no. of Huron K & capt. (possibly 13 "lost"), unspec. no. of Ot & Moh wounded & K | St. Law [between Mont & TR] | Ot were returning fur brigade. Huron were part of group, somewhat ahead of main body, paddled into ambush. Jesuit Garreau was also part of this advance group. Ot came to defense, but Moh had fortified position. Ot attacked it to no avail. Ot abandoned some supplies and siege. Moh apologized for killing the Jesuit. | JR 42:227-31, 235-39; 43:213; [Radisson], Explorations, 81-84 |
| 12 May 1657 | Onon vs. Huron | 1 Huron K | [Que] | Onon and Moh spent most of this year trying to lure Huron to relocate to Iroquoia. This Huron was most likely K when one of the Onon who came to bring Huron to Iroq tried to capture a Huron. | JR 43:43 |

Continued on next page

| Date | Groups Involved | Results | Location | Comments | Sources |
|---|---|---|---|---|---|
| 3 Aug 1657 | Onon vs. Huron | [7-13] Huron K, 40 capt.; 1 Iroq M K | Island on St. Law, 4 days journey above Mont | A group of about 50 Huron were going with 16 Sen and 30 Onon to relocate among Onon. Were attacked enroute. Radisson, who was along, put Iroq group at 80 and Huron at 100 F & 10-12 M. He also noted that by time of attack both groups had people leave. | *JR* 43:59; 44:69-77, 151; *Correspondance*, 591; [Radisson], *Explorations*, 51-55 |
| 25 Oct 1657 | Iroq [On] vs. Fr | 3 Fr M K | Mont | On and Onon were spotted in area prior to attack, but Moh said it was On who attacked. Radisson, among Moh at time, attributed this attack to the Anojot [Oneida]. | *JR* 43:59, 67; 44:85, 87-89, 99; Dollier, *Histoire*, 221; [Radisson], *Explorations*, 71 |
| 3 Nov 1657 | 9 Algk vs. Onon | 1 Onon scalped | Rich R. islands | Rec'd news this day. The Algk had set out 24 Oct. | *JR* 43:65, 69 |
| [Spring 1658] | Iroq [Moh?] vs. Mt | 3 Mt bands defeated | [Mistassini River] | The dating of this raid and Moh participation are based on very sketchy data. | *JR* 44:203-5; 45:233 |
| 13 June 1658 | 6 On Iroq vs. 3 Fr M | 3 Fr M capt. | TR | 2 Fr later released, 1 was K. | *JR* 44:101, 109, 111, 115, 125 |
| 13 July 1658 | Iroq vs. Mt & Algk | 1 Mt F K, 2 Algk F wounded | [Que] | Women working in field. | *JR* 44:101-3 |

Continued on next page

| Date | Groups Involved | Results | Location | Comments | Sources |
|------|----------------|---------|----------|----------|---------|
| 21 Aug 1658 | Iroq vs. 1 Fr | Fr M escaped | Cap Rouge | | JR 44:105 |
| 30 Aug 1658 | Iroq vs. Huron | 1 Huron capt. | Sillery | 4 Iroq capt. the Huron near Jesuit mill. | JR 44:107 |
| 16 Sept 1658 | Onon vs.? Fr | 11 Onon capt., 2 K | Mont | News rec'd this day. They all escaped 19 Oct. No details on how were capt. | JR 44:109-11, 119 |
| 25 Sept 1658 | On vs.? Fr | 5 On capt., 3 K, 1 released | TR | Prisoners arrived at Que this date. | JR 44:111, 117 |
| 20 Oct 1658 | Fr vs. Moh | 3 Moh capt. | [Que] | Moh were going to war at Tad when canoe broke down. Capt. when they came ashore. | JR 44:119 |
| 5 Nov 1658 | 12 Moh vs. Fr | 8 Fr [M] capt. | TR & LSP | 4 Fr capt. while working in field, and 4 as returned from hunting. 1 released. This was probably a Moh effort to get their people released. | JR 44:121 |
| [Winter 1658 to 1659] | Iroq [Moh] vs. [Mascouten] | Some Iroq losses | | End of Aug 1658 200 Iroq said to be going to war vs. [Mascouten]. In July 1659 Moh were condoled on losses suffered "last winter" vs. [Mascouten]. | JR 44:115; 45:101 |

Continued on next page

| Date | Groups Involved | Results | Location | Comments | Sources |
|------|-----------------|---------|----------|----------|---------|
| 27 June 1659 | Onon vs. Fr | 3 Fr capt. | Rich R. islands [near TR] | News arrived this day. 1 Fr M K, two others escaped. The Iroq had been spotted earlier in the month. It appears that they wanted to capture some Fr to exchange for Iroq of various tribes held by Fr. | JR 45:35, 97-105 |
| 10 Aug 1659 | Moh vs. Algk or Mt | 1 Algk or Mt F K, 1 Moh M K | Tad | News rec'd this day. Sources not conclusive about nationalty of F. Iroq was shot on the spot. | JR 45:107, 211 |

Continued on next page

| Date | Groups Involved | Results | Location | Comments | Sources |
|---|---|---|---|---|---|
| 21 Aug 1659 | Iroq vs. Sault Ind. (7 canoes) & Ot (6 canoes) | 18 Iroq K; 6 FIA K and 7 wounded | [Ott R.?] a days journey above Mont., below 40 ft. falls. | Fatalities were the result of battles with different Iroq bands. Radisson & Grosiliers were heading north with Sault Indians to trade. Met Ot and then ran into ambush Iroq had laid for Ot. Outnumbered, the Iroq left. Next day FIA ran into returning Iroq hunters and K 3 Iroq. FIA then encountered first Iroq group they thought had given up desire to fight. Rest of casualties took place during this battle. 21 August the Jesuits reported the arrival of unidentified FIA with 9 Iroq scalps. Radisson noted that this group took 10 scalps and capt. 4 Iroq during this battle. They were later K when more Iroq were encountered. FIA decided not to fight and got away during night. | JR 45:107; [Radisson], Explorations, 112-19 |
| 25 Aug 1659 | 60-100 Moh vs. Fr | 8 Fr capt. | Near TR | | JR 45:107-9, 117 |
| 12 Sept 1659 | 8 Iroq vs. Fr | 1 Fr M capt. | Cap Rouge | Fr were eel fishing. | JR 45:113 |
| [End of Sept] 1659 | Iroq vs. Fr | 1 Fr M K | TR | | JR 45:115 |

Continued on next page

| Date | Groups Involved | Results | Location | Comments | Sources |
|---|---|---|---|---|---|
| 1 Nov 1659 | FIA vs. Iroq [Moh] | 2 Iroq M K, 1 mc capt. | | This group of FIA had set out from Que 29 Aug 29 to raid toward TR and returned this day. The raid was probably to avenge the losses suffered 25 Aug. They had set out 17 canoes full of Algk and Huron. Given the length of time between departure and arrival they must have had to go to Iroquoia to make the raid. | JR 45:109, 117 |
| 15 May 1660 | [FIA] vs. Iroq | 4 Iroq K | | News rec'd this day. 3 Iroq K on the spot, 1 tortured to death. The FIA were from Tad, but said to be Algk. | JR 45:153; Correspondance, 619 |

Continued on next page

| Date | Groups Involved | Results | Location | Comments | Sources |
|------|-----------------|---------|----------|----------|---------|
| [End of May] 1660 | 500 Moh & 200 Onon vs. 40 Huron, 17 Fr & 4 Algk | 20-30 Huron capt., 12 Fr K, 5 Fr capt., 14-20 Iroq K, 19 wounded | la Chaudière Falls [Ott R.] | News rec'd 3 June at Mont, 8 June at Que. Iroq were coming to attack Fr. Huron had decided to go out to ambush Iroq returning from hunting. Fr decided to go along when all ran into Iroq. Some On along, but not clear how many of 700. This is the now legendary battle of Dollard des Ormeaux. The commonly held view is that the heroic defense prevented further incursions vs. New France. Further attack vs. the colony was prevented but, as Marie de l'Incarnation pointed out, because the goal of striking a blow at the Fr had been met, not out of fear of what more Fr could do. | JR 45:157, 245-61; Dollier, *Histoire*, 253-65; *Correspondance*, 622-28; *NYCD* 13:175; [Radisson], *Explorations*, 104-6 |
| 5 June 1660 | 8 Iroq vs. Fr | 1 Fr F K & 4 C capt., 7 Iroq K | Petite Cap [Que] | Iroq were former Huron. 8 Fr & 20 Mt and Algk went in pursuit. 3 Iroq drowned (presumably attempting to escape), 5 were capt, 4 of whom were tortured to death. The Fr F died of her wounds, her children were saved. | JR 45:157; *Correspondance*, 621 |

Continued on next page

| Date | Groups Involved | Results | Location | Comments | Sources |
|------|-----------------|---------|----------|----------|---------|
| [Between 8 & 19] July 1660 | Iroq vs. Algk | 1 Algk K, 1 capt | TR | Governor of Que, who happened to be at TR, gave chase with 100 others. Ran into Iroq ambush. Managed to get out with only 1 of party wounded. Radisson, describing what is certainly the same event, stated that 11 Iroq were K. It is hard to accept that the Jesuits would have overlooked such a significant number of dead, especially as it would redound to the governor's credit. | *JR* 45:159; [Radisson], *Explorations*, 107-9 |
| [Shortly after] 4 Aug 1660 | Fr vs. ? Cay | 12 Cay capt. | Mont | 50 Cay came, they said, in peace. Fr suspected otherwise and capt. 12 in order to negotiate release of Fr among Iroq. | *JR* 45:161; 46:117-19 |
| 15 Aug 1660 | 20-25 Iroq vs. Fr | 2 Fr M capt. | TR | News rec'd this day. | *JR* 45:161 |

Continued on next page

| Date | Groups Involved | Results | Location | Comments | Sources |
|---|---|---|---|---|---|
| [Before 19 Aug] 1660 | 100-150 Iroq vs. 500 FIA (Ot, Saulteux, Amikwa, Sioux & Ticacon [Kiskakon?]) | 5 Iroq [M] K, 2 FIA wounded | [Ott R] | Radisson, coming back to colony with this group, states that Iroq were outnumbered 5 to 1 and were too intimidated to attack at first, 30 L from Calumet Falls. Later on downriver, near the Long Sault, they set up an ambush, but were outnumbered, left their baggage, and got away during the night. These Iroq were probably remnants of the larger army that had come up to attack the colony. | [Radisson], *Explorations*, 100-104 |
| [Late Aug to early Sept] 1660 | 100 Onon vs. 300 Ot | 3 Ot [M] lost | [La Chaudière Falls, Ott R] | Onon attacked advance scouts of returning Ot fur brigade. Outnumbered, the Onon withdrew. Possibly part of same group above that wanted to avenge earlier losses. | *JR* 45:161-63; 46:121 |
| Feb 1661 | 160 Iroq vs. Fr | 13 Fr M capt., some later K | Mont | | *JR* 46:171, 207; Dollier, *Histoire*, 271 |
| Mar 1661 | Iroq vs. Fr | 6 Fr M capt. & 4 Fr M K, 1 Iroq M K | Mont | Dollier wrote that 260 Iroq were involved in this attack. | *JR* 46:207; Dollier, *Histoire*, 271 |
| 8 Apr 1661 | Onon vs. Fr | 14 Fr M capt. | TR | News rec'd this day. | *JR* 46:167 |

Continued on next page

| Date | Groups Involved | Results | Location | Comments | Sources |
|---|---|---|---|---|---|
| [8 Apr 1661] | 70–80 Moh vs. [28 Attikamek & 2 Fr M] | Almost all Att. K or capt., 2 Fr M K, 24 Iroq K | TR [St. Maurice R.] | Attacked group were traders returning to trade for furs. | JR 46:179, 209; Correspondance, 666 |
| [End of May 1661] | Iroq vs. 14 [Huron–Petun] | 4 M of attacked group K, [rest capt.?] | [Lake Superior] | Iroq "fell" upon this group. | JR 46:143 |
| [May 1661] | | | | During this month notices appear of conflict between the Upper Iroq tribes and the Susq. At the beginning of the month the assembly of Maryland agreed to furnish military aid to the Susq. This suggests that hostilities had already taken place. By the end of the month the Dutch authorities on the Hudson were apprised of Maryland's actions and were told that the Iroq and Susq were at war. No details as to causes or casualities. | Md. Archives 1:407; NYCD 12:344, 345-46 |
| 6 June 1661 | 60-70 Moh vs. Fr | 3 Fr M K | Tad | Fr were checking fishing lines. | JR 46:173-75 |
| 8 June 1661 | Iroq vs. Fr | 3 Fr M K | TR | News rec'd this day. | JR 46:175 |
| 10 June 1661 | Iroq vs. [Maryland] | Some farms of Finns & Swedes "ravaged" | [Maryland] | News rec'd this day. | NYCD 12:345 |

Continued on next page

| Date | Groups Involved | Results | Location | Comments | Sources |
|---|---|---|---|---|---|
| 18 June 1661 | [60-70 Moh] vs. [Fr or FIA?] | 15 [Fr or FIA] lost | Beaupré & île d'Orleans | 8 were from Beaupré & 7 from île d'Orleans. This was said to be same group that had hit at Tad 6 June. Target group unknown. | JR 46:179 |
| 22 June 1661 | 40 Iroq vs. 8 Fr M | 8 Fr M K | île d'Orleans | Leader of Fr had gone to warn a relative of Iroq presence. Ran into Iroq ambush. | JR 46:179, 211-15 |
| [June 1661] | Iroq [Moh] vs. Squirrel | [80 people capt. or K] Nation utterly defeated | [Between Lake Asssinca & Lake Mistassini] | Location is based on Historical Atlas of Canada, plate 18. | JR 46:289; 47:149-51; 56:183 |
| [Approx. 21 July 1661] | Moh vs. Fr | 1 Fr M capt. | TR | He was kept alive by the Moh. | JR 47:83 |
| [Mid- to late July 1661] | Susq vs. Cay | 3 Cay K | Near Cay villages | Cay were in their fields. | JR 47:71 |
| 1 Aug 1661 | [Moh] vs. Fr | 1 Fr M capt. | TR | Was encountered in Moh village. | JR 47:85 |

Continued on next page

| Date | Groups Involved | Results | Location | Comments | Sources |
|---|---|---|---|---|---|
| [29 Aug] 1661 | [40-50 Onon] vs. 9-14 Fr M | 2 Fr M K | Mont | The attack was led by Otreouati in revenge for being held in a Mont prison some time before. The Fr had gone to a field to reap some wheat. This attack took place at the same time as Garaconté, a fellow Onon, was trying to establish a firmer peace between Fr and Onon. | JR 46:189, 217-19; 47:71-73, 95; Dollier, Histoire, 275-77 |
| 25 Oct 1661 | [35 Oneida] vs. 14 Fr M | 3 Fr M K on spot, 2 capt. & later K; 1 Iroq M K | Mont | Fr had gone to cut stone on "île à la Pierre." On his way to Mont to negotiate peace Garaconté had gotten a band of On to agree not to attack Fr. Either this band had changed their minds, or another band struck the blow. | JR 46:189; 47:97, 157, 177; 50:55-57; Dollier, Histoire, 283-85 |
| 26 Oct 1661 | Iroq vs. [Delaware] | 12 [Delaware] K | Delaware R. | News reported this day. The Iroq were said to have attacked the "river-savages" who lived above the Swedish settlement [Altena?]. | NYCD 12:357 |

Continued on next page

| Date | Groups Involved | Results | Location | Comments | Sources |
|---|---|---|---|---|---|
| [End of 1661] | | | | Writing in the fall of this year two different sources put French losses to the Iroq at 100-114 people. The Jesuits wrote that the colony lost 114 people killed, 70 of them French. Marie de l'Incarnation wrote that the French had more than 100 people captured and killed. If we add up the numbers for this year we get only 39 killed and 22 captured for a total of 61 lost. If the generalized numbers are correct one must conclude that many raids went unrecorded, and what Iroq raids were chronicled were merely the major ones. There are references to this in the sources. At times, after describing a raid, a writer will note "that many more raids" or "many more captures" were made. | JR 46:219-21; Correspondance, 665 |
| [Winter 1661-1662] | Onon vs. [Shawnee] | Some F & C K | [Upper Ohio Valley] | This was a reprisal for Onon deaths incurred 8-9 years past when Onon had attacked Shawnee. | JR 47:145-47 |
| 7 Feb 1662 | 200 Onon vs. Fr | 4 Fr M K | Mont | Onon had attacked. Fr group of 26-27 went to aid of those being attacked. 4 Fr K were of this group. | JR 47:155, 277; Dollier, Histoire, 287 |
| [Late March to early April] 1662 | Iroq vs. Fr | 2 Fr wounded, unspecified no. of Iroq wounded | Mont | News rec'd this day, Easter Sunday. | JR 47:277 |

Continued on next page

| Date | Groups Involved | Results | Location | Comments | Sources |
|---|---|---|---|---|---|
| [30 April to 3] May 1662 | [200 to] 260 Mohawk vs. [Eastern Abenaki] | Some [Abenaki] K & capt. | Penobscott Fort | The English sources indicate the attack was vs. the North Indians, while the Jesuits noted a Moh party out to attack the Etchemins—a term they often used to refer to the Abenaki. The area of the fort is the tribal area of the Abenaki. There is also a reference to a Moh attack against an entire village of Abenaki. A house in the area of the fort was plundered. Not clear who it belonged to. | JR 47:139–41, 279; NYCD 13:226-27 |
| 6 May 1662 | Iroq vs. Fr | Several Iroq wounded, possibly 1 Iroq M K | Mont | Several other raids were said to have occurred, and some Fr K, but no details as to when. | Dollier, Histoire, 291 |
| Spring 1662 | Sauteur [Ojibwa] vs. 100 On & Moh | Almost all Iroq lost [K or capt.], a few escaped | [Lake Huron] | Iroq had gone to attack the Ot. While hunting for food were spotted and eventually attacked by the Ojibwa band. The Ojibwa had muskets. | JR 48:75-77 |
| 10-11 Sept 1662 | Iroq vs. [Fr?] | 2 [Fr?] M K | île d'Orleans | 7 canoes of Iroq. | JR 47:287 |
| 30 Sept 1662 | Iroq vs. Huron | 1 Huron M, F, & [fc] capt. | île d'Orleans | Thought to be by same group as above. | JR 47:291 |
| 6 Oct 1662 | Iroq vs. Fr | 2 Fr M K | Tad | News rec'd this day. | JR 47:291 |
| 6 Oct 1662 | Iroq vs. Hurons | 1 Huron M & F capt. | [Sillery] | Hurons were working their fields. | JR 47:291 |

Continued on next page

| Date | Groups Involved | Results | Location | Comments | Sources |
|------|-----------------|---------|----------|----------|---------|
| May [1663] | Moh vs. Huron | 1 Huron M K, 1 F wounded, 3 fc capt., 1 mc escaped | Mont | Moh said they came in peace. At night attacked people in whose cabin they were staying. 7 Moh had come but only 4 involved in the attack. | JR 48:87 |
| [5 May 1663] | 40 Iroq, mostly Moh, but with some On vs. Fr | 2 Fr M capt. | Mont | French were working in fields. One prisoner, the one given to Moh, was released when the Moh band fell into ambush of Algk. See below. | JR 48:93, 97, 105 |
| [Between 5 & 24 May] 1663 | Sillery Algk vs. [Moh] | 10 [Moh] K & scalped, 3 capt., 2 of whom later K | Lake Champlain | The Algk returned 24 May. They had set out, unaware of above raid, to strike a blow vs. Iroq. Had gone as far as Lake Champlain when spotted this group returning from New France with prisoner. The Algk had set out 3 weeks prior, but raid was obviously after 5 May since they released prisoner caught in that raid. | JR 47:303; 48:99-111 |
| [End of May to beginning of June] 1663 | Huron vs. 5 Onon | 1, possibly 2, Onon M K, rest wounded & turned over to Fr | [Mont] | The Huron attacked this group because they considered Onon to be spies & to avenge the loss caused by the Moh in the attack vs. their hosts May [1663]. See entry this date above. | JR 48:89-91 |
| [April] 1663 | 800 Iroq [Sen, Onon, & Cay] vs. Susq village | At least 25 Iroq K, 10 capt, plus unspecified number said to have been K | [Ohio River] | Susq village was better fortified than expected, so Iroq tried subtlety. 25 Iroq "ambassadors" capt. and K. Susq went out and engaged small groups of Iroq, capt. 10 more, and drove off Iroq. K unspecified number. | JR 48:7-79; NYCD 12:431 |

Continued on next page

| Date | Groups Involved | Results | Location | Comments | Sources |
|------|-----------------|---------|----------|----------|---------|
| 24 June 1663 | Susq vs.? Iroq | A few Iroq capt. | | News reported this day, but raid was recent. | *NYCD* 12:433 |
| [June?] 1663 | Moh vs. [Micmac or Nova Scotia colonists?] | | Nova Scotia | Governor Temple wrote 6 July 1663 to complain of Moh attack vs. "his people at their" fort. The raid was therefore earlier. Who was attacked is not clear. The Moh told him to keep out of their war with the [Abenaki], thus indicating that any attack against natives or colonists in that region was part of that conflict. | *NYCD* 13:297–98 |
| 23–25 July 1663 | Iroq vs. English | 4 English [M?] K | Maryland | News rec'd these days of deaths in two separate attacks. The attacks were either offshoots of Iroq-Susq hostilities, or deliberate Iroq attacks for English support of the Susq vs. the Iroq. | *NYCD* 12:435, 436 |
| 1 Sept 1663 | Moh vs. [Susq] & [Delaware?] River Indians | 3 [Susq] F K, 2 [Delaware?] River Indian [F] K | [Iroquoia?] | The Susq and [Delaware?] River Indians were K as returned from Moh. Had gone to make presents to Moh (of peace, to join them vs. rest of confederacy?). Moh decided to join rest of Iroq vs. Susq. | *NYCD* 12:439 |
| Autumn [Late Oct to Nov] 1663 | Moh vs. 2 Fr M | 2 Fr M capt. | TR | Prisoners were later freed and returned to Fr. | *JR* 49:119, 125, 135, 145–47 |

Continued on next page

| Date | Groups Involved | Results | Location | Comments | Sources |
|------|-----------------|---------|----------|----------|---------|
| [24 Nov to 12 Dec] 1663 | Iroq vs. [Sokoki] [Western Abenaki] | 30-40 [Sokoki] K, 20 Iroq wounded, unspecified no. of Iroq K, rumor had it at 200-300 | [Connecticut River] | The Iroq left 24 Nov and returned 11-12 Dec. The Sokoki had offered peace and the Moh wanted to accept, but the Onon and Sen did not. Moh later asked for Dutch aid to negotiate a peace and to get their people back. | NYCD 13:308-9, 355, 356, 378 |
| [Mid-May] 1664 | 100 FIA (Algk & Mt) vs. 30-33 Iroq Ambassadors | Some Iroq K & capt. | [St. Law?], "below the great sault" | The embassy was being led by Garaconté, and presumably was made up of several Iroq tribes. The FIA had gone out raiding in that area. One source suggests that intent was specifically to nab envoys. This implies an effort to jeopardize the peace process. FIA refused to heed pleas of Iroq that they came in peace, hacked up Iroq, and stole their goods. | JR 48:233-35; 49:139, 145-47; Correspondance, 728 |
| [Mid-May] 1664 | Iroq vs. Fr | 2 Fr fc capt. | île d'Orleans & TR | Women capt. in two separate raids, about the same time. 1 fc was 12 years old. | JR 49:119; Correspondance, 728 |
| 6 June 1664 | 160-200 Sen & On vs. Susq | 1 Sen, & 2 On [M] capt., 2 On [M] later K | Maryland | News reported this day. | Md. Archives 3:499-500 |
| 27 June 1664 | Sen vs. English | Some English K | [Maryland] | News reported this day. | Md. Archives 3:502-3 |

Continued on next page

| Date | Groups Involved | Results | Location | Comments | Sources |
|------|-----------------|---------|----------|----------|---------|
| [Aug?] 1664 | Iroq vs. Fr | 3–4 Fr M K or wounded, 1 Iroq M K | Mont | No clear date for this event, but precedes one in Aug. & since were hunting, it could also have been late summer. | Dollier, *Histoire*, 297 |
| Aug 1664 | Iroq vs. Fr. | 2 Fr M K | Mont | Shot dead in their canoes. | Dollier, *Histoire*, 297 |
| [Oct 1664 to before 6 Feb 1665] | Moh vs. [Pocumtuck] | 1 Pocumtuck M K & his wife & C capt., villages abandoned | [Pocumtuck villages] | Notice of this war by Moh vs. the [Sokoki], [Pocumtuck], and the [Penacook] was revealed 24 Sept 1664. On 6 Feb 1665, authorities reported the death of a Pocumtuck leader and the relocation of his tribe, that of the [Norwottucks], and also the abandoning of [Squakheag], a Sokoki area. It is not clear if these tribes were also hit, moved for fear of being attacked, or how permanent the moves were. The date is based on the earliest possible start date after the conference in Sept and the reporting of the results in early Feb. Raid was to avenge death of Moh ambassadors at the hands of one of these tribes. | *NYCD* 3:68; *Collections of the Mass. Historical Society*, 6:531 |

Continued on next page

| Date | Groups Involved | Results | Location | Comments | Sources |
|------|-----------------|---------|----------|----------|---------|
| Midwinter [1664-1665] | [30] Iroq vs. Mt | 11 Mt M & 1 F K, 5 Mt M capt., 2 escaped; 20 Iroq M K & 2 F capt. | Lake Piagouagami | 100 Moh and Onon had split up into 3 groups to go raiding. Data is for one of these, composition of group not clear, but about 30 of them. In first attack Iroq K 5 Mt M & 1 F. Learn of others, capt. 2 Mt M, 1 escaped and brought aid. Mt attack Iroq. Iroq K 4 Mt M & capt. 3 while losing 2 of their M K. 1 Mt escapes & brings aid. Mt attack Iroq & K 18 Iroq M, capt. 2 Iroq F, lose 2 of their M in fight and release their people held captive by Iroq. | JR 50:37-41 |
| [24 Apr 1665] | Iroq vs. 4 Fr | 2 Fr M K, 2 capt. | Mont | 4 Fr M were working on the hospital. 1 was K on the spot, 1 died of wounds, 2 were capt. 1 of these may have escaped. Around the same time as this raid a Fr M arrived at TR from Mont having escaped Iroq. | [Morin], Histoire simple et véritable, 137; JR 49:159 |
| [June to July 1665] | 20-30 Iroq vs. 300 Ot traders | Some K, but not clear from what group(s) | [Upper Ott R] | Iroq waiting to ambush Ot traders shortly after they left to go to New France to trade. When saw size of group encouraged Ot to proceed. After a few skirmishes Ot did just that. Date based on arrival of Ot in New France Aug. 3, and upon average of 30 days to make trip down. Place of ambush based on Ot tribal location and usual route taken to trade. | JR 49:163, 245-47 |
| July 1665 | Iroq vs. Fr | 1 Fr M capt. | île Ste. Thérèse | Sieur Le Moyne capt. He was returned by the Onon, but it is not clear which tribe he was capt. by. | Dollier, Histoire, 299-301; JR, 50:127 |

Continued on next page

| Date | Groups Involved | Results | Location | Comments | Sources |
|---|---|---|---|---|---|
| July 1665 | Iroq vs. Fr | Some Fr K & some capt. | TR | Raid took place shortly before arrival of De Tracy at TR around 23 July. | JR 49:239 |
| [Late July to early Aug 1665] | Iroq vs. 300 Ot traders | Some Ot M K | "Cap de massacre" [West end, LSP] | This is the same brigade of traders attacked June to July of this year. Not clear if Iroq attackers were the same ones that struck then. The Iroq in this attack just fired on a few canoes of stragglers and then fled. The date is based on the location of the attack and the fact that the Ot arrived at TR to trade 3 Aug. | JR 49:247-49 |
| 28 Oct 1665 | Iroq vs. 20 Nip M & families | 7 Nip M K, 12 Nip M capt. along with some F | "Toward the Petite Nation" | News rec'd this day. The location is as recorded. Both the Nip and Petite Nation were living, for most part, near TR. | JR 49:173 |
| 9 Jan to 8 Mar 1666 | 500 Fr vs. Moh | 4 Iroq & 6 Fr K | [Near Moh villages] | The villages were abandoned. Deaths took place during a small skirmish as Fr retreated, 20 Feb. The Fr deaths do not include the 60 or so who died of cold and hunger. | JR 50:131-35, 183 |
| [Mid- to late May] 1666 | Iroq vs. Fr | 1 Fr [M?] K | Mont | Rec'd news 4 June. This and the raid below took place in "past" 3 weeks. That puts them in mid- to late May. | JR 50:189 |
| [Mid- to late May] 1666 | Iroq vs. Fr | 1 Fr [M?] K | Ft. Chambly | See comment above. | JR 50:189 |

Continued on next page

| Date | Groups Involved | Results | Location | Comments | Sources |
|---|---|---|---|---|---|
| 11 July 1666 | Iroq vs. Hartford-area Indians | Some K & 9 capt. | | News reported this day. Raid was said to have taken place recently. The tribes located in this area were the Tunxis and the Podunk. | *NYCD* 3:120-21 |
| [Mid-July before] 20 July 1666 | Moh vs. Fr | 2-3 Fr M K, 4 Fr M capt. | Ft. Ste. Anne | News rec'd 20 July. | *JR* 50:139, 193 |
| 28 Sept to 5 Nov 1666 | 1,200 Fr & 100 Huron & Algk vs. Moh | 4 Moh villages destroyed, crops & supplies burned, villages looted | Moh villages | The Moh had intended to fight, but sight of massed army caused them to abandon those plans. Fr were unopposed. | *JR* 50:141-45, 203; *Correspondance*, 772-76 |
| [Late Aug to early Sept 1667] | Mah vs. Moh | 1 Moh F scalped, later died of wounds | Outside Gandaouagué | Date is based on Jesuits leaving Fort St. Anne 24 Aug and arriving among Moh shortly after. Jesuits were delayed at village while Moh went in pursuit of Mah, so raid was about time of their arrival. | *JR* 51:187-89 |
| [Fall, after mid-Sept, 1667] | Mah vs. Moh | 1 Moh M K | Outside Gandaouagué | Date based on internal references that suggest this raid occurred at least 20 days after the above raid. | *JR* 51:189-97 |
| 25 June 1668 | Moh vs. Nantick [Niantic?] | 1 Nantick M & F capt. | | News reported this day. Moh also killed livestock of English near Groton. | Conn. Archives, Indians, 1:Pt. 1, 8ff. |

Continued on next page

| Date | Groups Involved | Results | Location | Comments | Sources |
|---|---|---|---|---|---|
| Toward end of Oct 1668 | Onon vs. Susq | Some Susq capt., 1 Susq M & F K | | Prisoners arrived at Onon this time. At least 2 were tortured to death, but impression is left that more than this were capt. and tortured to death. | JR 52:161, 167-71, 173 |
| [Late June 1669] | Fr vs. 7 On & 1 Sen | 7 On [M] & 1 Sen [M] K, several Fr M K | Near Mont | Galinée left Mont 6 July and says the incident happened 8-15 days before his departure. The Fr attacked the Iroq to rob them of their pelts. The Fr M K were K by the French authorities for this crime which some thought might lead to war with the Iroq. | JR 53:33-35, 241; 54:113; Galinée, "Voyage de Dollier et Galinée," 8, 18 |
| [July to Aug 1669] | Susq vs. Sen | 10 Sen M K | [Near a Sen village] | | Galinée, "Voyage de Dollier et Galinée," 18, 20 |
| [Mid- to late Aug 1669] | Sen vs. [Shawnee] | 1 [Shawnee] M capt. & tortured to death | | The war party returned around this time. | Galinée, "Voyage de Dollier et Galinée," 32, 34 |
| 18 Aug 1669 | Mah vs. Moh | 4 Mah F & 6 M capt., 50 Mah M K, 40 Moh K | Moh village | The Mah attacked and the Moh then went in pursuit. Sometime after this the Moh went to avenge this but no engagement took place. | JR 53:137-59 |
| 26 Aug 1669 | 2 On vs. Susq | 1 On M K | [Susq village] | The survivor returned this day. Had gone to attack Susq. 1 On M capt. and tortured to death by Susq. | JR 53:243 |

Continued on next page

| Date | Groups Involved | Results | Location | Comments | Sources |
|---|---|---|---|---|---|
| 26 Aug 1669 | Iroq (4 On & 1 Sen) vs. [Shawnee] | 2 [Shawnee] capt. | | The Iroq returned around this date. There is no certainty as to when the raid was carried out. | *JR* 53:245; 54:113, 115 |
| 26 Aug 1669 | [60] [Amikwa] vs. 5 Iroq (3 On, 1 Onon, & 1 Sen) | 2 On, 1 Onon, & 1 Sen capt. or K | | Reported on this date by the above returning Iroq. He was the sole survivor of this attack. The party above was returning home when were attacked. Given Shawnee location, the Amikwa must have been out to attack some Iroq. The Shawnee were capt. as well. | *JR* 53:247; 54:113, 115 |
| [Fall to winter 1669] | 500 Sen & unspecified Number of Cay vs. [Shawnee] | | | 1 Sept Father Fremin noted the departure of these warriors. In July 1670 an Iroq leader defended Sen against charges that they had attacked Algk first and said they had only done injury to the [Shawnee]. This would indicate that some fighting occurred. | *JR* 53:47-49; 54:117 |
| [20 Sept 1669 to 27 Jan 1670] | [120] On, 50 Onon, & 10 Cay vs. Susq | 6 Susq M & 3 F capt., later 6 M & 1 F tortured to death | | These Iroq groups left 20 Sept and arrived with prisoners 27 Jan. The prisoners were divided among the tribes who had contributed warriors to raid. A Susq ambassador had been among Cay. When prisoners arrived he and his nephew were K. He had come to talk of peace. | *JR* 53:247, 253-55; 54:23, 29-31, 75 |

*Continued on next page*

| Date | Groups Involved | Results | Location | Comments | Sources |
|---|---|---|---|---|---|
| Mar 1670 | 20-22 Iroq (18-20 were Sen) vs. 106 Outagami [Fox] (100 F & C, & 6 M) | All Outagami K except 30 F capt. [70 F & C, & 6 M K] | Foot of Lake Michigan | 2 Iroq, escaped from Potawatomi, led Sen to 6 cabins of Outagami. Most M of that group were out hunting. After massacre some Algk pursued Iroq to no avail. See also raid below. | JR 53:39-49; 54:219-21, 227 |
| [Between Mar & 26 Apr 1670] | Algk [Mostly Ot] vs. Iroq [Sen] | Iroq all defeated, 3 Iroq scalped | | After the failure of the above pursuit, a group of Algk, mostly Ottawa but including their allies, went to avenge this injury. Attacked a group of Iroq hunters. Might have been against Sen. The date is based on time of above raid and the assumption that the 4 [Miami] who appeared among the Outagami with 3 Iroq scalps 26 Apr had gotten them in this reprisal raid. | JR 53:39-49; 54:219-21, 227, 265 |
| [Spring 1672] | Susq vs. On | 2 On F [K] | On village | F K fifty paces from village. | JR 56:37 |
| [Late Apr to late May 1672] | 20 Sen & 40 Cay vs. Susq | 1 Sen M K, 1 capt., 8 Cay M K, 15 wounded, 15-16 Susq M K | | Date is based on raid beginning Ascension Day, 40 days after Easter. Sen ran into group of 60 Susq boys, 15-16 years old, who attacked then went after the Cay. | JR 56:55-57 |
| [1674?] | Cay vs. Susq | 3 Susq K | | No details, it is simply observed in passing that 3 Susq prisoners were baptized before death at hands of torturers. | JR 58:227 |
| 6 Feb 1674 | Iroq vs. Mt [Porcupine tribe] | Massacre | [Lake St. Jean] | News reported this day. The defeat caused a general panic in the area. | JR 59:39-41 |

Continued on next page

| Date | Groups Involved | Results | Location | Comments | Sources |
|---|---|---|---|---|---|
| [1675] | Iroq vs. Susq | Susq utterly defeated | | The Jesuits note this year that since the Susq have been defeated the Sen have become increasingly insolent. There are no details as to what might have happened in this war, and there is a hint that it could have could have taken place from 1674 to 1675, but even this much is speculative. However, by Dec 1675 the Susq and Iroq held peace talks, and by May 1676 the Susq begin to relocate closer to the Iroq. | JR 58:237, 241; 59:251; NYCD 12:546, 553; Md. Archives 5:152-54 |
| [Winter 1675-76] | Moh vs. Narragansett | 11 Narragansett K | 5 K near Fort Albany, 6 at [Squakheag] | News reported 29 Apr 1676. | Collections of the Conn. Historical Society 21:241-42 |
| Feb [1676] | 300 Moh vs. King Phillip & 500 of his followers | Drove off Phillip, K some [possibly 79], capt. some | 40 miles west of Fort Albany | A report from Boston, 18 May refers to a Moh attack vs. the "enemy" and states the Moh K 79. This may be an exaggeration, but probably refers to the same raid. | NYCD 3:255; CSP 9:395 |
| 17 June 1676 | Onon vs. ? | 50 capt. from 2 different tribes, of whom 6 F, 5 M, 1 mc, 1 C K | 200 Leagues Southwest | The Onon return around this time. Other Iroq may have been involved. One of these groups of captives might have been Shawnee. Those K were tortured to death as group traveled through Sen villages on way to Onon. | JR 60:185; NYCD 3:252 |

Continued on next page

| Date | Groups Involved | Results | Location | Comments | Sources |
|---|---|---|---|---|---|
| 4 June 1677 | 80-100 Moh vs. Mah & North Indians [Western Abnk] | 18 people capt., most later returned | [Albany area] | Moh reproached for this attack this day. | NYCD 13:508; LIR, 40-41 |
| 27 June 1678 | 60 Moh vs. [Niantic] | 3 [Niantic] K; 3 M, 17 F, 2 mc, 2 [fc] capt. | 6 miles from Suddberry | The Moh return this day. Albany officials suspected most of the prisoners were later K. Niantic were [working] in a field when attacked. | Public Records of ...Conn. 3:262-63, 490; NYCD 13:520-27 |
| 7 Aug 1678 | 20 Moh vs. North Indians [Western Abnk] | 5 North Indians K, & 2 M, 1 F, & 3 mc capt. | | Moh return this day. 4 other North Indians had escaped. | NYCD 13:531 |
| 19 Aug 1678 | Sen & Susq vs. [Pisct] | Some Pisct K | | News reported this day. | Md. Archives 15:183 |
| [Between 3 May 1677 & before end of 1678] | Iroq vs. Ill | Iroq defeated | Ill territory | The Jesuits learned of this attack in [1678]. Father Allouez left the Ill after 3 May [1677] and made no mention of such an attack. It probably occurred after he left, but when that was and when in [1678] the Jesuits learned of it is not clear. | JR 60:165-67 |
| 10-12 May 1680 | 200-300 Susq & [Iroq] vs. Pisct | | [Pisct Fort] | There is no mention of casualties on either side. The Susq wanted revenge for some of their leaders K in earlier wars and prisoners held by Maryland freed. The Susq-Iroq group eventually withdrew. | Md. Archives 15:280, 281, 283 |

Continued on next page

| Date | Groups Involved | Results | Location | Comments | Sources |
|------|-----------------|---------|----------|----------|---------|
| Sept 1680 | 500-600 Iroq (Sen & Onon, at least) vs. Ill | 700-1,200 mostly F & C of Tamoroa Ill capt. or K; 30 Iroq M lost [K] | Grande Rivière [Ill territory] | Iroq took M & F as well as some trade goods Tonty had brought up. The process began in early Sept. Most Ill men were either at war or hunting. Iroq agreed to peace then pursued Ill as they left to go further north. Attacked the Tamoroa after they had split off from main group and were no longer expecting the attack. | AN, C11A 5:310; Margry, *Découvertes* 1:506-20, 584-88; Margry, *Relations*, 9-12 |
| [Dec 1680] | (400) Iroq vs. 2 cabins of Miami hunters | (30-40 Miami & Ill K; 300 capt; 180 Iroq K) unspecified number of Miami capt. & K, 13-14 "Cascacia" Ill K; 8 Iroq K | (Oumamis River) [St. Joseph's River] | The Iroq had detached themselves from army above or were the army in question. Iroq attacked Miami and proceeded to a Miami village. 100 "Cascacia" Ill returned from hunting, learned of Tamoroa defeat, and went in pursuit of Iroq. They were discovered and defeated. Iroq left with the Miami prisoners. This last part differs from Lahontan's account where the Iroq are said to have been defeated and the prisoners freed. His numbers also seem exaggerated. If the Iroq were bringing even half of the 1,200 Illinois reported capt. and K, they would hardly spare so large a detachment to raid. The data in parenthesis () is found in Lahontan's account. | AN, C11A 5:310; Margry, *Découvertes* 1:527-28; Lahontan, *New Voyages* 2:486-88 |
| 1 Jan 1681 | Susq & [Cay] vs. Mattawoman | Most of Mattawoman "cut off" | | | *Md. Archives* 15:329, 374, 382-84; 17:5 |

Continued on next page

| Date | Groups Involved | Results | Location | Comments | Sources |
|------|----------------|---------|----------|----------|---------|
| 18 June 1681 | 200 Susq & [Cay] vs. Pisct | 13 Pisct capt. | [Pisct Fort] | News reported this day. The original intent had been to attack Pisct, but for some reason talks were held. Pisct capt. were probably envoys in the talks. | *Md. Archives* 15:353, 359, 374, 375 |
| [24-30 Aug] 1681 | 300 Iroq (70-100 were Moh, the rest Cay, On, Onon,) vs. Pisct | 1 Pisct M K & 9 M, 4 F, & 4 fc capt. | [Pisct Fort] | Spokesmen for the On and Onon stated that they came to raid to capture people to bolster their population because they feared hostilities with the Sen. | *Md. Archives* 17:3, 5, 14, 15 |
| [Late Aug to mid-Sept 1681] | | | | Throughout this period the Iroq are accused of various raids against Marylanders, especially in Charles County. It is hard to determine how to assess these. It is by no means certain that the Iroq were responsible for the attacks. In the past they had been blamed for attacks and later exonerated. In Virginia, too, the authorities recognized that often the Iroq were blamed for acts based solely on rumor. The hostile acts were probably committed by local tribes using the Iroq threat as a means to exact their own revenge. Certainly the Maryland authorities recognized that even in the two to three attacks that are probably legitimately attributable to the Iroq, these are but offshoots of the major group noted above, and that the Iroq were more interested in freeing captives held by Marylanders than in stealing their linen. | *Md. Archives* 17:18-25, 27-28; *CSP* 11:93 |

Continued on next page

| Date | Groups Involved | Results | Location | Comments | Sources |
|---|---|---|---|---|---|
| 1681 | Iroq vs. Ill | 700-900 Ill capt., 300-600 K | [Ill territory] | There is no clear indication of when this happened. The first notice of it was Aug 1682, but the raid was said to have occurred in 1681. | JR 62:71, 159-61, 185; Margry, Relations, 22 |
| 6 Feb 1682 | Sen vs. ? | 35 people capt. at one location & 4-5 from another | | News reported this day. Writing from Mt. Paradise, Virginia, C. Jones notes 35 capt. in an attack 300 miles SSW from his location and 4-5 capt. from some villages "under the Mountains" 500 miles away. Not clear if in same direction. | CSP 11:193 |
| Summer 1682 | Onon vs. Pisct | 3 Pisct capt. (2 of whom were F), & some K | | On deny that the Pisct prisoner they have was brought by their warriors. They make no denial about the K Pisct. This would lead one to conclude that Onon were primarily responsible. The Onon K their two F capt. | Md. Archives 17:214, 215; JR 62:59 |
| [Between 4 & 18 June] 1682 | 100-104 Iroq vs.? | Iroq defeated? | | This is date Tonty encountered Iroq toward "Ouabache." In one version of this event Tonty has Iroq out to raid vs. Tamoroa Ill. In an earlier version he stated Iroq were defeated by "Scioux." It is not clear if the Iroq were out vs. "Scioux" or if meeting was accidental, or he or his transcriber made an error in the group's name. | Margry, Relations, 21; Margry, Découvertes 1:611 |

Continued on next page

| Date | Groups Involved | Results | Location | Comments | Sources |
|------|-----------------|---------|----------|----------|---------|
| [Early to mid-July] 1682 | 50 On vs. Choptank | 54 Choptank capt., & several English K | [Choptank village] | News reported 4 Aug with notice that raid had occurred about three weeks prior. 14 captives were eventually returned. The rest refused to leave the On. Apparently several Englislh were also K, and their properties looted of tobacco. | *Md. Archives* 17:214, 229, 369; *NYCD* 13:565; *JR* 62:67 |
| 25 Aug 1682 | Iroq vs. [Erie] | 600 Erie (M, F, & C) surrendered | Near Virginia | This news reported this day. The Jesuits noted that the Erie surrendered rather than be forced to relocate. This does not really seem like a raid, but does indicate that the threat of force is what produced the Erie move. | *JR* 62:71 |
| 25 Aug 1682 | Onon vs. [Miami] | At least 6 Miami M & 1 F capt., 4 of the M & the 1 F were tortured to death | | Prisoners reported arriving around this date. 3 M and 1 F capt. by one group, 3 M capt. by another. Apparently more Miami were K during the attacks, but numbers not specified. | *JR* 62:73, 79, 81, 87, 91, 93 |
| 15 Sept 1682 | On vs. Dowaganhaes [Algk] | 50 Dowaganhaes capt. | | The On report this news this day and state that warriors had done this lately. This is not a reference to the raid vs. the Choptank. At the time this news was announced, those out vs. the Choptank had yet to return. Dowaganhaes was a general term used by the Iroq to designate Algk speaking groups. | *Md. Archives* 17:215 |

Continued on next page

| Date | Groups Involved | Results | Location | Comments | Sources |
|---|---|---|---|---|---|
| 15 or 20 Feb 1683 | 400 Outagami [Fox] vs. 1000 Iroq | 500 Iroq M K; 100 Fox M K & 30 wounded | Fox hunting area | No other source makes note of this massive defeat of the Iroq. It is extremely unlikely that such an event would go unnoticed by French and English authorities. Nor does it seem plausible that 400 Fox would risk attacking an army of 1,000. Lahontan makes mention of this event in connection with his voyage down the mythical Long River. This account, it would appear, is equally dubious. | Lahontan, *New Voyages* 2:488-94 |
| Aug 1683 | Iroq vs. English of Virginia | 5-6 English K, 2-3 Iroq [M] K, & 300 head of cattle | Head of Rappahannock River | Iroq apparently went on a rampage and English were K only when tried to protect their property and fired on Iroq, who returned the fire. | L/R, 70-71 |
| 21 Nov 1683 | Sen vs. Chickahominy [and/or] Rappahannock | Many K. Of one group attacked, only 3 people survived | Chick. [and/or] Rap. Fort | News reported this day, but appears to have been a recent raid. | L/R, 125; CSP 11:549, 551 |
| End of Feb 1684 | 200 Sen & Cay vs. 14 Fr traders | 7 canoes of goods pillaged, Fr detained, but eventually released | Toward Ill | These Iroq were on their way to attack Fort St. Louis. The traders were attacked because they were carrying guns and ammunition to the enemies of the Iroq. | AN, C11A 6:261, 265, 269, 273; Colden, *Five Indian Nations*, 60-62; Wraxall, *Indian Affairs*, 12-13 |

Continued on next page

| Date | Groups Involved | Results | Location | Comments | Sources |
|---|---|---|---|---|---|
| 20-21 Mar 1684 | 200 Sen & Cay vs. Fr | Fr Fort attacked, Iroq driven off | Fort St. Louis | This attack took place after the above attack vs. the traders. The Iroq were upset at the Fr having a Fort in enemy territory. | AN, C11A 6:261, 269; Margry, Découvertes 1:614; Margry, Relations, 22 |
| July to Aug 1684 | 1,800 Fr & FIA vs. Iroq | Fr make peace | | The intended attack vs. the Iroq by la Barre came to nothing. That is, it was launched, but the differences were resolved peacefullly. | AN, C11A 6:267, 287-88, 299-300, 388-91 |
| [July to Aug? 1684] | Iroq vs. [Appamatuck] | | [James River] | This raid took place at or shortly after the time of the conference between Iroq and the governor of Virginia in July. | LIR, 85, 87, 88 |
| [July to Aug? 1684] | [On] Iroq vs. English in Virginia | 3 Indian boys, servants of Englishman, capt. | Near Appamatock River Falls | This raid happened at about same time as above raid. The group was probably an offshoot of the one vs. Appamatuck. The Iroq excuse themselves of this action by saying the warriors had yet to learn of peace. (See above.) 2 of the boys went to On and 1 to Moh, thus suggesting they were probably the ones who attacked. The Moh, however, denied taking part. | LIR, 85 |
| [July to Dec? 1684] | Iroq vs. [Nottoway] | 1 Nottoway K | South side, James River | Raid seems to have taken place after the Virginia-Iroq conference of July and sometime before 1685. | LIR, 85 |
| [July to Dec.? 1684] | Iroq vs. [Nansatico] | 1 Nansatico capt. | [R]appahannock R. | On date see above. | LIR, 85 |

Continued on next page

| Date | Groups Involved | Results | Location | Comments | Sources |
|---|---|---|---|---|---|
| Spring 1685 | Iroq vs. [Saponi] | Some Saponi wounded & 1 capt. | Below the mountains | | LIR, 85 |
| [Mid-July] 1685 | Iroq vs. English in Virginia | 1 Indian girl, servant of Englishman, capt. | Near Appamatock River Falls | This was the same Englishman that had lost 3 M servants to the Iroq sometime last year. The raid was by a small group. | LIR, 85 |
| 21 May 1686 | Sen vs. [Wyandot] | 70 Wyandot capt. | | News reported this day. The raid could have been either in the winter of 1685 or early spring of this year. 5 captives later released. | LIR, 100 |
| 4 Nov 1686 | Iroq vs. Ounicanicks [Miami?] | 500 Miami capt., 29 Iroq [M] K | [Miami territory] | News reported this day. Father Lamberville, writing from among the Onon, leaves the impression that the raid was sometime this year. 2 Iroq were K during capture of Miami, and 27 were K when the Touloues [?] and Ill attacked Iroq to try to free prisoners. However, the impression was left that the captives did make it to Iroquoia. The attacking Iroq group may have been the Sen. The document, however, is too vague to make this any more than conjecture. | CSP 12:276 |
| End of Mar 1687 | 60 [Iroq, possibly Sen] vs. [Appamatuck] & English of Virginia | 3 English K, several Appamatuck K & several wounded, 5-6 Sen K | Head of James River | The attacked group were deer hunting. The Iroq apologized for killing the English—they claimed that they thought them to be Indians. A messenger sent to get aid was killed as he returned to battle scene. Iroq then left. On identity of Iroq see below. | LIR, 135-36 |

Continued on next page

| Date | Groups Involved | Results | Location | Comments | Sources |
|---|---|---|---|---|---|
| 27 June 1687 | 300 [Iroq, Sen, &/or On] vs. Waynoake [Weanock] & English of Virginia | 6 Weanock F & 1 mc capt., English homes ransacked & looted of, among other things, clocks | Head of James River | In the LIR the Sen are clearly designated as attackers in this and in above raid. In another document the On are castigated for this attack and it was they who returned six prisoners. Later the governor of Virginia complained about both these attacks but stated that he did not know which Iroq group was responsible. It is not clear if Robert Livingston confused the Virginia term Sinnikus (or one of its many variants) for Seneca. Sinnikus was often used as a general term for all Iroq. Or it may have been that both groups participated in this raid and that he had this information. The same may be true for the raid noted above. | LIR, 125, 137-38; CSP 12:429-30 |
| July to Aug 1687 | 2,000 Fr & FIA vs. Sen & Cay | 6-7 Fr & 5 FIA M K, 11-15 FIA & 15 Fr M wounded; 28-50 Sen M K, 60 wounded, 200 Cay (150 F & C, & 50 M) capt., 1 M & 1 F K, Sen villages looted & destroyed | Sen villages | On the way south to Sen, Denonville's army capt. some Cay villagers, and possibly destroyed their villages on the north shore of Lake Ontario. All the killing took place when the Fr army was ambushed on their way to the Sen villages. The abandoned villages were destroyed. Lahontan, as usual, has higher mortality figures. Those presented here are based on the official Fr accounts. | AN, C11A 9:32-38, 61-77, 104-20; Baugy, Journal, 68-109; JR 63:269-81; Lahontan, New Voyages 1:121-22, 129; Margry, Relations, 26 |
| [Between mid-Aug & Sept] 1687 | Iroq vs. Fr | 9 Fr M K | Between Cataraqui & Mont | | JR 63:279 |

Continued on next page

| Date | Groups Involved | Results | Location | Comments | Sources |
|------|-----------------|---------|----------|----------|---------|
| 7 Sept 1687 | 60 Iroq vs. Fr | 3 Iroq M K, 1 Indian capt. K & 1 F K | île St. Hélène, Mont | Iroq attacked a house. It is not clear what the Indians capt. by the Iroq were doing there, or if capt. There. | JR 63:279; AN, C11A 9:142 |
| [Sept to Oct] 1687 | Iroq vs. Fr | [9] Fr M K | | The Iroq are said to have attacked and burned Fr property. In several raids have K 18 Fr M. If the raid in which 9 Fr M were K is excluded, we may conclude that in the process of these "burning" raids 9 more Fr have been K. | JR 63:279, 287 |
| [Approx. 22-27 Oct] 1687 | 200 Iroq vs. Fr. | 5-6 Fr M K, some wounded; 3 Iroq M K, some wounded | Mont | | JR 63:289; AN, C11A 9:142; 10:148 |
| 8 Nov 1687 | Moh vs. Fr | 1 Fr M & 1 F capt. & several other Fr K; 2 Moh K | Fort Chambly | News reported this day. This group may have captured some Fr. The Albany authorities mention M F & C being sent by the Moh. But it is not clear if these are Fr or are Moh being sent to English for protection while Moh are out warring. | L/R, 139 |
| [Late 1687] | 40 Iroq (Moh, Onon, & On) vs. Fr | 1 Fr F & 3 Fr M capt. | Near Fort Frontenac | The 3 Fr M were soldiers. The Fr F & 12 other Fr captives were released in 1688. | AN, C11A 10:86-87, 89 |
| [Late Dec] 1687 | 22 Huron vs. 40-64 Sen hunters | 14 Sen M & 4 F capt., 2 Sen escaped, the rest [20-44] K; 3 Huron [M] K | [50 L south of Fort St. Joseph] | The Huron were from Michilimackinac. The higher figures and the number of capt. were furnished by Lahontan. | AN, C11A 10:70; Lahontan, New Voyages 1:141-42 |

Continued on next page

| Date | Groups Involved | Results | Location | Comments | Sources |
|---|---|---|---|---|---|
| [Late Dec] 1687 | 22 Huron vs. 40-64 Sen hunters | 14 Sen M & 4 F capt., 2 Sen escaped, the rest [20-44] K; 3 Huron [M] K | [50 L south of Fort St. Joseph] | The Huron were from Michilimackinac. The higher figures and the number of capt. were furnished by Lahontan. | AN, C11A 10:70; Lahontan, *New Voyages* 1:141-42 |
| Spring 1688 | 25-30 Iroq vs. 2 Fr M | 2 Fr M K | | The 2 K were stragglers, part of a convoy of 120 returning from Fort Frontenac. Iroq made no attempt at the larger group. | AN, C11A 10:88 |
| [Spring] 1688 | 60 Iroq vs. Miami | 59 Miami M & F capt. | [Miami territory] | The returning Iroq war party was attacked and the captives freed when they ran into a group of Fr and FIA who had set out to strike some blow vs. the Iroq. See raid of 28 July-4 Aug 1688. | Lahontan, *New Voyages* 1:157-60 |
| [Spring to summer] 1688 | Ill vs. Iroq | 12 Iroq capt., 6 later K | | Some 13 Ill parties, 300 M in all, had left in Jan to raid vs. Iroq. This was result of one raid. | Margry, *Découvertes* 3:589 |
| [Summer] 1688 | 300 Onon vs. 80 Miami warriors | 4 Miami K | [North shore Lake Erie?] | The Miami had set out to attack Iroq. Were dissuaded by Fr authorities and were attacked as made way back to Fort St. Joseph. | Lahontan, *New Voyages* 1:161-63 |

Continued on next page

| Date | Groups Involved | Results | Location | Comments | Sources |
|---|---|---|---|---|---|
| [Summer] 1688 | Iroq vs. Fr | Fr & Fr settlements attacked | | Near La Presentation a canoe with 3 Fr M, stragglers from a supply convoy to Fort Frontenac, was attacked. No details as to outcome. At same time groups of Iroq, the Moh are specifically noted, "ravage" the countryside at St. François, Rivière de Loups, Sorel, Contrecoeur, and St. Ours. It is unlikely the Moh were doing this alone. Moreover, two armies of about 600 Iroq each were spotted in the colony. | AN, C11A 10:88-89 |
| 28 July-4 Aug 1688 | Fr. & FIA (40 Sauteurs & unspecified number of Fr & Ot) vs. 60 Iroq | 15 Iroq [M] K, 5 wounded & 12 capt.; 4 Sauteurs K; captives Iroq had were freed | South shore, Lake Erie | Fr and FIA had gone out to raid at a Cay fishing site. Spotted large Iroq group and decided to abandon plans. On way back came upon Iroq returning with Miami captives. The casualties were result of two separate engagements between these two groups. | Lahontan, *New Voyages* 1:155-60 |
| [Late summer to early fall] 1688 | Huron vs. 4 Iroq | 1 Iroq [M] K | [Possibly Near Mont] | The Huron Le Rat attacked what turned out to be 4 members of Otreouati's peace delegation. Lahontan has 40 Iroq attacked by 100 of Le Rat's men. | AN, C11A 10:90, 100-101; Lahontan, *New Voyages* 1:220-23 |
| [Late summer to early fall] 1688 | FIA (Moh from Prairie de-la-Madeleine) vs. Iroq | 4 Iroq scalped [K] | St. Law | The FIA were Moh from Prairie de-la-Madeleine. This raid was said to have taken place around the same time as that noted above. | AN, C11A 10:90 |
| 30 Oct 1688 | Abnk vs. Iroq | 7 Iroq M K | Chambly River | News reported this date. The raid was probably carried out earlier, but there is nothing in the document to suggest when. | AN, C11A 10:90 |

Continued on next page

| Date | Groups Involved | Results | Location | Comments | Sources |
|---|---|---|---|---|---|
| [Winter 1688-1689] | Ill vs. Iroq | At least 80 Iroq capt., possibly all K | [Iroq lands?] | Writing in Mar 1689 Tonty reports that Ill have brought 80 Iroq prisoners, out of which they made a "bonne grillade." More were K during the battle. It is implied that the Sen were the target group. | Margry, Decouvertes 3:564 |
| [Before 5 Aug, probably late July,] 1689 | 300 Iroq vs. Fr | 4 Fr. M capt. | Fort Frontenac | The 300 Iroq were part of the army on their way to attack La Chine. The Iroq did not attack the Fort. It is not clear under what circumstances Fr. Millet and the 3 others were capt. | JR 64:67-75 |
| 5 Aug 1689 | 1,200-1,500 Iroq vs. Fr | 200 Fr K, 120-130 Fr M F & C capt., houses & fields burned | La Chine | Although various sources note this destruction, none provide exact figures on how many M F and C were capt. or K, nor are any Iroq losses reported. It seems extremely unlikely that some Iroq were not K. After this the Iroq continued to harrass the Fr and capt. Fr M and F, but the sources provide no data as to how many, or in what areas. | JR 64:71; NYCD 3:599, 620-21; Lahontan, New Voyages 1:224-25; AN, C11A 10:219, 244 |
| Early Oct 1689 | Sen vs. 30 Fr soldiers | 12-18 Iroq [M] K, 3 capt. & later tortured to death | "sur un lac" [LSP?] | The French claim 18 Iroq were K, but the Sen put the number at 12. It is not certain, but the Fr might have been out on patrol for Iroq in light of their continual depredations against the colony. | AN, C11A 10:244; 11:9 |

Continued on next page

| Date | Groups Involved | Results | Location | Comments | Sources |
|------|-----------------|---------|----------|----------|---------|
| 13 Nov 1689 | 150 Iroq (On & Onon) vs. Fr | At least 8 Fr capt., 4 later K, & 4 were returned; houses burned | [Lachenaie] & île Jésus | Only 2 people from Lachenaie escaped. The 8 capt. were taken by the Onon. The number taken by the On is not specified. | AN, C11A 10:207; 11:9 |
| 2 June 1690 | 13 canoes of Iroq [Moh?] vs. 149-170 Fr | 4 Fr [M] K, some wounded; over 30 Iroq K, some wounded, 4 Iroq (2 M & 2 F) capt., 1 M later K | 3 L above "les chats" [Ott R.] | The Fr were enroute to Michilimackinac when were lured into an ambush by Iroq. Fr then sent men in behind Iroq and trapped them in a cross fire. 4 canoes of Iroq escaped. If these were the large Iroq war canoes, the Iroq party could have been over 130 people strong. Since F were along, they may have been hunting as well. The Iroq group may have been Moh. See second [June] 1690 raid below. | AN, C11A 11:15, 86; Colden, *Five Indian Nations*, 121-22 |
| [June] 1690 | Iroq vs. [Fr?] | 15-16 [Fr?] capt. & later K | "Rivière Puante," opposite TR | The captives were K by Iroq in order to make a faster escape. Were being pursued. This raid was said to have occurred prior to the one below. On reasons for date, see below. The source does not make clear who was capt. Since most attacks seem directed against the Fr, and the source is referring to attacks vs. the colony, it is assumed that Fr were the target. | AN, C11A 11:19; Colden, *Five Indian Nations*, 122 |

Continued on next page

| Date | Groups Involved | Results | Location | Comments | Sources |
|------|-----------------|---------|----------|----------|---------|
| [June] 1690 | 25 Fr vs. Iroq [Moh?] | 25 Iroq M K; 12 Fr [M] K | Point-aux-Trembles | The Iroq, thought to be the survivors from the 2 June raid, were planning some action vs. Fr. They were spotted and 25 Fr set up an ambush. Iroq charged Fr, casualties were inflicted, and both sides retreated. An English document, dated 7 July 1690, states that the Moh had fought the Fr and lost 55 K. This is the total K for this and the 2 June raid. If this reference is to either or both of these raids, then these Iroq were the Moh. Since this group was believed to be remnant of that of 2 June group, that would make them Moh as well. This raid is dated in June because of location--not far for fugitives of 2 June raid to travel--and because for Boston to be aware of either of the raids in question so early in July, the raids had to have been in June. | AN, C11A 11:19; CSP 13:296; Colden, *Five Indian Nations*, 122 |
| [Summer?] 1690 | Iroq vs. [Fr] C | 5-6 Fr C capt., 4 later freed, 1 K; 1 Iroq [M] K, 3 Iroq [M] capt. & K | Sorel, near Fort | [Fr] C were capt. as herded cattle. 1 C K as Iroq fled Fr pursuers. 1 Iroq K during pursuit. 4 "Iroq" were later capt., one, it turns out, was an Englishman. It is implied they were part of group that capt. Fr C. All 4 were K. | AN, C11A 11:19; Colden, *Five Indian Nations*, 122 |

Continued on next page

| Date | Groups Involved | Results | Location | Comments | Sources |
|---|---|---|---|---|---|
| 4 Sept 1690 | 167 [Iroq] & English vs. Fr | 21 Fr M (11 farmers, 10 soldiers), 4 Fr F capt. Later 2 Fr M & 4 Fr F K; 1-6 Iroq K; 150 cattle K | "La Fourche," 1/4 L from Prairie de-la-Madeleine | The French source attributes this as an Iroq raid, but the group was composed of 125 [Iroq] and 42 English [Dutch from Albany led by P. Schuyler. In his account he stated that attack took place 23 Aug and that only 1 Iroq was K. | AN, C11A 11:27; O'Callaghan, *Documentary History* 2: 285-88 |
| 22 Sept 1690 | 34 Fr vs. Iroq | [18] Fr [M] K or capt. | Fort near LSP | Fr discovered Iroq, muster 34 M to pursue. Attacked Iroq who fled to join up with a larger group. Pursuing Fr get caught, "no more that half escaped." | AN, C11A 11:28 |
| [Winter 1690 to 1691] | FIA (Indians from Michilimackinac) vs. Iroq | 15-20 Iroq K | [Iroq lands] | Champigny learned from the Moh in Apr 1691 that FIA had struck a blow vs. Iroq and 15-20 people were K. In a May 1691 conference at Michilimackinac FIA reported that they had already begun their attacks vs. the Iroq and that the Ill and Miami were also out vs. Iroq. More precise identification of group and time does not seem possible. | AN, C11A 11:49, 258 |
| [Late March to before 5 Apr] 1691 | 120 Moh & 20 Dutch vs. FIA (Indians of the Sault & La Montagne) | 10 FIA capt | Fort Chambly area | FIA were capt. as were hunting. All were returned. Purpose of capture was apparently to initiate peace talks. | AN, C11A 11:46-47, 258; AN, C11E 10:9-11; *JR* 64:57-61 |

*Continued on next page*

| Date | Groups Involved | Results | Location | Comments | Sources |
|---|---|---|---|---|---|
| 7-8 May 1691 | 800-1,000 Iroq vs. Fr | 2-3 Fr K, 5-6 Fr capt., 25 houses burned | Mont [See "Comments"] | The areas hit include "lower end of Montreal Island," La Chine, Rivière-des-Prairies, and Point-aux-Trembles. After this initial assault, which may have been by only 400 of the army, the Iroq broke up into smaller groups to raid in area of Mont and shores opposite the island. Some Fr capt. as attempted spring planting. | AN, C11A 11:49-50, 202, 251 |
| [Spring to summer] 1691 | Iroq vs. FIA F | Some FIA F capt., 2-3 FIA [M] wounded; some Iroq "lost" [K] | Near La Montagne | Iroq, likely offshoot of larger army, capt. the F as they worked in the fields. Help came and rest of casualties were in the ensuing fighting. | AN, C11A 11:51 |
| [Spring to summer] 1691 | 200 Fr vs. 30-50 On | 4-5 Fr K; 5 On capt. 4 later K, 1 On escaped, rest [24-44] died in fighting or in burning house | Repentigny | On—again, likely offshoot of larger army—were spotted by Fr patrol, who were soon joined by another patrol. Attacked sleeping On. Those few On that were not capt. or escaped were K during fighting trying to escape the fire the Fr had set to the house they were in, or died in the flames. Governor Callières of Mont claimed only 30 On were in house. | AN, C11A 11: 52-53; 12:97 |
| [Late Nov to mid-Dec] 1691 | 10 Iroq [Moh] vs. FIA | 4 FIA MC & 1 FIA F capt. | Prairie [de-la-Madeleine?] | Raid is first reported 30 Dec and Fr "Relations" ending [12 Nov] make no mention of this. The Indians were led by Caristasie, a Moh. His son was also along. | NYCD 3:815 |

Continued on next page

| Date | Groups Involved | Results | Location | Comments | Sources |
|---|---|---|---|---|---|
| [Late Nov to mid-Dec] 1691 | 29-34 Iroq (at least 18 Moh & 11 On) vs. 22-23 FIA (one source suggests these were Moh) | 8 FIA M K, 6 FIA M & 10 F capt.; 15-17 Iroq [M] K, 2 Iroq [M] wounded, 14 Iroq [M] capt., 4 Iroq [M] escaped | Sorel to Chambly & Lake Champlain | Raid took place after the one above. Caristasie and his son met this group as were returning and were persuaded to join this group of 18 Moh and 11 On going up to raid vs. Fr. Iroq attacked 2 cabins of FIA hunters, K 4 M and capt. 6 M and 10 F. Iroq lost 1 On K and 2 Iroq were wounded. A FIA escaped, went for help. 40 Sault St. Louis FIA and possibly some Fr, went after Iroq and caught them on Lake Champlain. 4 more FIA M were K and Iroq had 15-16 of their people K and 14 capt. The 16 FIA capt. were released. | AN, C11A 12:25, 93, 97; *NYCD* 3:815, 817 |
| Beginning of Mar 1692 | 120 Fr & 205 FIA vs. 50 Sen | 24 Sen K, 16 capt. & 10 escaped; 5 FIA [M] K, 1 Fr [M] K & 5 of Fr & FIA group wounded | île de Tonniate, 50 L from Mont [Gonanaque area, possibly Wells Island] | Fr and FIA set out in Feb to raid vs. Iroq. Came upon Sen as Sen were hunting. Fr and FIA freed 3 Fr capt. Sen had with them. 1 captive, Sieur de la Plante, had been a captive for 3 years. | AN, C11A 12:25, 93, 97-98 |
| Apr 1692 | Iroq vs. FIA | 1 FIA K | Rivière St. François, above TR | | AN, C11A 12:93 |

*Continued on next page*

| Date | Groups Involved | Results | Location | Comments | Sources |
|------|-----------------|---------|----------|----------|---------|
| End of May 1692 | Iroq [Onon] vs. Algk ("têtes de Boule") & 36 Fr | 21 Fr & 3 Algk "lost," 15 as capt. | Long Sault [Ott R] | This group of Iroq were said to be same ones defeated later this year by Vaudreuil. That group was said to have been Onon and 140-150 strong. The Iroq took ammunitions and merchandise which the Algk had traded for. Not clear how many of the 29 canoes of Algk that had come to trade were attacked. Fr officials claim intent of Iroq was to blockade the Ott R to prevent Ott Algk coming to trade and Fr from going to them. Probably to prevent the Ott Algk from being furnished with the very type of war supplies the Iroq took from this group. | AN, C11A 12:25, 93-94, 97-98 |
| Early July 1692 | Iroq [Onon] vs. Fr | 2 Fr farmers [M] capt. | Near Fort Roland, 4 L above Mont | Iroq said to be of same group as that later identified as Onon. | AN, C11A 12:94 |
| [Early July] 1692 | Iroq [Onon] vs. Fr | 9 Fr [farmers M] capt. | Lachenaie | Raid said to have occurred after above one. Iroq said to be of same group as that later identified as Onon. The Fr sent out parties, as had in early Apr when news of a large Iroq party was rec'd. On each occasion the Fr withdrew when they realized they were outnumbered. | AN, C11A 12:94 |
| [July] 1692 | Iroq [Onon] vs. Fr | 2 Fr [farmers M] capt. & burned a barn | Île Jèsus | Raid took place after the one above. Iroq said to be of same group as that later identified as Onon. In this and the above 2 raids it is uncertain how many of the 140-150 Iroq were taking part. | AN, C11A 12:94 |

Continued on next page

| Date | Groups Involved | Results | Location | Comments | Sources |
|------|-----------------|---------|----------|----------|---------|
| 28 July 1692 | 39 Moh & Mah vs. 33 Fr | 4 Fr M K & 2 wounded | LSP, Richelieu Islands | | AN, C11A 12:94 |
| [After 28 July] 1692 | 39 Moh & Mah vs. Fr or FIA | 1 Fr or FIA F (15-16 yrs old) capt.; 1 Moh or Mah wounded | St. François | Raid was carried out after above one, by same group. The girl's mother was also capt., but escaped when the Indian carrying her was wounded by a shot. | AN, C11A 12:94 |
| [July to before 5 Aug] 1692 | 400-500 Fr [& FIA] vs. 140-150 Onon | 20 Iroq lost, 9 Iroq F & 4 Iroq C capt.; 10 Fr M K, 4 FIA K, 6 of FR & FIA wounded | Long Sault [Ott R] | Took place after raids in early July and before 5 Aug when Ot brigade arrived unmolested down that river. After attacking in the colony the Iroq had returned to what was obviously a fortified hunting camp. The Fr hoped to exact revenge, free their people that had been captured, and get at what furs the Iroq had taken. Fr freed 6-12 of their people, plundered the Iroq camp, but were unable to find the two large caches of Iroq furs. Frontenac wrote that group was 200 strong and most were K or capt., but none of the other, more detailed accounts bear this out. The 200 figure is possible if one includes the 60 F and 20 C said to have been part of the Iroq camp. | AN, C11A 12:25, 94, 98-99 |

Continued on next page

| Date | Groups Involved | Results | Location | Comments | Sources |
|---|---|---|---|---|---|
| [Jan to Oct 1692] | FIA vs. Iroq | 42 Iroq K or capt. | [Iroq hunting areas & villages] | Raids were likely carried out during the winter of 1691 to 1692, or in the spring of 1692. In "past year" 800 FIA (Mississauga, Huron, Ill, Ot, & Upper Nations) in variously sized parties attacked Iroq as they hunted near their villages. Have "defeated" 42 Iroq, including those capt. and scalped. | AN, C11A 12:24, 95 |
| [Mid-Oct to before 11 Nov] 1692 | 400 Iroq (Cay, Onon, & Sen) vs. FIA | Some K on both sides; 5-6 [Fr or FIA?] capt. or K | Fort of the Sault [Mont] | Date is based on date of Frontenac's last letter which did not mention the raid and date of the report in which this raid was reported. Iroq did not attack the fort. People were K in some skirmishes. This was apparently part of a larger effort that came to nothing. Another army of 400 (Moh, Mah, & English) also came up, but when they discovered that the other group had retreated, they left as well. Some 40-50 stayed in area and raided in small bands. 5-6 people were capt. Or K by one of these groups. | AN, C11A 12:46-47 |

*Continued on next page*

| Date | Groups Involved | Results | Location | Comments | Sources |
|---|---|---|---|---|---|
| Feb 1693 | 425-430 Fr (100 soldiers, the rest [325-330] habitants & officers]) & 200 FIA (Huron, Iroq, & Abnk) vs. Moh | 3 Moh villages plundered & destroyed, supplies destroyed, 18-30 Moh K, 280-300 Moh capt. (80-100 M, 180-200 F, C, & old M): 14-27 Fr & FIA K, 17 wounded | Moh villages | The Fr attack vs. the villages was successful, most of the men were off warring or hunting. As the Fr retreated they were engaged by group of Iroq and English. It was here that the Fr and FIA suffered their casualties. As a result of this attack some 40-50 Moh captives were released. Because of poor food supplies and other difficulties, only 58 Moh captives made it to New France. The others were either released or escaped. | AN, C11A 12:185-91, 256-58, 318; Colden, *Five Indian Nations*, 144-47 |
| [Spring to summer], after May, 1693 | Iroq vs. 18-20 Fr & 20 FIA (Christian converts) | 3 Fr [M] K & some capt. | Rapids, head of Mont Island [La Chine?] | The party left in May and was sent to Michilimackinac to bring back men to colony. They were attacked on their trip back to the colony. 1 Iroq was capt., but it turned out he was a Sault Indian who had earlier been capt. by the Iroq. | AN, C11A 12:193, 258-59; Colden, *Five Indian Nations*, 150 |
| Before 25 June 1693 | Nip vs. Iroq (3 canoes) | 1 canoe of Iroq defeated | Fort Frontenac area | The Nip had come down with 60 Amikwa to raid vs. Iroq. | AN, C11A 12:198-99 |
| Early Aug 1693 | Iroq [Moh?] vs. Fr | 1 Fr M K, 2 Fr M capt., 1 of whom later died | St. François | Iroq attacked about 15-16 Fr and capt. the siegneur of place [Crévier]. He later died of his wounds. | AN, C11A 12:260; CSP 14:177, 178 |
| [Winter to spring] 1694 | Fr & FIA vs. Iroq | 3 Moh capt., some Iroq K | Iroq villages | Fr authorities stated that parties of Fr and FIA have been out vs. Iroq and some Iroq have been K and capt. In one raid 15 Sault Indians and 2 Fr returned 15 Apr with 3 Moh capt. and some scalps. Details of other raids were not recorded. | AN, C11A 13:5; 14:74 |

*Continued on next page*

| Date | Groups Involved | Results | Location | Comments | Sources |
|---|---|---|---|---|---|
| 5 Nov 1694 | Ill vs. Iroq | 400–500 Iroq K or capt. | | Date news reported. There is no specific time frame for when this action was to have taken place. It is most likely a cumulative total for 1 or 2 years. This news was furnished to Frontenac and Champigny by a Jesuit living among the Ill. | AN, C11A 13:19–20 |
| Before 15 Apr 1695 | 15 FIA (Indians of the Sault) & 2 Fr vs. Moh | 3 Moh capt. | [Moh lands] | The group of FIA returned this date. This group likely set out early this year. | AN, C11A 14:74 |
| Spring 1695 | 100–150 Iroq (Sen & Onon) vs. Wagenhaws [General name for AlgK] | 10 Wagenhaws capt., 9 later K | St Law, Fort Frontenac area | The group was coming down to colony. In Wraxall the impression is left that two raids took place: one in which a group of Wagenhaws were entirely defeated by 100 Iroq, and one in which some Sen and Onon capt. 10 Wagenhaws. In Colden this is all given as one incident. Because Wraxall is not precise enough to justify interpreting this as two raids, I have followed Colden's version. | Wraxall, *Indian Affairs*, 28; Colden, *Five Indian Nations*, 181 |
| Spring 1695 | 200–400 Iroq (Sen & Cay) vs. Fr & Miami | 50–60 Iroq [M] lost [K], 30 wounded; 3 Miami F & 3–4 C capt. | Post in Miami country [Fort St. Joseph] | A group of 200 Sen and Cay were reported to have set out to attack the Miami. The Fr report the Iroq group that struck them was 250 strong. The commander put the group at 300–400 Iroq. It is assumed these were the same groups. The Iroq first capt. the Miami F and C working in the fields, then attacked the fort. | AN, C11A 13:340; 14:76, 80–82 |

Continued on next page

| Date | Groups Involved | Results | Location | Comments | Sources |
|---|---|---|---|---|---|
| June 1695 | Iroq vs. FIA & Fr | 1 Fr M K: [6 Iroq K or wounded?] | Lake of Two Mountains | The Iroq attack at village of Lake of Two Mountains results unknown. 1 Fr & 7 FIA set out [to avenge this] & run into 15 Iroq. Fr M was K. FIA claim to have K 6 Iroq. Since they did not have scalps, it is possible Iroq were only wounded. | AN, C11A 14:78-79 |
| [June 1695] | Iroq vs. Fr | 3 Fr [M] K | Rivière-des-Prairies | Raid said to have taken place about same time as that above. | AN, C11A 14:79 |
| 13 June 1695 | 2 Moh vs. 2 Fr | 1 Fr [M] wounded; 2 Iroq [M] wounded, 1 later capt. by FIA | Lake Champlain | | AN, C11A 14:77 |
| July 1695 | Iroq vs. 10-13 canoes of Fr & FIA | 1 FIA K, 1 FIA & 1 Fr wounded | | This group, possibly traders, were coming from the upper country. | AN, C11A 14:80 |
| 12 or 13 Aug 1695 | 30 Iroq vs. Fr | 1 Fr F & 1 Fr M K; 2 Fr F, 1 M, & 4 C capt. | "Tremblay" [Point-aux-Trembles?] | In one account 8 people were said to have been capt. | AN, C11A 13:343; 14:83 |
| [Early to mid-Aug] 1695 | 5 FIA vs. Iroq | 1 Sen F K, 2 capt.; 1 Onon M K; 1 FIA M K, 1 wounded & 1 capt. | Between On & Onon villages | The FIA came upon the Sen F as they traveled between Onon and On villages. 3 Onon came upon body of F and pursued FIA. Onon lost 1 K when engaged FIA. Other 2 Onon went to On for help and pursued FIA. FIA incurred losses in that fight. | LIR, 172-74 |

Continued on next page

| Date | Groups Involved | Results | Location | Comments | Sources |
|------|----------------|---------|----------|----------|---------|
| 22 Aug 1695 | 13 Algk vs. Moh | 2 Moh scalped [K], 3 Moh F [2 were "girls"] capt. | | Group of Algk return this date. No indication of when raid took place. | AN, C11A 14:62 |
| 29 Aug 1695 | Iroq vs. Fr | 2 Fr [M?] K & 4 capt. | Prairie de-la-Madeleine | Fr were taken during harvest time. | AN, C11A 14:90 |
| 29 Aug 1695 | Iroq (Moh and/or On) vs. Fr | 1 Fr [M?] K | Boucherville | The Moh and/or the On were said to be involved in this raid. | AN, C11A 14:90 |
| 31 Aug 1695 | Iroq (Moh and/or On) vs. Fr | 3 Fr [M?] capt. | Cap-St.-Michel | The Moh and/or the On were said to be involved in this raid. | AN, C11A 14:90 |
| [Sept] 1695 | FIA [Sault Indians] vs. Onon | 1 Onon F & 2 M capt. & later K; some FIA K | Near Onon village | The FIA had set out to raid vs. Iroq. Capt. the 3 Onon but were pursued and K the Onon. Only 1 of the unspecified number of FIA returned. Survivor returned this date. | AN, C11A 14:92 |
| [Sept] 1695 | Fr & 10-12 FIA vs. Iroq [Moh and/or On] | 5 Iroq [M] K, 1 capt. & later died; 2 Fr [M] K; 2 Iroq [M] capt. & 2 scalped [K] | [Boucher ville] | Upon learning of Iroq presence in Boucherville area Fr sent out a party to attack them. 5 Iroq and 2 Fr K during this attack. 1 Iroq captive later died of wounds. FIA of Sault went in pursuit of others and returned with 2 scalps and 2 captives. Iroq are identified based on group known to have been in area at time. | AN, C11A 14:92-94, 95 |

Continued on next page

| Date | Groups Involved | Results | Location | Comments | Sources |
|---|---|---|---|---|---|
| [Winter 1695 to spring 1696] | 200 Algk (Ot & Potawatami—30 of the latter are identified) vs. Iroq | 30-50 Iroq K [30 scalps taken], 40 [M] drowned [not clear if drowned are included in the K total], 34-52 M, F, & C capt., Iroq goods & beaver, 400-500 pelts, taken | | The attack took place as Iroq were returning to Iroquoia after hunting. It was likely in the spring but not a certainty. In one version the Ot are said to attack the Iroq they had hunted with. In another account it is suggested Ot had been hunting with Iroq and decided to attack after met Potawatami on way to attack. Another source states Iroq had been hunting with the Huron. Some Ot could have been part of the Huron party. The Huron became aware of plans to attack the Iroq and tried to warn them. | AN, C11A 14:43, 45, 119-21, 183 |
| Mar 1696 | 300 Fr & FIA vs. Iroq | 7 Iroq capt. (1 M, 1 F, & 1 C are identified), 4 later K; 3 Fr [M] K | Between Ott R. & Rich R. | Of the capt. Iroq 4 are identified as Onon and were K. 2 Sen were spared as was the C, a grandson of Garaconté. | AN, C11A 14:36 |
| Mid-May 1696 | Fr & FIA vs. Iroq | 3 Iroq [M] K & scalped | | | AN, C11A 14:183 |

*Continued on next page*

| Date | Groups Involved | Results | Location | Comments | Sources |
|---|---|---|---|---|---|
| Mid-May 1696 | Fr & FIA vs. Iroq | 8 Iroq capt. | | This raid took place three days after the above one. It is implied that this and above raid were by same group. They left from Fort Frontenac. Thus raids may have been into Iroq territory. | AN, C11A 14:183 |
| May 1696 | [Fr & FIA] vs. Moh | 2 Moh [M] capt. | | In this raid and the one below the attacking group is not stated. Since Fr and FIA were usually raiding in joint parties, it was assumed reasonable to credit them with being the ones carrying out the raids. | AN, C11A 14:37 |
| [May 1696] | [Fr & FIA] vs. Moh | 2 Moh [M] capt. | Near village of the Sault | Date is based on observation that this raid took place about same time as the one above. | AN, C11A 14:37 |
| [May] 1696 | Iroq vs. Fr | 2 Fr M capt. | Lachenaie | | AN, C11A 14:37 |
| [May] 1696 | Iroq vs. Fr | 1 Fr wounded | Longueuil | This attack was not carried out by same group that struck at Lachenaie. | AN, C11A 14:37 |

Continued on next page

| Date | Groups Involved | Results | Location | Comments | Sources |
|---|---|---|---|---|---|
| July to Aug 1696 | 2,150 Fr & FIA (500 of this total were FIA) vs. Onon & On | Onon & On villages, crops, & supplies destroyed, 4 Iroq M K, 1 Iroq F capt.; 1 Fr M & 3 FIA K | Onon & On villages | The Iroq were aware of Fr plans and had abandoned their villages. All the Fr found were 2 old people at Onon, the M they K. The 1 Fr M and 2-3 FIA K by the Onon were stragglers from the army. In these little incursions 3 more Onon were K. | AN, C11A 14:48, 55, 60, 119-20, 148-49, 184, 193; JR 65:27-29 |
| [July to Aug] 1696 | Iroq vs. [Fr or FIA] | 20-30 people [Fr or FIA] capt. | Between TR & LSP | This was said to have taken place about the time of Fr attack of that year. The time is not specified, nor is it clear who was capt. or if it was the result of one or more raids. Attributed to the Moh. | JR 65:29 |
| Sept 1696 | Iroq vs. Fr | 1 Fr M capt. | Fort Frontenac | A group of soldiers was attacked. All but 1 made it safely back into the fort. | AN, C11A 15:6 |
| 2 July 1697 | 6 Iroq vs. Fr | 1 Fr M, 1 fc, & 1 mc K | Prairie St. Lambert [Mont] | The mc died of wounds. | AN, C11A 15:10 |

Continued on next page

| Date | Groups Involved | Results | Location | Comments | Sources |
|---|---|---|---|---|---|
| [Fall] 1697 | FIA vs. Sen or Sen vs. FIA | Over 100 Sen [M] capt. or K, 40 Iroq K, 15 capt.; 4 FIA (Miami) K | | Writing in the Fall, French authorities claim that since the Spring FIA have taken over 100 Sen. In one raid the Miami K 40 Sen, capt. 15, and lost only 4 K. In the Fr sources the group is not identified, but in an English account of what is most certainly the same incident the Cay tell the Albany authorities it was the Miami. The Sen were said to have fought the Miami and suffered their losses as they retreated. | AN, C11A 15:13-14, 96; NYCD 4:294 |
| Fall 1697 | Iroq vs. [Fr] | 1 [Fr] K, 1 scalped but lived; 2 Iroq [M] K | Prairie de-la-Madeleine | | AN, C11A 15:13 |
| Fall 1697 | 34 Algk vs. 30-40 Onon | 18-20 Iroq K, 8 (6 M & 2 F) capt.; 6 [M] Algk K, 4 wounded | Ft Frontenac area | Onon were hunting. Algk had set out to raid vs. Iroq and capt. 1 Onon F. Onon attacked to get back F. Only 20 of Onon group were M. | AN, C11A 15:25-26, 166 |
| [Nov] 1697 | Huron vs. 20 Iroq | Iroq were defeated | | Iroq were said to be heading off to attack Ot when were surprised by Huron. | AN, C11A 15:98 |
| 14 Sept 1699 | Dowaganhaes [Algk] vs. Sen | 5 Sen [M] K & scalped | Near Sen village | The Sen group was out hunting. | NYCD 4:597; CSP 17:475 |

Continued on next page

| Date | Groups Involved | Results | Location | Comments | Sources |
|---|---|---|---|---|---|
| Spring 1700 | Iroq (Sen) vs. Miami | 58 Iroq capt. or K | Miami area | Iroq went to area under pretext of hunting. | AN, C11A 18:146-47, 155 |
| Spring 1700 | Ot vs. 28 Iroq | 9 Iroq K, 17 capt. | Ot hunting area | Iroq were hunting when were attacked by the Ot. Ot claimed not to know of ongoing peace efforts. | AN, C11A 18:78 |
| 26 or 27 Sept 1700 | Dionndades [Huron-Petun] vs. Onon, On, & Sen | 3 Sen F & 2 M K | Iroq villages | A combined Iroq force was sent off to avenge this simultaneous attack vs. these three Iroq tribes. | NYCD 4:768, 800, 805 |
| 27 Aug 1701 | Iroq (On) vs. Ondadeonwas | 1 Ondadeonwas capt. | "Behind" Carolina & Maryland | The On arrived with the prisoner this day. | NYCD 4:918 |

# Iroquois Population Losses to 1701

The following table lists Iroquois population losses by year. The figures in the Captured, Killed, and Lost columns represent losses incurred as a result of warfare. They were derived from table D.1. In each column distinction is made between losses suffered due to enemy-initiated attacks and casualties that resulted from raids begun by the Iroquois. The numbers in brackets represent losses due to Iroquois-initiated raids. "Other Causes" lists all Iroquois deaths due to natural causes. These causes include illnesses the Iroquois normally contracted and diseases introduced by Europeans. These figures were taken from table A.2 and from the discussion of epidemics in appendix B. Little is known of the impact of disease among the Iroquois until the Jesuits established permanent missions among the Iroquois in the late 1660s. This means that population decline due to natural causes and disease are seriously underrepresented in this table. On the limitations of the data on disease and mortality, see the discussions in appendixes A and B. The years marked with an asterisk indicate that epidemic disease struck sometime during that year.

Iroquois Population Losses to 1701

| Year | Captured | Killed | Lost | Other Causes | Total |
|---|---|---|---|---|---|
| 1603 | | 100 | | | 100 |
| 1609 | 10-12 | 50 | | | 60-62 |
| 1610 | 15 | | | | 15 |
| 1615 | 13 | 4 | | | 17 |
| 1623 | | 60 | | | 60 |
| 1627 | 3 | | | | 3 |
| 1635 | 1 | | | | 1 |
| 1636 | 7 | 2 | 28 | | 37 |
| 1637 | 13 | 2 | | | 15 |
| 1638 | 80 | | | | 80 |
| 1639* | 12 | | | | 12 |
| 1640* | 2 | | | | 2 |
| 1641* | 4 | 1 | | | 5 |

Continued on next page

| Year | Captured | Killed | Lost | Other Causes | Total |
|---|---|---|---|---|---|
| 1642 | | [6] | 2 | | 8 |
| 1643 | | 1; [2] | | | 3 |
| 1644 | 3 | | | | 3 |
| 1645 | 2 | 11-13 | | | 13-15 |
| 1646* | 1 | | | | 1 |
| 1647* | [2] | 10; [5] | | | 17 |
| 1648 | 2; [19-22] | 1; [17-19] | | | 39-44 |
| 1649 | [30] | 7; [140] | | | 177 |
| 1650 | 1; [7] | [36] | [200] | | 244 |
| 1651 | 1 | 2 | | | 3 |
| 1652 | | [7] | [130] | | 137 |
| 1653 | 7; [1] | 81; [6] | | | 95 |
| 1654 | 8; [1] | 14 | | | 23 |

Continued on next page

Table E.1 continued

| Year | Captured | Killed | Lost | Other Causes | Total |
|---|---|---|---|---|---|
| 1655* | [5] | [2] | | | 7 |
| 1656 | | [1] | | | 1 |
| 1657 | | 1; [1] | | | 2 |
| 1658 | 3; [16] | [5] | [2] | | 26 |
| 1659 | 1 | 2; [19] | | | 22 |
| 1660* | 12 | 4; [25-31] | | | 41-47 |
| 1661* | | 3; [26] | | 120 | 149 |
| 1662* | | [1] | 90-100 | 1,000 | 1,091-1,101 |
| 1663* | 6-7; [10] | 13-14; [25] | | | 54-56 |
| 1664 | 2; [3] | 2; [23] | | | 30 |
| 1666 | | 4 | | | 4 |
| 1667 | | 2 | | 43 | 45 |
| 1668* | | | | 240 | 240 |

Continued on next page

| Year | Captured | Killed | Lost | Other Causes | Total |
|------|----------|--------|------|--------------|-------|
| 1669 | | 58; [1] | 4 | 205 | 268 |
| 1670 | | 3 | | 74 | 77 |
| 1671 | | | | 187 | 187 |
| 1672* | [1] | 2; [8] | | 85 | 96 |
| 1673 | | | | 164 | 164 |
| 1674 | | | | 113 | 113 |
| 1675 | | | | 179 | 179 |
| 1676* | | | | 284 | 284 |
| 1677 | | | | 180 | 180 |
| 1678 | | | | 248 | 248 |
| 1679* | | | | 213 | 213 |
| 1680 | | [8] | [30] | | 38 |
| 1682* | | | | 70 | 70 |

Continued on next page

| Year | Captured | Killed | Lost | Other Causes | Total |
|---|---|---|---|---|---|
| 1683 | | [2-3] | 500 | | 502-503 |
| 1686 | | [29] | | | 29 |
| 1687 | 218 | 48-94; [13-14] | | | 279-326 |
| 1688 | 18 | 33 | | | 51 |
| 1689 | | [15-21] | | | 15-21 |
| 1690* | 2; [3] | 40-45; [36-41] | | 500 | 581-591 |
| 1691 | 1; [14] | 28-48; [17-19] | [2-3] | | 62-85 |
| 1692 | 29 | 24 | 62 | | 115 |
| 1693 | 280-300 | 18-30 | | | 298-330 |
| 1694 | 3 | 2 | 400-500 | | 405-505 |
| 1695 | 44-62; [1] | 45-65; [6] | [50-60] | | 146-194 |
| 1696 | 16 | 11 | | | 27 |
| 1697 | 23 | 58-60; [2] | 60-65 | | 143-150 |

Continued on next page

| Year | Captured | Killed | Lost | Other Causes | Total |
|------|----------|--------|------|--------------|-------|
| 1699 | | 5 | | | 5 |
| 1700 | 17 | 14 | | | 31 |
| TOTAL | 855-892; [108] | 1,270-1,378; [486-509] | 724-839; [414-425] | 3,905 | 7,762-8,056 |

# *Iroquois Warfare: The Human Toll*

The following tables list the price Iroquois warfare exacted on the human populations of the Northeast. Table F.1 lists the total number of people captured, killed, or lost to the Iroquois due to Iroquois-initiated warfare. Tables F.2 and F.3 present the results of Iroquois raiding against the French and the Hurons.

Table F.2 lists only losses incurred due to Iroquois attacks against groups composed solely of French. Only those captured, killed, or lost as a result of direct Iroquois attacks were listed. These limitations were necessary if one hoped to contend, based on this data, that Iroquois attacks against the French were indeed meant to strike some blow against them. If the attacked group contained a variety of other peoples, one could not be assured which ones the Iroquois had targeted. These same criteria apply to the Huron data in table F.3. French and Huron losses resulting from attacks against groups that they were part of, and from raids initiated by the French and/or Hurons, are discussed following the respective tables.

The data in all three tables was taken from table D.1. Years marked with an asterisk indicate that disease or epidemic struck sometime during that year.

Population Losses to the Iroquois to 1701

| Year | Captured | Killed | Lost | # of Raids |
|------|----------|--------|------|------------|
| 1616 | 1 | | | 1 |
| 1631 | 2 | 1 | | 1 |
| 1633 | | | 2-3 | 1 |
| 1634* | 100 | 200 | | 1 |
| 1635 | | 44 | | 2 |
| 1636* | | 14 | | 2 |
| 1637 | 30 | 3 | | 3 |
| 1638 | | | | 1 |
| 1639* | | 4-5 | | 1 |
| 1640* | | 2 | | 3 |
| 1641* | 32 | 2 | | 3 |
| 1642 | 51-56 | 8 | | 10 |
| 1643 | 21-22 | 28 | 20 | 8 |
| 1644 | 33-37 | 10 | | 10 |

Continued on next page

| Year | Captured | Killed | Lost | # of Raids |
|------|----------|--------|------|------------|
| 1645 | | 6 | | 4 |
| 1646* | 9 | 1 | | 5 |
| 1647* | 143-164 | 12-13 | | 10 |
| 1648 | 28 | 14 | 740 | 8 |
| 1649 | 19 | 237 | 400 | 6 |
| 1650 | 15 | 16 | 19 | 18 |
| 1651 | 28-29 | 11 | | 19 |
| 1652 | 567-667 | 37 | | 29 |
| 1653 | 13 | 30 | | 16 |
| 1654 | 1 | 1 | | 3 |
| 1655* | 4 | 8 | | 6 |
| 1656 | 2 | 13 | 84-98 | 6 |
| 1657 | 40 | 11-17 | | 3 |
| 1658 | 12 | 1 | | 9 |

Continued on next page

| Year | Captured | Killed | Lost | # of Raids |
|------|----------|--------|------|------------|
| 1659 | 12 | 8 | | 6 |
| 1660* | 32-42 | 16 | 3 | 6 |
| 1661* | 33 | 47 | 121-123 | 19 |
| 1662* | 7 | 10 | | 8 |
| 1663* | 7 | 39-49 | | 8 |
| 1664 | 9 | 20-21 | | 7 |
| 1665 | 17 | 13 | | 6 |
| 1666 | 13 | 6-7 | | 4 |
| 1668* | 4 | 2 | | 2 |
| 1669 | 4 | 8 | | 5 |
| 1670 | 30 | 76 | | 1 |
| 1672* | | 15-16 | | 1 |
| 1674 | | 3 | | 2 |
| 1675 | | 11 | | 2 |

Continued on next page

| Year | Captured | Killed | Lost | # of Raids |
|------|----------|--------|------|------------|
| 1676* | 37 | 92 | | 2 |
| 1677 | 18 | | | 1 |
| 1678 | 30 | 10 | | 4 |
| 1680 | | 13-14 | 700-701, 200 | 3 |
| 1681 | 730-930 | 300-600 | | 6 |
| 1682* | 746-747 | 9 | | 7 |
| 1683 | | 5-6 | | 2 |
| 1684 | 4 | 1 | | 6 |
| 1685 | 2 | | | 2 |
| 1686 | 570 | | | 2 |
| 1687 | 13 | 32-33 | | 8 |
| 1688 | 59 | 6 | | 4 |
| 1689 | 128-138 | 200 | | 4 |
| 1690* | 23-24 | 26-27 | | 4 |

Continued on next page

| Year | Captured | Killed | Lost | # of Raids |
|---|---|---|---|---|
| 1691 | 33-34 | 10-11 | | 5 |
| 1692 | 29 | 14 | | 8 |
| 1693 | 3 | 5 | | 2 |
| 1695 | 21-22 | 19 | | 10 |
| 1696 | 23-33 | | | 4 |
| 1697 | | 4 | | 2 |
| 1700 | | | 58 | 1 |
| 1701 | | | | 1 |
| TOTAL | 3,791-4,157 | 1,738-2,065 | 2,150-2,667 | 7,679-8,889 |

Note: The above totals do not include those losses to the Iroquois that resulted from attacks initiated by their enemies. If those numbers are included (19 captured; 278-293 killed; 127-128 lost), the toll the Iroquois exacted on their foes climbs to 8,103-9,329 people.

French Population Losses to the Iroquois to 1701

| Year | Captured | Killed | Lost | # of Raids |
|------|----------|--------|------|------------|
| 1633 |          | 2-3    |      | 1          |
| 1641 | 2        |        |      | 1          |
| 1642 | 1        |        |      | 1          |
| 1643 | 2-3      | 3      |      | 1          |
| 1644 |          | 6      |      | 4          |
| 1646 | 2        |        |      | 1          |
| 1647 |          |        |      | 1          |
| 1648 |          | 1      |      | 2          |
| 1649 | 1        |        |      | 1          |
| 1650 |          | 4      | 9    | 4          |
| 1651 |          | 6      |      | 9          |
| 1652 | 3        | 9      |      | 7          |
| 1653 | 4        | 8      |      | 9          |
| 1654 | 1        | 1      |      | 2          |

Continued on next page

| Year | Captured | Killed | Lost | # of Raids |
|------|----------|--------|------|-----------|
| 1655 | 4 | 8 | | 5 |
| 1657 | | 3 | | 1 |
| 1658 | 11 | | | 5 |
| 1659 | 12 | 1 | | 4 |
| 1660 | 6 | 1 | | 2 |
| 1661 | 33 | 27 | | 11 |
| 1662 | 8 | | | 5 |
| 1663 | 4 | | | 2 |
| 1664 | 2 | 5-6 | | 3 |
| 1665 | 5 | 4 | | 3 |
| 1666 | 4 | 4-5 | | 3 |
| 1684 | | | | 2 |
| 1687 | 6 | 27-28 | | 6 |
| 1688 | | 2 | | 2 |

continued on next page

| Year | Captured | Killed | Lost | # of Raids |
|------|----------|--------|------|------------|
| 1689 | 128-138 | 200 | | 4 |
| 1690 | 23-24 | 26-27 | | 4 |
| 1691 | 5-6 | 2-3 | | 1 |
| 1692 | 13 | 4 | | 4 |
| 1693 | 1 | 2 | | 1 |
| 1695 | 14 | 8 | | 6 |
| 1696 | 3 | | | 3 |
| 1697 | | 4 | | 2 |
| TOTAL | 298-311 | 368-374 | 9 | 123 |

*Note:* The result of Iroquois attacks was the removal of 675-694 people from the various French communities along the St. Lawrence River. If one includes French losses incurred during attacks against the French and their Indian allies, or attacks against Indian groups that resulted in French deaths (45 captured; 36 killed), and French losses due to their own attacks against the Iroquois (57-59 killed; 18 lost), then the total human toll of Iroquois warfare was 831-852 French lives.

Huron Population Losses to the Iroquois to 1701

Table F.3

| Year | Captured | Killed | Lost | # of Raids |
|------|----------|--------|------|------------|
| 1634 | 100 | 200 | | 1 |
| 1636 | | 12 | | 1 |
| 1637 | 30 | 1 | | 1 |
| 1639 | | 4-5 | | 1 |
| 1640 | | 2 | | 2 |
| 1642 | 2 | 3 | | 6 |
| 1643 | 10 | 22 | 20 | 4 |
| 1644 | 26-30 | 3 | | 4 |
| 1645 | | 4 | | 3 |
| 1646 | 5 | | | 3 |
| 1647 | 14 | 6-7 | | 4 |
| 1648 | 24 | 11 | 740 | 5 |
| 1649 | 2 | 232 | 400 | 2 |
| 1650 | 15 | 3 | 10 | 9 |

Continued on next page

| Year | Captured | Killed | Lost | # of Raids |
|---|---|---|---|---|
| 1651 | 6 | 2 | | 5 |
| 1652 | 7 | 6 | | 8 |
| 1653 | 8 | | | 5 |
| 1656 | | 3 | 71-85 | 3 |
| 1657 | 40 | 8-14 | | 2 |
| 1658 | 1 | | | 1 |
| 1662 | 5 | | | 2 |
| 1663 | 3 | 1 | | 1 |
| TOTAL | 300-304 | 523-531 | 1,242-1,255 | 73 |

Note: If one includes Huron losses incurred when the Hurons were part of other groups (60-70 captured; 10 killed), and those sustained during Huron-initiated raids (3 killed; 100 lost), the total population drain due to Iroquois warfare was 2,237-2,273. This figure represents about one quarter of the Hurons' population.

# Notes

1. A good introduction to all aspects of the history and culture of the Iroquois is the series of chapters in Trigger, ed., *Handbook*. The bibliography there and that in Weinman, *Bibliography*, are good points of departure for works on specific aspects of Iroquois history and culture. The most recent overviews of the Iroquois and their world are Richter, *Ordeal*, and Snow, *Iroquois*. On Iroquois migrations see Snow, "Migration in Prehistory."

## CHAPTER ONE. IROQUOIS-FRENCH HISTORY AND HISTORIANS

1. For the impact of these factors on the image of Indians presented by historians of New France see Trigger, *Natives and Newcomers*, 20–39. On the influence of nationalism in Quebec historiography see Gagnon, *Quebec and Its Historians* (both vols.); Ouellet, "La modernisation de l'historiographie."

2. See for example Garneau, *Histoire*; Ferland, *Cours d'histoire*; Faillon, *Histoire*.

3. With few exceptions, all the major works that preceded his, in which one can find aspects of Hunt's thesis, are listed in his bibliography. Nonetheless, the novelty of Hunt's work was not in the ideas he espoused but in how he used them to explain Iroquois warfare and history from, allegedly, the Iroquois perspective.

4. Eccles, "History of New France," 163–75.

5. Parkman to George Ellis, [1864], in Parkman, *Letters* 1:175–84; Jennings, "Francis Parkman," 316–20; Eccles, "History of New France," 172–73.

6. Parkman, July, [18]44, in Parkman, *Journals* 1:257.

7. Hunt thought Parkman's focus on the Iroquois was to "furnish a lurid background

of fire, blood, and villainy against which to draw in bold lines the failure of New France" (Hunt, *Wars of the Iroquois*, 187).

8. Parkman to E. G. Squier, 2 Apr. 1850, in Parkman, *Letters* 1:68. After spending a few weeks with a Dakota tribe, Parkman wrote, "For the most part, a civilized white man can discover very few points of sympathy between his own nature and that of an Indian. . . . Nay, so alien to himself do they appear, that, after breathing the air of the prairie for a few months, he begins to look upon them as a troublesome and dangerous species of wild beast" (*Oregon Trail*, 267–68). This is a revised version; in the original serialized publication of this book, and in the first book versions, he finished off this thought with, "and if expedient, he could shoot them with as little compunction as they themselves would experience after performing the same office upon him"; see Feltskoq, ed., *Oregon Trail*, 627; for Parkman's views on blacks see Parkman to G. Hale, 6 Oct. [1844], in Parkman, *Letters* 1:18; Parkman to G. Cary, 15 Dec. 1844, in Parkman, *Letters* 1:20; journal entry for 1 Oct. 1846, in Parkman, *Journals* 2:483.

9. Parkman, *Pioneers of France*, 207, 208, 213.

10. Parkman, *Pioneers of France*, 344; Parkman, *Jesuits*, lxi, 115, 212; Parkman, *Old Régime*, 5.

11. Parkman, *Jesuits*, 213; *Count Frontenac*, 175; *Pioneers of France*, 366.

12. Parkman, *La Salle*, 192–93. This work first appeared under this title in 1879. The first version of this work was titled *The Discovery of the Great West: A Historical Narrative*, published in 1869. After Parkman gained access to documents that further illuminated La Salle's role in the West, he revised the work and changed the title.

13. Jennings, "Francis Parkman," 305–28. According to Jennings, the purpose was to justify the genocidal Indian policy of the American government (316–18). On the relationship between images of the Indian and government policy, see Berkhofer, *White Man's Indian*, 113–75.

14. Parkman, *Jesuits*, lxv–lxvi, lxxxix, 447

15. Parkman, *Jesuits*, xliii, n.1.

16. More than one contemporary rejected Morton's "scientific" findings; see Wilson, "Supposed Prevalence." Justin Winsor lists others critical of Morton, and stated that it "is certainly evident that skull capacity is no sure measure of intelligence" (Winsor, "Progress of Opinion," in Winsor, ed., *Narrative and Critical History* 1:372, n.14).

17. Parkman, *Jesuits*, 336, 337, 434, 436, 448.

18. Parkman, *Jesuits*, 436–45, quotes on 436.

19. Parkman, *Jesuits*, 211, 241. In accepting Champlain's attacks as the cause of Iroquois hostility toward New France, Parkman was probably following his Quebec contemporaries Faillon and Ferland, whose works he read and used; see Parkman to Ferland, 10 Sept. 1856; Parkman to Shea, 26 July 1858; Parkman to Casgrain, 28 Mar. 1866; in Parkman, *Letters* 1:119–20, 132; 2:7–8.

20. Parkman was not the first to dwell on Iroquois "ferocity." Bacqueville de la Potherie, a contemporary of the Iroquois and historian of New France, assessed Iroquois character and its impact on their relations with native groups in the following terms: "They have an insatiable [desire] for human blood, and, in consequence of this, are ir-

reconcilable enemies of all the nations in this vast country" (La Potherie au Ministre, 11 aôut 1700, AN, CIIA 18:147). Parkman saw and ordered this document transcribed from the Archives Nationales, but it is not clear if he was influenced by it prior to writing *Jesuits*. The Abbé Casgrain, a friend of Parkman's, wrote that Parkman visited the Paris archives in 1858–59 (Casgrain, *Parkman*, 33), but Parkman himself made no mention of working there during that trip. See letters of Parkman from Paris to various people in Parkman, *Letters* 1:133–38. In his book, La Potherie modified his view and wrote that the Iroquois, while fierce, were not "always thirsting for human blood" (La Potherie, *Histoire* 3:n.p. [preface]).

21. See for example Hunt, *Wars of the Iroquois*, 5, 7, 187; Jennings, *Ambiguous Iroquois Empire*, 18, 100.

22. George Bancroft commended Parkman for, among other things, "excellent judgment," while L. H. Morgan, often called the father of American anthropolgy, thought the *Jesuits* a "splendid contribution to American History and Ethnology." Bancroft to Parkman, May 1867, and Morgan to Parkman, 5 June [1867?], in Parkman, *Letters* 2:14.

23. Parkman, *Discovery of the Great West*, 203. This passage remained unaltered when Parkman revised this book and published it in 1879 as *La Salle and the Discovery of the Great West*.

24. Parkman, *Count Frontenac*, 79–80.

25. It did not take long for this interpretation to work its way into histories of English-Iroquois, French-Iroquois, and Iroquois-Native relations written by Americans. With the publication of Winsor's *Narrative and Critical History* in the mid- to late 1880s it seems to have established itself as a significant interpretive model. See for example Andrew M. Davis, "Canada and Louisiana," in Winsor, ed., *Narrative and Critical History* 5:2, and George E. Ellis, "The Red Indian of North America in Contact with the French and English," in Winsor, ed., *Narrative and Critical History* 1:283, 285, 286. Indeed, Parkman's work served as a basis for Ellis's analysis (1:316–17, 317 n.1). This stress on the role of the fur trade and the Iroquois seeking to take commercial advantage of it are clearly the product of Parkman's influence. In 1747 Colden had stressed the importance of the fur trade to the English and how significant the Iroquois were in that trade, but the emphasis was on how important the trade was to New York, not how central it was to accounting for Iroquois wars (Colden, *History*). The importance of the Iroquois to New York's trade was made clear in the book's subtitle and in documents appended to the 1747 edition.

26. Eccles, *Essays*, xi.

27. He compiled the abridgement to make a case for the need for an agent to handle relations between the colony of New York and her native allies.

28. He did not define what he meant by the term *middleman*. Webster's *Seventh New Collegiate Dictionary* gives the following definition for the term: "a dealer or agent intermediate between the producer of goods and the retailer or consumer." The purpose of the activity is to make some material gain in the process of carrying out the transactions. The meaning of the term has not changed over the years, and it seems safe to assume that it was this practice that McIlwain had in mind. The universality of the phrase probably accounts for why he did not explain it.

29. McIlwain, introduction to Wraxall, *Indian Affairs*, xlii–xliv.

30. See chapter 4. It seems worth stressing here, however, that the term *middleman* was not coined until almost the nineteenth century. There is a danger of anachronism in using this term, with its modern frame of reference and associations, to describe seventeenth-century Iroquois behavior. Indeed, it may very well be anachronistic to use it to describe even European trading practices in the seventeenth century. In New France, for example, notions of honor and rank conditioned most aspects of life including economic behavior. See Miquelon, *New France*, 227–58; Moogk, "Rank in New France."

31. A few decades earlier French-Canadian historian Benjamin Sulte made a similiar unsupported claim (Sulte, "La guerre des Iroquois," 63–92).

32. This view is strengthened when one takes into account the 1869 version of this interpretation. Moreover, Parkman did not support his views with documentary evidence.

33. McIlwain, in Wraxall, *Indian Affairs*, xliv n.1.

34. Charlevoix, *Histoire* 3:387–88. This passage bears a striking resemblance to Parkman's analysis. It is not unlikely that Parkman was influenced by Charlevoix on this point.

35. Kellogg, *French Régime*, 222, 243; Innis, *Fur Trade*, 20 (to his credit, Innis tried to show how native culture had been altered and weakened by contact with Europeans; see 15–21); Brebner, *Explorers*, 142.

36. Hunt, *Wars of the Iroquois*, 4–5. As Hunt dramatically put it, "old institutions and economies had profoundly altered or disappeared completely at the electrifying touch of the white man's trade" (5).

37. Conrad Heidenreich, for example, has shown that it took several years of concerted effort to get the Hurons to come to trade with the French and that when they did appear it was as much to form a political alliance as it was to trade (Heidenreich, *Huronia*, 232–37).

38. Hunt, *Wars of the Iroquois*, 11, 12, 19, 34, 135, 159.

39. Hunt was particularly disdainful of Parkman's "insensate fury" argument and wished to show that the Iroquois had perfectly "rational" reasons for their wars (*Wars of the Iroquois*, 5).

40. Hunt, *Wars of the Iroquois*, 21. Like some later writers, he defined self-interest in only economic terms. See for example Trigger, "Early Native North American Responses," 1195–215.

41. Trelease, "The Iroquois," 32–51, quote on 37.

42. See Trelease, "The Iroquois," 36, 50; *American Anthropologist* 42 (Oct.–Dec. 1940): 662–64; *American Historical Review* 46 (Jan. 1941): 415–16; *Mississippi Valley Historical Review* 27 (Sept. 1940): 287–88; *Canadian Historical Review* 31 (June 1940): 211–12. Reviewers greeted Hunt's book with a critical eye. Yet while they were quick to point out the strong economic bias and monocausal nature of his interpretation, they were also in accord that it was an important contribution to the history of the Iroquois and the colonial era. Hindsight reveals that they seriously underestimated the impact of *Wars of the Iroquois*. Hunt died 18 April 1947 at the age of 48. He appears not to have elaborated on or revised his views in print after 1940.

43. These points will be discussed in later chapters, but see also Snyderman, "Behind the Tree of Peace"; Richter, "War and Culture."

44. Robert A. Goldstein's *French-Iroquois Diplomatic and Military Relations*, as the title indicates, also focused on French relations with the Iroquois. The book was published in 1969 but, with the exception of a few titles, most of the works in the bibliography date from 1940 and prior, and it was probably written in that decade (205–8). This is a superficial and highly derivative work. The list of sources is a mere three pages long and contains no manuscript sources and no material on the French that had not appeared in translation. For a work that purported to deal with relations from the French perspective, these were not minor omissions. Goldstein accepted Hunt's thesis wholesale while shifting the focus of Hunt's work to the French from the Iroquois. For him the cause of the Iroquois-Hurons war was the Iroquois desire to become middlemen in the fur trade. The introduction of European goods had destroyed old skills and led them to become dependent on trade goods. The struggle to control the fur trade, added to the hostility still felt at Champlain's actions, accounted for Iroquois wars against New France (10, 24, 60, 62).

45. Desrosiers, *Iroquoisie*, 7–8, 91–92, 109, 131, 226, 235, 255.

46. Desrosiers, *Iroquoisie*, 25, 38, 39, 184, 185, 207, 209. Desrosiers seems to have decided out of hand that the French and Iroquois could not have worked out some peaceful settlement.

47. Desrosiers did not try to ascribe all actions to one motive and often suggested that cultural considerations or noneconomic motives influenced Iroquois behavior; see his analysis of the 1645 Mohawk treaty efforts, "La rupture de la paix de 1645."

48. For Desrosiers the gaining of goods was to elevate Iroquois culture above the primitive (*Iroquoisie*, 10–11, 209), rather than for Hunt's less well-defined "survival" motive, but he, too, stressed the dependence on European goods as a motive for war.

49. Gagnon, *Quebec and Its Historians, 1840 to 1920*, 113.

50. Groulx, *Histoire*, 64, 65, 100, 125–31. Groulx did not link the Iroquois desire for mastery over other tribes to the fur trade.

51. Lanctot, *History* 1:170, 179–80, 202–3, 229–30, 248, 333, 2:126. Jean Leclerc, in his biography of Denonville, *Le Marquis de Denonville*, also recognized various motives for Iroquois wars, but in the end he too made it all part of economic warfare. For him the power of the Iroquois came from their role as middlemen, but their success changed them and they became "more militaristic, even imperialistic . . . in order to realize their economic objectives" (52).

52. Trudel, *Beginnings*, 57, 149, 217–24.

53. Gagnon, *Quebec and Its Historians: The Twentieth Century*, 35, 40–50.

54. Eccles, *Frontenac* 4; *Canadian Frontier*, 112–16, 218; *France in America*, 45 n.37, 90, 262.

55. In an introduction written for a new edition of *Canadian Frontier*, he questioned the economic motivation interpretation. In a 1986 review of Trigger's *Natives and Newcomers*, Eccles lambasted Trigger because his interpretation of Iroquois-native relations was "little more than a version of the discredited thesis of" Hunt (381).

56. Eccles, "Fur Trade," 343; *France in America*, 46–47, 91, 95–96.

57. For examples of those who subscribe to Hunt's thesis, see Perdue, "Cherokee Relations with the Iroquois in the Eighteenth Century," in Richter and Merrell, eds., *Beyond the Covenant Chain*, 136; and Havard, *La Grande Paix*, 46, 92–93.

58. See Richter, *Ordeal*, esp. 50–74; Jennings, *Ambiguous Iroquois Empire*, 85, 93, 100; Aquila, *Iroquois Restoration*, 37; Delâge, *Le Pays renversé*; Trigger, *Natives and Newcomers*, 260–62, and *Children*, esp. 2:617–33; Tooker, "Iroquois Defeat," 115–17.

59. Richter, *Ordeal*, 32–38, 50–74.

60. Conrad Heidenreich, "History of the St. Lawrence–Great Lakes Area to A.D. 1650," in Ellis and Ferris, eds., *Archaeology of Southern Ontario*, 475–92; Campeau, *La Mission des Jésuites*, 289–90, 345–49; Snow, *Iroquois*, 109–11, 114–15, 127. Heidenreich's current work represents a rejection of the Beaver Wars interpretation that he accepted in his 1970 monograph, *Huronia*.

61. Heidenreich has gone the furthest in this regard. Others have questioned the Beaver Wars interpretation but offer fanciful and unsupported explanations in its stead. See for example Schlesier, "Epidemics," 129–45, in which the author tries to draw a direct cause and effect relationship between disease and Iroquois warfare against the French but overlooks several epidemics and the fact that most diseases that afflicted the Iroquois came from their allies, not the French. Also in this category of interesting but unproven is Mathew Dennis's thesis that the Iroquois warred against Indian and European in order to extend to them the benefits of peace (*Cultivating*).

62. If after 1940 and into the 1990s specialists on the Iroquois and other native groups continued to argue that the Five Nations waged war for economic ends, it should come as no surprise that historians of New France accepted these views. After all, they were usually writing general political or economic histories of the colony and were not particularly sensitive to the native side of events. In recent years work on New France has been in the nature of local or specialized studies, most with strict social or economic focuses. While many of these works are important contributions to the historiography of New France, natives rarely enter the picture, and when they do they are quickly relegated to the background. See for example Dechêne, *Habitants*.

CHAPTER TWO. GOVERNMENT AND SOCIAL ORGANIZATION

1. Wallace, *Death and Rebirth*, 30, 34, quote on 36. Cornelius Jaenen has also noted this and suggested that independence of action was so rampant that it sometimes threatened established authority (*Friend and Foe*, 92).

2. Journal of Frederick Post, 1758, in Thwaites, ed., *Early Western Travels* 1:230. Writing around 1780 the Moravian missionary David Zeisberger echoed these sentiments (Zeisberger, *History*, 18). An anonymous French observer, writing about 1762, noted that while the Iroquois were proud, they were not vain ("Mémoire sur les coutumes" 1:471–72; this document has been published in translation, see Cardy, "Iroquois"). Cardy claims that the document was written in the Bastille in 1763 and first appeared in print in 1804. It must have been written early in, or before, 1762 since it first appeared in two parts in the April (123–47) and May (5–24) 1762 installments of the

French annual *Journal étranger*. A more accurate publication record of the document and another conclusion as to who penned it can be found in Duchet, "Bougainville."

3. Lafitau, *Moeurs* 2:61.

4. Zeisberger, *History*, 125: "Fear of disgrace keeps them from open wrong-doing for they do not wish to have a bad name."

5. Father Cholenec, in [Dablon], *Relation of 1676 and 1677*, *JR* 60:287. See also Jean de Lamberville to [Father Superior], 25 Aug. 1682, *JR* 62:63; Zeisberger, *History*, 83. The definitive studies of this cultural trait are Fenton, "Iroquois Suicide," and "A Further Note."

6. Father Cholenec, in [Dablon], *Relation of 1676 and 1677*, *JR* 60:287; Journal of Frederick Post, 1758, in Thwaites, ed., *Early Western Travels* 1:231.

7. Zeisberger, *History*, 19. Father Le Jeune noted this behavior among the Montagnais (*Relation of 1634*, *JR* 6:231), and Father Brébeuf observed it among the Hurons ("Huronia Report," *JR* 10:211). Subtle slander through humor and sorcery were the ways to release pent-up anger against someone; see Hallowell, "Some Psychological Characteristics," 211–16.

8. La Potherie, *Histoire* 3:28; Journal of Frederick Post, 1758, in Thwaites, ed., *Early Western Travels* 1:231; Zeisberger, *History*, 19, 77.

9. Lafitau, *Moeurs* 1:300.

10. Father Cholenec, in [Dablon], *Relation of 1677 and 1678*, *JR* 1:59.

11. "Mémoire sur les coutumes," 442–43.

12. [Dablon], *Relation of 1670–71*, *JR* 54:281; Father Millet [1674], in [Dablon], *Relation of 1673–74*, *JR* 58:185; [Raudot], *Relation*, 186; "Mémoire sur les coutumes," 442.

13. Lafitau, *Moeurs* 2:102.

14. Vaudreuil et Raudot au Ministre, 13 nov. 1708, AN, C11A 28:62; [Raudot], *Relation*, 189; Galinée, "Voyage de Dollier et Galinée," 16. At a conference with the Iroquois in 1700, some Iroquois leaders told the English authorities that they could not confirm their request to send one hundred warriors to staff a proposed fort "because it is the young men [who] must do the service, and they must be consulted about it" (Conference, [2 Aug.–4 Sept.] 1700, NYCD 4:737).

15. Lafitau, *Moeurs* 1:293; Father Frémin, quoted in [Le Mercier], *Relation of 1667–68*, *JR* 51:213–15.

16. "Mémoire sur les coutumes," 446.

17. The Iroquois were considered very generous by their French neighbors. See [Raudot], *Relation*, 190; "Mémoire sur les coutumes," 472; "Nation Iroquoise," 11 (this document was written sometime in the seventeenth century by a Frenchman who was captured by the Iroquois; at some later point a cover and the title "Nation Iroquoise" were added).

18. Father Frémin, quoted in [Le Mercier], *Relation of 1667–68*, *JR* 51:213–15.

19. By the same token, war chiefs did not order their men to war so as not to be held accountable to their families in the advent of the death of a warrior ("Mémoire sur les coutumes," 446–47).

20. Lafitau, *Moeurs* 1:293.

21. Each sociopolitical group among the Iroquois conducted its affairs as if indepen-

dent of all other groups and informed others of their decisions only if they felt it might be of concern to them (Lafitau, *Moeurs* 1:287; "Nation Iroquoise," 5).

22. [Raudot], *Relation*, 185; "Nation Iroquoise," 4. Even among Christianized mission Iroquois, decisions continued to be made by the whole group. At councils held to convince the community to undertake a given course, speakers continued to take their guidance from elders (Father Chauchetière, "Narration annuelle de la Mission du Sault depuis la fundation jusques à l'an 1686," *JR* 63:163).

23. J. Megapolensis, "A Short Account of the Mohawk Indians, 1644," *NNN*, 179; [Raudot], *Relation*, 186. This continued to be a feature of Iroquois politics; see Morgan, *League*, 111; E. Tooker, "The League of the Iroquois: Its History, Politics, and Ritual," in Trigger, ed., *Handbook*, 422.

24. Indeed, even when a decision was made to war, the war chiefs were asked to go to war and efforts were made to persuade them to do so, but the war chiefs decided for themselves whether they would engage in hostilities ("Nation Iroquoise," 6).

25. Zeisberger, *History*, 116.

26. Lafitau, *Moeurs* 1:308; "Mémoire sur les coutumes," 441; [Raudot], *Relation*, 185.

27. In what follows I have tried to rely only on seventeenth- and eighteenth-century sources. For more detailed discussions on various aspects of council procedures, terms, and ceremonies based on nineteenth- and twentieth-century fieldwork among the Iroquois, see Jennings, ed., *History and Culture*. Fenton has concluded, based mostly on modern evidence, that part of the procedures of councils was derived from the Iroquois Condolence Council (W. N. Fenton, "Structure, Continuity, and Change in the Process of Iroquois Treaty Making," in Jennings, ed., *History and Culture*, 18–21).

28. La Potherie, *Histoire* 3:31; Father Millet, in [Dablon], *Relation of 1673-74*, *JR* 58:187.

29. Father Millet, in [Dablon], *Relation of 1673-74*, *JR* 58:189. Father Millet does not describe the ceremonies.

30. When these procedures were not followed, the Iroquois were quick to complain. On one occasion, when the Iroquois came to meet with the French and were not saluted with the usual gunfire, General Montcalm noted in his journal that "they insinuated modestly . . . that they were surprised at not being received with the usual ceremonies" (Journal du Marquis de Montcalm, 1756–1757, in H. R. Casgrain, ed., *Collection des manuscrits* 7:123).

31. Father Millet, in [Dablon], *Relation of 1673-74*, *JR* 58:189.

32. Untitled document [1666], AN, CIIA 2:264v; this document, a description of the Iroquois clan system, is not dated or signed; it follows documents dated 1666 and takes its tentative date from that; it has been translated and published; see "The Nine Iroquois Tribes," *NYCD* 9:47–51. The original French word *famille*, meaning "family," and in this case "clan," has been erroneously translated as "tribe." The editor's notes should also be disregarded.

33. Untitled document [1666], AN, CIIA 2:264v; La Pause, Relation de l'Ambassade des Cinq Nations, *RAPQ*, *1932-33*, 328. This practice was also followed at Iroquois-European councils, although there, who spoke first depended on a variety of factors. The

most important determinants seem to have been who initiated the conference and who was acting as host. See Michael K. Foster, "On Who Spoke First at Iroquois-White Councils: An Exercise in the Method of Upstreaming," in Foster, Campisi, and Mithun, eds., *Extending the Rafters*, 183–207.

34. Untitled document [1666], AN, CIIA 2:264v; E. Tooker, "The League of the Iroquois: Its History, Politics, and Ritual," in Trigger, ed., *Handbook*, 429.

35. Bartram, *Observations*, 74; see also La Pause, Relation de l'Ambassade des Cinq Nations, *RAPQ*, *1932–33*, 329; "Nation Iroquoise," 5. When a tribe made a proposition for which delegates had not received instructions, the adjournment was probably even longer.

36. Zeisberger, *History*, 143.

37. Bartram, *Observations*, 90. For a fuller discussion of Iroquois oratory, see Robie, "Kiotsaeton's Three Rivers Address," and Reynolds, "Persuasive Speaking."

38. David De Vries, "Korte Historiael," *NNN*, 230–31; conference, Governor Burnet and the Five Nations, Aug. 1721, in Colden, *Letters and Papers* 1:132.

39. Lafitau, *Moeurs* 1:308; Zeisberger, *History*, 32, 94. For detailed descriptions of these belts, see the journal of Conrad Weiser [1748], in Thwaites, ed., *Early Western Travels* 1:30; Zeisberger, *History*, 95. On the uses and history of wampum see Ceci, "Value of Wampum"; Speck, "Functions of Wampum"; Vachon, "Colliers et ceintures de porcelaine dans la diplomatie indienne," and "Colliers et ceintures de porcelaine chez les indiens de la Nouvelle-France." For an interesting discussion on how the Iroquois viewed the role of wampum, see Michael K. Foster, "Another Look at the Function of Wampum in Iroquois-White Councils," in Jennings, ed., *History and Culture*, 99–114.

40. Lafitau, *Moeurs* 1:310; La Pause, Relation de l'Ambassade des Cinq Nations, *RAPQ*, *1932–33*, 325; Wraxall, *Indian Affairs*, 60. On the size of the belts, see also La Potherie, *Histoire* 1:333.

41. Wraxall, *Indian Affairs*, 93, 94.

42. [Vimont], *Relation of 1644–45*, JR 27:253; Zeisberger, *History*, 97.

43. "Continuation of Colden's History," in Colden, *Letters and Papers* 9:416, 418, 419.

44. Father Millet, in [Dablon], *Relation of 1673–74*, JR 58:185, 187; La Pause, Relation de l'Ambassade des Cinq Nations, *RAPQ*, *1932–33*, 332. At village councils they would indicate which family had provided the wampum.

45. At conferences with Europeans, for example, the Iroquois appointed one speaker to state the Confederacy's views, but each tribe still had a speaker present its particular contribution or viewpoint on that Confederacy decision. See for example "Answer of the Five Nations," 23 Sept. 1689, *LIR*, 154–58.

46. Colden, *History of the Five Nations*, 2; Lafitau, *Moeurs* 1:287.

47. E. Tooker, "The League of the Iroquois: Its History, Politics, and Ritual," in Trigger, ed., *Handbook*, 430.

48. Wraxall, *Indian Affairs*, 165; conference, 7 Sept. 1726, *NYCD* 5:789.

49. "Report of Some Onondaga Sachems," 26 Apr. 1700, *NYCD* 4:658.

50. "Conference with Five Nations," 30 June 1700, *NYCD* 4:694.

51. Wraxall, *Indian Affairs*, 165–69; "Conference with Iroquois," 7–14 Sept. 1726, *NYCD* 5:789–90.

52. La Potherie, *Histoire* 4:193–94. This was a view shared by other French observers; see [Raudot], *Relation*, 185; "Nation Iroquoise," 10.

53. Lafitau, *Moeurs* 1:297. The extent of that power is still being debated. Recently, Francis Jennings has taken umbrage at earlier writers for their acceptance of what he calls the myth of the Iroquois Empire (Jennings, *Ambiguous Iroquois Empire*). Along similar lines see Lebman, "The End of the Iroquois Mystique."

54. Lafitau, *Moeurs* 1:308.

55. Fenton, "Iroquois Culture Patterns," in Trigger, ed., *Handbook*, 309–10.

56. Colden, *Five Indian Nations*, 1–2; Lafitau, *Moeurs* 1:287; La Potherie, *Histoire* 1:360–61; "Nation Iroquoise," 4v-5.

57. Untitled document [1666], AN, CIIA 2:264. See also E. Tooker, "The League of the Iroquois: Its History, Politics, and Ritual," in Trigger, ed., *Handbook*, 426–28.

58. Lafitau, *Moeurs* 1:287; La Potherie, *Histoire* 1:360–61.

59. Longhouses in villages were grouped according to clan affiliation; each longhouse also had its clan symbol painted over the entrance (La Potherie, *Histoire* 1:360–61; untitled document [1666], AN, CIIA 2:264v; diary of Cammerhoff and Zeisberger, 1750, in Beauchamp, ed., *Moravian Journals*, 69). There is some evidence to suggest that among the Mohawks, at least, villages were occupied, or dominated, by one clan (J. Megapolensis, "A Short Account of the Mohawk Indians, 1644," *NNN*, 178–79; [van den Bogaert], "Narrative of a Journey into the Mohawk and Oneida Country, 1634–35," *NNN*, 144). One French source claims that before the formation of the Iroquois confederation, each village was occupied by a single clan (untitled document [1666], AN, CIIA 2:264v). It was the obligation of one moiety to mourn the death of someone from the other ("Continuation of Colden's History," in Colden, *Letters and Papers* 9:363–64; *LIR*, 201).

60. Albany Conference, 29 Aug. 1700, in Wraxall, *Indian Affairs*, 34–37, quote on 35. For a longer version of this conference, see *NYCD* 4:727–46. The same quotation, with minor variations, is on 736.

61. Colden, *Five Indian Nations*, 1–2. See for example "Deed from the Five Nations to the King," *NYCD* 4:910, and "Acte authentique des six nations iroquoises sur leur indépendance," 2 Nov. 1742, *RAPQ*, *1921–22*, unnum. plate following 108. French and English authorities wrote the names of the native delegates on conference transcripts and pointed to where they should make a mark to testify to their presence at the conference and to their agreement with the matters recorded in the transcripts.

62. For example, it was the obligation of those who had marriage ties to a clan, not actual members of the clan who had lost a member, to avenge a death (Lafitau, *Moeurs* 2:99).

63. For a similar interpretation see Campisi, "Iroquois," 108. For a different view of the role of clans, one that holds that their function was not to maintain genealogical connections but originated to facilitate trade over North America, see Tooker, "Clans."

64. Lafitau, *Moeurs* 1:72.

65. Colden, *Five Indian Nations*, 9; Bartram, *Observations*, 91.

66. See for example, "Conference, River Indians and Five Nations," 10 Aug. 1747, in Colden, *Letters and Papers* 3:415–16; "Indian Conference," 26 Dec. 1755, and "Indian Conference," 19 Feb. 1756, in Johnson, *Papers* 9:332–33, 364. Indeed, one of the matters public speakers had to be well versed in was "what title to apply to . . . other nations, whether brother or nephew or uncle" (Zeisberger, *History*, 142). The calling of the English "brother" or "brethren" and the French "Father" was a conscious choice and signified how the Iroquois viewed their relationship to these powers. Thus in the case of the English, the Iroquois viewed themselves as equals, while with the French they acknowledged respect—rather more likely due to their military might than from affection. This latter point can be inferred from the fact that the "father figure," as represented by age and wisdom, was respected among Indians (Lafitau, *Moeurs* 1:291). It did not, however, carry all the emotional connotations associated with the word in Western culture. More directly, as noted by an Abenaki speaker who came to treat for peace with the Mohawks in October 1700, "To call you Brethren is nothing in comparison to Father, therefore we take you as Fathers" (*NYCD* 4:758).

67. Morgan, *League*, 83. Fenton, in "Iroquoian Culture Patterns" (in Trigger, ed., *Handbook*, 310), appears to doubt this was the case. He does not suggest any reasons, however, and concludes by stating that if this was true, it is no longer practiced among modern Iroquois. It is important to note that even if the moieties were not exogamous, they still served an integrative function by providing the Mohawks and Oneidas with the same social structures as the other tribes in the Confederacy, and thus the same linking process.

68. "Continuation of Colden's History," in Colden, *Letters and Papers* 9:363–64; "Indian Conference," 18–19 Feb. 1756, in [Johnson], *Papers* 9:356–57.

69. Fenton, "Iroquoian Culture Patterns," in Trigger, ed., *Handbook*, 314.

70. "Nation Iroquoise," 9v–10; "Mémoire sur les coutumes," 460–61.

71. [Le Jeune], *Relation of 1656–57*, *JR* 43:271.

72. This is not a particularly novel assertion. Fenton is only the latest in a long line of distinguished anthropologists to note that "Iroquois political organization extends the basic patterns of social structure" (W. N. Fenton, "Structure, Continuity, and Change in the Process of Iroquois Treaty Making," in Jennings, ed., *History and Culture*, 12). Nineteenth- and early-twentieth-century studies of the League of the Iroquois all detail the role of clans in its workings; see Morgan, *League*; Hale, *Iroquois Book*; Parker, *Constitution*. What follows here, however, is based directly on seventeenth-century evidence about how the clan system worked at the local government level.

73. The evidence on which the following paragraph is based was culled from: "Nation Iroquoise," 4–5; Father Millet, in [Dablon], *Relation of 1673–74*, *JR* 58:185–89; [Raudot], *Relation*, 185–87; "Mémoire sur les coutumes," 442–43.

74. E. Tooker, "The League of the Iroquois: Its History, Politics, and Ritual," in Trigger, ed., *Handbook*, 424–26; Hewitt, "Status," 479.

75. Fenton, "Iroquoian Culture Patterns," in Trigger, ed., *Handbook*, 314; Lafitau, *Moeurs* 1:287, 291; La Potherie, *Histoire* 3:29.

76. E. Tooker, "The League of the Iroquois: Its History, Politics, and Ritual," in Trigger, ed., *Handbook*, 428; Campisi, "Iroquois," 168.

77. E. Tooker, "The League of the Iroquois: Its History, Politics, and Ritual," in Trigger, ed., *Handbook*, 421, 424–28.

78. D. K. Richter, "Ordeals of the Longhouse: The Five Nations in Early American History," in Richter and Merrell, eds., *Beyond the Covenant Chain*, 11–27.

79. Indeed, differences in languages developed among the five tribes; see F. G. Lounsbury, "Iroquoian Languages," in Trigger, ed., *Handbook*, 335–36.

80. Whether the Confederacy was formed to stop intertribal feuding, either for defense or to expedite war, is not as important in this context as the fact that it was created; see W. N. Fenton, "Problems in the Authentication of the League of the Iroquois," in Campisi and Hauptman, eds., *Neighbours and Intruders*, 261–68, in which he traces the various stages of the League's development. He also deals with the problem of a founding date for the League and concludes that trying to establish one is probably futile since the evidence is scant and contradictory.

CHAPTER THREE. WARFARE PART ONE

1. "Conference [with the Five Nations, 10–21 July] 1701," *NYCD* 4:899.

2. Compiled from table D.1. The Iroquois waged war in small groups rather than in one large army. Even in intertribal wars, when fighting parties were larger, the Iroquois tended to send out one group after the return of the first or to send them to different areas. See for example the raids in 1653 against various groups in different locations (table D.1). This practice is reflected in the high number of raids. Lafitau remarked that warring was so ubiquitous that there were almost always some parties in the field (Lafitau, *Moeurs* 2:101).

3. "Nation Iroquoise," 5–6; see also "Mémoire sur les coutumes," 442.

4. "Nation Iroquoise," 8; "Mémoire sur les coutumes," 446–47.

5. Lafitau, *Moeurs* 2:101.

6. Livingston to Schuyler, 23 Aug. 1720, *NYCD* 5:559–61. Livingston complained about the constant state of warfare and the readiness of the youth to engage in it.

7. Colden, *Five Indian Nations*, 6; Lafitau, *Moeurs* 2:111–13; Zeisberger, *History*, 103. The latter stated that hogs were used more often. This was probably because hogs were more widely available after 1750 (when Zeisberger lived among the Iroquois) and became preferred because they carried more meat. Zeisberger noted that dogs were still used, but usually more than one at a time because "Indian dogs are very lean" (103).

8. "Nation Iroquoise," 6v.

9. Colden, *Five Indian Nations*, 7; Lafitau, *Moeurs* 2:114–15; Zeisberger, *History*, 103.

10. Colden, *Five Indian Nations*, 7; Lafitau, *Moeurs* 2:114–15. Part of the reason for leaving in ceremonial finery was for the benefit of the attendant villagers; the other was to emphasize the solemnity and grandeur of the mission.

11. "Mémoire sur les coutumes," 448.

12. Untitled document [1666], AN, CIIA 2:265; Colden, *Five Indian Nations*, 7–8; Lafitau, *Moeurs* 2:37; Zeisberger, *History*, 114.

13. "Relation officielle de l'entreprise de Cavelier de La Salle de 1679–1681," in Margry, *Découvertes* 1:519. The Iroquois sometimes "recorded" their martial exploits with body tattoos ([Radisson], *Explorations*, 27). At times the Iroquois left a war club beside a corpse to indicate who the attacker had been (untitled document [1666], AN, CIIA 2:265; [Relation of 1694–95], AN, CIIA 14:90v).

14. Cammerhoff and Zeisberger in their diary of 1750 noted a clearing filled with trees marked in this way. Their Cayuga guide pointed out two trees that outlined his martial deeds (Beauchamp, ed., *Moravian Journals*, 41).

15. Lafitau, *Moeurs* 2:115–16.

16. J. Megapolensis, "A Short Account of the Mohawk Indians, 1644," NNN, 176; Spangenberg's journal, 1745, in Beauchamp, ed., *Moravian Journals*, 10; Bartram, *Observations*, 62; Colden, *Five Indian Nations*, 9; "Mémoire sur les coutumes," 447.

17. For a discussion of the marginal effectiveness of muskets, see Given, *A Most Pernicious Thing*. Given makes a strong case that muskets and arquebuses were cumbersome weapons with many limitations, but he fails to explain convincingly why they were so eagerly sought after by natives.

18. Zeisberger, *History*, 23. Iroquois canoes were fragile and rarely lasted more than one year, but Zeisberger claimed that the Iroquois knew how to keep their "canows water-tight so that they do not leak" (23). He should have known since he spent a great deal of time traveling in them and helped to build canoes on more than one occasion; see the diary of Zeisberger and Frey, 1753, in Beauchamp, ed., *Moravian Journals*, 189.

19. Diary of Zeisberger and Frey, 1753, in Beauchamp, ed., *Moravian Journals*, 156, 159, 160.

20. Diary of Cammerhoff and Zeisberger, 1750, in Beauchamp, ed., *Moravian Journals*, 27, 33, 37, 38; "Nation Iroquoise," 8; Zeisberger, *History*, 40. Both missionaries and their Iroquois guides did this. On many occasions they were spared the trouble of constructing their own by coming across "abandoned huts." Bartram described how his Iroquois guides erected one of these lean-tos (*Observations*, 39–40). A similar method of stripping bark was most probably used when that material was needed to make canoes.

21. Zeisberger, *History*, 40.

22. Untitled document [1666], AN, CIIA 2:265; "Mémoire sur les coutumes," 448.

23. [Le Jeune], *Relation of 1640–41*, JR 20:63.

24. [Vimont], *Relation of 1642*, JR 22:247–49; "Mémoire sur les coutumes," 448; Lafitau, *Moeurs* 2:141. Despite this, the Iroquois did not post guards at night. Instead they relied on the report of the scout who was sent ahead to check that the intended campsite was safe. Nor did they post guards when returning with prisoners. However, the Iroquois faith in their methods of securing prisoners was not always well founded. On at least one occasion the captives turned on their sleeping "hosts" and killed them all (Spangenberg's journal, 1745, in Beauchamp, ed., *Moravian Journals*, 10).

25. The Iroquois' unwillingness to provide convenient targets particularly frustrated the French. In one instance, Governor Frontenac complained that the Iroquois, "barbarians that they are" ["sauvages comme ils sont"], hid in the woods and did not come out

into the open "where we would not fail to charge them" (Frontenac au Ministre, 11 nov. 1692, AN, CIIA 12:46–48v). The wisdom of Iroquois strategy seems to have escaped Frontenac.

26. Boucher, *Histoire véritable*, 122; "Mémoire sur les coutumes," 448; [Vimont], *Relation of 1642–43*, JR 24: 277; Henri Tonti, "Mémoire envoyé en 1693," in Margry, *Relations*, 9. Two partial studies of Iroquois military tactics in the seventeenth century are Otterbein, "Why the Iroquois Won," and "Huron vs. Iroquois." In the former article, Otterbein concluded that Iroquois strategy, not weapons superiority, accounted for Iroquois successes against native foes. In the latter work he provides one example of this assertion. For a discussion of Iroquois weapons and tactics during the war of 1812, see Benn, "Iroquois Warfare."

27. It is not clear how shields had been used by the Iroquois. If they were used only to block arrow volleys and then discarded for close fighting, their having fallen into disuse would not entail greater casualties during hand-to-hand fighting.

28. [Lalemant], *Relation of 1647*, JR 32:21; Dollier, *Histoire du Montréal*, 127, 175. The dead were cremated.

29. The records do not indicate if the same procedures were followed when hundreds of captives were taken.

30. On the method of binding prisoners, see untitled document [1666], AN, CIIA 2:263. The torments were minor only in comparison to what would follow for those destined to be tortured.

31. Prisoners were bound hand and foot to stakes as in a St. Andrew's cross (Lafitau, *Moeurs* 2:148–49; La Potherie, *Histoire* 2:23). Father Jogues, who was captured by the Iroquois, described this as the way he was tied while he was in the village proper and not while en route ("Narré de la prise de père Isaac Jogues," RAPQ, 1924–25, 8).

32. Untitled document [1666], AN, CIIA 2:265v.

33. Journal of Frederick Post, 15 July to 20 Sept. 1758, in Thwaites, ed., *Early Western Travels* 1:190; Zeisberger, *History*, 104; diary of Cammeroff and Zeisberger, 1750, in Beauchamp, ed., *Moravian Journals*, 37.

34. [Le Mercier], *Relation of 1669–70*, JR 54:23; Colden, *Five Indian Nations*, 9; Lafitau, *Moeurs* 2:153.

35. "Nation Iroquoise," 8v; Lafitau, *Moeurs* 2:152; La Potherie, *Histoire* 2:23; "Mémoire sur les coutumes," 449.

36. Lafitau, *Moeurs* 2:149–50.

37. Jean de Lamberville to [Father Superior], 25 Aug. 1682, JR 62:79; see also "Nation Iroquoise," 8v.

38. [Le Mercier], *Relation of 1669–70*, JR 54:23–25.

39. "Narré de la prise de père Isaac Jogues," RAPQ, 1924–25, 7. The narrative was written by Father Buteux, who was killed by the Iroquois in 1652. This process remained more or less the same into the eighteenth century. See Lafitau, *Moeurs* 2:149–50; journal of Frederick Post, Oct. 1758–Jan. 1759, in Thwaites, ed., *Early Western Travels* 1:254; Zeisberger, *History*, 105–6.

40. Lafitau, *Moeurs* 2:152. James Lynch has suggested that one reason prisoners could be harshly treated in the period shortly after capture was because they had yet to be

adopted into a family ("Iroquois Confederacy," 86–88). On the adoption and treatment of nonnative captives, see Axtell, *European*, 168–205.

41. Galinée, "Voyage de Dollier et Galinée," 30; "Mémoire sur les coutumes," 450.

42. [Radisson], *Explorations*, 16–24, 69; Lafitau, *Moeurs* 2:153. In escaping, or in killing some Mohawks in the process, Radisson had forfeited his status as a member of his mother's clan.

43. Boucher, *Histoire véritable*, 117.

44. Colden, *Five Indian Nations*, 4, vi. Lafitau felt that Iroquois warfare "exposes their courage to the rudest tests, furnishes them frequent occasions to put in its brightest light all the nobility of their sentiments and the unshakeable firmness of a truly heroic greatness of mind" (*Moeurs* 2:98).

45. Thomas Gage to Johnson, 7 Oct. 1771, in [Johnson], *Papers* 12:994–95.

46. Joseph Brant and John Norton, quoted in Boyce, "Glimpse," 290, 293.

47. Lafitau, *Moeurs* 2:102–3; see also Zeisberger, *History*, 19; La Potherie, *Histoire* 3:28.

48. Conference, July 1704, in [Cadillac], [Papers of Cadillac] 33:191.

49. Adventure raids were usually undertaken as a result of a vision in a dream (see La Potherie, *Histoire* 2:20). On the various roles of dreams in Iroquois society see Wallace, *Death and Rebirth*, 59–75.

50. Lafitau, *Moeurs* 2:99; see also "Nation Iroquoise," 8. On the Athonni, see La Potherie, *Histoire* 1:360.

51. Lafitau, *Moeurs* 2:243; Barclay to Colden, 7 Dec. 1741, in Colden, *Letters and Papers* 8:282.

52. Fenton, "Iroquoian Culture Patterns," in Trigger, ed., *Handbook*, 311–12.

53. Lafitau, *Moeurs* 2:152.

54. Lafitau, *Moeurs* 2:156, 101. Charles Le Moyne de Longueuil, the French Indian agent to the Onondagas, recognized that the problem was complex. In his efforts to keep that tribe from waging war, he addressed his appeal to all the parties involved in the process: "Children I desire that the young men shall be obedient and do what the old Sachims shall order . . . the sqaas . . . should give good advice to the young men" ("Propositions of the French at Onondaga," [reported] 7 May 1711, *NYCD* 5:243–44).

55. Speech to Six Nations, Acting Governor George Clarke, Albany, [12] Aug. 1740, *NYCD* 6:173. The document dates this opening speech as being on 16 August and the response on 12 August. The latter is probably the correct date for the opening speech, and 16 August for when the transcripts of the conference were completed.

56. Lafitau, *Moeurs* 2:102.

57. [Conference], 14 June 1712, in Wraxall, *Indian Affairs*, 93.

58. [Report to Albany Indian Commissioners], 26 July 1738, in Wraxall, *Indian Affairs*, 210–11. English efforts in July 1738 to bring about peace between the Senecas and the Catawbas were halted after a Seneca was murdered by some Catawbas. The Senecas quickly sent out a small raiding party to make the Catawbas atone. Wraxall also reported that a much sought-after treaty between the Ottawas and the Iroquois, concluded on 9 June 1710, barely lasted into the new year because of the Iroquois need to avenge a few murders (72–73, 80).

59. Journal of Conrad Weiser, 1748, in Thwaites, ed., *Early Western Travels* 1:33–34.

60. Fenton, "Iroquois Suicide," 134.

61. "Nation Iroquoise," 7.

62. Scalps were one of the material signs of a successful raid ([Le Mercier], *Relation of 1669–70, JR* 53:245; La Potherie, *Histoire* 2:22). See also Knowles, "Torture," 152. While scalps could be used to replace the dead, that is, "scalps which take the place of a captive and replace a person," it is most likely that in such cases the scalp served more as a sign that the death of the person had been avenged (Lafitau, *Moeurs* 2:163). For a discussion on the various ways in which scalps were taken see Nadeau, "Indian Scalping Technique." On the longevity of this native practice, see Axtell, *European and the Indian*, 16–35.

63. "Mémoire sur les coutumes," 448; Colden, *Five Indian Nations*, 9.

64. La Pause, Mémoire sur la campagne à faire en Canada, l'année 1757, *RAPQ, 1932–33*, 338; see also La Pause, Relation de l'Ambassade des Cinq Nations, *RAPQ, 1932–33*, 308–9. After chasing Braddock's defeated army, the Indians returned with spoils of war, some prisoners, and "infinite number of scalps." Zeisberger noted the persistence of this attitude into the 1780s. "If they can bring back a captive or a scalp they regard themselves as amply rewarded for all weariness and need they have suffered and danger to which they have been exposed" (*History*, 40–41).

65. Knowles, "Torture," 151–225; Trigger, *Huron*, 47–53. While much of value can be extracted from these works, the focus of each is not to explain Iroquois torture. Knowles was concerned with documenting the various methods of torture and in tracing links between them in order to ascertain questions of diffusion. Trigger's work dealt mostly with the Huron. Richter's *Ordeal* devotes one paragraph to the role of torture (69–70).

66. Richter, *Ordeal*, 69–70. Wallace has suggested that warfare in general served to maintain social equilibrium by providing a way to release tensions (*Death and Rebirth*, 44–48).

67. A Huron explained his nation's attitude to prisoners: "We have nothing but caresses for them a day before their death, even when our minds are filled with cruelties, the severity of which we afterward find all our pleasure in making them feel" ([Lalemant], "Huron Report, 1641–42" *JR* 23:93).

68. Lafitau, *Moeurs* 2:156.

69. Boucher, *Histoire véritable*, 125–126; Galinée, "Voyage de Dollier et Galinée," 30–32; [Le Mercier], *Relation of 1669–70, JR* 54:27.

70. [Le Mercier], *Relation of 1668–69, JR* 52:167–69; [Radisson], *Explorations*, 16–24.

71. [Le Mercier], "Huron Report, 1637," *JR* 13:61.

72. Galinée, "Voyage de Dollier et Galinée," 34; "Wentworth Greenhalgh's Journal of a Tour to the Indians of Western New-York," *NYCD* 3:252; "Mémoire sur les coutumes," 454; Lafitau, *Moeurs* 2:157.

73. [Radisson], *Explorations*, 21; Galinée, "Voyage de Dollier et Galinée," 34.

74. Jean de Lamberville to [Father Superior], 25 Aug. 1682, *JR* 62:87, 91; "Mémoire sur les coutumes," 451; Lafitau, *Moeurs* 2:155.

75. One of the difficulties that will face any researcher tackling this problem is how to deal with disparate descriptions of the torture process. Are they different because they reflect dissimilar practices or because some observers omitted aspects included in the reports of others? Prisoners captured as part of an adventure raid were treated differently from those brought in as part of a revenge raid ("Nation Iroquoise," 8; Galinée, "Voyage de Dollier et Galinée," 30–34; "Mémoire sur les coutumes," 450). Different torture processes may reflect this. Without knowing the reasons for the raid, one cannot properly evaluate what the evidence on torture reveals.

76. Lafitau, *Moeurs* 2:156–57. See also Father Millet's observation in [Le Mercier], *Relation of 1668–69*, *JR* 52:169. Father Le Mercier, writing over thirty years before, had noted that the Hurons burned the legs first "so that . . . [the prisoner] might hold out until daybreak" ([Le Mercier], "Huron Report, 1637," *JR* 13:61, 67).

77. See the personal accounts in [Bressani], *Breve Relatione*, *JR* 39:55–77; [Lalemant], *Relation of 1647*, *JR* 31:39–51; [Le Mercier], *Relation of 1652–53*, *JR* 40:133–37; [Radisson], *Explorations*, 16–24.

78. Indeed, the most common torture method was to burn the victim slowly. The "effectiveness" of these methods is suggested by victims sometimes enduring for days. See [Raudot], *Relation*, 184; "Mémoire sur les coutumes," 452. However, after several days of torture, as the anonymous author of the latter work observed, the body of the victim was "nothing more than a shapeless mass" (451).

79. Father Poncet recalled how one Iroquois wanted to place the stub of his finger in his pipe in order to stem the flow of blood ([Le Mercier], *Relation of 1652–53*, *JR* 40:133–35). La Potherie (*Histoire* 2:25) noted that this was the purpose of putting burning sand and ashes on the victim's head after he was scalped. "After they have roasted [*grillé*] him well, they lift his scalp . . . [and pour] a bowl full of burning sand onto his head to stop the blood [flow]." The Hurons also used fire in torture to the same end ([Lalemant], "Huron Report 1642–43," *JR* 26:191).

80. Father Poncet, in [Le Mercier], *Relation of 1652–53*, *JR* 40:133–35; Father Jogues, in [Lalemant], *Relation of 1647*, *JR* 31:45.

81. "Nation Iroquoise," 8. As one Iroquois speaker explained, it is the "Custom to give such Prisoners as are taken of the Enemy, to those families that have lost their relatives in battle, who have the sole disposal of them, either to kill them or keep them alive" (Onondaga speaker, Albany Conference, 20 Aug. 1711, *NYCD* 5:269).

82. J. Megapolensis, "A Short Account of the Mohawk Indians, 1644," *NNN*, 175; "Nation Iroquoise," 7; Lafitau, *Moeurs* 2:195. Some prisoners were not adopted immediately ([Lalemant], *Relation of 1647*, *JR* 31:53). This may have been part of some test of suitability or some prisoners might have been deliberately set aside to be exchanged for Iroquois taken captive by other groups.

83. Boucher, *Histoire véritable*, 125–26; Lafitau, *Moeurs* 2:156. Interestingly enough, the torture of the prisoner did not end the obligation to replace the dead, which continued, wrote Lafitau, "until life is given a person representing the one whom they wish to resuscitate" (156).

84. In one case, a woman who had been given a captive to replace her son could not bear to see the captive live (Galinée, "Voyage de Dollier et Galinée," 30). In another,

some eight people were killed in revenge for the death of one Oneida warrior ("Nation Iroquoise," 7v).

85. La Potherie, *Histoire* 3:46, 47; Lafitau, *Moeurs* 2:171–72; "Mémoire sur les coutumes," 450; Colden, *Five Indian Nations*, 9. When whole tribes were taken, they were often allowed to live in their own village and given a kinship term to symbolize their relationship to the Iroquois. Thus the Wyandots were called "nephews" and in turn called the Six Nations "uncles" after they were adopted in 1748 (journal of Conrad Weiser, 1748, in Thwaites, ed., *Early Western Travels* 1:35–36). More significant was the adoption of the Tuscaroras. In 1713–14 the Iroquois began receiving refugee Tuscaroras (an estimated five hundred families), and in 1722–23 this group was formally adopted into the Five Nations and given a position in one of the moieties. The Confederacy even went so far as to change its name to that of Six Nations in order to acknowledge the position among them of the new tribe (David Landy, "Tuscarora among the Iroquois," in Trigger, ed., *Handbook*, 519–20). On the reasons for adopting people and tribes among the Iroquois, see Lynch, "Iroquois Confederacy," 83–99.

86. La Potherie, *Histoire* 3:43–44; Lafitau, *Moeurs* 2:172; Zeisberger, *History*, 40–41.

87. Bartram, *Observations*, 91. See also "Mémoire sur les coutumes," 452.

88. Lafitau, *Moeurs* 2:98. Recently it has been suggested that "slavery was practiced by Northern Iroquoians in the context of what has been previously and exclusively described as an adoption complex" (Starna and Watkins, "Northern Iroquoian Slavery"). This too may have may been a reason to gain captives.

89. *Journal des pères Jésuites*, JR 45:155, 157.

90. [Ragueneau], *Relation of 1651–52*, JR 38:49, 51. See also Baugy, *Journal*, 50–52.

91. [Le Mercier], *Relation of 1664–65*, JR 49:233.

92. [Le Mercier], *Relation of 1653–54*, JR 41:49. The Jesuits felt Iroquois peace efforts in the 1650s were merely attempts to garner French aid and to take the Hurons in the colony to Iroquoia to swell Iroquois warrior ranks ([Le Jeune], *Relation of 1657–58*, JR 44:151).

93. [Court Minute], 22 Aug. 1681, *Md. Archives* 17:3–5.

94. Lalemant, "Huron Report, 1639–40," in [Le Jeune], *Relation of 1640*, JR 19:81. It is important to note that he penned this observation before the Huron-Iroquois wars reached their nadir. Recollet missionary Gabriel Sagard, writing in 1623 before the French had witnessed large-scale native warfare, also remarked that the goal of Iroquoian warfare was to exterminate their enemies (Sagard, *Long Journey*, 163). See also Lafitau, *Moeurs* 2:145.

95. "Propositions made by . . . the [Five Nations]," 10 [June] 1711, NYCD 5:274. In NYCD the date is given as "Albany, 10th, 1711" and follows some material dated late August. Wraxall (*Indian Affairs*, 87–90) puts this conference in June of that year. This makes more sense than the NYCD implied date of August.

96. Father Jogues, in [Vimont], *Relation of 1642–43*, JR 24:297.

97. [Lalemant], *Relation of 1659–60*, JR 45:207. Father Le Jeune also commented on the diversity of groups found among the Five Nations. Iroquois villages, he noted, "con-

tain more Foreigners than natives of that country. Onnontaghé counts seven different nations, who have come to settle in it; and there are as many as eleven in Sonnontouan'' ([Le Jeune], *Relation of 1656–57*, JR 43:265).

98. Huron speaker, in [Le Mercier], *Relation of 1664–65*, JR 49:233; journal of Fathers Frémin, Pierron, and Bruyas, in [Le Mercier], *Relation of 1667–68*, JR 51:187; Father Bruyas to [Father Superior?], 21 Jan. 1668, in [Le Mercier], *Relation of 1667–68*, JR 51:123; [Le Mercier], *Relation of 1668–69*, JR 52:179.

99. [Raudot], *Relation*, 184.

100. Hale, *Iroquois Book of Rites*, 88–89, 95; Parker, *Constitution*, 50–52; [Chief John Gibson et al.], "The Traditional Narrative of the Origin of the Confederation of the Five Nations," [1900], in Parker, *Constitution*, 101, 105, 111.

101. Parker, *Constitution*, 52; Hale, *Iroquois Book of Rites*, 92, 94.

102. See Dennis, *Cultivating*, esp. 76–115.

103. [Norton], *Journal*, 105.

104. On the impact of Iroquois wars on the human geography of the Northeast, see Campeau, *Catastrophe démographique*; C. Heidenreich in Harris, ed., *Historical Atlas*, plates 18, 37–39.

CHAPTER FOUR. WARFARE PART TWO

1. Colden, *Five Indian Nations*, 11; B. G. Trigger, "Early Iroquoian Contacts with Europeans," in Trigger, ed., *Handbook*, 344–56; T. J. Brasser, "Early Indian-European Contacts," in Trigger, ed., *Handbook*, 78–88. For a more speculative and impassioned discussion of this matter, see Jennings, *Invasion*, 3–174. The most comprehensive and nuanced discussion of the impact of cultural contact on natives and Europeans is Axtell, *Invasion Within*.

2. James A. Tuck, "Northern Iroquoian Prehistory," in Trigger, ed., *Handbook*, 322–33; Niemczycki, "Seneca Tribalization."

3. Hunt, *Wars*, 20, 22; Snyderman, "Behind the Tree of Peace," 7–8; Trigger, *Huron*, 42–44; Richter, *Ordeal*, 54, 74. This view has not been restricted to explanations of Iroquois warfare. It has also been used to account for changes in native warfare in general; see Innis, *Fur Trade*, 20; Jaenen, *Friend and Foe*, 127–38.

4. James A. Tuck, "Northern Iroquoian Prehistory," in Trigger, ed., *Handbook*, 326; Wright, *Ontario Iroquois*, 22; Finlayson, 1975 and 1978 Rescue Excavations, 438–40; [Cartier], *Voyages*, 155–56.

5. [Cartier], *Voyages*, 177–78. For a similar view see Abler, "European Technology." Abler contends that there is strong evidence to suggest that postcontact warfare was no more violent than that in the precontact period.

6. The ready exception to this is the work of Fenton, who has devoted his life to the study of the Iroquois and to showing how continuity and adaptation played a role in their survival. A full bibliography of his important contributions in this area can be found in Foster, Campisi, and Mithune, eds., *Extending the Rafters*, 401–17.

7. Axtell, *European and the Indian*, 256.

8. Wallace, "Some Psychological Determinants," 59.

9. Lafitau, *Moeurs* 2:30. See also A. van der Donck, "A Description of the New Netherlands . . . [Amsterdam, 1656]," in *New York Historical Society Collections* 1:194, 195.

10. Lafitau, *Moeurs* 2:116.

11. Drunken binges lasting three to four days—until the alcohol was used up—invariably led to murders and accidental deaths (Fathers Frémin, Pierron, and Bruyas, in [Le Mercier], *Relation of 1667–68*, JR 51:217; [Dablon], *Relation of 1679*, JR 61:161; Father Jean de Lamberville to [?], 25 Aug. 1682, JR 62:67).

12. Boucher, *Histoire véritable*, 116–17; Father Carheil, in [Le Mercier], *Relation of 1668–69*, JR 52:193; Father Lamberville, in [Dablon], *Relation of 1679*, JR 61:173; Father Trouvé, in Dollier, *Histoire du Montréal*, 355. On native alcohol use and its impact see Mancall, *Deadly Medicine*.

13. "Mémoires sur les coutumes," 475.

14. Axtell, *Invasion Within*. On the Jesuits as initiators of change in general see Axtell, *Beyond 1492*, 152–70.

15. [De Quen], *Relation of 1655–56*, JR 135. Father Brébeuf wrote that one obstacle to conversion was that he could not get the Indians to understand Christian concepts as understood by Christian thinkers. The Indians took the expressions he used and related them to their cosmology ([Le Jeune], *Relation of 1635*, JR 8:133).

16. [Le Mercier], *Relation of 1668–69*, JR 52:153.

17. See table A.2. The Jesuits did not consider this a failure. In baptizing an Iroquois they had saved a soul from eternal damnation, and this was what they had come to do.

18. Axtell, *Invasion Within*, 71–127. Axtell has argued convincingly that most healthy adult converts to Christianity adopted their new religious beliefs sincerely (*After Columbus*, 100–121).

19. Kuhn, "Trade and Exchange," 1–2, 14–18; Dean R. Snow, "Iroquois Prehistory," in Foster, Campisi, and Mithune, eds., *Extending the Rafters*, 257.

20. Dennis (*Cultivating*, 154–79, 213–71) provides countless examples of this process, although the conclusions he draws from them are suspect.

21. "Information furnished . . . by Mr. Miller [to Commissioners for Trade and Plantations]," 4 Sept. 1696, NYCD 4:183; Robert Livingston to the Lords of Trade, 13 May 1701, NYCD 4:876.

22. Yet for all that, Indians did not stop producing clay kettles or forget how to cook with them (Sagard, *Long Journey*, 84, 102, 109; [Le Jeune], *Relation of 1633*, JR 5:97).

23. Colden, *Five Indian Nations*, 2. Even presents given to Iroquois leaders by Europeans were shared among all the people ("Information furnished . . . by Mr. Miller [to Commissioners for Trade and Plantations]," 4 Sept. 1696, NYCD 4:183; Robert Livingston to the Lords of Trade, 13 May 1701, NYCD 4:876).

24. [Le Jeune], *Relation of 1656–57*, JR 43:271; Lafitau, *Moeurs* 2:184; Colden, *Letters and Papers* 9:363–64. This continued to hold true even for converted Iroquois. See Father Chauchetiére, "Narration annuelle de la Mission du Sault depuis la fondation jusques à l'an 1686," JR 63:165.

25. Noble, "Some Social Implications," 23; James A. Tuck, "Northern Iroquoian Prehistory," in Trigger, ed., *Handbook*, 332–33; Axtell, *European and the Indian*, 115–16.

26. Axtell, *European and the Indian*, 121–22; La Potherie, *Histoire* 3:8; [Raudot], *Relation*, 188.

27. Kuhn, "Trade and Exchange," 64, 66.

28. J. Megapolensis, "A Short Account of the Mohawk Indians, 1644," *NNN*, 176.

29. [Le Jeune], *Relation of 1634*, *JR* 6:297–99.

30. Letter from Father Bruyas, 21 Jan. 1668, *JR* 51:129. The Iroquois were not alone in questioning Europeans' materialism; see Axtell, *After Columbus*, 142–43.

31. [Le Jeune], *Relation of 1656–57*, *JR* 43:271. This attitude, and the interdependent nature of the clan system and its obligations, worked against the development of individual "capitalist" behavior necessary to theories of the Iroquois being middlemen or fighting to gain goods.

32. "Nation Iroquoise," 11; Boucher, *Histoire véritable*, 114–15; Father Trouvé, in Dollier, *Histoire du Montréal*, 357; [Raudot], *Relation*, 190.

33. Father Trouvé, in Dollier, *Histoire du Montréal*, 357; Barclay to Colden, 7 Dec. 1741, in Colden, *Letters and Papers* 8:279.

34. "Mémoire sur les coutumes," 472; Barclay to Colden, 7 Dec. 1741, in Colden, *Letters and Papers* 8:279.

35. Lafitau, *Moeurs* 1:91.

36. Lafitau, *Moeurs* 2:71; Zeisberger, *History*, 30.

37. Colden, *Five Indian Nations*, 3.

38. Spangenberg's journal, 1745, in Beauchamp, ed., *Moravian Journals*, 7.

39. Zeisberger, *History*, 121.

40. [Raudot], *Relation*, 61, 62.

41. The debate over Iroquois dependency has not really risen above this level. No Iroquoianist has offered a nuanced definition such as that in White, *Roots of Dependency*, xvii–xix. The closest that the Iroquois have come to being put into the Wallerstein model of world economic development—of subsistence economies being exploited, changed, and made dependent on newly emerging capitalist societies—is Delâge, *Le Pays renversé*. Delâge looks at early native-European relations in Canada as a means to test a theory of "unequal exchange" and how the participation of the Iroquois and Hurons in this exchange system made them part of the new European economy and led to cultural change and dependence. Unfortunately, Delâge, like his less methodologically sophisticated predecessors, reduces everything to a matter of economics, and Iroquois warfare is explained as simply a desire to control the fur trade. Iroquois society, he argues, was altered by the unequal nature of the exchange process, which led to the development of a market-driven economy, and Iroquois wars were fought over the furs needed to participate in the rewards of the New World economy.

42. Richter is only the latest in a long line to argue that it did; see his *Ordeal*, 76, 87, 104, 180.

43. Gov. Fletcher to the Committee of Trade, 9 Oct. 1693, *NYCD* 4:57; Gov. Fletcher to Duke of Shrewsbury, 30 May 1696, *NYCD* 4:149.

44. See for example Hunt, *Wars of the Iroquois*; Trigger, *Children of Aataentsic*; Richter, *Ordeal*.

45. Havard, *La Grande Paix*, 92–93.

46. Trigger, *Children of Aataentsic*, 634, 658, 661. Even writers who feel non-economic motives were of significance do not fail to claim that attacks against fur brigades and traders were to steal the furs or goods they carried. See Richter, *Ordeal*, 57, 64, 144; Jennings, *Ambiguous Iroquois Empire*, 93.

47. See for example Trigger, *Natives and Newcomers*, 263. After describing some raids, and without citing any evidence, he assumes that theft took place and that "seizure of furs and European goods appears to have been an important objective of these raids."

48. See appendix D for a discussion of the sources, methods, and limitations of the data used here. Unless otherwise indicated, the data that follow were culled from table D.1.

49. This is not to suggest that in other raids goods or furs were not taken; after all it was common practice to loot those defeated in war. But this practice can hardly be said to be the only motive for every raid. Between 1600 and 1666 at least 33 percent of Iroquois attacks against the Hurons were against women farming or men fishing. Little material wealth could be expected from such raids.

50. While it is possible that goods were taken in the other raids, it is equally possible that none were taken.

51. [Lalemant], *Relation of 1647–48*, *JR* 32:179.

52. Champlain, *Works* 1:137.

53. Jonas Michalelus to A. Smoutious, [11 Aug.] 1628, *NNN*, 131; W. Kieft to K. V. Rensselaer, 11 Sept. 1642, in [van Rensselaer], *Van Rensselaer-Bowier Manuscripts*, 625; Stuyvesant to directors, 26 Apr. 1664, *NYCD* 13:372–73; "Information furnished . . . by Mr. Miller [to Commissioners for Trade and Plantations]," 4 Sept. 1696, *NYCD* 4:183.

54. In July 1648 some Iroquois had come north to the Three Rivers area to try to free some of their people held by the French. When they spotted a few Huron canoes, they attacked them. Unfortunately for the Iroquois, those canoes were followed by the larger Huron fur brigade. The Iroquois were defeated and plundered of their possessions (table D.1, [17 or 18 July] 1648). A similar mistake against an Ottawa fur brigade was rectified before the Iroquois sustained any losses (table D.1, [late Aug. to early Sept.] 1660).

55. Table D.1, [late Aug. to mid-Sept.] 1681.

56. Calvert [et al.] to Chickley, 13 Sept. 1681, *Md. Archives* 17:22–23.

57. See the various letters introduced into Council in the *Md. Archives* 17:18–25.

58. "Order in Council," 26 Sept. 1681, *Md. Archives* 17:27–28; "Declaration," 8 Oct. 1681, *Md. Archives* 17:37–42.

59. Table D.1, 27 June 1687.

60. Table D.1, 19–20 May 1656.

61. This may also have been true of the three other attacks against homes of French settlers in which goods were taken; see table D.1, 6 Mar. 1647; [2 May] 1650; 6 May 1651. Despite numerous references to these three attacks, the information is too scant to allow one to arrive at a firm conclusion about Iroquois intent. The attacks may have been part of a general policy of harassment against the French (table D.1, entries of Iroquois vs. French, 1647–54), and some of the captured in these raids were subject to severe torture, but it cannot be denied that theft may have been intended as well.

62. Table D.1, 2 Aug. 1642.

63. Table D.1, 20 Aug. 1642.

64. Marie de l'Incarnation à la Mère Ursule de Ste.-Catherine, 29 Sept. 1642, *Correspondance*, 168.

65. Faillon (*Histoire* 2:3) also read Marie de l'Incarnation to have stated that firearms, powder, and ammunition were taken. These, he wrote, were what the Hurons "venaient de se pourvoir dans leur traite" (came to provide themselves with in their trade).

66. [Le Jeune], *Relation of 1640–41*, JR 21:23–53.

67. Campeau, *La Mission des Jésuites*, 347.

68. The extent of the French gun trade in this period remains uncertain. See chapter 8 and Trigger, *Children of Aataentsic*, 627–32.

69. Table D.1, [15 Sept.] 1643. In this instance I have assumed that "lost" meant the Iroquois took the supplies rather than that they fell into a river.

70. Table D.1, [28–30] Apr. 1644.

71. [Vimont], *Relation of 1643–44*, JR 26:29–31.

72. Table D.1, 30 Mar. 1644.

73. [Vimont], *Relation of 1643–44*, JR 26:35.

74. Table D.1, 18 May 1656.

75. [Le Jeune], *Relation of 1656–57*, JR 43:187, 189; Marie de l'Incarnation à son fils, 14 août 1656, *Correspondance*, 583–84.

76. Table D.1, 19–20 May 1656.

77. In one incident the Iroquois took some prisoners and some furs. In another they took the supplies that the fleeing group left behind, as well as some twenty captives or scalps (table D.1, 9 May 1643, [late July to early Aug.] 1643).

78. See the first two entries under this date in table D.1.

79. Table D.1, second entry dated 9 June 1643.

80. [Vimont], *Relation of 1642–43*, JR 24:277. Dollier, in his *Histoire du Montréal*, states that it was the Hurons who told the Iroquois of the French presence at Montreal. It is unlikely that the Iroquois were unaware of this. This "treachery" on the part of the Hurons was probably invented by Dollier in order to justify Governor Maisonneuve's awarding the abandoned furs to his men rather than returning them to their rightful owners. Some Hurons had escaped the Iroquois ambush (109, 111).

81. Table D.1, [spring-summer 1647].

82. Father Vimont is one of the few Iroquois contemporaries to claim that theft was a goal of Iroquois raiding. Not surprisingly, he made that observation in 1643 when four of the six successful attacks against fur brigades took place. Significantly, he did not repeat that observation, and he claimed this to be a motive only of Mohawk raids—he did not ascribe this motive to the other Iroquois tribes. More importantly, he recognized that the Mohawk goal was to gain furs to trade for guns so that the Mohawk could "ravage everything and become masters everywhere" ([Vimont], *Relation of 1642–43*, JR 24:271).

83. Table D.1, end of Feb. 1684.

84. It is not clear, but it seems that this represents the cost of the goods taken, not their expected sale price. It is hard to conceive of even seven large trading canoes taking that much worth of kettles. Kettles cost about one livre per livre weight. Guns cost about ten

livres each ("Estat des marchandises nécessaires pour la traité du fort Bourbon," [1697], AN, CIIA 15:258).

85. [Conference], 5 Aug. 1684, in Colden, *Five Indian Nations*, 61–63. See also [conference], 5 Aug. 1684, in Wraxall, *Indian Affairs*, 12–13.

86. Table D. I, end of May 1692.

87. The Iroquois launched thirty-seven raids against the French and their allies during this decade (table D. I, 1690 to 1701).

88. Frontenac au Ministre, 15 Sept. 1692, AN, CIIA 12:25; "Relation de ce s'est passé en Canada au sujet de la guerre. . . , par Champigny," 5 Oct. 1692, AN, CIIA 12:94, 98; Calliere [au Ministre], 20 Sept. 1692, AN, CIIA 12:97–98.

89. Table D. I, 16 Mar. 1649, Apr. 1680. The other attack against a village in which goods were taken was against the North Indians (Abenaki). Houses in the area of the fort were plundered, but it is not clear to whom they belonged (table D. I, [30 Apr.–3 May 1662]).

90. Sahlins, *Stone Age Economics*, 185–86 n. 1–2.

91. Trigger, "Alfred G. Bailey," 16–19. This theme has been elaborated in Trigger, "Early Native North American Responses." By labeling his interpretation rational he implies that the views of others are not. Indeed, in one article he compared those who did not follow the "rationalistic" approach to Francis Parkman because "they share with Parkman a minimization of aboriginal rationality" ("Alfred G. Bailey," 18).

92. Trigger, "Early Native North American Responses," 1202, 1211–12.

93. On the vagueness of Trigger's definitions, see Axtell, "Columbian Encounters," 346.

94. Father Ragueneau also remarked on the fact that the Iroquois stole goods from the Hurons. Again, he wrote shortly after the period of the few successful attacks. More to the point, he wrote that the Hurons "too have had, in their turn, successes in warfare, have put to flight the enemy, and have carried off their spoils and some number of captives" ([Ragueneau], "Huronia Report, 1645–46," JR 29:247, 251).

95. Dickinson, "Annaotaha et Dollard."

96. [Le Mercier], *Relation of 1665–66*, JR 50:141–45, 203; Marie de l'Incarnation à son fils, 12 Nov. 1666, *Correspondance*, 772–76. The same thing happened in the July–August 1687 attack against the Senecas and in the February 1693 attack against the Mohawks (Denonville au Ministre, 25 aôut 1687, AN, CIIA 9:61–77; "Acte de prise de possession du pays des Iroquois dit sonont8ans, 19 juillet 1687," AN, CIIA 9:41; Baugy, *Journal*, 105; Father Bechefer à Monsieur Cabart de Villermont, 19 Sept. 1687, JR 63:275; "Relation de ce qui s'est passé en Canada," [Sept. 1692–Nov. 1693], AN, CIIA 12:187).

CHAPTER FIVE. THE EARLY WARS

1. See for example the Iroquois raid against the Saponi (table D. I, spring 1685). In some cases even the group attacked remains a mystery (table D. I, 17 June 1676). In all there were eleven instances, just over 3 percent of all raids, for which it was not possible to determine the identity or composition of the group the Iroquois attacked.

2. [Vimont], *Relation of 1642*, JR 22:207–15; [Lalemant], *Relation of 1645–46*, JR 29:173.

3. "Relation de Père Denis Jamet, Recollet du Québec au cardinal de Joyeuse, 15 juiellet 1615," in Le Blant and Baudry, eds., *Nouveaux documents*, 350. Jamet wrote that his informant could recall seeing the village of those defeated by the Iroquois. Depending on the informant's age, that places the defeat of the St. Lawrence group in the latter half of the 1500s.

4. Marc Lescarbot, "La Conversion des sauvages qui on este baptizes en la nouvelle-france cette année, 1610," in MNF 1:90–91.

5. Champlain, *Works* 2:77, 91.

6. There seems to be an assumption by historians that because the Iroquois may have been involved in the wars, and appear to have won, they began the hostilities. They may have become engaged in warfare in the St. Lawrence valley in retaliation for raids against them by the tribes living there.

7. [Cartier], *Voyages*, 171.

8. B. Trigger and J. Pendergast, "Saint Lawrence Iroquoians," in Trigger, ed., *Handbook*, 357–61.

9. St. Lawrence Iroquoian pottery has been found in sixteenth-century Five Nations sites; see Kuhn et al., "Evidence."

10. A short but extremely useful critique and overview of the archaeological work on the St. Lawrence Iroquoians and the various theories derived from it is James B. Jamieson, "The Archaeology of the St. Lawrence Iroquoians," in Ellis and Ferris, eds., *Archaeology*, 385–404.

11. [Cartier], *Voyages*, 177–78.

12. B. Trigger and J. Pendergast, "Saint Lawrence Iroquoians," in Trigger, ed., *Handbook*, 357–61.

13. [Cartier], *Voyages*, 203, 54–63, 177–78. Cartier speculated that the reference to the southern origins of this group meant they came from Florida. That deduction was based on Stadaconans' responses to questions about oranges and other fruits. It is extremely unlikely that the Stadaconans knew what an orange looked like, even if Cartier drew one for them. Moreover, Florida was more than a thirty-day canoe trip from Quebec, and there was not much need of furs there.

14. [Norton], *Journal*, 87.

15. [Radisson], *Explorations*, 46–48; Lafitau, *Moeurs* 1:86; Colden, *Five Indian Nations*, 22–23; Morgan, *League*, 5–8; [Le Jeune], *Relation of 1636*, JR 9:159.

16. The Iroquois initiated only one of the eleven raids recorded between 1603 and 1628 (table D.1, 1603–28). In 1660 Father Lalemant recorded an account of Iroquois-Algonquin hostilities that once again placed the Iroquois (in this case, specifically the Mohawks) on the defensive from Algonquin attacks around 1600 ([Lalemant], *Relation of 1659–60*, JR 45:205).

17. See Trigger, ed., *Handbook* under the names of the various tribes. See also Pendergast, "Huron-St. Lawrence Iroquois Relations."

18. Pendergast and Jamieson, looking at the same evidence on St. Lawrence Iroquoians and working from similar assumptions, came to different conclusions about the

significance of St. Lawrence Iroquoian pipes on Huron sites (Pendergast, "Huron–St. Lawrence Iroquois Relations," 34; James B. Jamieson, "The Archaeology of the St. Lawrence Iroquoians," in Ellis and Ferris, eds., *Archaeology*, 403).

19. [Radisson], *Explorations*, 46–48; Colden, *Five Indian Nations*, 22–23; "Mémoire sur les coutumes," 444; Morgan, *League*, 5–8; [Norton], *Journal*, 105–10.

20. Hunt, *Wars of the Iroquois*, 17, 21; Trigger, *Children of Aataentsic*, 223. Both writers, however, fail to explain why the Iroquois did not participate in the St. Lawrence fur trade after having defeated those who had stood in the way of that ambition. See Conrad Heidenreich, "History of the St. Lawrence–Great Lakes Area to A.D. 1650," in Ellis and Ferris, eds., *Archaeology of Southern Ontario*, 483.

21. Desrosiers, *Iroquoisie*, 13; B. Trigger and J. Pendergast, "Saint Lawrence Iroquoians," in Trigger, ed., *Handbook*, 361. Early historians of New France also accounted for Donnacona's behavior by reference to desires to take advantage of the French (Faillon, *Histoire* 1:15; Ferland, *Cours d'histoire* 1:27).

22. Certainly the discussion in the preceding chapters should allow one to at least call into question the monocausal nature of this view.

23. [Cartier], *Voyages*, 52, 120–21, 142, 150.

24. "Examination of Newfoundland Sailors Regarding Cartier," 23 Sept. 1542, in Biggar, ed., *Collection of Documents*, 447–67.

25. [Cartier], *Voyages*, 250.

26. Trudel, *Beginnings*, 54–70.

27. Conrad Heidenreich, "History of the St. Lawrence–Great Lakes Area to A.D. 1650," in Ellis and Ferris, eds., *Archaeology of Southern Ontario*, 480–81.

28. Richard Hakluyt to Sir Francis Walsingham, 7 Jan. 1584, *CSP* 9:24. He does not mention how long it took to accumulate that store of furs.

29. The value of beaver was calculated on the following basis: one pound sterling was worth about six Dutch guilders during the 1600s (Cristoph and Cristoph, eds., *Andros Papers*, xxvi). In the same period, beaver sold in New Netherland for about six to eight guilders (directors to Stuyvesant, 4 Apr. 1652, *NYCD* 14:165–74).

30. On the high price of furs and pelts before 1600, see Axtell, *After Columbus*, 162–64; on sixteenth-century trade in general, see 149–81.

31. Marcel Trudel quotes, and seems to accept, Hakluyt's assertion that in 1584 five fur-laden ships arrived in France from the St. Lawrence area (Trudel, *Beginnings*, 58). This seems far-fetched. Even after the French established and organized the St. Lawrence trade, two ships were most often enough to take all the furs traded (C. Lalemant to J. Lalemant, Aug. 1626, *JR* 4:207).

32. "Arrêt du Conseil d'Etat permettant. . . ," 6 oct. 1609, in Le Blant and Baudry, eds., *Nouveaux documents* 1:191–93. On the selling price of beaver in this period, see "Vente par Jean Sorel. . . ," 2 mars 1609, in Le Blant and Baudry, eds., *Nouveaux documents* 1:182. Eccles (*France in America*, 15) and Trudel (*Beginnings*, 91) state that this right was granted in 1607. I have followed them in this matter.

33. "Vente par Jean Sorel. . . ," 2 mars 1609, in Le Blant and Baudry, eds., *Nouveaux documents* 1:182. "Prêt de 772 livres. . . ," 23 dec. 1609, in Le Blant and Baudry, eds., *Nouveaux documents* 1:200.

34. "Procuration donnée par Pierre de Gua. . . ," 20 oct. 1607, in Le Blant and Baudry, eds., *Nouveaux documents* 1:145–56. The early Dutch trade does not seem to have been of much greater volume. The Dutch fur take in 1614, from one years' trading by three different traders on the Hudson and down toward Delaware, does not appear to have exceeded twenty-five hundred pelts (Hart, *Prehistory*, 31–32, 80–86).

35. Trudel, *Beginnings*, 57–58.

36. Champlain, *Works* 2:339–45.

37. Conrad Heidenreich, "History of the St. Lawrence–Great Lakes Area to A.D. 1650," in Ellis and Ferris, eds., *Archaeology of Southern Ontario*, 481; James B. Jamieson, "The Archaeology of the St. Lawrence Iroquoians," in Ellis and Ferris, eds., *Archaeology*, 403; Pendergast, "Huron-St. Lawrence Iroquois Relations," 24–25; J. V. Wright, "Archaeology of Southern Ontario to a.d. 1650: A Critique," in Ellis and Ferris, eds., *Archaeology of Southern Ontario*, 502. This lack of material is even more telling when one considers the various nontrade ways by which European items entered native societies. See Pendergast, "Introduction of European Goods."

38. [Cartier], *Voyages*, 129, 132–34, 133, 140, 143, 161, 259, 264–65. This desire was not confined to Donnacona. As Cartier passed upriver, at least one other native leader sought and made an alliance with Cartier.

39. It was common practice to put on public displays of and for natives brought to France (Dickason, *Myth of the Savage*, 205–17). Taignoagny and Domagaya did, in fact, describe French firearms to their father ([Cartier], *Voyages*, 134).

40. [Cartier], *Voyages*, 151, 162–65.

41. [Cartier], *Voyages*, 217, 259, 264–65.

42. Forbes, "Two and a Half Centuries," 5–6.

43. Champlain, *Works* 1:137. Some years later French Indian allies made this same observation (3:31). It seems worth stressing here that this blockade of the St. Lawrence began long before it became the regular route for taking furs to New France.

CHAPTER SIX. "BUT ONE PEOPLE"

1. Parkman, *Jesuits*, lxvi n. 1; Hunt, *Wars of the Iroquois*, 6.

2. Morgan, for no apparent reason, placed the figure at 25,000 (*League*, 27). Trigger (*Children of Aataentsic*, 98) also without explanation placed it at 20,000. My own calculations put the Iroquois population at 23,000 to 25,000 (see appendix C). Recent work on the Mohawk population seems to point to a growing willingness to accept higher population figures, especially in the pre-epidemic era; see Starna, "Mohawk Iroquois Populations," and Snow, "Microchronology." Dean Snow puts the Mohawk population at 2,000 people for the years 1666–79 (1603); my calculations put the Mohawk population in these years at 2,700 (table C.4).

3. The Jesuits early on recognized that Iroquois raiding exacted a heavy toll on the Confederacy ([Le Jeune], *Relation of 1656–57*, JR 43:265; Father Pierron, in [Le Mercier], *Relation of 1669–70*, JR 53:155).

4. See tables A.2 and E.1. Based on table A.2, assuming that the Jesuits managed to baptize more or less the same percentage of dying Iroquois during epidemic and non-

epidemic periods, the evidence suggests a significant death rate due to epidemic disease over the long run, but there are not huge population declines per epidemic. However, if the Jesuits did not manage to baptize the same percentage of people in epidemic years as in nonepidemic years, that leaves one no further ahead when trying to assess the impact of epidemics on the Iroquois.

5. Among the health problems indigenous to precontact Iroquoians were tuberculosis, arthritis, infections of all types from open wounds and broken bones, and probably syphilis (Larocque, "Les maladies").

6. This may seem far-fetched, but it seems to be a conservative approach. For example, it is by no means certain that the Jesuits baptized all those on the verge of death, or the same ratio of dying Iroquois in epidemic years as in nonepidemic years. Thus the 2,002 baptized dead in this twelve-year period probably underrepresents the actual number of deaths.

7. The Hurons, Eries, and Neutrals were some of the tribes Father Lalemant found among the Iroquois by 1660 ([Lalemant], *Relation of 1659–60*, JR 45:207).

8. See table D.1, July 1648; 16–19 Mar. 1649; autumn [prior to 30 Aug. 1650]; spring [1651]; [winter 1652]; [fall 1654 to winter 1655]; [Apr.] 1663; Sept. 1680; [approx. Dec. 1680]; 1681; 25 Aug. 1682; 4 Nov. 1686.

9. Table F.3. While not all the Hurons were killed off by 1663, they were no longer the focus of Iroquois aggression. Moreover, while some most certainly died at the hands of the Iroquois after this date, it was often when they took part in attacks launched by the French and their Indian allies. The records often do not mention what native groups were part of the attacking party, nor the breakdown of losses by tribe.

10. Heidenreich, *Huronia*, 98.

11. *Journal des pères Jésuites, 1651*, JR 36:141–43; [Le Jeune], *Relation of 1656–57*, JR 44:21; [Dablon], *Relation of 1672–73*, JR 57:193.

12. On the village populations see Heidenreich, *Huronia*, 102.

13. Father Frémin, in *Relation of 1669–70*, JR 54:81. On Gandougaraé as the refugee village, see also Thomas Abler and Elisabeth Tooker, "Seneca," in Trigger, ed., *Handbook*, 505–6.

14. Galinée, "Voyage de Dollier et Galinée," 24; "Journal of Wentworth Greenhalgh," NYCD 251–52.

15. See appendix C and the discussion there.

16. Journal of Fathers Frémin, Pierron, and Bruyas, in [Le Mercier], *Relation of 1667–68*, JR 51:187.

17. Fenton and Tooker, "Mohawk," 467.

18. "Wentworth Greenhalgh's Journal of a Tour to the Indians of Western New-York," NYCD 3:250.

19. Hurons were found living among these other tribes, but the data do not permit one to attempt population estimates ([De Quen], *Relation of 1655–56*, JR 42:73).

20. Father Jogues, in [Vimont], *Relation of 1642–43*, JR 24:297.

21. The Hurons from the villages of St. Michel and St. Jean Baptiste serve as the most dramatic examples of large groups relocating to the Iroquois before the rest of their nation was destroyed, but there are hints in the historical record that individuals and small

groups of Hurons went over to the Iroquois for similar reasons (*Journal des pères Jésuites, 1651, JR* 36:143; [Le Jeune], *Relation of 1656–57, JR* 44:21; [Dablon], *Relation of 1672–73, JR* 57:193; Dollier, *Histoire du Montréal*, 139). The result of this process of voluntary defections, or of not resisting their captors once caught, wrote Dollier, was that the Iroquois strength was increased (139).

22. [Ragueneau], *Relation of 1649–50, JR* 35:219.

23. [Ragueneau], *Relation of 1650–51, JR* 36:183.

24. *Journal des pères Jésuites, 1653, JR* 38:199 (emphasis in original).

25. [Le Jeune], *Relation of 1656–57, JR* 43:187.

26. *Journal des pères Jésuites, 1654, JR* 44:19. The Hurons, however, did not respond quickly enough to the Mohawks' offer to relocate peacefully and "inhabit but one land and be but one people with them." In 1656 some Hurons were attacked and taken to Mohawk villages as captives because the Mohawks felt the Hurons were reneging on the agreement made in November of 1653 ([De Quen], *Relation of 1655–56, JR* 42:231; [Le Jeune], *Relation of 1656–57, JR* 43:117, 119, 189, 213).

27. *Journal des pères Jésuites, 1656, JR* 42:253.

28. Table D.1; unless otherwise indicated, the following data were also taken from this source. Only rarely was the St. Lawrence Algonquin group identified by name in the sources. Most often the French simply indicated that they were Algonquins who lived near their settlements.

29. Jean de Lamberville to [Father Superior], Onondaga, 25 Aug. 1682, *JR* 62:71.

30. The Neutrals allowed the Hurons to take captive a Seneca in one of their villages ([Ragueneau], "Huronia Report, 1647–48," *JR* 33:81–83). Father Lafitau wrote that Father Garnier had informed him that the war started when "war games" led to an Iroquois death, which the Iroquois then sought to avenge (Lafitau, *Moeurs* 2:105–6). John Norton tells of a similar tradition as the cause of the wars against the Susquehannocks ([Norton], *Journal*, 209–10).

31. [Le Mercier], *Relation of 1653–54, JR* 41:79–83. Norton, without mentioning the role of Huron refugees, also attributes this war to the Eries' failure to make reparations for the Seneca death (*Journal*, 206).

32. *Journal des pères Jésuites, 1651, JR* 36:143.

33. [Council minute], 13 June 1678, *Md. Archives* 15:175; [conference, 19 Mar. 1679], *Md. Archives* 15:239; Capt. R. Brandt to [Charles Calvert], 16 May 1680, *Md. Archives* 15:283; [council minute], 23 Aug. 1681, *Md. Archives* 17:6.

34. Vachon, "The Mohawk Nation."

35. "Mémoire sur les coutumes," 464.

36. François Marguerie, in [Le Jeune], *Relation of 1640–41, JR* 21:37.

37. Talon au Roy, 10 oct. 1670, AN, CIIA 3:101–2; "Narrative of Governor Courcelles Voyage to Lake Ontario," 1671, *NYCD* 9:80; Frontenac au Ministre, 2 nov. 1672, AN, CIIA 3:240. The reports of these three men are those most often cited by modern scholars to support claims that the Iroquois encroached on the lands of others and that they had run out of furs on their own lands. Modern writers have apparently accepted the assumption that informed these seventeenth-century reports.

38. Talon au Roy, 10 oct. 1670, AN, CIIA 3:96–97. On Colbert's opposition and Talon

and Frontenac's effort to expand the trade, see Eccles, *Canada Under Louis XIV*, 59–76, and *Frontenac*, 75–126.

39. La Potherie, *Histoire* 4:179.

40. [Radisson], *Explorations*, 27–35. Some five decades later, in the spring of 1700, the Senecas used a hunting trip toward the country of the Miamis as a pretext for a raid against that tribe (La Potherie au Ministre, 11 aôut and 16 oct. 1700, AN, CIIA 18:147, 155). French allies also did this. In August of 1633 some Hurons headed off into the Lake Champlain area to hunt beavers and Iroquois (*Mercure François*, 19:862).

41. Father Chauchetière, "Narration annuelle de la Mission du Sault depuis la fondation jusques à l'an 1686," *JR* 63:153, 155, 175; [Le Mercier], *Relation of 1669–1670*, *JR* 54:117; Galinée, "Voyage de Dollier et Galinée," 38; Lahontan, *New Voyages*, 323; "Relation de [1695–96]," AN, CIIA 14:36.

42. [Vimont], *Relation of 1642–43*, *JR* 24:231; [Vimont], *Relation of 1643–44*, *JR* 25:107; [Lalemant], *Relation of 1645–46*, *JR* 29:147; Father Poncet, in [Le Mercier], *Relation of 1652–53*, *JR* 40:151–53; [Le Mercier], *Relation of 1653–54*, *JR* 41:67; *Journal des pères Jésuites, 1665*, *JR* 49:171.

43. W. N. Fenton, "Northern Iroquoian Culture Patterns," in Trigger, ed., *Handbook*, 298.

44. Starna and Relethford, "Deer Densities."

45. [Lalemant], *Relation of 1645–46*, *JR* 28:287; A. van der Donck, "A Description of the New Netherlands . . . [Amsterdam, 1656]," in *New York Historical Society Collections* 1:169; [Dablon], *Relation of 1671–72*, *JR* 56:49.

46. Lafitau, *Moeurs* 2:69–70; Fenton, "Northern Iroquoian Culture Patterns," in Trigger, ed., *Handbook*, 302; Starna, Hamell, and Butts, "Northern Iroquoian Horticulture."

47. Van Rensselaer to Willem Kieft, 25 May 1640, in [van Rensselaer], *Van Rensselaer-Bowier Manuscripts*, 472–85.

48. Hunt, *Wars of the Iroquois*, 34.

49. For the document in question see "Memorial presented by K. van Rensselaer to the Assembly of the Nineteen of the West India Company, Nov. 25, 1633," in [van Rensselaer], *Van Rensselaer-Bowier Manuscripts*, 235–50.

50. Van Rensselaer to Kieft, 25 May 1640, in [van Rensselaer], *Van Rensselaer-Bowier Manuscripts*, 483–84.

51. [van den Bogaert], *Journey*, 1.

52. See appendix (1 Nov. 1633) added to the letter of Mr. Joachim to the States General, 27 May 1634, NYCD 1:81; Wouter van Twiller to directors of West India Company, 14 Aug. 1636, trans. A. J. F. van Laer, *New York State Historical Association Quarterly Journal* 1, no. 18 (1919): 49; "Ordinance Prohibiting Trade in Furs (1638)" and "Ordinance Against Clandestine Trade, 7 June 1638," in van Laer, ed. and trans., *New York Historical Manuscripts* 4:3–4, 10–12. For people charged with illegal trade see "Ordinance Against Clandestine Trade, 7 June 1638," in van Laer, ed. and trans., *New York Historical Manuscripts* 4:33–34, 37–40, 250, 252–53.

53. Van Rensselaer to Toussaint Muyssart, 20 Apr. 1641, and van Rensselaer to Arent van Curler, 18 July 1641, in [van Rensselaer], *Van Rensselaer-Bowier Manuscripts*,

546–47, 562. This activity also suggests that, his protestations to the contrary, van Rensselaer was diverting furs from the company.

54. "Memorial presented by K. van Rensselaer," 25 Nov. 1633, in [van Rensselaer], *Van Rensselaer-Bowier Manuscripts*, 248. Eight years later van Rensselaer still had "not given up the hope, if the Lord will grant me a few years more, of diverting to the colony a large part of the furs of the savages who now trade with the French in Canada" (van Rensselaer to Toussaint Muyssart, 6 June 1641, in [van Rensselaer], *Van Rensselaer-Bowier Manuscripts*, 553).

55. [Directors to Stuyvesant], 6 June 1653, *NYCD* 13:35. The Mohawks naturally opposed granting their foes access to the Dutch. The Iroquois could not be certain the Dutch would not sell guns to their foes, and access to the Dutch would also provide Iroquois enemies with an opportunity to be among the Iroquois and carry out reprisal raids under the pretext of coming to trade.

56. Hunt, *Wars of the Iroquois*, 33. On the Dutch fur trade and sources, see table 6.3.

57. Champlain, *Works* 5:73–74, 77; untitled document, AN, CIIA 1:66; [Vimont], *Relation of 1644–45*, JR 27:245–91; Marie de l'Incarnation à son fils, 14 sept. 1645, *Correspondance*, 257.

58. *Journal des pères Jésuites, 1646*, JR 28:149–51.

59. [Lalemant], *Relation of 1645–46*, JR 28:299.

60. [Vimont], *Relation of 1644–45*, JR 27:245.

61. Talon au Roy, 10 oct. 1670, AN, CIIA 3:101–2; "Narrative of Governor Courcelles Voyage to Lake Ontario, 1671," *NYCD* 9:80.

62. K. van Rensselaer to Johannes de Laet, 6 Oct. 1636, in [van Rensselaer], *Van Rensselaer-Bowier Manuscripts*, 334.

63. References other than De Laet give slightly different totals for some of the same years. In a letter to the States General, Peter Schagere puts the number of beaver pelts for 1626 at 7,246 and those of otter at 853 (Schagere to States General, [5 Nov. 1626], *NYCD* 1:37). Wassenaer ("Historisch Verhael," *NNN*, 87) wrote that two ships returned with 10,000 pelts from New Netherland in 1628. Capt. John Mason, in a letter to Secretary Coke (2 Apr. 1632, *CSP* 1:144) reported that the Dutch had shipped 15,000 beaver skins in 1632. Rather than the slight differences, what is remarkable is how closely the disparate sources agree on the volume of trade.

64. K. van Rensselaer to Willem Kieft, 25 May 1640, in [van Rensselaer], *Van Rensselaer-Bowier Manuscripts*, 483. In 1629 the Assembly of the Nineteen informed the States General that the New Netherland fur trade could at best be valued at 50,000 guilders (23 Oct. 1629, *NYCD* 1:40). The actual average value of skins in the period from 1624 to 1629 was 40,636 guilders.

65. Directors to Stuyvesant, 4 Apr. 1652, *NYCD* 14:167.

66. [Deposition of Symon Groot], 2 July 1688, *LIR*, 144. The Dutch often used "Sinnekes," or a variant spelling of this word, to refer to one or more of the four Iroquois tribes to the west of the Mohawks. It is not clear what tribe Groot meant.

67. A. van der Donck, "A Description of the New Netherlands . . . [Amsterdam, 1656]," in *New York Historical Society Collections* 1:210, 221.

68. It is even more suspect when one considers that the Iroquois were too busy warring to do much trapping and trading during most of the decade.

69. Bellomont to the Lords of Trade, 28 Nov. 1700, *NYCD* 4:789. Bellomont claimed that one year the Dutch exported sixty-six thousand beaver pelts.

70. [Furs shipped from Fort Orange], 20 June to 27 Sept. [1657], in J. Pearson, ed., *Early Records of the City and County of Albany [1654–1678]*, vol. I, [1869], in Munsell, ed., *Collections* 4:244; the list in question is also referred to in an editorial note in *NYCD* 13:27. In both the published reference to this list and the list itself the total of furs shipped is put at 40,940. However, if one adds up the daily shipments, the total comes to 37,640.

71. Stuyvesant to Directors, 6 Oct. 1660, *NYCD* 14:484.

72. "Description of the Towne of Mannadens, 1661," *NNN*, 424.

73. For example, Governor Dongan claimed that New York's fur trade averaged around "35 or 40000 Beavers besides Peltry"; Instructions from Governor Dongan to Captain Palmer, 8 Sept. 1687, *NYCD* 3:476. He does not explain who brought the furs in and from where. On the illegal trade from New France in the 1670s see, Norton, *Fur Trade*, 121–22.

74. "Invoice of Goods sent to the Colony," 20 Apr. 1634, and "Account of Ammunition for Rensselaers Steyn," 10 Sept. 1643, in [van Rensselaer], *Van Rensselaer-Bowier Manuscripts*, 264, 265, 706; [court minute], 1648, in van Laer, ed., *Minutes of the Court of Rensselaerswyck*, 211.

75. "Journal of New Netherland, 1647," *NNN*, 274.

76. A. van der Donck, "A Description of the New Netherlands . . . [Amsterdam, 1656]," in *New York Historical Society Collections* 1:210. In 1634 one Mohawk hunter was said to have trapped 120 beavers ([van den Bogaert], *Journey*, 5–6).

77. Archeological evidence reveals that firearms, or parts therefrom, start showing up in the villages of the tribes west of the Mohawks in the period 1625 to 1650 (Bradley, *Evolution*, 142–45; Wray, "Volume of Dutch Trade Goods," 104; Puype, *Dutch and Other Flintlocks*, 68). Firearms only show up in large numbers on sites dated from 1650 to 1687.

78. Almost any conference between the Iroquois and their European allies touches on trade matters.

79. Rich, Ray, and Freeman have shown that, unlike most modern consumers, Indians had fixed demands. When prices of goods dropped and the Indians could get more for the same furs than previously, they did not necessarily increase the amount they purchased. They simply brought in fewer furs to purchase what they required (Rich, "Trade Habits"; Ray and Freeman, *"Give Us Good Measure,"* esp. 218–28).

80. "Minutes of the Court of Ft. Orange," 6 Sept. 1659, *NYCD* 13:109. For a slightly different version of this speech see van Laer, ed., *Minutes of the Court of Fort Orange* 2:211–13.

81. At least this was true at the start of their dealings with the English. Later in the century the relationship changed to include military cooperation.

82. "Conference of the Earl of Bellomont with the Indians," Aug. 1700, *NYCD* 4:733. See also "Acte authentique des six nations sur leur indépendance," 2 Nov. 1748, *RAPQ, 1921–22*, following 108. The Iroquois again stress that a desire to trade for guns first induced them to establish trade ties to Europeans.

83. [Conference minute], 7 July 1712, in Wraxall, *Indian Affairs*, 95. For a slightly different version of this speech see "Continuation of Colden's History," in Colden, *Letters and Papers* 9:411.

CHAPTER SEVEN. THE FAILURE OF PEACE

1. Hostile relations with the Iroquois helped shape the military nature of New France and affected almost every facet of life in the colony; see Eccles, *Canadian Frontier*.

2. The need to build and maintain forts, reaffirm alliances with gift exchanges, outfit allies for war, and send the occasional army against the Iroquois all used up limited French resources. In the first nine months of 1691, warring cost New France over sixty thousand livres, and Champigny had to budget twenty-four thousand livres for presents to French allies (Champigny au Ministre, 12 oct. 1691, AN, CIIA 11:281–82). Even when the French fought the English and the Iroquois, French authorities still claimed that warring against the Iroquois caused the greater part of the expenses (Champigny au Ministre, 14 oct. 1698, AN, CIIA 16:102–3). French authorities continually bemoaned these costs; see Desbarats, "Cost."

3. See table F.2; unless otherwise indicated, the data that follow were taken from this source.

4. The French were attacked sixteen times when they were part of combined French and native groups; indeed, the Iroquois attacked the French more than any other group.

5. If one includes French losses sustained as a result of their own attacks against the Iroquois, the total human cost of Iroquois warfare was 831–52 French removed from their population.

6. Dickinson, "La Guerre iroquoise," 36.

7. Belmont de Vachon, *Histoire*, 36.

8. Dickinson, "La Guerre iroquoise," 36.

9. The Iroquois attacked groups composed solely of French eighty-eight times up to 1666, and only thirty-five times from then to 1701. As figure 7.1 shows, the post-1666 raids were concentrated in the years 1687 to 1697.

10. Large groups, on the order of one to two hundred, while not unheard of, were rarer; see table D.1, "Iroq. vs Fr."

11. See table D.1, entries dated 22 Aug. 1653 and [end of May] 1660. In the latter raid five hundred of the seven-hundred-strong Iroquois army were Mohawks.

12. Untitled document, AN, CIIA 1:66; Champlain, *Works* 5:74–79, 117, 130; 6:33–34; [Le Jeune], *Relation of 1632*, JR 5:29; [Le Jeune], *Relation of 1634*, JR 7:215; [Brebeuf], "Huronia Report, 1635," JR 8:69, 115, 117; [van den Bogaert], "Narrative of a Journey into the Mohawk and Oneida Country, 1634–35," NNN, 139; [Le Jeune], *Relation of 1635*, JR 8:25.

13. Before 1640 the French native allies took the war to the Iroquois. After that date the balance shifted in favor of the Iroquois; see figure 7.2.

14. [Le Jeune], *Relation of 1640–41*, JR 21:27–59.

15. Champlain, *Works* 5:74. The Jesuits also approved of peaceful relations because

they would gain access to more natives and thus reap a richer harvest of souls (Le Jeune to Father Provincial, [Aug.] 1634, *JR* 6:59).

16. [Champlain], ["Relation du Sieur de Champlain en Canada, 1633"], *Mercure françois*, 19:841–43, 858–59.

17. [Vimont], *Relation of 1642*, *JR* 22:35. The Jesuit concern was for their missions, not for the fur trade.

18. Lahontan, *New Voyages* 1:394; Eccles, *Canadian Frontier*, 135.

19. Eccles, *Frontenac*, 66, 99–100.

20. See figure 7.2. A complete set of data of French fur receipts does not exist. While the available information is scattered, it suggests that the wars of the Iroquois did not prevent a growth in the number of furs traded to New France. For example, in 1626, Charles Lalemant observed that 12,000 to 15,000 furs were traded annually in New France and that 22,000 was a good year (C. Lalemant to J. Lalemant, Aug. 1626, *JR* 4:207). At approximately 1.5 pounds per beaver pelt (Innis, *Fur Trade*, 4), that is 18,000 to 22,000 pounds of furs annually, or 33,000 pounds in a good year. In 1645, 30,000 pounds, or roughly 20,000 furs, were traded (*Journal des pères Jésuites, 1645*, *JR* 27:85). In 1653 the French took in 68,000 pounds of furs, or approximately 45,000 pelts (Thomas Wien and James Pritchard, in Harris, ed., *Historical Atlas*, plate 48). Interestingly enough, these figures also help put to rest the myth that Iroquois attacks against fur brigades seriously impeded the flow of furs to New France.

21. Montmagny appears not to have worried that if peace was established among them all, his native allies might want to trade with the Dutch and the English.

22. Father Jogues, in [Lalemant], *Relation of 1647*, *JR* 31:29.

23. [Radisson], *Explorations*, 58. The bracketed words were added by the editor of Radisson's manuscript either to fill in a missing word or to reflect what he thought the word or words were. The original text is in badly written English. It is possible that Radisson wrote the word *weapons* or *help*, or meant either one, rather than *guns*. In any case, the meaning of the passage remains that if the French had helped the Iroquois against their foes, they would not have warred against the French.

24. [Vimont], *Relation of 1642*, *JR* 22:35. On the origins and purpose of Montreal see Dollier, *Histoire du Montréal*. Dechêne, *Habitants*, provides a more secular history of Montreal.

25. This matter will be discussed below, but since Fort Richelieu was created to hinder the passage of the Iroquois one may assume that, given its location, the Iroquois were aware of this purpose and resented it.

26. Forbes, "Two and a Half Centuries," 5–6; Champlain, *Works* 5:73–74, 77.

27. See for example the maps in Heidenreich, "Analysis."

28. The Iroquois complained throughout the century about the French trading guns to Iroquois enemies. The strongest evidence of a French gun trade is for the period after 1650. This will be discussed below.

29. [Le Jeune], *Relation of 1640–41*, *JR* 21:27–59.

30. [Council minute], General Court, 25 Oct. 1644, in *Public Records* 1:113–14.

31. Campeau, *La Mission des Jésuites*, 347. Trigger has argued that this type of trade did not provide the Hurons with many guns because they were sold only to individuals, a

Huron had to be a Christian trader to come get his gun, and there were never more than 120 Christian Huron traders (*Children of Aataentsic* 2:633). However, there is no reason why a Huron convert, even if he was not a trader by capacity, could not accompany a fur brigade to New France in order to purchase his allotted gun. By 1643 there were 300 active Christians among the Hurons (Campeau, *La Mission des Jésuites*, 238). Even if only half of them were male, that would be 150 Hurons with guns. That figure does not include others who converted after 1643 nor those who might have obtained guns illegally.

32. Marie de l'Incarnation à la Mère Ursule de Ste.-Catherine, 29 sept. 1642, *Correspondance*, 168.

33. Campeau, *La Mission des Jésuites*, 187–89, 211.

34. [West India Company] to P. Stuyvesant, 7 Apr. 1648, *New York Historical Society Collections* 2:310; "Journal of New Netherland," NNN, 273–74.

35. "Ordinance prohibiting the sale of fire arms to Indians," 31 Mar. 1639, in van Laer, ed. and trans., *New York Historical Manuscripts* 4:42–43; "ordinance," 18 July 1641, in [van Rensselaer], *Van Rensselaer-Bowier Manuscripts*, 565–66; "ordinance," 10 Oct. 1642, in [van Rensselaer], *Van Rensselaer-Bowier Manuscripts*, 626–27. In one instance Dutch authorities felt constrained to illustrate the gravity of the problems gun sales produced by mentioning that the king of France had complained to Holland about the impact of gun sales to natives ("ordinance," 23 Feb. 1645, in van Laer, ed. and trans., *New York Historical Manuscripts* 4:256–57).

36. "Propositions submitted by the Honorable Director General Stuyvesant," 23 June 1648, in van Laer, ed. and trans., *New York Historical Manuscripts* 4:525–26; "Propositions," 1 Aug. 1648, in van Laer, ed. and trans., *New York Historical Manuscripts*, 546–48, 549.

37. [Le Jeune], *Relation of 1640–41*, JR 21:37; [Vimont], *Relation of 1642*, JR 22:251.

38. [Vimont], *Relation of 1642–43*, JR 24:271; J. Megapolensis, "A Short Account of the Mohawk Indians, 1644," NNN, 176.

39. See table C.4. How many more they obtained before the trade was legalized, and to what extent the other four Iroquois tribes participated in this trade, is open to speculation. The Iroquois were not the only native groups who had guns. In 1637 the Abenakis were reported to have some, and in 1643 the government of Maryland prohibited the sale of guns to Indians without license because of the possible harm to the colony due to "the great number of gunnes, now in the hands and use of Indians, in and about this colony" ([Le Jeune], *Relation of 1637*, JR 12:189; [proclamation, 2 Jan. 1643], *Md. Archives* 3:144).

40. [Le Jeune], *Relation of 1657–58*, JR 44:217.

41. As Father Le Jeune astutely observed, the other tribes had a hand in Mohawk wars but it was at the initiative of the Mohawks ([Le Jeune], *Relation of 1640–41*, JR 21:21).

42. This was apparently the motive behind attempts, in the mid-1650s, to lure the remnants of the Huron nation to Iroquoia ([Le Mercier], *Relation of 1653–54*, JR 41:49). Other observers commented on this purpose for raiding against French native allies in the 1680s.

43. In 1641 the French became regular targets of the Iroquois and were struck 5 times

in 1644. In the years prior to 1641 the Iroquois had never launched more than 3 raids per year against native groups. In 1642 they struck French native allies 8 times; in 1643, 7 times; and in 1644, 5 times; see figure 6.1. The decrease in attacks against native groups in 1644 seems to be due to more raids being carried out against the French in that year.

44. [Vimont], *Relation of 1643–44*, JR 26:63, 67–71.

45. *Journal des pères Jésuites, 1646*, JR 28:149–51. In May 1646 the Algonquins again urged the French not to exclude them from the peace ([Lalemant], *Relation of 1645–46*, JR 29:299).

46. *Journal des pères Jésuites, 1646*, JR 28:149–51.

47. [Vimont], *Relation of 1644–45*, JR 27:262; Marie de l'Incarnation à son fils, 14 sept. 1645, *Correspondance*, 257.

48. [Lalemant], *Relation of 1645–46*, JR 28:275. The other tribes in the Confederacy seem not to have wanted to conclude formal peace, probably because they were not as concerned with the French as they were with the Hurons.

49. A standard interpretation of what this treaty was about and why it was broken is George Hunt's in *Wars of the Iroquois*, 77–86. Leo-Paul Desrosiers ("La rupture") and Bruce Trigger (*Children of Aataentsic*, 647–58) dispute Hunt's economic interpretation and present their own economic version of events.

50. In July 1643 some twelve Iroquois were held off in their bid to defeat seven Algonquins because the Algonquins were more effective in their use of guns than the Iroquois ([Vimont], *Relation of 1642–43*, JR 24:289–91).

51. [Vimont], *Relation of 1644–45*, JR 27:269.

52. [Lalemant], *Relation of 1645–46*, JR 29:57.

53. [Lalemant], *Relation of 1647*, JR 30:115–17, 227–29; Marie de l'Incarnation à son fils, [summer] 1647, *Correspondance*, 323–35.

54. [Lalemant], *Relation of 1647*, JR 30:229. Even during his captivity in 1642, Father Jogues had been considered a sorcerer and was accused of bringing bad luck to the hunters he accompanied as a servant (31:73).

55. Marie de l'Incarnation à son fils, [summer] 1647, *Correspondance*, 325; [Lalemant], *Relation of 1647*, JR 30:227.

56. The sources do not often enough identify the attacking Iroquois tribe by name. When they do, it still appears to be the Mohawks that attack the French and one of the other tribes that raid against New France's native allies; see table D.1, entries for 1646 to 1649.

57. The Jesuits suggested that the Onondagas receptivity to Huron peace overtures in 1648 may have been due, in part, to Mohawk arrogance ([Ragueneau], "Huron Report, 1647–48," JR 33:123).

CHAPTER EIGHT. CONFLICT AND UNCERTAINTY

1. [Le Mercier], *Relation of 1652–53*, JR 40:89–91, 185–91; *Journal des pères Jésuites, 1653*, JR 38:179, 183.

2. [Le Mercier], *Relation of 1652–53*, JR 40:93. The Jesuits were, however, pragmatic men, and they understood that some Iroquois saw their missions and presence

among them as part of the price of ensuring peace with New France (Father Pierron, in [Le Mercier], *Relation of 1669–70*, JR 53:223, 225). Leo-Paul Desrosiers provides the most detailed discussion of the events surrounding this treaty, and what led to the Onondagas' decision; see his "Les Onnontagués" and "La paix-miracle."

3. On the Erie attacks see table D.1, entries for 1652–54. On the allied army, estimated at one thousand strong, see *Journal des pères Jésuites, 1653*, JR 38:181.

4. [Le Mercier], *Relation of 1653–54*, JR 41:83; [Le Jeune], *Relation of 1657–58*, JR 44:151.

5. [De Quen], *Relation of 1655–56*, JR 42:53, 57.

6. [Le Mercier], *Relation of 1653–54*, JR 41:201–3; [Le Jeune], *Relation of 1656–57*, JR 43:129; [Le Jeune], *Relation of 1657–58*, JR 44:151. These views have had some influence on the historiography of this event. Desrosiers ("La paix-miracle," 88) and Hunt (*Wars of the Iroquois*, 74) concluded from these statements that the Mohawks charged tolls. Gustave Lanctot (*Histoire*, 268) thought the Mohawks were middlemen between the western tribes and the Dutch at Fort Orange.

7. Heidenreich, *Huronia*, 221–22.

8. The date of the earliest treaty between the Iroquois and the Dutch is unknown. A document used as evidence to support claims of a treaty made in 1613 between the Dutch and Mohawks has been shown to be a forgery (Gehring, Starna, and Fenton, "Tawagonshi Treaty"). Daniel Richter has suggested that the first treaty was made sometime around 1618 between the Mohawks and a Dutch trader and that a formal treaty with the Dutch government and all Five Nations was made in 1642 ("Rediscovered Links"). Whether or not the first treaty was concluded in 1618, it seems likely that the first one between the Mohawks, Onondagas, Oneidas, and Dutch authorities was made in 1634–35 during van den Bogaert's visit to these tribes rather than in 1642 ([van den Bogaert], *Journey*, 15–19).

9. [Lalemant], *Relation of 1661–62*, JR 47:205.

10. [Court minute, 15 July 1654], in van Laer, ed. and trans., *Minutes of the Court of Fort Orange* 1:170.

11. "Resolution to Provide the Mohawks with . . . Powder and Lead, 1654," NYCD 13:35.

12. [Le Mercier], *Relation of 1653–54*, JR 41:87. Father Jogues's efforts, in 1645, to establish direct Onondaga-French relations had upset the Mohawks for similar reasons ([Lalemant], *Relation of 1645–46*, JR 29:57). On the process of Confederacy council protocol, and the status of the five tribes within it, see E. Tooker, "The League of the Iroquois: Its History, Politics, and Ritual," in Trigger, ed., *Handbook*, 422–29.

13. [Le Mercier], *Relation of 1652–53*, JR 40:91; *Journal des pères Jésuites, 1653*, JR 38:183.

14. [Le Mercier], *Relation of 1652–53*, JR 40:163.

15. [Le Jeune], *Relation of 1656–57*, JR 43:99.

16. [Ragueneau], *Relation of 1651–52*, JR 38:61–62.

17. *Journal des pères Jésuites, 1653*, JR 38:191–95; [Le Mercier], *Relation of 1652–53*, JR 40:103–13. It is not clear what part of the non-Mohawk component, if any, the Senecas made up.

18. *Journal des pères Jésuites, 1653*, JR 38:195. They were later released and their presents returned to them ([Le Mercier], *Relation of 1652–53*, JR 40:183).

19. *Journal des pères Jésuites, 1653*, JR 38:189; Dollier, *Histoire du Montréal*, 181–83.

20. [Le Mercier], *Relation of 1652–53*, JR 40:115.

21. The French did, however, give the Mohawks guns as presents ([Le Jeune], *Relation of 1655–56*, JR 43:165, 171, 113).

22. *Journal des pères Jésuites, 1653*, JR 38:199; [Le Mercier], *Relation of 1653–54*, JR 41:47. Father Le Mercier reported that some Hurons were convinced that the Mohawks' only motive for continuing peace talks with the French was "to conceal their game, and to afford them more means of speaking with us [the Hurons] without suspicion and of conducting this whole affair [the secret offer to the Hurons] smoothly and effectively." The Onondagas do not appear to have thought of this, and it was not an original strategy of theirs. It was only in January 1654 that they came to the French and asked for a treaty similar to that which they learned the Mohawks had made (*Journal des pères Jésuites, 1654*, JR 41:19).

23. "Propositions made . . . on the Part of the Maquaas," 25 Dec. 1653, in van Laer, ed. and trans., *Minutes of the Court of Fort Orange* 1:90.

24. Marie de l'Incarnation à son fils, 12 oct. 1655, *Correspondance*, 564.

25. [De Quen], *Relation of 1655–56*, JR 42:93.

26. Copies of two letters sent from New France, [1655], JR 41:217; [Le Jeune], *Relation of 1656–57*, JR 43:99–101.

27. If so, they would not have been the last to try this. In October 1656, following in the footsteps of the Mohawks and Onondagas, the Oneidas tried to lure some Hurons to their villages (*Journal des pères Jésuites, 1656*, JR 42:253).

28. Letter of Father Ragueneau, 9 Aug. 1657, in [Le Jeune], *Relation of 1656–57*, JR 44:69.

29. On the efforts to attract the Hurons see *Journal des pères Jésuites, 1656*, JR 42:253; *Journal des pères Jésuites, 1657*, JR 43:59–61; [Le Jeune], *Relation of 1656–57*, JR 43:117–19, 187; Father Ragueneau's letter, 9 Aug. 1657, appended to [Le Jeune], *Relation of 1656–57*, JR 44:69–77; [Le Jeune], *Relation of 1657–58*, JR 44:151; Marie de l'Incarnation à son fils, 15 oct. 1657, *Correspondance*, 591–92; [Radisson], *Explorations*, 45–55. The struggle for the Hurons in New France is summarized in Trigger, *Children of Aataentsic*, 801–15. Campeau (*Gannentaha*, 1–53) covers these events, as well as the establishment and abandonment of the first Jesuit mission among the Iroquois.

30. A Dutch document dated 6 Jan. 1654 but found between two others dated Jan. 1655 records that the Mohawks asked the Dutch to help them "compose difficulties which have arisen" because the Mohawks have killed a chief of the "Sinekens of Onnedaego" ([court minute], 6 Jan. 1654, in van Laer and Pearson, eds., *Early Records* 1:217). Since that chief was killed in the fall of 1654 as he returned with Father Lemoyne (Campeau, *Gannentaha*, 19), the actual date for this document should be 6 Jan. 1655. On the killing of the Senecas see [Le Jeune], *Relation of 1656–57*, JR 43:101, 103.

31. [Le Jeune], *Relation of 1656–57*, JR 43:109.

32. [Le Jeune], *Relation of 1656–57*, JR 43:107–9, 169.

33. "Propositions of Three Mohawk Castles," [16–22] June 1657, NYCD 13:73. See also van Laer, ed. and trans., *Minutes of the Court of Fort Orange* 2:45, 47–48.

34. [Council minute], 27 July 1660, NYCD 13:186.

35. True, there were several more attempts at peace in 1658 and 1659, but these were half-hearted efforts designed to regain Iroquois from various tribes who had been captured when the Iroquois had attacked New France ([council minute], 13 Aug. 1658, NYCD 13:88–89; *Journal des pères Jésuites, 1658*, JR 44:113–15, 121, 125; *Journal des pères Jésuites, 1659–60*, JR 45:81–87, 103).

36. See table D.1, entries for 1658 to 1662. On the marked increase in raiding against the French starting in 1658, see figure 7.1.

37. [Le Jeune], *Relation of 1640–41*, JR 21:27–59.

38. [Le Jeune], *Relation of 1657–58*, JR 44:157–65; Campeau, *Gannentaha*, 42.

39. [Le Jeune], *Relation of 1660–61*, JR 47:69–79; see also table D.1, [29 Aug.] 1661.

40. [Lalemant], *Relation of 1663–64*, JR 49:143.

41. This is the now famous battle of Dollard des Ormeaux against the Iroquois; see table D.1, [end of May] 1660. There were some Oneidas among the seven hundred Iroquois, but the sources do not indicate how many. The original target was Quebec, but the French forced the Iroquois' hand when they went out from Trois Rivières to try to steal the Iroquois' furs (*Journal des pères Jésuites, 1659–60*, JR 45:153; Marie de l'Incarnation à son fils, 25 juin 1660, *Correspondance*, 619). Campeau (*Gannentaha*, 56) suggests that the orginal goal of the attack was to capture the remaining Hurons.

42. [Lalemant], *Relation of 1659–60*, JR 46:121, 123.

43. Father Lemoyne to Father [Lalemant], 25 Aug. and 11 Sept. 1661, in [Le Jeune], *Relation of 1660–61*, JR 47:69–70.

44. French explorer and trader Pierre Radisson was only one of the many inhabitants of New France who were captured and adopted by the Mohawks. Revenge and capture may also have been a goal of other tribes in their raids against the French.

45. Marie de l'Incarnation à son fils, 2 nov. 1660, *Correspondance*, 648. Her emphasis on land as a buffer and means of sustenance addresses the continuing importance of territory in Iroquois policy.

46. "Propositions made by . . . the Mohawks," 19 Nov. 1655, in van Laer and Pearson, eds., *Early Records* 1:237.

47. [Le Mercier], *Relation of 1653–54*, JR 41:61–65.

48. [De Quen], *Relation of 1655–56*, JR 42:229.

49. [Radisson], *Explorations*, 99, 103. The fact that French traders should fear Iroquois wrath for trading guns to French allies indicates that the French knew this practice upset the Iroquois.

50. [Lalemant], *Relation of 1662–63*, JR 48:75; *Journal des pères Jésuites, 1665*, JR 49:245.

51. On the early Jesuit mission to Onondaga and their hopes of extending their ministry to the other tribes see Campeau, *Gannentaha*, 20–44. On the Jesuits' methods of converting natives to Christianity see Gagnon, *La Conversion*; Axtell, *Invasion Within*, 43–127. A good brief overview of the Jesuits' methods for bringing about change, and of their efficacy, is Axtell, *Beyond 1492*, 152–70.

52. [Lalemant], *Relation of 1659–60*, JR 46:117; [Le Jeune], *Relation of 1660–61*, JR 47:69–79, 97–103; [Lalemant], *Relation of 1663–64*, JR 49:139–49; *Journal des pères Jésuites, 1664*, JR 48:239.

53. *Journal des pères Jésuites, 1658*, JR 44:113.

54. Assembly Proceedings, 2 May 1661, *Md. Archives* 1:407; [Lalemant], *Relation of 1662–63*, JR 48:77. As early as 1642 the Maryland Assembly had prohibited "lending arms to Indians" (Assembly Proceedings, 26 July 1642, *Md. Archives* 1:134). This would seem to suggest that arms trading was taking place. In 1650, when colonists were allowed to trade freely with the Indians, the prohibition on trading arms was repeated ("An Act Concerning Trade with Indians," [Apr. 1650], *Md. Archives*, 307).

55. For these raids and their results see table D.1, entries for 1661 to 1664. The Onondagas and Cayugas took part in the Senecas' wars against the Susquehannocks.

56. [Lalemant], *Relation of 1662–63*, JR 48:79–81; *Relation of 1663–64*, JR 49:139–43. Between 1660 and 1663 the Iroquois were struck by three epidemics of smallpox (see the discussion in appendix B and table B.1).

57. "Letter of the Town Council of New Amsterdam," 16 Sept. 1664, NNN, 452; "Report of the Surrender of New Netherland by Peter Stuyvesant," 16 Oct. 1665, NNN, 458–66.

58. [Lalemant], *Relation of 1661–62*, JR 47:217. *Profit* in the above quote should be read to mean "advantage" or "benefit" in a general sense, rather than profit as in modern usage, meaning the part of a price above the cost of a given good.

59. Table D.1, entries for 1664 to 1666. The sources only identify the specific tribe once. In that instance, the Iroquois tribe in question was the Mohawks.

60. Eccles's *Canada Under Louis XIV* and *Frontenac* remain the definitive studies of the political and military history of New France in the second half of the seventeenth century.

61. [Le Mercier], *Relation of 1665–66*, JR 50:135–39; *Journal des pères Jésuites, 1666–67*, JR 50:191. The Mohawks confirmed their peace with the French in 1667.

62. Goldstein, *French-Iroquois Diplomatic and Military Relations*, 98, 101; Eccles, *France in America*, 70.

63. Table D.1, entries for 1667 to 1677. The Mahicans (*Loups* in French sources) were proving to be particularly difficult on the Iroquois. See also [Le Mercier], *Relation of 1666–67*, JR 51:83, 203, 243. A peace between the Mohawks and the Mahicans, made in 1666, apparently broke down ("Peace between the Maquase and the Mahicanders," 31 Aug.–10 Sept. 1666, LIR, 34–35).

64. "Articles between Colonel Cartwright and the New York Indians," 24 Sept. 1664, NYCD 3:67.

65. Norton, *Fur Trade*, 43, 83–85.

66. Table D.1, entries for 1668 to 1684. As we have already seen in chapter 3, the wars against the Piscataways in the early 1680s were the result of the recently adopted Susquehannocks using their new military strength to exact revenge on their old foes.

67. Various priests played key roles as emissaries and interpreters but, unfortunately, the exact role of the Jesuits in French-Iroquois political affairs in the seventeenth century

has yet to be studied systematically. In "Iroquois versus Iroquois" Richter outlines the divisive impact the Jesuits had on Iroquois society.

CHAPTER NINE. "YOUR FYRE SHALL BURN NO MORE"

1. "Mémoire pour éclaircir les dispositions," [1682], AN, CIIA 6:21; De Meulles au Ministre, 12 nov. 1682, AN, CIIA 6:85.

2. "Dans l'assembleé tenue 10 octobre, 1682," AN, CIIA 6:68–70. The Jesuits also recorded this meeting; see "Assembly at Quebec," 10 Oct. 1682, JR 62:157.

3. Broshar, "First Push"; Buffinton, "Policy of Albany"; Eccles, "Fur Trade." La Barre, for example, focused on the threat to the fur trade because he was so concerned with profiting from it. Baron Lahontan charged that La Barre's 1684 expedition against the Iroquois was a mere cover for a trading venture. The Intendant De Meulles reported that La Barre used his military supply convoys to transport trade merchandise for his personal ventures (Lahontan, *New Voyages* 1:86; De Meulles au Ministre, 10 oct. 1684, AN, CIIA 6:389). See also Robert la Roque de Roquebrune, "Le Febvre de la Barre," *Dictionary of Canadian Biography* 1:442–46. Eccles (*Frontenac*, 157–72) presents a more sympathetic account of La Barre's actions.

4. Monseignat, "Relation de ce qui s'est passé de plus remarquable en Canada," [Nov. 1689 to Nov. 1690], AN, CIIA 11:7–8; "Answer of the Five Nations," 23 Sept. 1689, LIR, 157.

5. [Dablon], *Relation of 1670–71*, JR 54:263–65. Onnontio was the name the Iroquois gave to all French governors; it means "great mountain" and was a literal translation of Montmagny, the name of the first French governor with whom they had sustained contact.

6. "Relation officielle de l'enterprise de Cavelier de La Salle de 1979 a 1681," in Margry, *Découvertes* 1:469.

7. "Instructions que Sieur de la Barre," 24 juillet 1684, AN, CIIA 6:269; [conference with Iroquois], 5 Aug. 1684, in Colden, *Five Indian Nations*, 61; Lahontan, *New Voyages* 1:81. The Iroquois did not change their story about why they attacked this convoy. In 1687 they again repeated to English authorities that they had attacked the French because they were carrying arms to Iroquois foes ("Information given by the [Iroquois]," 2 Aug. 1687, in Records of the States of the United States, Pennsylvania: Penn Manuscripts, Indian Affairs, 1:1).

8. "Estat des marchandises nécessaires," [1697], AN, CIIA 15:258. These prices do not include the cost of holsters/scabbards for the guns and pistols or that of premade lead balls. In the same year, 1,200 livres weight of kettles was worth 1,320 livres. Since guns were more valuable than kettles (about 10 livres worth to 1 livres worth respectively), it would require a larger number of kettles than guns to make up the same value of cargo. It is unlikely that seven canoes—the number attacked in the 1684 convoy—could carry that many kettles.

9. White (*Middle Ground*, 136) estimates that the French traded 320–440 guns a year in the *pays d'en haut* during the 1670s and 680–800 a year in the 1680s and 1690s.

10. Champigny au Ministre, 5 nov. 1687, AN, CIIA 9:192–93; "Estat des marchandises est Munitions distribuées, 1693," AN, CIIA 12:[290].

11. [Conference with the Iroquois], 5 Aug. 1684, in Colden, *Five Indian Nations*, 61; Lahontan, *New Voyages* 1:81; See also [conference with the Iroquois], 5 Aug. 1684, 'in Wraxall, *Indian Affairs*, 12–13.

12. C. Heidenreich (in Harris, ed., *Historical Atlas*, plate 37) provides a comprehensive list of French forts, indicating when they were established and the years they were occupied; plates 37–38 show the geographical distribution of most of the forts listed.

13. On the origins of France's imperial policy toward the English colonies in America see Eccles, *Frontenac*, 334–37; *Canada Under Louis XIV*, 246–48. As Eccles points out, this strategy of Versailles's, undertaken "to achieve the ends of France in Europe rather than France in North America," merely recognized the reality that had developed in New France during the closing decades of the seventeenth century as the colony's leaders and businessmen sought to protect their trade interests (*Canada Under Louis XIV*, 246).

14. Frontenac au Ministre, 2 nov. 1672, AN, CIIA 3:240; "Voyage de Monsieur Le Comte de Frontenac au Lac Ontario en 1673," AN, CIIA 4:12.

15. Lahontan, *New Voyages* 1:273–74.

16. [conference minute], 15 juin 1688, AN, CIIA 10:48.

17. "Answer of the Six Nations," 13 Feb. 1688, NYCD 3:534. The view expressed in this quotation supports the contention that wars were not fought for land per se. If conquest of a tribe was grounds for claiming rights over their land, the Iroquois would question not the French tactic but only their claim to have conquered the Iroquois. This, in turn, suggests that Iroquois concerns over lands, and wars to that effect, were to protect what they considered theirs and to keep it for their uses, rather than to conquer tribes for their land.

18. "Abstract of the Proposalls," 2 Aug. 1684, NYCD 3:347.

19. [Conference], [4] Oct. 1683, NYCD 14:772.

20. [Conference with the Iroquois], 5 Aug. 1684, in Colden, *Five Indian Nations*, 61; "Propositions of the Five Nations," 5 Aug. 1687, NYCD 3:442; "Gov. Dongan's Proposals [to the Iroquois]," 25 Apr. 1687, LIR, 113.

21. Dongan to the Lord President, 19 Feb. 1688, NYCD 3:510; [conference with the Iroquois, 20–27 July 1698], in *Propositions Made by the Five Nations*, 5; [conference with the Five Nations], 10–21 July 1701, NYCD 4:900, 905, 907; "Conference [with Iroquois et al., 9 July to 15 Aug.] 1701," NYCD 4:988. These concerns continued well into the eighteenth century; see for example [conference with the Iroquois], 7–14 Sept. 1726, NYCD 5:790.

22. Eccles, *Canada Under Louis XIV*, 103.

23. "Voyage de Monsieur Le Comte de Frontenac, 1673," AN, CIIA 4:21.

24. "Present Conditions of the Missions, 1675," [Father Dablon], JR 59:251; Father Jean Enjalran to [Father General], 13 Oct. 1676, JR 60:135.

25. Le Roy à Frontenac, 28 avril 1677, Archives Nationales, Paris, Archives des Colonies, series B, 7:95; Eccles, *Frontenac*, 194.

26. [Conference with the Iroquois, 20–27 July 1698], in *Propositions Made by the*

*Five Nations*, 5; [conference with the Five Nations], 10–21 July 1701, *NYCD* 4:907; [conference], 16 Aug. 1694, in Wraxall, *Indian Affairs*, 26. Colden (*History*, 171–75) has a more detailed version of the 16 Aug. 1694 conference.

27. In the metaphorical speech of the Iroquois, to establish a "fire" is to claim that place for oneself or one's tribe. To "extinguish" or "put out" a fire is to leave that place or remove from it those who had lived there. A useful overview of this and other metaphors of Iroquois speech is "Glossary of Figures of Speech," in Jennings, ed., *History and Culture*, 115–24.

28. [Conference at Onondaga], 22 Jan. 1690, in Colden, *Five Indian Nations*, 111. This statement and others like it seem to suggest that the Iroquois considered the closing of the fort to have been the result of the 1689 attacks against the colony that began with the capture of some people near Fort Frontenac.

29. This was the name the Iroquois applied to New York governor Benjamin Fletcher.

30. This term, *people of the longhouse*, is the Iroquois name for themselves.

31. "Message from the Governor of Canada to the Five Nations and their Answer," [31 Jan.–4 Feb.] 1695, *NYCD* 4:122.

32. [Conference], 20 Aug. 1694, in Colden, *Five Indian Nations*, 177–78; [conference], 18 Sept. 1695, in Wraxall, *Indian Affairs*, 27–28; [conference with the Iroquois, 20–27 July 1698], in *Propositions Made by the Five Nations*, 10–11.

33. La Potherie, *Histoire* 4:179.

34. Father Jean Enjalran to unknown, 13 Oct. 1676, *JR* 60:145. By 1682 the Mohawks alone accounted for at least one hundred of the Iroquois to be found at the missions of Praire-de-la-Madeleine and St. François Xavier du Sault ([Dablon], *Relation of 1679*, *JR* 61:241; Claude Chauchetière to [Father Superior], 14 Oct. 1682, *JR* 62:169).

35. B. G. Trigger, in Harris, ed., *Historical Atlas*, plate 47.

36. "Conference [with the Five Nations, 10–21 July] 1701," *NYCD* 4:907; see also Richter, "Iroquois versus Iroquois," 11–12.

37. "Presens des onontaguéz," 5 sept. 1684, AN, CIIA 6:299–300. This is the official version of the treaty signed by La Barre. Lahontan, who was part of the French force, gives a much less flattering version of what transpired (*New Voyages* 1:75–84). Colden (*History*, 65–71) paraphrases Lahontan. Even in La Barre's account the fact that the Iroquois had the upper hand is evident in their metaphors and light sarcasm. In their opening speech they offer La Barre an "unpleasant drink" to rid the French of all that they suffered on their trip ("Presens des onontaguéz," 5 sept. 1684, AN, CIIA 6:299). They knew the French had no choice but to take the bitter medicine. La Barre even had to give approval for the Iroquois war against the Illinois. When told the Iroquois were going to continue hostilities against that group, all he could do was ask them to be careful not to strike against the French in Illinois country.

38. "Answer of the [Five Nations]," 6 Aug. 1687, Records of the States of the United States, Pennsylvania: Penn Manuscripts, Indian Affairs, 1:3.

39. Duchesneau, "Mémoire pour faire connoistre," 13 nov. 1681, AN, CIIA 5:309; Jean de Lamberville to [Father Superior], 25 Aug. 1682, *JR* 62:73–87, 95. In response to the questions about why the Iroquois warred against the Illinois, the Onondaga leader

Teganissorens is reported to have answered, "they deserve to die; they have killed my people [*il m'a tué*]; one can offer no other response" (Belmont, *Histoire du Canada*, 16). This dramatic answer accurately reflects the role of revenge in the start of these hostilities. The Iroquois war against the Ottawas probably started in a similar fashion as the Five Nations pursued the remnants of the Huron nation into Ottawa lands.

40. Jean de Lamberville to [Father Superior], 25 Aug. 1682, *JR* 62:81; Father Thiery Beschefer to Father Provincial, 21 Oct. 1683, *JR* 62:213.

41. "Relation officielle de La Salle," in Margry, *Découvertes* 1:505; [conference minute], 31 Mar. 1687, in Richter, "Rediscovered Links," 78; [conference with the Iroquois], 5 Aug. 1684, in Colden, *Five Indian Nations*, 61; "Propositions of the Five Nations," 5 Aug. 1687, *NYCD* 3:442; "Gov. Dongan's Proposals [to the Iroquois]," 25 Apr. 1687, in *LIR*, 113.

42. [Conference], [4] Oct. 1683, *NYCD* 14:772; "Journal of Messrs. Bleeker and Schuylers Visit to Onondaga," [2–29 June 1701], *NYCD* 14:891; Lahontan, *New Voyages* 1:82. Lahontan suggests that the wars started because the Illinois and Miamis overhunted Iroquois lands. This may have been true, but it is likely that the wars began as a result of deaths that occurred when one group attacked the other as they hunted near each other.

43. Lahontan, *New Voyages* 1:323; "Relation [de ce qui s'est passé en Canada, 1695–1696]," AN, CIIA 14:36; Callières et Champigny au Ministre, 18 oct. 1700, AN, CIIA 18:3; Colden, *Five Indian Nations*, 181. Lahontan, like many other French writers, thought that the Iroquois were forced to range out of their lands to go to these areas. As far as the Iroquois were concerned, these were their lands.

44. "Robert Livingston's Report of his Journey to Onondaga," [Apr. 1700], *NYCD* 4:650; La Potherie, *Histoire* 4:254–55.

45. La Potherie, *Histoire* 4:179, 182–83, 203–4, 207, 221–22, 254–55.

46. Table F.1. Of that number, all but aproximately 210 (about 8.7 percent) were Indians (table F.2).

47. Jean de Lamberville to Gov. Frontenac, 20 Sept. 1682, *JR* 62:153. For similar views see [Gov. La Barre], "Dans l'assembleé tenue 10 octobre 1682," *JR* 62:68–70; Lahontan, *New Voyages* 1:395; Baugy, *Journal*, 50–52. The Iroquois continued to practice this strategy in the eighteenth century; see [conference at Onondaga], 6–10 June 1710, in Wraxall, *Indian Affairs*, 71–74.

48. See for example the efforts to get the Hurons, Ottawas, Ojibwas, Missisaugas, and Iroquois living on the reserves in New France to make peace with the Iroquois and/or relocate to Iroquoia ([conference], 3 Feb. 1690, in Wraxall, *Indian Affairs*, 15; [conference], 22 Jan. 1690, in Colden, *Five Indian Nations*, 106–12; "Relation de ce qui s'est passé de plus considérable en Canada," [1690–91], AN, CIIA 11:46; Champigny au Ministre, 10 mai 1691, AN, CIIA 11:256; Père Bruyas à Frontenac, 4 avril 1691, Archives Nationales, Paris, Archives des Colonies, series CIIE 10:9–11; Callières au Ministre, 19 oct. 1694, AN, CIIA 13:105; Frontenac et Champigny au Minstre, 10 nov. 1695, AN, CIIA 13:296; "Propositions of the Five Nations," 30 June 1700, *NYCD* 4:694–95; "Conference [with the Iroquois, 26 Aug. to 4 Sept.] 1700," *NYCD* 4:732, 736. In one instance, when the English asked the Iroquois to capture some Jesuits, the Iroquois responded that

this was not a wise policy since it might alienate some of the tribes they were trying to lure closer to them and who listened to the priests.

49. [Conference minute], 23 Sept. 1678, in Richter, "Rediscovered Links," 76; "Propositions to the Five Nations," 5 Aug. 1687, *NYCD* 3:442–43; Groenendyke and Provoost to Commissioners, 16 June 1700, *NYCD* 4:691; "Conference [with the Iroquois, 26 Aug.–4 Sept.] 1700," *NYCD* 4:741. If there is still any doubt that the Iroquois did not serve as middlemen in the fur trade between Albany and the western tribes, this policy of the Iroquois should put it to rest. If the Iroquois brought in the furs of the western tribes they would hardly have allowed, or encouraged, those tribes to have direct access to their suppliers. Economically, the Iroquois had much to lose if they did. They would have lost their alleged middleman's profit and would have allowed former foes access to their land and its resources. The only reason for allowing the western tribes access to Albany, and taking such a security risk, was because the benefit to be gained—the weakening of the French—was worth the price.

50. [Barrillion et Bonrepaus?], "Mémoire pour Monseigneur le Marquis De Seignelay," 1687, AN, CIIA 9:249; [Denonville], "Mémoire instructif de L'Estat des affaires de la Nouvelle France," 10 août 1688, AN, CIIA 10:67.

51. "Propositions of the Five Nations," [June–July 1693], *NYCD* 4:45.

52. "Answer of the [Five Nations]," 6 Aug. 1687, Records of the States of the United States, Pennsylvania: Penn Manuscripts, Indian Affairs, Penn Manuscripts, 1:3. He was quick to add, however, that since the French were so actively supporting their native allies, the English might like to consider doing likewise.

53. In 1687 Denonville had amassed an army of two thousand to war against the Iroquois (table D.1, July to Aug. 1687). In their 1689 attack against Lachine, the best the Confederacy could do was a force of twelve hundred to fifteen hundred (table D.1, 5 Aug. 1689). However, the overall population of New France, about fifteen thousand in 1690, was comparable to or slightly lower than that of the Iroquois. On the French population see Hubert Charbonneau and R. C. Harris, in Harris, ed., *Historical Atlas*, plate 46; on the Iroquois population see appendix C.

54. "Answer of the Five Nations," 23 Sept. 1689, in *LIR*, 155; [Propositions of the Mohawks], 25 Mar. 1690, in Colden, *Five Indian Nations*, 117, 119; "Proposals of the Commissioners . . . to the Indians," 3 May 1690, *NYCD* 3:714; "Answer of the Five Nations," 2 June 1691, *NYCD* 776–77; "Propositions of the Senecas and Mohawks," 4 Sept. 1691, *NYCD* 3:807; "Answers of the Five Nations," 6 June 1692, *NYCD* 3:842–44; "Answer of the Five Nations to Governor Fletcher," 25 Feb. 1693, *NYCD* 4:22–23.

55. The Iroquois complained that they received little ammunition for their beaver pelts. This stinginess, they said, was not all in line with the English requests for them to prosecute the war ("Answer of the Five Nations," 2 June 1691, *NYCD* 3:774–77).

56. Journal of Benjamin Bullivant, [13 Feb.–19 May] 1690, *CSP* 13:264. These complaints led to renewed requests by the king for the other colonies to contribute more to the war effort. But while some colonies were offended by the Iroquois' charges, little more concrete help was offered and the king's requests went unheeded ([Board of Trade to Nicholson], 2 Sept. 1697, *Md. Archives* 23:207–12; Robert Treat and Council to . . .

Fitz John Winthrop, 12 Nov. 1696, and Fitz John Winthrop to King William, [n.d.], in *Collections of the Connecticut Historical Society* 24:126–27, 128–29.

57. Council Minutes, 17 Aug. 1692, 22 Mar. 1693, Records of the States of the United States, New York: Journal of the Legislative Council, [1691–1743], 18, 54; Governor Fletcher to the Committee of Trade and Plantations, 28 Mar. 1694, *NYCD* 4:84–85; Earl of Bellomont to the Lords of Trade, 13 Apr. 1699 and 28 Feb. 1700, *NYCD* 4:487, 608.

58. "Answer of [the Five Nations]," 14 Aug. 1692, in *LIR*, 165; see also [conference, 2–4 June 1691], in Colden, *Five Indian Nations*, 125.

59. "Comparative Population of Albany and the Indians in 1689 and 1698," 19 Apr. 1698, *NYCD* 4:337.

60. The estimate of 2,550 warriors is often considered high because the Iroquois were thought to have lost many people in the wars up to 1689. However, as noted above, both the statistical data and the accounts of French observers indicate that the Iroquois had significantly bolstered the size of their forces with the capture of other native groups.

61. This total does not include the five hundred estimated deaths due to disease in 1690.

62. Eccles, *Frontenac*, 244–72.

63. [Conference], 22 Jan. 1690, in Colden, *Five Indian Nations*, 111; Council Minute, 11 Dec. 1693, Records of the States of the United States, New York: Executive Council Records, 7:36; "Journal of Major Dirck Wessel's Embassy to Onondaga," [Aug. 1693], *NYCD* 4:59–63; "Propositions of the Five Nations," [2–9 Feb.] 1694, *NYCD* 4:85–87; "Message from the Governor of Canada to the Five Nations and their Answer," [31 Jan.–4 Feb.] 1695, *NYCD* 4:120–22; "Propositions Made by the [Onondagas]," 4 June 1697, *NYCD* 4:279.

64. Champigny au Minstre, 11 aôut 1695, AN, CIIA 13:339; Champigny au Ministre, 6 nov. 1695, AN, CIIA 13:360.

65. Sanonguirese, [conference, 1–3 Oct. 1696], *NYCD* 4:237, 240.

66. "Deed of the Five Nations to the King of their Beaver Hunting Ground," 19 July 1701, *NYCD* 4:908–11; Peter Wraxall, "Some Thoughts upon the British Indian Interest in North America," [1755], *NYCD* 7:18; Seneca speaker in "Schuyler's Journal of a Visit to Seneca Country," 23 Apr. 1720, *NYCD* 5:545. The Iroquois had tried this approach in the early 1680s as a means to protect their interests in the Susquehanna valley from the encroachments of Pennsylvania. "Abstract of the Proposalls of the Onouendages and Cayouges," 2 Aug. 1684, *NYCD* 3:347; "Propositions of the Cayugas and Onondagas," 26 Sept. 1683, in van Laer and Pearson, eds., *Early Records* 2:198. In 1726 they again deeded part of their lands to the English in the hopes they would stop French encroachment. This time it was to try and stop the building of the French fort at Niagara. "Deed in Trust from three of the Five Nations of Indians to the King," 14 Sept. 1726, *NYCD* 5:800–801.

67. "Conference [with the Five Nations, 10–21 July] 1701," *NYCD* 4:906.

68. For a more detailed study of this point, and the 1701 treaties in general, see Brandão and Starna, "Treaties of 1701."

69. The Iroquois openly acknowledged their division between those who would fol-

low the advice of the English and those who wanted to accept French proposals ("Propositions of the Five Nations," 30 June 1700, *NYCD* 4:694).

70. The diplomatic efforts of this period are remarkably complex. The various reports, journals, and conference records found in *NYCD* vol. 4, esp. 372–565, cover the events from the viewpoint of the Iroquois and the English. The French side is presented in [conference with the Iroquois], 18 juillet 1700, AN, CIIA 18:81–83; [conference with the Iroquois], 3–9 sept. 1700, AN, CIIA 18:84–88; La Potherie au Ministre, 16 oct. 1700, AN, CIIA 18:150–59; La Potherie, *Histoire* 4:193–266. Brandão and Starna, "Treaties of 1701"; Havard, *La Grande Paix*; Haan, "Problem of Iroquois Neutrality"; and Wallace, "Origins of Iroquois Neutrality" discuss the events leading to the treaties of 1701.

71. [Conference with the Onondagas and Oneidas], 3 Feb. 1699, in Wraxall, *Indian Affairs*, 31.

72. On continued Iroquois distrust of the French see La Potherie, *Histoire* 4:170–71.

73. "Instructions for the Earl of Bellomont," 31 Aug. 1697, *NYCD* 4:290; on Iroquois land swindles, see "Fraudulent Purchase of Land from the Mohawk Indians," 31 May 1698, *NYCD* 4:345–47. The Iroquois also complained that the English had gotten rich off their hunting and were still charging too much for trade goods ([conference, 13–14 June 1699], *NYCD* 4:571). So upset were the Iroquois with the prices that the English at Albany charged that some tribes concluded trade arrangements with Pennsylvania to avoid trading at Albany ([minute of Indian affairs], 23 Aug. 1699, in Wraxall, *Indian Affairs*, 33; Council Minute, 30 Aug. 1699, Records of the States of the United States, New York: Executive Council Records, 8, pt. 1:131).

74. By 1750 this view seems to have been quite common (Cayuga speaker, conference, 15 May 1750, *NYCD* 10:206; see also Wraxall, "Some thoughts on the British Indian Interests," [1755], *NYCD* 7:18).

APPENDIX A. REBIRTH AND DEATH

1. Pouliot (*Études sur les Relations des Jésuites*, 7) says the purpose of the *Relations* was to attract benefactors for the missions in New France and to inspire missionary zeal. He also notes the imprecise nature of Jesuit figures in this regard (223).

2. [Dablon], *Relation of 1679*, JR 61:163. As to the "goodly part" that died, Father Dablon makes no attempt to put a number to that expression.

3. [Le Mercier], *Relation of 1668–69*, JR 52:159.

4. [Dablon], *Relation of 1673–74*, JR 58:225.

5. Pouliot, *Études sur les Relations des Jésuites*, 223, 224, 308 n.1–2.

6. During the years in question the Iroquois lost, either captured or killed, seventy people in warfare. Most were males; see table D.1, entries for 1667–79.

7. To gain a sense of how significant a portion of the overall population this was, see appendix C.

APPENDIX B. EPIDEMICS AND DISEASE

1. Schlesier, "Epidemics and Indian Middlemen," 142.

2. Richter, *Ordeal*, 58–59; B. Trigger, "Early Iroquoian Contacts with Europeans,"

in Trigger, ed., *Handbook*, 352; Snow and Starna, "Sixteenth-Century Depopulation," 144.

3. See Henige, "Primary Source"; Snow and Lamphear, "European Contact."

4. See the comments of Dobyns, Snow, Lamphear, and Henige in Dobyns et al., "Commentary."

5. [van den Bogaert], "Narrative of a Journey into the Mohawk and Oneida Country, 1634–35," *NNN*, 139–62.

6. Le Mercier, "Huron Relation of 1636–37," in [Le Jeune], *Relation of 1637*, JR 14:9. Snow and Starna ("Sixteenth-Century Depopulation," 144) put this epidemic in 1637, but the Huron were first struck by this disease in September of 1636. If they picked up the contagion from the Mohawk, then the latter must have been hit by it in 1636.

7. Le Mercier, "Huronia Report, 1636–37," in [Le Jeune], *Relation of 1636–37*, JR 13:37–45.

8. Trigger, *Children of Aataentsic*, 526, 544–45.

9. *Annales de l'Hôtel-Dieu*, 24–25.

10. Lalemant, "Huronia Report, 1640–41," in [Le Jeune], *Relation of 1640–41*, JR 21:211.

11. [Lalemant], *Relation of 1647*, JR 30:229, 273, 31:121, quote on 30:273; Marie de l'Incarnation à son fils, [summer] 1647, *Correspondance*, 323.

12. [Le Jeune], *Relation of 1656–57*, JR 43:291.

13. *Annales de l'Hôtel-Dieu*, 198.

14. *Dictionary of Canadian Biography* 1:635.

15. See the letter in [Le Jeune], *Relation of 1660–61*, JR 47:69–93.

16. [Lalemant], *Relation of 1661–62*, JR 47:193, 205.

17. [Le Mercier], *Relation of 1664–65*, JR 50:59, 63. Writing two years earlier, Lalemant gives figures that come close to one thousand baptized (*Relation of 1661–62*, JR 47:193, 205; *Relation of 1662–63*, JR 48:83).

18. [Lalemant], *Relation of 1662–63*, JR 48:79, 83. Lalemant added that French captives among the Iroquois had baptized three hundred children and a like number of adults as a result of disease (83).

19. [Le Mercier], *Relation of 1669–70*, JR 54:79, 81.

20. [Dablon], *Relation of 1672–73*, JR 57:81, 83.

21. [Dablon], *Relation of 1676 and 1677*, JR 60:175.

22. "Message from the Sachims of Onondage," 6 Oct. 1679, *LIR*, 51–52; "The Oneydes Answer," 31 Oct. 1679, *LIR*, 55–57.

23. He wrote that there was a "grande quantité" of dead (Frontenac au Roi, 6 nov. 1679, AN, CIIA 5:12). Snow and Starna ("Sixteenth-Century Depopulation," 144) claim that this epidemic lasted during the winter of 1679–80, but the source they cite suggests otherwise. Under the entry of 23 Mar. 1680, Jasper Danckaerts wrote that the news from Albany was that a great number of Indians had died of smallpox in the early part of winter ([Danckaerts], *Journal of Jasper Danckaerts*, 181). The winter obviously started in 1679, and that this was when the disease was raging is confirmed by the messages of the Iroquois. Moreover, Danckaerts noted the disease almost everywhere he went in 1679

but made no mention of it in 1680 except to state that it "had prevailed so much the last year" (50, 58, 141, 149, quote on 239).

24. Jean de Lamberville to [Father Superior], 25 Aug. 1682, *JR* 62:97, 99.

25. Council of Connecticut to the Council of Massachusetts, 28 May 1690, *Collec-tions of the Connecticut Historical Society* 21:320; Monseignat, "Relation de ce qui s'est passé de plus remarquable en Canada," [Nov. 1689 to Nov. 1690], AN, CIIA 11:38.

26. There is evidence that as early as 1634 some Mohawk relocated to avoid disease ([van den Bogaert], "Narrative of a Journey into the Mohawk and Oneida Country, 1634–35," *NNN*, 141).

## APPENDIX C. POPULATION ESTIMATES

1. At least the process by which things are dug up, categorized, and dated is scientific. The speculations and theorizing based on that unearthed data can often be less disciplined and balanced than that of historians.

2. Heidenreich, *Huronia*, 99. In the *Relation of 1667–68* (*JR* 52:49), Le Mercier cites a letter of 8 November in which Bishop Laval writes that the natives usually have two to three children and "rarely do they exceed the number of four." Pierre Radisson, however, claimed that his adopted Mohawk mother had nine children. Two girls died at an unspecified age, and three sons were killed in war (*Explorations*, 26–27).

3. Heidenreich, *Huronia*, 99; Starna, "Mohawk Iroquois Populations," 377, 379. Dean Snow and William Starna depart from most other studies in suggesting an average of six hearths per Mohawk longhouse in the postcontact period ("Sixteenth-Century Depopulation," 144).

4. Radisson observed that his adopted father, still an active warrior, had five sons who were also warriors. Radisson makes no mention of any of them being married (*Explorations*, 26).

5. Many warriors married old, which would limit how many children they could father ("Mémoire sur les coutumes," 453, 455).

6. [Le Mercier], *Relation of 1668–69*, *JR* 52:193.

7. Galinée, "Voyage de Dollier et Galinée," 24.

8. [Dablon], *Relation of 1671–72*, *JR* 56:27.

9. Father Garnier to Gov. Frontenac, 6 July 1673, *JR* 57:27.

10. Starna, "Mohawk Iroquois Population," 375.

11. To determine a true mortality rate one would have to know how many people contracted a disease and how many from among them died. Here, as in most studies of this nature, *mortality rate* actually refers to the overall decline in population as the result of an epidemic or of several epidemics over time.

12. Indeed, even the high Mohawk mortality rate can be skewed by comparing a high preepidemic population with a postepidemic population that is lower than it might be; see Snow and Starna, "Sixteenth-Century Depopulation," 146, 147–48. While the preepidemic figure appears reasonable, the population for the Mohawk in 1644 is based on multiplying the warrior total by 5, rather than 8, as my calculations suggest.

13. They may have lost as many as thirteen hundred warriors in the last twelve years of the century (table D.1, entries for period 1689 to 1701).

### APPENDIX D. THE STATISTICS OF WAR

1. Untitled document, AN, CIIA 1:66–69.

2. O'Callaghan, preface to *NYCD* vol. 1; [van den Bogaert], *Journey*, xxiii.

3. The Dutch did not make much effort to convert the Iroquois and did not send missionaries to live among them. Later on the English, feeling threatened by the Jesuit impact on the Iroquois, tried to establish missions. But the ministers usually wanted too much money and too many creature comforts to overcome their reluctance to live among the "savages." On the unsuccessful English missionary effort during the years of this study, see Axtell, *Invasion Within*, 254–59.

4. The following refers not to interpretative differences but rather to factual data. Although at times, arriving at a "fact," such as a date, could be a matter of interpretation.

5. Thanks to Professor C. E. Heidenreich for his inestimable help in identifying native groups and geographical locations based on often sketchy details.

# Bibliography

ARCHIVAL SOURCES

Archives de la Compagnie de Jésus au Canada Français, Maison des Jésuites, Ste. Jér-
   ôme, Quebec
   Fonds Garneau
Archives Nationales, Paris, France
   Archives des Colonies, series B, Lettres Envoyées
   Archives des Colonies, series CIIA, Correspondence General, Canada
   Archives des Colonies, series CIIE, Des Limites des Postes
Bibliothèque Mazarin, Paris
   "Abregé des vies et moeurs et autres Particularitez de La Nation Irokoise laquelle est
   diviseé en Cinq villages. Sçavoir Agnez, Onney8t, Nontagué, Goyog8an et Son-
   nont8ans," ms 1964
Records of the States of the United States [on microfilm, comp. W. S. Jenkins]
   Connecticut Archives: Indians
   Massachusetts: Legislative Records; Executive Council Records
   New York: Journal of the Legislative Council; Executive Council Records
   Pennsylvania: Penn Manuscripts, Indian Affairs

OTHER SOURCES

Abler, Thomas. "European Technology and the Art of War in Iroquoia." In *Cultures in
   Conflict: Current Archaeological Perspectives*. Ed. D. C. Tkaczuk and B. C. Viv-
   ian. Proceedings of the Twentieth Annual Conference of the Archaeological Association of the University of Calgary, 1989: 273–82.
*Les Annales de l'Hôtel-Dieu de Quebec*. Ed. A. Jamet. Quebec, n.p., 1939.

Aquila, Richard. "Down the Warriors Path: The Causes of the Southern Wars of the Iroquois." *American Indian Quarterly* 4 (Aug. 1978): 211–21.

—————. *The Iroquois Restoration: Iroquois Diplomacy on the Colonial Frontier, 1701–1754.* Detroit: Wayne State University Press, 1983.

*Archives of Maryland.* Ed. W. H. Browne et al. Vols. 1–26. Baltimore: Maryland Historical Society, 1883–1906.

Axtell, James. *After Columbus: Essays in the Ethnohistory of Colonial North America.* New York: Oxford University Press, 1988.

—————. *Beyond 1492: Encounters in Colonial North America.* New York: Oxford University Press, 1992.

—————. "Columbian Encounters: Beyond 1492." *William and Mary Quarterly* 49 (April 1992): 335–60.

—————. *The European and the Indian: Essays in the Ethnohistory of Colonial North America.* New York: Oxford University Press, 1982.

—————. *The Invasion Within: The Contest of Cultures in Colonial North America.* New York: Oxford University Press, 1985.

Bachman, Van Cleaf. *Peltries or Plantations: The Economic Policies of the Dutch West India Company in New Netherland, 1623–1639.* Baltimore: Johns Hopkins University Press, 1969.

Bartram, John. "Observations on the Inhabitants, Climate, Soil, Rivers, Productions, and other matters worthy of Notice Made by Mr. John Bartram In his Travels From Pensilvania to Onondago, Oswega, and the Lake Ontario In Canada" [London, 1751]. In *A Journey to Onondaga in 1743 by John Bartram, Lewis Evans, and Conrad Weiser.* Barre MA: Imprint Society, 1973.

Baugy, Louis Henri, dit Chevalier de. *Journal d'une expédition contre les Iroquois en 1687.* Paris: Ernest Leroux, 1883.

Beauchamp, W. M., ed. *Moravian Journals Relating to Central New York, 1745–66.* New York: Onondaga Historical Association, 1916.

Belmont de Vachon, François. *Histoire du Canada, [1608–1700].* Société littéraire et historique du Québec, 1840.

Benn, Carl. "Iroquois Warfare, 1812–14." In *War Along the Niagara: Essays on the War of 1812 and Its Legacy.* Ed. Arthur R. Bowler. Youngstown OH: Old Fort Niagara Association, 1991.

Berkhofer, Robert F. *The White Man's Indian.* New York: Alfred A. Knopf, 1978.

Biggar, H. P., ed. *A Collection of Documents Relating to Jacques Cartier and the Sieur de Roberval.* Publication of the Public Archives of Canada, no. 14. Ottawa, 1930.

Bonvillain, Nancy. "Missionary Role in French Colonial Expansion: An Examination of the Jesuit Relations." *Man in the Northeast* 29 (spring 1985): 1–14.

Boucher, Pierre. *Histoire véritable et naturell des moeurs & productions du pays de la Nouvelle France, vulgairement dite le Canada.* Paris: 1664. Reprint, Quebec: Société Historique de Boucherville, 1964.

Boyce, Douglas. "A Glimpse of Iroquois Culture History through the Eyes of Joseph Brant and John Norton." *American Philosophical Society Proceedings* 117 (Aug. 1978): 286–94.

Bradley, James W. *Evolution of the Onondaga Iroquois: Accommodating Change, 1500–1655*. Syracuse NY: Syracuse University Press, 1987.

Brandão, J. A., and William A. Starna. "The Treaties of 1701: A Triumph of Iroquois Diplomacy." *Ethnohistory* 43 (spring 1996): 209–44.

Brebner, J. B. *The Explorers of North America: 1492–1806*. 1933. Reprint, New York: Doubleday, 1955.

Broshar, Helen. "The First Push Westward of the Albany Traders." *Mississippi Valley Historical Review* 7 (Dec. 1920): 228–41.

Buffinton, A. H. "The Policy of Albany and English Westward Expansion." *Mississippi Valley Historical Review* 8 (Mar. 1922): 327–66.

[Cadillac]. [Papers of Cadillac and Others Pertaining to the Founding and Early History of Detroit]. *Michigan Pioneer and Historical Society Collections*. Vols. 33, 34. 1904, 1905.

*Calendar of State Papers, Colonial Series, America and the West Indies*. Ed. W. Sainsbury et al. 44 vols. London: Her Majesties Stationary Office, 1896–.

Campeau, Lucien. *Catastrophe démographique sur les Grand Lacs*. Montreal: Éditions Bellarmin, 1986.

———. *Gannentaha: Première mission iroquoise (1653–1665)*. Montreal: Éditions Bellarmin, 1983.

———. *La mission des Jésuites chez les Hurons, 1634–1650*. Montreal: Éditons Bellarmin, 1987.

Campeau, Lucien, ed. *Monumenta Novae Franciae, I: Première mission d'Acadie, 1602–1616*. Rome: Monumenta Historica Societatus Iseu; Quebec: Presses de l'Université de Laval, 1967.

———. *Monumenta Novae Franciae, II: Etablissment à Quebec, 1616–1634*. Rome: Monumenta Historica Societatus Iseu; Quebec: Presses de l'Universite de Laval, 1979.

Campisi, Jack. "The Iroquois and the Euro-American Concept of Tribe." *New York History* 58 (Apr. 1982): 165–82.

Campisi, Jack, and Laurence Hauptman, eds. *Neighbours and Intruders: An Ethnohistorical Exploration of the Indians of Hudson's River*. Mercury Series, Canadian Ethnology Service, paper 39. Ottawa: National Museum of Man, 1978.

Cardy, Michael. "The Iroquois in the Eighteenth Century: A Neglected Source." *Man in the Northeast* 38 (fall 1989): 1–20.

[Cartier, Jacques]. *The Voyages of Jacques Cartier*. Ed. H. P. Biggar. Publications of the Public Archives of Canada, no. 11. Ottawa, 1924.

Casgrain, H. R. *Francis Parkman*. Quebec: C. Darveau, 1872.

Casgrain, H. R., ed. *Collection des manuscrits du Maréchal Lévis*. 12 vols. Montreal: C. O. Beauchemin, 1889–95.

Ceci, Lynn. "The Value of Wampum Among the New York Iroquois: A Case Study in Artifact Analysis." *Journal of Anthropological Research* 38 (spring 1982): 97–102.

[Champlain, Samuel]. *The Works of Samuel de Champlain*. Ed. H. P. Biggar. 6 vols. Toronto: Champlain Society Publications, 1922.

Charlevoix, Pierre François-Xavier. *Histoire et description générale de la Nouvelle France, avec le journal historique d'un voyage fait par ordre du Roi dans l'Amérique septentrionale*. 6 vols. Paris: Chez Giffart, 1744.

Christoph, Peter R., and Florence A. Christoph, eds. *The Andros Papers, 1674–1676: Files of the Provincial Secretary of New York during the Administration of Governor Sir Edmund Andros*. Vol. 1. Syracuse NY: Syracuse University Press, 1989.

Clermont, Norman. "Une figure Iroquoise, Garakonté." *Recherches amérindiennes au Québec* 7 (1978): 101–7.

Colden, Cadwallader. *The History of the Five Indian Nations of Canada Which are dependant on the Province of New-York in America and are a Barrier between the English and the French in that Part of the World*. London: 1747. Reprint, Toronto: Coles Publishing, 1972.

————. *The Letters and Papers of Cadwallader Colden*. 9 vols. New York Historical Society Collections, vols. 50–56, 67–68. New York, 1917–23, 1934–35.

*Collections of the Connecticut Historical Society*. Vols. 21 and 24. Hartford, 1924, 1932.

*Collections of the Massachusetts Historical Society*. 4th ser. Boston, 1863.

*Colonial Records of Pennsylvania: Minutes of the Provincial Council of Pennsylvania, 1683–1717*. Vols. 1–2. Philadelphia, 1852.

Crosby, Alfred W. *The Columbian Exchange: Biological Consequences of 1492*. Westport CT: Greenwood, 1972.

Cutcliffe, Stephen. "Colonial Indian Policy as a Measure of Rising Imperialism: New York and Pennsylvania, 1700–1755." *Western Pennsylvania Historical Magazine* 64 (July 1981): 237–67.

————. "Indians, Furs, and Empire: The Changing Policies of New York and Pennsylvania, 1674–1768." Ph.D. diss., Lehigh University, 1976.

[Danckaerts, Jasper]. *The Journal of Jasper Danckaerts, 1679–1680*. Ed. J. B. Bartlett and J. F. Jameson. New York: Charles Scribner's Sons, 1913.

————. "Observations of the Indians from Jasper Danckaerts's Journal, 1679–1680," Ed. Charles T. Gehring and Robert S. Grumet. *William and Mary Quarterly*, 3d ser., 44 (January 1987): 104–20.

Dechêne, Louis. *Habitants et marchands de Montréal au XVIIe siècle*. Montreal: Librairie Plon, 1974.

Dêlage, Denys. *Le Pays renversé: Amérindiens et européens en Amérique du nord-est, 1600–1664*. Montreal: Boréal Express, 1985.

Dennis, Matthew. *Cultivating a Landscape of Peace: Iroquois-European Encounters in Seventeenth-Century America*. Ithaca NY: Cornell University Press, 1993.

Desbarats, Catherine M. "The Cost of Canada's Native Alliances: Reality and Scarcity's Rhetoric." *William and Mary Quarterly*, 3d ser., 52 (Oct. 1995): 609–30.

Desrosiers, Léo-Paul. "Les années terribles." *Cahiers des dix* 26 (1961): 55–90.

————. "Denonville." *Cahiers des dix* 23 (1958): 107–38.

————. "L'expédition de M. de la Barre." *Cahiers des dix* 22 (1957): 105–35.

————. "Frontenac, l'artisan de la victoire." *Cahiers des dix* 28 (1963): 93–145.

————. "Il y a trois cents ans." *Cahiers des dix* 25 (1960): 85–101.

———. *Iroquoisie, 1534–1645.* Vol. 1. Montreal: Études de l'Institut d'Histoire de l'Amérique française, 1947.

———. "Iroquoise, terre française." *Cahiers des dix* 20 (1955): 33–59.

———. "Négociations de paix (1693–1696)." *Cahiers des dix* 21 (1956): 55–87.

———. "Les Onnontagués." *Cahiers des dix* 18 (1953): 45–66.

———. "La paix de 1667." *Cahiers des dix* 29 (1964): 25–45.

———. "La paix-miracle (1653–1660)." *Cahiers des dix* 24: 85–112.

———. "Préliminaires du massacre de Lachine." *Cahiers des dix* 19 (1954): 47–66.

———. "Revers et succès (1662–1663)." *Cahiers des dix* 27 (1962): 77–95.

———. "La rupture de la paix de 1645." *Cahiers des dix* 17 (1952): 169–81.

Dickason, Olive. *The Myth of the Savage, and the Beginnings of French Colonialism in the Americas.* Edmonton: University of Alberta Press, 1984.

Dickinson, John A. "Annaotaha et Dollard vus de l'autre côté de la palissade." *Revue d'histoire de l'Amérique française* 35 (Sept. 1981): 163–78.

———. "La Guerre iroquoise et la mortalité en Nouvelle-France, 1608–1666." *Revue d'histoire de l'Amérique française* 36 (June 1982): 31–54.

Dobyns, Henry F., et al. "Commentary on Native American Demography." *Ethnohistory* 36 (summer 1989): 285–306.

Dollier de Casson, François. *Histoire du Montréal.* Ed. and trans. Ralph Flenley as *A History of Montreal, 1640–1672.* London: J. M. Dent and Sons, 1928.

Duchet, Michèle. "Bougainville, Raynal, Diderot et les sauvages du Canada: Une source ignorée de l'*Histoire des deux Indes.*'" *Revue d'histoire de la France* 2 (avril–juin 1963): 228–36.

Eccles, W. J. "A Belated Review of Harold Adams Innis, *The Fur Trade in Canada.*" *Canadian Historical Review* 60 (Dec. 1979): 419–41.

———. *Canada Under Louis XIV, 1663–1701.* Toronto: McClelland and Stewart, 1964.

———. *The Canadian Frontier, 1534–1760.* 1969. Reprint, Albuquerque: University of New Mexico Press, 1978.

———. *Essays on New France.* Toronto: Oxford University Press, 1987.

———. *France in America.* Rev. ed. Markham ON: Fitzhenry and Whiteside, 1991.

———. *Frontenac: The Courtier Governor.* 1959; Toronto: McClelland and Stewart, 1965.

———. "The Fur Trade and Eighteenth-Century Imperialism." *William and Mary Quarterly*, 3d ser., 40 (July 1983): 341–62.

———. "The History of New France According to Francis Parkman." *William and Mary Quarterly*, 3d ser., 18 (Apr. 1961): 162–75.

———. Review of B. G. Trigger, *Natives and Newcomers. William and Mary Quarterly*, 3d ser., 42 (July 1986): 480–83.

Eid, Leroy. "'National' War Among Indians of Northeastern North America." *Canadian Review of American Studies* 16 (1985): 125–54.

———. "The Ojibwa-Iroquois War: The War the Five Nations Did Not Win." *Ethnohistory* 26 (fall 1979): 297–324.

Ellis, Chris J., and Neal Ferris, eds. *The Archaeology of Southern Ontario to A.D. 1650.*

Occasional Publication of the London Chapter, Ontario Archaeological Society, Publication no. 5. London ON, 1990.

Faillon, Étienne-Michel. *Histoire de la colonie française en Canada* [1534–1682]. 3 vols. Villemarie, France: Bibilothèque Paroissiale, 1865–66.

Feltskoq, E. N., ed. *The Oregon Trail*, by Francis Parkman. Madison: University of Wisconsin Press, 1969.

Fenton, William. "A Further Note on Iroquois Suicide." *Ethnohistory* 33 (fall 1986): 448–57.

———. "Iroquois Suicide: A Study in the Stability of a Culture Pattern." Bureau of American Ethnology Bulletin. Washington DC, 1941: 79–138.

Ferland, J. B. A. *Cours d'histoire du Canada*. 2 vols. Quebec: Augustin Coté, 1861, 1865.

Fernow, Berthold, ed. *The Records of New Amsterdam, 1653 to 1674*. 7 vols. New York: Knickerbocker Press, 1897.

Finlayson, William D. *The 1975 and 1978 Rescue Excavations at the Draper Site: Introduction and Settlement Patterns*. Mercury series, Canadian Ethnology Service, paper 130. Ottawa: National Museum of Man, 1985.

Foster, M. *From the Earth to beyond the Sky: An Ethnographic Approach to Four Longhouse Iroquois Speech Events*. Mercury series, Canadian Ethnology Service, paper 20. Ottawa: National Museum of Man, 1974.

Foster M., J. Campisi, and M. Mithune, eds. *Extending the Rafters: Interdisciplinary Approaches to Iroquoian Studies*. Albany: State University of New York Press, 1984.

Forbes, Allan. "Two and a Half Centuries of Conflict: The Iroquois and the Laurentian Wars." *Pennsylvania Archeologist* 40 (Dec. 1970): 1–20.

Gagnon, François-Marc. *La Conversion par l'image: Un aspect de la mission des Jésuites auprès des indiens du Canada au XVIIe siècle*. Montreal: Éditions Bellarmin, 1975.

Gagnon, Serge. *Quebec and Its Historians: 1840 to 1920*. Montreal: Harvest House, 1982.

———. *Quebec and Its Historians: The Twentieth Century*. Montreal: Harvest House, 1985.

[Galinée, René Bréhant de]. "Ce qui s'est passé de plus remarquable dans le voyage de M.M. Dollier et Galinée (1669.1670)." Ed. James H. Coyne. *Ontario Historical Society Papers and Records*. Vol. 4. Toronto, 1903.

Garneau, François-Xavier. *Histoire du Canada*. 5th ed. 2 vols. Paris: Librairie Félix Arcan, 1913, 1920.

Gehring, Charles T., William A. Starna, and William N. Fenton. "The Tawagonshi Treaty of 1613: The Final Chapter." *New York History* 68 (Oct. 1987): 373–93.

Given, Brian. *A Most Pernicious Thing: Gun Trading and Native Warfare in the Early Contact Period*. Ottawa: Carlton University Press, 1994.

Goldstein, Robert A. *French-Iroquois Diplomatic and Military Relations, 1609–1701*. The Hague: Mouton, 1969.

Groulx, Lionel. *Histoire du Canada français*. 2 vols. Montreal: Fides, 1976.

[Guyart, Marie]. *Marie de L'Incarnation, Ursuline (1599–1672), Correspondance*. Ed. Guy Oury. Abbaye Saint-Pierre, France: Solesmes, 1971.

Haan, Richard. "The Covenant Chain: Iroquois Diplomacy on the Niagara Frontier, 1697–1730." Ph.D. diss., University of California, 1976.

———. "The Problem of Iroquois Neutrality: Suggestions for Revision." *Ethnohistory* 27 (fall 1980): 317–30.

Hale, Horatio. *The Iroquois Book of Rites*. Philadelphia, 1883. Reprint, Toronto: Coles, 1972.

Hallowell, A. I. "Some Psychological Characteristics of the Northeastern Indians." In *Man in Northeastern North America*. Ed. F. Johnson. Papers of the Robert S. Peabody Foundation for Archaeology, vol. 3. Andover MA: Philips Academy, 1946.

Harris, R. Cole, ed. *The Historical Atlas of Canada: From the Beginning to 1800*. Toronto: University of Toronto Press, 1987.

Hart, Simon. *The Prehistory of the New Netherland Company: Amsterdam Notarial Records of the First Dutch Voyages to the Hudson*. Amsterdam: City of Amsterdam Press, 1959.

Havard, Gilles. *La Grande Paix de Montréal de 1701: Les voies de la diplomatie franco-amérindienne*. Montreal: Recherches amérindiennes au Québec, 1992.

Heidenreich, Conrad. "An Analysis of the Seventeenth-Century Map 'Nouvelle France.'" *Cartographica* 25 (1988): 67–111.

———. *Huronia: A History and Geography of the Huron Indians, 1600–1650*. Toronto: McClelland and Stewart, 1971.

Henige, David. "Primary Source by Primary Source? On the Role of Epidemics in New World Depopulation." *Ethnohistory* 33 (summer 1986): 293–312.

Hewitt, J. N. B. "Era of the Formation of the League of the Iroquois." *American Anthropologist* 7 (Jan. 1894): 61–67.

———. "Legend of the Founding of the Iroquois League." *American Anthropologist* 5 (1892): 131–48.

———. "The Status of Women in Iroquois Polity before 1784." *Smithsonian Institution Annual Report, 1932*. Washington DC: Smithsonian Institution, 1933.

Hodge, Frederick. *Handbook of American Indians North of Mexico*. 2 vols. Bureau of American Ethnology Bulletin 30, in 2 parts. Washington DC, 1907, 1910.

Hunt, George T. *The Wars of the Iroquois: A Study in Intertribal Trade Relations*. Madison: University of Wisconsin Press, 1940.

Innis, H. *The Fur Trade in Canada*. Rev. ed. Toronto: University of Toronto Press, 1956.

Jaenen, C. *Friend and Foe: Aspects of French-Amerindian Cultural Contact in the Sixteenth and Seventeenth Centuries*. Toronto: McClelland and Stewart, 1976.

Jameson, J. F., ed. *Narratives of New Netherland, 1609–1664*. 1909. Reprint, New York: Barnes and Noble, 1959.

Jennings, Francis. *The Ambiguous Iroquois Empire: The Covenant Chain Confederation of Indian Tribes with English Colonies, from Its Beginnings to the Lancaster Treaty of 1744*. New York: W. W. Norton, 1984.

———. "The Constitutional Evolution of the Covenant Chain." *American Philosophical Society Proceedings* 115 (Apr. 1971): 88–96.

———. "Francis Parkman: A Brahmin among the Untouchables." *William and Mary Quarterly*, 3d ser., 42: (July 1985): 305–28.

———. *The Invasion of America: Indians, Colonialism and the Cant of Conquest.* New York: W. W. Norton, 1976.

———. "A Vanishing Indian: Francis Parkman Versus His Sources." *Pennsylvania Magazine of History and Biography* 87 (July 1963): 306–23.

Jennings, Francis, ed. *The History and Culture of Iroquois Diplomacy.* Syracuse NY: Syracuse University Press, 1985.

Jennings, F., and W. Fenton, eds. *The Iroquois Indians: A Documentary History of the Six Nations and Their League.* 50 reels. Chicago: D'Arcy McNickle Center for the History of the American Indian at the Newberry Library, 1984.

[Johnson, William]. *Papers of Sir William Johnson.* Ed. James Sullivan et al. 14 vols. Albany: University of the State of New York, 1921–65.

*Journal of the House of Burgesses of Virginia, 1619–1776.* Ed. H. R. McIlwaine. 13 vols. Richmond: 1905–15.

*Journals of the Council of the State of Virginia.* Ed. H. R. McIlwaine. 2 vols. Richmond: 1931–32.

Kellogg, Louise. *The French Régime in Wisconsin and in the Northwest.* 1925. Reprint, New York: Cooper Square, 1968.

Knowles, Nathaniel. "The Torture of Captives by the Indians of Eastern North America." *American Philosophical Society Proceedings* 82 (Mar. 1940): 151–225.

Konrad, Victor. "An Iroquois Frontier: The North Shore of Lake Ontario during the Late Seventeenth Century." *Journal of Historical Geography* 7 (Apr. 1981): 129–44.

Kuhn, Robert. "Trade and Exchange Among the Mohawk-Iroquois: A Trace Element Analysis of Ceramic Smoking Pipes." Ph.D. diss., State University of New York, 1985.

Kuhn, Robert, et al. "The Evidence for a St. Lawrence Presence on Sixteenth-Century Mohawk Sites." *Northeast Anthropology* 45 (spring 1993): 77–86.

Lafitau, J. F. *Moeurs des sauvages ameriquains comparées aux moeurs des premier temps.* 2 vols. 1727. Ed. W. N. Fenton, trans. E. L. Moore as *Customs of the American Indians Compared with the Customs of Primitive Times.* 2 vols. Champlain Society Publication, vols. 48–49. Toronto: 1974, 1977.

Lahontan, Louis-Armand, Baron de. *New Voyages to North America.* Ed. R. G. Thwaites. 2 vols. Chicago: A. C. McClurg, 1905.

Lanctot, Gustave. *Histoire du Canada: Des origines au régime royal.* Montreal: Librairie Beauchemin, 1960.

———. *A History of Canada, [1534–1760].* 3 vols. Toronto: Clark, Irwin, 1963–65.

La Potherie, Le Roy de, [dit, Bacqueville de la Potherie] Claude-Charles. *Histoire de l'Amérique septentrionale.* 4 vols. Paris: 1722.

Larocque, Robert. "Les maladies chez les iroquoiens préhistoriques." *Recherches amérindiennes au Québec* 10 (1980): 165–80.

Le Blant, R., and R. Baudry, eds. *Nouveaux documents sur Champlain et son époque,* *vol. 1, 1560–1622.* Publication des Archives Publiques du Canada, no. 15. Ottawa, 1967.

Lebman, J. David. "The End of the Iroquois Mystique: The Oneida Land Cession Treaties of the 1780s." *William and Mary Quarterly,* 3rd ser., 47 (October 1990): 523–47.

Leclerc, Jean. *Le Marquis de Denonville, gouverneur de la Nouvelle-France, 1685– 1689.* Montreal: Fides, 1976.

*Legislative Journals of the Council of Colonial Virginia, [1680–1774].* Ed. H. R. McIl-waine. 3 vols. Richmond: 1918–19.

Lincoln, Charles, ed. *Narratives of the Indian Wars, 1675–1699.* New York: Charles Scribner's Sons, 1913.

[Livingston, Robert]. *The Livingston Indian Records.* Ed. L. Leder. Gettysburg: Penn-sylvania Historical Association, 1956.

Lurie, N. O. "Indian Cultural Adjustment to European Civilization." In *Seventeenth-Century America: Essays in Colonial History.* Ed. J. S. Morton. Chapel Hill: Uni-versity of North Carolina Press, 1959.

Lynch, James. "The Iroquois Confederacy and the Adoption and Administration of Non-Iroquoian Individuals and Groups Prior to 1756." *Man in the Northeast* 30 (fall 1985): 83–99.

Mancall, Peter C. *Deadly Medicine: Indians and Alcohol in Early America.* Ithaca NY: Cornell University Press, 1995.

Margry, Pierre, ed. *Découvertes et établissements des français dans l'ouest et dans le sud de l'Amérique septentrionale, 1614–1754.* 6 vols. Paris: D. Jouaust, 1876–86.

———. *Relations et mémoires inédits pour servir à l'histoire de la France dans les pays d'outremer.* Paris: Challamel Aimé, 1867.

McManus, John. "An Economic Analysis of Indian Behaviour in the North American Fur Trade." *Journal of Economic History* 32 (Mar. 1972): 36–53.

"Mémoire sur les coutumes et usages des cinq nations iroquoises du canada." In *Vari-étés litteraires ou Recueil de pièces, tant originales que traduites, concernant la phi-losophie, la littérature et les arts.* Ed. J.-P. Baptiste and F. Arnaud. 4 vols. Paris, 1804. Reprint, Geneva: Slatkine Reprints, 1969.

*Mercure françois.* Vol. 19. Paris: 1633.

*Minutes of the Council and General Court of Colonial Virginia, 1620–1632, 1670– 1676.* Ed. H. R. McIlwaine. Richmond: 1924.

Miquelon, Dale. *New France, 1701–1744: "A Supplement to Europe."* Toronto: McClelland and Stewart, 1987.

Moogk, Peter N. "Rank in New France: Reconstructing a Society from Notarial Records." *Histoire sociale-Social History* 8 (May 1975): 34–53.

Morgan, L. H. *The League of the Iroquois.* Rochester NY: Sange and Brother, 1851.

Morgan, W. T. "The Five Nations and Queen Anne." *Mississippi Valley Historical Review* 13 (Sept. 1926): 169–89.

[Morin, Marie]. *Histoire simple et véritable.* Ed. Ghislaine Legendre. Montreal: Les Presses de l'Université de Montréal, 1979.

Munsell, J., ed. *Collections on the History of Albany, from Its Discovery to the Present Time*. 4 vols. Albany: J. Munsell, 1865–71.

Nadeau, Gabriel. "Indian Scalping Technique in Different Tribes." *Bulletin of History of Medicine* 10, no. 2 (July 1941): 178–94.

Naroll, Raoul. "The Causes of the Fourth Iroquois War." *Ethnohistory* 16 (1969): 51–81.

*New Jersey Archives, First Series: Documents Relating to the Colonial History of the State of New Jersey, 1631–1703*. Vols. 1–2. Newark: New Jersey Historical Society, 1880, 1881.

*New York Historical Society Collections*, 2d ser., vol. 1–2. 1841: n.p.

Niemczycki, Mary Ann. "Seneca Tribalization: An Adaptive Strategy." *Man in the Northeast* 36 (fall 1988): 77–87.

Noble, W. C. "Some Social Implications of the Iroquois *in situ* Theory." *Ontario Archeology* 13 (June 1969): 16–28.

[Norton, John]. *The Journal of Major John Norton, 1816*. Ed. Carl F. Klinck and James J. Talman. Toronto: Champlain Society, 1970.

Norton, Thomas E. *The Fur Trade in Colonial New York, 1686–1776*. Madison: University of Wisconsin Press, 1974.

O'Callaghan, E. B., ed. *The Documentary History of the State of New York*. 4 vols. Albany: Weed, Parsons, 1849.

———. *Documents Relative to the Colonial History of the State of New York*. 15 vols. Albany: Weed, Parsons, 1856–83.

Otterbein, K. "Huron *vs.* Iroquois: A Case Study in Inter-tribal Warfare." *Ethnohistory* 26 (spring 1979): 141–52.

———. "Why the Iroquois Won: An Analysis of Military Tactics." *Ethnohistory* 11 (winter 1964): 56–63.

Ouellet, Fernand. "La modernisation de l'historiographie et l'émergence de l'histoire sociale." *Recherches sociographiques* 21 (1985): 11–83.

Paltsits, Victor Hugo, ed. *Minutes of the Executive Council of the Province of New York: The Administration of Francis Lovelace, 1668–1673*. 2 vols. Albany: State of New York, 1910.

Parker, A. C. *The Constitution of the Five Nations*. New York Museum Bulletin 184, 1916.

Parkman, Francis. *Count Frontenac and New France Under Louis XIV*. 1877. Reprint, Boston: Little, Brown, 1905.

———. *Discovery of the Great West: A Historical Narrative*. London: John Murray, 1869.

———. *The Jesuits in North America in the Seventeenth Century*. 1867. Reprint, Toronto: George N. Morang, 1907.

———. *The Journals of Francis Parkman*. Ed. Mason Wade. 2 vols. London: Eyre and Spottiswoode, 1947.

———. *La Salle and the Discovery of the Great West*. 1879. Reprint, Boston: Little, Brown, 1907.

————. *Letters of Francis Parkman*. 2 vols. Ed. Wilbur R. Jacobs. Norman: University of Oklahoma Press, 1960.

————. *The Old Régime in Canada*. Boston: Little, Brown, 1874.

————. *The Oregon Trail: Sketches of Prairie and Rocky Mountain Life*. 1849. Reprint, Boston: Little, Brown, 1882.

————. *Pioneers of France in the New World*. 1865. Reprint, Boston: Little, Brown, 1909.

Pendergast, James. "Huron–St. Lawrence Iroquois Relations in the Terminal Prehistoric Period." *Ontario Archaeology* 44 (1985): 23–39.

————. "The Introduction of European Goods into the Native Community in the Sixteenth Century." *Proceedings of the 1992 People to People Conference*. Ed. Charles F. Hayes 3d, 7–18. Rochester Museum and Science Center, Research Records, no. 23. Rochester NY, 1994.

————. "Were the French on Lake Ontario in the Sixteenth Century?" *Man in the Northeast* 29 (spring 1985): 71–85.

Penn, William. *Correspondence between William Penn and James Logan and Others, 1700–1750*. Pennsylvania Historical Society Memoirs, vols. 9 and 10. Philadelphia, 1870, 1872.

————. *The Papers of William Penn, 1644–1718*. Ed. M. M. Dunn and R. Dunn. 4 vols. Pennsylvania: University of Pennsylvania Press, 1981–87.

Pouliot, L. *Études sur les Relations des Jésuites de la Nouvelle-France, 1632–1672*. Paris: Descleé de Brouwer et Cie., 1940.

*Propositions Made by the Five Nations . . . [to the] Earl of Bellomont*. New York: William Bradford, 1698.

*Public Records of the Colony of Connecticut*. Ed. J. H. Trumbull et al. Vols. 1–4. Hartford, 1850–68.

Puype, Jan Piet. *Dutch and Other Flintlocks from Seventeenth-Century Iroquois Sites*. Proceedings of the 1984 Trade Gun Conference, part 1. Rochester Museum and Science Center, Research Records, no. 18. Rochester NY, 1985.

Quinn, David B., and M. Alison, eds. *The English New England Voyages, 1602–1608*. Second series, no. 161. London: Hakluyt Society, 1983.

[Radisson, Pierre Esprit]. *The Explorations of Pierre Esprit Radisson*. Ed. Arthur T. Adams. Minneapolis: Ross and Haines, 1961.

*Rapport de l'archiviste de la province de Québec*.

[Raudot, Antoine]. *Relation par lettres de l'amerique septentrionale*. Ed. Camille de Rochemontiex. Paris: Letouzey et Ané, 1904.

Ray, A. J., and D. Freeman. *"Give Us Good Measure": An Economic Analysis of Relations between the Indians and the Hudson's Bay Company before 1763*. Toronto: University of Toronto Press, 1978.

Reynolds, Wynn. "Persuasive Speaking of the Iroquois Indians at Treaty Councils, 1678–1776." Ph.D. diss., Columbia University, 1957.

Rich, E. E. "Trade Habits and Economic Motivation among the Indians in North America." *Canadian Journal of Economics and Political Science* 26 (Feb. 1960): 35–53.

Richter, Daniel K. "Iroquois versus Iroquois: Jesuit Missions and Christianity in Village Politics, 1642–1686." *Ethnohistory* 32 (1986): 1–16.

———. *The Ordeal of the Longhouse: The Peoples of the Iroquois League in the Era of European Colonization*. Chapel Hill: University of North Carolina Press, 1992.

———. "Rediscovered Links in the Covenant Chain: Previously Unpublished Transcripts of the New York Indian Treaty Minutes, 1677–1691." *Proceedings of the American Antiquarian Society* 92, pt. 1 (Apr. 1982): 45–85.

———. "War and Culture: The Iroquois Experience." *William and Mary Quarterly*, 3d ser., 40 (Oct. 1983): 528–59.

Richter, Daniel K., and James Merrell, eds. *Beyond the Covenant Chain: The Iroquois and Their Neighbors in Indian North America, 1600–1800*. Syracuse NY: Syracuse University Press, 1987.

Robie, Harry. "Kiotsaetson's Three Rivers Address: An Example of 'Effective' Iroquois Oratory." *American Indian Quarterly* 6 (fall–winter 1982): 238–53.

Sagard, Gabriel. *Histoire du Canada*. Paris: 1636.

———. *The Long Journey to the Country of the Hurons*. Ed. G. M. Wrong. Trans. H. H. Langton. Champlain Society Publication, vol. 25. Toronto, 1939.

Sahlins, Marshall. *Stone Age Economics*. Chicago: Aldine, 1972.

Schlesier, Karl. "Epidemics and Indian Middlemen: Rethinking the Wars of the Iroquois, 1609–1653." *Ethnohistory* 23 (spring 1976): 129–45.

Sempowski, Martha, et al. "The Adams and Culbertson Sites: A Hypothesis for Village Formation." *Man in the Northeast* 35 (spring 1988): 95–108.

Snow, Dean. *The Iroquois*. Cambridge MA: Blackwell, 1994.

———. "Microchronology and Demographic Evidence Relating to the Size of Pre-Columbian North American Indian Populations." *Science* 268 (16 June 1995): 1601–4.

———. "Migration in Prehistory: The Northern Iroquoian Case." *American Antiquity* 60 (1995): 59–79.

Snow, Dean, and Kim Lanphear. "European Contact and Indian Depopulation in the Northeast: The Timing of the First Epidemics." *Ethnohistory* 35 (winter 1988): 15–33.

Snow, Dean, and William A. Starna. "Sixteenth-Century Depopulation: A View from the Mohawk Valley." *American Anthropologist* 91 (Mar. 1989): 142–49.

Snyderman, George. "Behind the Tree of Peace: A Sociological Analysis of Iroquois Warfare." *Pennsylvania Archaeologist* 18 (fall 1948): 3–93.

———. "Concepts of Landownership among the Iroquois and Their Neighbours." Bureau of American Ethnology Bulletin 149. Washington DC, 1951: 15–34.

Speck, F. G. "The Functions of Wampum Among the Eastern Alongkian." *American Anthropological Association Memoirs* 6 (1919): 3–71.

Starna, William. "Mohawk Iroquois Populations: A Revision." *Ethnohistory* 27 (fall 1980): 371–82.

Starna, William, and John H. Relethford. "Deer Densities and Population Dynamics: A Cautionary Note." *American Antiquity* 50 (1985): 825–32.

Starna, William, and Ralph Watkins. "Northern Iroquoian Slavery." *Ethnohistory* 38 (winter 1991): 34–57.

Starna, William, George Hamell, and William L. Butts. "Northern Iroquoian Horticulture and Insect Infestation: A Cause for Village Removal." *Ethnohistory* 31 (summer 1984): 197–207.

Sulte, Benjamin. "La guerre des Iroquois, 1600–1653." *Mémoires de la Société Royale du Canada*, 2d ser., vol. 3, sect. 1 (1897): 63–92.

Thwaites, R. G. *France in America*. 1905. Reprint, New York: Cooper Square, 1968.

Thwaites, R. G., ed. *Early Western Travels, 1748–1846*. 38 vols. Cleveland: Arthur H. Clark, 1904–7.

———. *The Jesuit Relations and Allied Documents, 1610–1791*. 73 vols. Cleveland: Burrows Bros., 1896–1901.

Tooker, E. "Clans and Moieties in North America." *Current Anthropology* 12 (June 1971): 357–76.

———. *An Ethnography of the Huron, 1615–1649*. Midland ON: Huronia Historical Development Council, 1967.

———. "The Iroquois Defeat of the Huron: A Review of Causes." *Pennsylvania Archaeologist* 33 (July 1963): 115–23.

Trelease, A. W. *Indian Affairs in Colonial New York: The Seventeenth Century*. Ithaca NY: Cornell University Press, 1960.

———. "The Iroquois and the Western Fur Trade: A Problem in Interpretation." *Mississippi Valley Historical Review* 49 (June 1962): 32–51.

Trigger, Bruce. "Alfred G. Bailey—Ethnohistorian." *Acadiensis* (spring 1989) 18: 2–21.

———. *The Children of Aataentsic*. 2 vols. Montreal: McGill-Queens University Press, 1976.

———. "Early Native North American Responses to European Contact: Romantic versus Rationalistic Interpretations." *Journal of American History* 77 (Mar. 1991): 1195–1215.

———. *The Huron: Farmers of the North*. Toronto: Holt, Rinehart, and Winston, 1969.

———. "The Mohawk-Mahican War (1624–28): The Establishment of a Pattern." *Canadian Historical Review* 52 (Sept. 1971): 276–86.

———. *Natives and Newcomers: Canada's Heroic Age Reconsidered*. Montreal: McGill-Queen's University Press, 1985.

———. "Order and Freedom in Huron Society." In *Perspectives on the North American Indians*. Ed. M. Nagler. Toronto: McClelland and Stewart, 1972.

Trigger, Bruce, ed. *Handbook of North American Indians*. Vol. 15, *The Northeast*. Washington DC: Smithsonian Institution, 1978.

Trudel, Marcel. *The Beginnings of New France, 1524–1663*. Toronto: McClelland and Stewart, 1973.

———. *Les débuts du régime seigneurial au Canada*. Montreal: Éditions Fides, 1974.

Tuck, James. *Onondaga Iroquois Prehistory: A Study in Settlement Archaeology*. Syracuse NY: Syracuse University Press, 1971.

Vachon, André. "Colliers et ceintures de porcelaine chez les indiens de la Nouvelle-France," *Cahiers des dix* 35 (1970): 251–78.

———. "Colliers et ceintures de porcelaine dans la diplomatie indienne." *Cahiers des dix* 36 (1971): 179–92.

Vachon, Robert. "The Mohawk Nation and Its Communities." *Interculture* 25 (winter 1992): 14–20.

[van den Bogaert, Harmen Meynderstsz]. *A Journey into Mohawk and Oneida Country, 1634–1635: The Journal of Harmen Meyndertsz van den Bogaert.* Ed. Charles T. Gehring and William A. Starna. Syracuse NY: Syracuse University Press, 1988.

van Laer, A. J. F., ed. and trans. *Court Minutes of Albany, Rensselaerswyck, and Schenectady, 1668–1685.* 3 vols. Albany: University of the State of New York, 1926, 1928, 1932.

———. *Minutes of the Court of Fort Orange and Beverwyck, 1652–60.* 2 vols. Albany: University of the State of New York, 1920, 1923.

———. *Minutes of the Court of Rensselaerswyck, 1648–52.* Albany: University of the State of New York, 1922.

———. *New York Historical Manuscripts: Dutch.* 4 vols. Baltimore: Genealogical Publishing, 1974.

van Laer, A. J. F., and Jonathan Pearson, eds. *The Early Records of the City and County of Albany, [1654–78].* 4 vols. Albany: State University of New York, 1869, 1919.

[van Rensselaer, Jeremias]. *The Correspondence of Jeremias van Rensselaer, 1651–1674.* Ed. and trans. A. J. F. van Laer. Albany: University of the State of New York, 1932.

[van Rensselaer, Killiaen]. *Van Rensselaer-Bowier Manuscripts: The Letters of Killiaen van Rensselaer, 1630–1643, and Other Documents Relating to the Colony of Rensselaerswyck.* Ed. and trans. A. J. F. van Laer. New York State Library Bulletin, History, no. 7. Albany: University of the State of New York, 1908.

[van Rensselaer, Maria]. *The Correspondence of Maria van Rensselaer, 1669–1689.* Ed. and trans. A. J. F. van Laer. Albany: University of the State of New York, 1935.

Wallace, A. F. C. *The Death and Rebirth of the Seneca.* New York: Vintage Books, 1972.

———. "Origins of Iroquois Neutrality: The Grand Settlement of 1701." *Pennsylvania History* 24 (July 1957): 223–35.

———. "Some Psychological Determinants of Culture Change in an Iroquoian Community." In *Symposium on Local Diversity in Iroquois Culture.* Ed. W. N. Fenton. Bureau of American Ethnology Bulletin 144. Washington DC, 1951: 58–76.

Weinman, Paul L. *A Bibliography of the Iroquoian Literature.* New York State Museum and Science Service, Bulletin 411. Albany, 1969.

White, Richard. *The Middle Ground: Indians, Empires, and Republics in the Great Lakes Region, 1650–1815.* New York: Cambridge University Press, 1991.

———. *Roots of Dependency: Subsistence, Environment, and Social Change among the Choctaws, Pawnees, and Navajos.* Lincoln: University of Nebraska Press, 1983.

Wilson, D. D. "Supposed Prevalence of One Cranial Type throughout the American

Aborigines." *Canadian Journal of Industry, Science and Art* n.s. (November 1857): 406–35.

Winsor, Justin, ed. *Narrative and Critical History of America*. 8 vols. Boston: Houghton, Mifflin, 1884–89.

*The Winthrop Papers, 1498–1649*. 5 vols. Boston: Massachusetts Historical Society, 1929–47.

Wraxall, Peter. *An Abridgement of the Indian Affairs Contained in Four Folio Volumes, Transacted in the Colony of New York from the Year 1678 to the Year 1751*. Ed. C. H. McIlwain. Cambridge MA: Harvard University Press, 1915.

Wray, Charles F. "The Volume of Dutch Trade Goods Received by the Seneca Iroquois, 1600–1687 A.D." *New Netherland Studies* 84 (June 1985): 100–112.

Wray, Charles F., et al. *The Adams and Culbertson Sites*. Rochester Museum and Science Center, Research Records, no. 23. Rochester NY, 1987.

Wright, J. V. *The Ontario Iroquois Tradition*. National Museum of Canada Bulletin, no. 210. Ottawa, 1966.

Zeisberger, David. *History of Northern American Indians*. Ed. A. Butler Hulbert and W. N. Schwarze. Ohio Archeological and Historical Society Publications, vol. 19. Columbus, 1910: 1–189.

# Index